Weimar Etudes

Henry Pachter.

WEIMAR ETUDES

HENRY PACHTER

New York   Columbia University Press   1982

Library of Congress Cataloging in Publication Data

Pachter, Henry Maximilian, 1907–1980
Weimar études.

Includes bibliographical references and index.
1. Germany—Politics and government—1918–
1933.   2. Germany—Intellectual life.
3. Pachter, Henry Maximilian, 1907–1980
I. Title.
DD240.P25   943.85   82-1122
ISBN 0-231-05360-6   AACR2
ISBN 0-231-05361-4 (pbk.)

Columbia University Press
New York and Guildford, Surrey

Clothbound editions of Columbia University Press books are Smyth-sewn
and printed on permanent and durable acid-free paper.

Contents

Illustrations

A Note on the Manuscript

Over the past few years, Henry Pachter was involved in gathering his essays on the Weimar period to form a book. This was perhaps his favorite project, and in Stephen Eric Bronner of the Department of Political Science at Rutgers University—once his student, later his colleague, and always a friend—he found a man with whom he could discuss the enterprise and from whom he could get criticism and advice.

Unfortunately, Henry Pachter did not live to see the completion of this work and so it comes out posthumously. In effect, a share of the book belongs to Professor Bronner, who selected, edited, and coordinated the material. Entrusted with my husband's literary estate, Professor Bronner sought to follow Henry Pachter's outlines for the present volume. Also, numerous unpublished manuscripts were among my husband's literary legacy, and Professor Bronner sought to reconstruct some of them for publication.

Where changes have been made in the already published pieces, they were made either to avoid repetition or on simple stylistic grounds. Certain other changes were made in accordance with my husband's unpublished notes; here I would like to thank Charles Webel and Joan McQuary of Columbia University Press for their editorial suggestions and advice.

Some articles which Henry Pachter had hoped to include were never completed. There was to be an analysis of "Jewish Writers in Germany" along with sketches on Arnold Brecht, Walter Benjamin, and Karl Korsch—"the most wayward of them all." A piece on the "Spirit of Weimar" was also to be included. But we hope that this very spirit will become visible even in this foreshortened collection.

Hedwig Pachter
August 1981

Foreword

Walter Laqueur

THE need to preface a book is not readily obvious except in
the rare instance of a very young man who has made an important contribution in one genre or another, where a few
words of recommendation by a leading figure in the field may
do no harm. This hardly applies in the present case, nor have
I been asked to write a eulogy: Henry Pachter was allergic
to any kind of pomposity, however well meant, and would
have loathed it. Others who knew him better have written
about him.*

I have read most of his books and articles, but I never lived
in New York for any length of time and our paths seldom
crossed. Yet, I know that he genuinely cared about young
people and exerted considerable influence over some of them.
They in turn liked him, a phenomenon not that frequent these
days. I also know that the current volume was dear to Henry
Pachter, and that he was working on it when he died. This is
of interest since there was on occasion something unfinished
in his books. Sometimes I even had the impression that he
shied away from writing about the very subjects that were
closest to his heart. The same is true, incidentally, with regard to some of his contemporaries: I do not profess to have

* See, for instance Stanley Plastrik in Dissent (Spring 1981); Martin Jay and Robert
Boyers in Salmagundi (Spring–Summer 1981); and Stephen Eric Bronner in Telos
(Winter 1980–81).

xi

a psychological explanation. It certainly was not laziness, a subject on which Henry Pachter once wrote a provocative little essay. Perhaps it was a lack of self-discipline, but there may have been perfectly good reasons which one doesn't know and on which it is fruitless to speculate.

On the other side of the ledger there was so much that was attractive in Henry Pachter: a restless, original, inquisitive mind, great intellectual integrity, a culture widely ranging over many fields, an enormous vitality and fearlessness, attitudes so old-fashioned as to be almost avant-garde. On many occasions he must have sorely tried the patience of his younger friends who admired these and other qualities and above all perhaps the fact that the commitment to the ideals of freedom and justice of his younger years never weakened. But they still could not quite stomach his contempt for some of the cult figures of the 1960s and early 1970s, his lack of reverence vis-à-vis the pseudo-profundity of some of his own contemporaries who had acquired something akin to guru status, at least for a while. What, above all, were they to make of his "cold war stance" and his "anti-Sovietism"? They explained it, I suppose, as part of the trauma of the late 1930s; the Moscow trials and the Hitler-Stalin pact, which Henry Pachter, like most of his contemporaries, had never quite overcome. They probably thought that his basic political attitudes had frozen sometime in 1939—or at most in 1953. Was he not aware that Stalin was dead and the cold war over and done with? But they were willing to forgive these minor eccentricities.

Henry Pachter, on the other hand, must have been exasperated from time to time: Why can't young people learn from the experiences of the past? Why do they have to repeat all the errors of their elders? Not being a patient man by nature, it must have been difficult for him to accept that youth is always the season of credulity, and that every generation has to make its own mistakes. Experience cannot be bequeathed.

On occasion he would overplay the part of a gadfly or go off on a tangent; he that is without a sin let him first cast a stone——Resentment made him sometimes curiously blind.

This is true, for instance, with regard to nationalism: about the destructive force of nationalism in the twentieth century—in the first world as well as in the second and the third—there was no room for differences of opinion. But to note the fact is one thing, to get emotional about it is another. Such anger does not do much harm, but it is about as effective as polemicizing against rain, or storm, or hail. On major issues, however, Henry Pachter was usually right: his "cultural conservatism," sadly noted by some of his younger friends, was not a symptom of old age—there were few men as youthful in spirit as Henry at seventy. Rather, it was the reaction of an honest critic, appalled by the great amount of rubbish that has been passed off lately for avant-garde culture.

Politics, however, in the widest sense remained his main interest. Yet the milieu from which he came, the German Jewish middle class, was certainly not deeply interested in political philosophy and even less in political practice. Politicization came to these circles only after the first world war, or to be precise in the late 1920s; it is too often forgotten that up to the Great Depression, cultural rather than political problems were the main issues of controversy and dominated public debate. In the same way that young men and women had joined the youth movement in the 1920s, they turned to radical politics after 1930. It was equally obvious that this political commitment to the extreme Left, if not necessarily always to the changing Communist party line, should persist for at least a decade. Hitler was the main enemy, not Stalin.

To generalize about Henry Pachter's generation is dangerous and not only because a generation is always an elusive category. There were four distinct age groups in the German Jewish emigration. First, their were those born before the turn of the century, who had grown up in that secure and orderly world about which the author writes in his recollections, who served in the war and left Germany already well established in their professions. They were the least adaptable and frequently had the greatest difficulties after their emigration. Henry Pachter belonged to the second group—those born, roughly speaking, between 1900 and 1912. They were too young to have fought in the first world war, their formative years were during the Weimar Republic, their formal education was finished when they left Germany, but they were only at the beginning of their professional careers. The subsequent generation, to which I belong, were those born between the outbreak of the first world war and the middle 1920s. They remember the last years of Weimar (the younger vaguely, the older more distinctly), but they remember most clearly the rise of Nazism. They were as a rule too young to have engaged in active politics before 1933 and did not have to escape at once. Their education was unfinished when they left, alone or with their parents. Last, there is the fourth generation, those born in the late 1920s and after, who may have some faint childhood memories of the country of birth, but whose ties to Germany by language, culture, and most other ways are weak. Their formative years were in their country of adoption.

If one considers the present collection, these distinctions are of more than actuarial interest. There is a great deal of difference whether someone left his country of birth in his early teens or early twenties, a fact that becomes palpably obvious if one compares their writings on Germany in later years—it is not so much a matter of knowledge but of perspective. The older ones like Henry Pachter had been more involved in the controversies of that period, they had stronger predilections and more pronounced prejudices, but they had also a feel for the period which cannot apparently be acquired by studying the diplomatic documents of the time, or even all the contributions to the *Zeitschrift für Sozialforschung* and *Die Gesellschaft*.

The case of the youth movement of which Henry Pachter was a member is an obvious example. It is possible to comment sensibly, even shrewdly, about it for those writing from a distance, but some deeper understanding will usually be missing. Perhaps it can be acquired by a great effort of imagination, but this is rare, and imagination may easily lead into the wrong direction. What has just been noted may apply to all emigrations but it is apparently more true with regard to emigrants from Germany than to others. I knew not a few Russians who had been very young when they left their native country during the civil war. But they grew up in Paris and Berlin so deeply steeped in things Russian that the distance between them and the generation of their parents was much smaller. Most of those who had left Germany, on the other hand, did not really contemplate returning, hence their wish to integrate themselves fully in the new country.

Many of Henry Pachter's generation have already disappeared. The names of some of them are household words, others are known only in a small circle. If their life had proceeded undisturbed by the great storms of world politics, many of them would have become first-rate professional men and women, university teachers, journalists, scientists, businessmen, perhaps even politicians. But I wonder whether it would have been a very interesting generation. They were uprooted, they had to make a second, and sometimes third, start in their lives, they had to confront new societies and cultures, not to mention the necessity to earn a living. All this made an enormous difference. On one hand, a heavy price had to be paid for the uprooting which, psychologists assure us, is not to be recommended as far as mental hygiene is concerned, but I have always doubted Adorno's lamentations about the "damaged lives" of the emigrés. There were compensations which become clear in what inspires these essays: a cosmopolitan attitude (in the best sense), an absence of cultural or political parochialism, an intellectual curiosity which did not come to an end at the age of twenty-five as it so often does, a breadth of cultural interests quite uncommon nowadays. Many of these emigrés had a classical education, they spoke three or four languages and read more; if they were not playing the piano or violin they were passionately interested in other arts—in short they had *Allgemeinbildung*, they were educated people.

The concept of generation is both an old and a new one. Comte (and many after him) thought that a generation was the span of thirty years, an insight that had not been unknown in biblical times. This may have been true, though not invariably so, in an age of continuity. At other times a new generation may appear every year or two—or only after a century. Dilthey, in his essay on Novalis, was perhaps the first to point out that a generation was not just a chronological-metrical concept, but that it involved a deeper relationship. Those concerned had been subject to the same leading influences in their most impressionable years. What these influences were for Henry Pachter's generation becomes clear again in this volume, which is not to say that all, even within that relatively small group, moved in the same direction. Some joined the extreme left, others became Zionists, yet others saw fulfillment outside public affairs, even though very few of them became totally apolitical. Yet they still had a great deal in common, more with each other than with those who preceded or succeeded them, which is the ultimate sign of recognition for a generation. The fact that they had lived through a very stormy period of world history made them good political seismographs. Having faced the mortal danger of fascism, having been betrayed by the god (or several gods) that failed, they became sensitive (sometimes even hypersensitive) not just vis-à-vis danger to their own survival, but the wider dangers to the basic values in which they believed. As Pachter recognized, this sensitiveness did not necessarily make them political geniuses; some of them were inclined toward exaggeration and alarmism.

Political judgment is not only based on the study of Hobbes, Marx, and other political philosophers. It involves experience and is based on instinct, difficult to define and analyze but nonetheless of crucial importance. Last, it is based on common sense which, clearly, is by no means as common as commonly believed. In Henry Pachter's generation, better political judgment was usually found among those who had not just been politically committed but politically active. For they had learned certain basic lessons they were unlikely to forget. *Bis peccare in bello non licet;* already the ancients knew that in war it is not permitted twice to err—and the same is true in politics.

Sooner or later the story of the generation of 1932 will be written, just as the generations of 1898 and 1914 have come to preoccupy historians and sociologists. Such intellectual and social identikit pictures are of a certain use despite the inevitable distortion. From this it will emerge (I suspect) that many of them remained basically romantics and optimists almost to the very end, much in contrast to successive generations. With all their *Kulturpessimismus* they still believed that they were the harbingers of a better future—*mit uns zieht die neue Zeit*. They entered the sorrowful city but they did not abandon all hope. Perhaps I unduly generalize; but I am sure that it was true with regard to Henry Pachter.

Weimar Etudes

PRELUDE

[1]

Empire and Republic: Autobiographical Fragments

PART I

The Crisis of Europe

IT has been said that those who did not experience French society before the Great Revolution never knew how beautiful life could be, while those who were born after the first world war never knew how secure life could be. Of course there were riots and strikes, the Balkan and colonial wars, naval races and diplomatic crises, the rise in the cost of living, the recessions—all of which greatly disturbed the domestic and external peace of the prewar generation. But the question is not whether there actually were problems deep enough to justify fear; after all, there were numerous avant-gardists who experienced the crisis of culture long before the war. The question is whether people generally felt that they could cope with those conflicts. That undoubtedly was the case before World War I— and was no longer the case thereafter.

My own recollection of the prewar days is that of a well-protected childhood in the midst of an expanding empire, a recollection of well-being and of a trustworthy world. I do not think that many Europeans who were born after the war have similar reminiscences: that sense of security never returned.

I was seven years old when the first world war began. I remember that we were on vacation at a seaside resort and that my father said: "They have killed the Archduke Franz Ferdinand." Every schoolboy knew that Franz Ferdinand was the heir to the Austrian throne, a nephew of the old Emperor Franz Joseph, whose only son had shot himself. It was a great tragedy for the ancient house of the Habsburgs, whose empire had now shrunk to the dominions of Austria, Bohemia, and Hungary.

Although it was still one of the five or six great powers of Europe, in the world of the twentieth century Austria retained the quality of "yesterday." Where we Germans strove for efficiency, the Austrians were *gemütlich*; where we emphasized discipline, they displayed charm. This, along with the blue Danube and the Strauss waltzes, the coffeehouses and the court theater, gave the monarchy a nineteenth-century flavor. In fact, when I was in Vienna some years ago, I was astonished to find that picture postcards of the "Old Emperor" in his magnificent uniform were still being sold, that the museums still exhibited a baroque splendor and little modern art, and that despite a furious pursuit of construction projects the city still retained that old world quality.

While other modern countries tended toward becoming nation states, the Old Emperor ruled over a Babylonian mixture of nationalities. Germans and Hungarians were the master races; Czechs, Slovaks, Ruthenians, Croats and Serbs, Bosnians, and Poles were considered second- and third-rate subjects of the emperor. The well-born looked down on the minorities, who in turn looked beyond the empire's borders for support—to Serbia, Poland, and even Russia.

Franz Ferdinand's assassins were Pan-Slav army officers who belonged to a secret organization called the Black Hand. Probably they meant to provoke Austria to war, and Austria obliged: The Vienna court presented Serbia with an ultimatum it could not possibly have accepted. Russia, allied with Serbia, began to mobilize; thereupon Germany, Austria's ally, also began to mobilize—and so the infernal machine of nineteenth-century alliances unleashed its fury.

My father said: "If there is war, we Germans must stand by our allies, the Austrians." The papers were already proclaiming our unstinting Nibelungen loyalty: "The Austrians are our brothers." Although I was only seven years old, I replied to my father's explanation about the Nibelungen with the statement: "But we won't be as stupid as they." I remember distinctly that I said this, and even the place where I was when I said it. The dunes at that sea resort were decorated with all sorts of patriotic monuments, and we were standing before two pieces of field artillery captured from the Danes in the 1864 war. A young couple had just passed by; first the husband took a picture of his bride sitting on the gun, and then she took his picture standing next to the gun, with his chin thrust forward.

Many others had pictures taken of themselves standing on that rampart, looking fiercely out at the sea. We were a very patriotic people and very proud of our army. One could not enter a peasant's house without noticing, exhibited on the wall on the place of honor over the sofa, the photo of the husband or son as a soldier—or even of his whole platoon—usually framed in a mat that held the inscription: "In memory of my service time."

Militarism and chauvinism were part of our education. We hated the French and worshiped the army. Even the hit songs our maids crooned often glorified the soldier's calling. I too was very proud of our soldiers—not just out of patriotism but because of my own private loyalty. In Berlin we lived across the street from an army barracks, and from our window I could watch the dragoons drill. On special occasions they would ride out in full regalia, with flags and music, a great spectacle for us children; once a year the emperor would visit the barracks. Then, of course, we would stand on the sidewalk waiting for him, and when he whizzed by we would shout hurrah.

I must admit that I never saw much of him, but that didn't matter because at home I had an emperor all my own. He was the biggest of my toy soldiers, he wore the uhlan uniform, and he was riding a white horse.

Here I must mention a detail about my cavalry soldiers. They could be mounted and taken off their horses. But to hold them in the proper riding position, each had a plug sticking out under his behind which fitted into a hole in the horse's saddle. With ordinary cavalrymen I considered this a mere convenience; but I was always embarrassed by the fact that the emperor, too, had such a protuberance sticking out between his legs. I felt it was improper for an emperor to have a penis, or something that reminded me of a penis, and I don't think it ever occurred to me that an emperor, too, has to go to the bathroom—that would have affected my respect for authority.

But on that memorable day in July 1914, my militaristic education left no doubt that our emperor was honor bound to accept the challenge. So my father thought as well. He packed our things and took us home to Berlin, for of course one does not vacation in a sea resort when war is about to break out. Twenty-five years and twenty-five days later, after Hitler and Stalin had signed the pact that was portending war—I was then living in Paris—I said to my wife: "This may be our last chance ever to have a vacation. Let's go to the seashore once more before it's too late."

By that time, I knew that war would be a long, painful ordeal involving all nations and shaking the fates of millions of people. In 1914, no one expected anything of the sort. The soldiers marched out of Berlin with flowers stuck in their rifle barrels, singing gay songs, waving to the throbbing crowds, and assuring them: "In four weeks we'll be back." We thought of war as a temporary interruption of normal life; some even looked upon it as a pleasant diversion from boring routines. Our teachers were able to quote the greatest German poets to that effect: war brings out the best in man and a nation without war soon loses its virtue. Field Marshal von Hindenburg wrote to his wife—and the letter was published in the newspapers—that the war was as good for his health as taking the waters.

People who were less inclined to heroism were assured that business would continue as usual. Much later, when the war had shown its true face, such pronouncements were sharply criticized. But the initial responses were the fruit of naiveté rather than cynicism; they simply expressed a national mood which everyone shared.

In the Social Democratic pub my father attended, no one thought of the war as the preordained outgrowth of the capitalist system, and no one predicted that the war would result in the final crisis of capitalism. Few knew of the works—by Karl Kautsky, Rosa Luxemburg, and Rudolf Hilferding—that showed how war grows out of the system. Fewer still knew about the obscure Russian who was writing an essay under the pseudonym of Lenin, *Imperialism, the Highest Stage of Capitalism,* to prove that this war was an intrinsic product of capitalist development that would usher in the overthrow of the bourgeoisie.

Strangely enough, however, the economic interpretation of the war was immediately expounded by the patriotic writers who were trying to explain the conflict to young people. I had several such books—written for children—harping on three themes: Germany was the victim of encirclement; the war was a blessing in disguise since it united all Germans; the war was caused by England's jealousy of Germany's commercial successes. None of these contentions seemed plausible to me, especially since the teacher told us that all we cared for was honor, glory, and justice—for all of which we needed power. These were deemed worthy motives, and our slogans exalted war as an enjoyable activity, pleasing to God. Yet, no one wished to take responsibility for the outbreak of the war, and the emperor even called God to witness that he had not wanted it.

The spirit of the nation was best expressed by a slogan attributed to the crown prince: "Let them have it!" At school we followed the slogan. We rooted for our brave soldiers and we gloried in their victories. We collected gold coins and aluminum foil, because it became clear all too soon that Germany was not at all prepared for a prolonged war. Quickly enough, rationing began: bread, meat, clothing could be bought only with coupons.

In my father's shop, the workers were not quite so patriotic. The typesetters and printers were all Social Democrats, and they took a slightly bemused attitude when I appeared with my patriotic flag or collection box. The workers felt that the war was benefiting the rich, and they were especially bitter about the war profiteers. But, as Social Democrats, many continued to support the war against barbarian czarism—the bastion of world reaction.

The enormous gap between the classes became an embarrassment to the wartime government. Through official and informal channels the nation was exhorted to forget class divisions and to unite against the foreign enemy. In war, we were told, class differences would fall away; there would be no distinction between high-born and low-born in the trenches.

I had a book entitled *Franz and Hans of the Front House and the Rear House*. Middle-class people in Berlin, I should explain, lived in the apartments facing the street while low-income families lived in the rear houses facing drab courtyards and dingy walls. We knew some front-house people, or had a nodding acquaintance with them, but we had no truck with any rear-house people. Now suddenly we were being asked to form a united front against the archenemy. The emperor, who had once called the Social Democrats "rabble without a fatherland," now solemnly urged them to save the fatherland.

The emperor's challenge put all possible opponents on the defensive. The Social Democratic party proved to be patriotic; for the duration of the war it proclaimed a "civil truce," a *Burgfrieden*, in the class war. Among the vast majority, no one wished to appear as a traitor; everyone was eager to show patriotism beyond the call of duty. Thus the young Reichstag deputy Ludwig Frank, a Jew and a socialist, volunteered and died in the first battle; he believed that "a new society [was] being built in the comradeship of the trenches," and a similar tune was struck by the young French Catholic writer Charles Péguy.

Later there emerged a left wing which opposed the war

and condemned those Social Democrats who had supported it. This group was to call itself the "Independent Social Democratic Party." Still further to the left was the Spartacus League, led by Karl Liebknecht and Rosa Luxemburg. Some of the renowned war resisters were Jews, and later it was said that Jews had not behaved like worthy Germans during the war. But most Jews did support the war, and Ludwig Frank became a hero to those who hoped to affirm their right to be Germans.

Among the people I knew, only an aunt of mine had her doubts. When the first victory bulletins appeared in "extra editions," she said skeptically: "Provided it is true." But after a while, even she could not deny that we were winning the war. We had overrun Belgium; our troops were deep inside France; our submarines were strangling England's imports; in the battle of Tannenberg we had stopped the Russian steamroller and taken a hundred thousand prisoners, some of whom could soon be seen as farm workers and in the salt mines. Hindenburg, the great marshal, and his chief of staff, Ludendorff, were liberating Poland, Kurland, and other Baltic areas from the czarist yoke.

Soon I was to see how important these Eastern conquests were to us. When my father was drafted, he became book-keeper in a supply depot deep in Poland; from there he was able to send us a goose or a few pounds of flour once in a while, a supplement, sorely needed, to our meager rations. We had no farm connections whatsoever, and my mother would have starved to death rather than buy food on the black market. But, through my father's letters, we all became aware of the occupation regime's corruption and the arbitrariness of the officers' caste. Army officers expected Polish Jews to step into the gutter when they met on a sidewalk, and they had a quick hand on the riding whip when they thought someone was a bit too slow.

As the war drew into its fourth year, my father's letters reflected the weariness of the soldiers. After a revolution knocked the czar out of the war, there seemed to be little reason to continue the slaughter. My father even wrote an

allegorical tale or parable predicting a peace founded on reconciliation. I found it among his papers much later; it was so
ineptly written that, I had to admit, it could not be published.

An Aborted Revolution

Peace did not come by negotiation. It was achieved by the
defeat of Germany and the victory of the Western allies, who
were strengthened through America's entry into the war. The
German people did not know that by winning so many battles they had lost the war.

Unable to overrun the French and take Paris quickly, the
German armies were stopped and had to dig into the trenches.
Then the news of glorious victories gave way to terse bulletins of defeat and surrender. Erich Maria Remarque later took
the title of his world-famous *All Quiet on the Western Front*
(*Im Westen nichts Neues*) from one of those stereotyped bulletins symbolizing the hopelessness of our efforts and the futility of our sacrifice.

The war of matériel became a war of attrition and mutual
starvation. Desperately we tried to strangle England with our
U-boat blockade; I remember a front-page cartoon showing an
Englishman with his neck in the noose, the rope being pulled
by two U-boats. Such propaganda assurances, however, could
hardly conceal from us the fact that it was rather England
that had blockaded us. We were hungry. Even the slim rations to which we were entitled were often unavailable. We
learned how many things, including shoes, could be made of
paper and how many different dishes—entrée and dessert not
excluded—could be made from turnips. And these were not
the turnips one can find at a New York greengrocer's, but
wartime turnips that were grown as large as possible and that
tasted like wood.

People were becoming discontented. One day I heard the
word "strike" for the first time; my mother said it was a very
bad thing. A Jewish boy in my school told somebody that we
were losing the war; another said the crown prince was hav-

ing affairs with French girls. Our principal called an assembly and made a solemn speech against defeatists and grousers. I didn't know whom to believe.

Our office apprentice came home on leave from the Western front and told horror stories. In his sector our armies were retreating, yielding territory but leaving no house or tree standing. He was disgusted with our tactics and approved of soldiers who simply went AWOL. I thought all this was horrible if true; talking about it made it even more horrible. But, then, there were still people who talked of "peace through victory" and of annexing occupied territory.

On November 9, 1918, revolution came to Germany—a catastrophe which we had thought could happen only in faraway countries. I was too young to understand the upheaval. Although my mother said that at last the war and all the worrying were over, I regretted the emperor's flight and the breakdown of his order. To me, revolution meant soldiers who went around with their rifles upside down and their coats unbuttoned; noisy, disorderly demonstrations in the streets; breakdown of communication; and rumors everywhere. We heard of irregular troops holding this or that government building, but no one could tell whose side they were on. Red flags and posters; strikes, shouts, and occasional shooting; officers from whose uniforms the epaulets had been torn; no policeman with his familiar spiked helmet in sight; it seemed there were only soldiers with red arm bands.

I wrote to my father, who was still in Poland: "Do you too have to wear a red cockade?" hoping he didn't. Most of the kids in my class were faithful to the monarchy. We could not believe that our glorious armies had been defeated.

We lined the streets when the soldiers came marching home—somber, their heads down. We cheered them because our teachers had told us that our soldiers had been "unconquered in the field." This assertion was technically true. Our army had still been deep in enemy territory but the supply lines had broken down, the reserves were exhausted, and morale had hit zero. Had the Allies waited another week before granting Hindenburg an armistice, the field marshal would not have been able to withdraw from France in an orderly manner. But they demanded only a speedy retreat.

This technical detail came to be the source of all subsequent nationalist propaganda. "Unconquered in the field," the German army was defeated by a "stab in the back" that came from the Jews and Social Democrats who had "betrayed" the fatherland on the "home front."

There was only one way the Socialists could have met the charge—by pleading guilty. They should have bravely confronted their accusers and flung a "Yes" into their faces: Yes, *we* ended a cruel and senseless war which *your* kind criminally started but did not know how to win or end. Had they answered in this fashion, they might have given the new republic a noble, humane meaning and rallied all brave and decent people to its flag. Indeed, the great historian Arthur Rosenberg—who was to become my teacher and friend—has argued that such a republic could have told the Allies: This is a different Germany, a Germany that cannot be held responsible for the kaiser's militarism. And had the Allies then, nevertheless, imposed a conquerors' peace, as they did at Versailles, the republic would have been entitled to proclaim revolutionary resistance.

But sober council prevailed. The Social Democrats tried to deny the charge, tried to prove that they had been good patriots, and some of them even sued for slander those who had charged them with the crime of sanity. In short, they conceded that their enemies had a sound case, and thus they surrendered their argument before the oratorical duel had even begun. In this match, the greater demagoguery of the right emerged triumphant. The nationalists spoke of "November criminals," referring to the date of the revolution that would install the Weimar Republic; indeed, they attacked the new president, Friedrich Ebert—probably the most reluctant revolutionary in history—who had never wanted a revolution, and to whom power had only come through the emperor's flight.

Had the Social Democrats assumed responsibility for the revolution, they would have wiped out their shame of 1914;

they might even have reconciled the Independent Social Democrats. They could have forged a new unity of the working class to give the revolution the impetus it lacked. They could have indicted the war criminals, made a clean sweep of the old officer caste and the reactionary bureaucrats, dispossessed the Junkers, and broken up the big estates in eastern Germany. But Ebert's concern was to maintain public order and assure supplies for the population. He was not prepared for the turbulent process that creates a new society. To bring the soldiers home safely, he needed the closest collaboration with the generals, but he failed to curb their private plans to organize counterrevolutionary troops. Under his very eyes, the generals recruited volunteers and openly indoctrinated them to meet the threat of a socialist revolution.

The counterrevolutionary soldiers marched through the streets of Berlin with swastikas painted on their helmets. This was where I got my first glimpse of the emblem. People explained that it was an ancient symbol of racial purity; those of sound hearing sensed that the next word would be "anti-Semitism." Since Jews were prominent in the republican parties and had taken a hand in founding the Republic, monarchists soon began to speak of the "Jew republic."

My mother somehow instinctively reacted against these mercenary hoodlums who posed as defenders of law and order; but when Karl Liebknecht and Rosa Luxemburg were killed, she said: "They had it coming to them." Meanwhile my father had come home from the East, had talked to me, and converted me to the Republic. He was for Ebert and a liberal democracy. He hated Rosa Luxemburg and all who would prevent an orderly transition to a new normalcy. With the princes and generals gone, he looked forward to the establishment of a strong social and democratic state—severe against its enemies on the right and left, but just toward peaceful citizens.

In this, he followed the majority, who above all wanted peace and stability. I saw Social Democratic demonstrators carrying large signs inscribed: "Ebert, Get Tough!" When the Communists—at the time called Spartacists—seized the building of the Social Democratic daily *Vorwärts* in Berlin, we were all for law and order, along with Ebert and his mercenaries who quelled the uprising.

The idea of occupying newspaper buildings was crazy and had no strategic value whatsoever. Paul Frölich, the biographer of Rosa Luxemburg and at the time a member of the Communist party's leading cadre, told me later that no one had given the order; he was convinced the uprising had been sparked by agents provocateurs. Rosa Luxemburg, too, knew that it was premature and ill-considered. But she could not allow the masses to make their own mistakes without interfering; she had to be with them, like a mother whose children threaten to wade into a treacherous pool.

Visiting the *Vorwärts* scene, I suddenly heard the burst of a machine gun behind me and took cover. A crowd of workers in blue shirts gathered around an army officer and tore the epaulets from his shoulders, shouting disdainfully: "Noske! Noske!"—the name of the Social Democratic minister whose nickname was "the bloodhound" and who had called in the troops against the revolutionary workers.

Soon the forces of order, including my family, rallied around Noske and the Republic. The revolutionary institutions, the "councils," that had sprung up at the front and at home, began to wither away, and a new constitution stabilized the social balance. But few accepted the new colors of the Republic, the venerable black, red, and gold; the boys in my high-school class openly referred to the republican flag as black, red, and shit. It was never displayed at school assemblies because it passed for controversial. On election day, each party would fly its favorite flag from balconies and windows. At those times, I had to admit that my art teacher was right when he said that black, white, and red was more pleasing to the eye. It was a pretty sight indeed—but not from a republican point of view.

The Democrats

At the age of thirteen, I began the first of my numerous political engagements. I worked for the Democratic party, a republican, liberal-bourgeois group which was "left" in all matters of cultural freedom, freedom of the press, and other civil liberties. They were free-trade advocates, anti-militarist, anti-agrarian, anti-monopolist, and sincerely democratic. In the revolution of 1918–1919 they were a party of the center, defending the principles of property, and in all conflict situations they preached moderation and order.

As a young boy, of course, I somewhat exaggerated their virtues. To me they were the heirs of the March 1848 barricades, militantly fighting the Junkers' obscurantism, chauvinism, and militarism. They would bring radical reform into the administrative and educational apparatus, giving the young their share in decision-making processes. I also hoped that the Democratic party would repudiate the humiliating clauses of the Versailles Treaty, which threatened the life of the young republic that they championed.

There were a number of like-minded comrades in the Democratic party, young and romantic, and even the (Roman Catholic) Center party had a similar group. But in both parties the young activists were outmaneuvered by the moderate leaders who opted for slow reform and fulfillment of the Versailles Treaty. Center, Social Democrats, and Democrats formed the Weimar Coalition. The flag mirrored the parties: black (the traditional color of clericalism) for the Center, red for the Socialists, and gold for the Democrats. That coalition might have given the Republic a chance if only it had been granted a little time. But through inflation, reparations, foreign occupation, and depression, the coalition lost its majority in the Reichstag. Only in Prussia did it provide a stable administration until, in 1932, the government was forcibly overthrown.

It is easy to speculate about what might have been. There were radical wings in all parties. The two socialist parties might have formed a coalition with the Eastern-oriented left wing of the Center, the radical patriots among the Democrats, and even with like-minded army circles and the so-called National-Bolshevists. But the Independent Socialists were committed to pacifism and the regular Social Democrats to Western parliamentarism, so the idea of a national and social revolution never got off the ground; it would be revived later by the Communists and the Nazis.

Such speculations, however, give way before the real accomplishments of the Republic. While it failed to establish a republican army and judiciary or to smash the old bureaucratic government machinery, it did abolish the preeminence of the military and the aristocracy; it brought the middle class to power. It expanded the public sphere throughout Germany and made democratic government possible in Prussia and other once-reactionary states (*Länder*).

The government was a compromise of many social and regional, religious and political traditions; today we would call it pluralistic: a neutral state subject to the pressures of forces outside the realm of politics—business and labor, the army, the farm lobby, the private militias, etc.—most of which stood in fundamental opposition to one another. The Democratic party echoed our schools, where we learned that capitalism stands for the freedom of the individual. I had some nagging doubts when I saw the "freedom" of the workers.

Many of us felt that the Republic gave expression to what divided the people rather than to what would unite them. For this reason, some soon joined the radical left and others the radical right. Whatever the differences between them, these radical parties promised us a genuine experience of community, the true *Gemeinschaft*—a magic word which fascinated all who came from the youth movement. Many believed that only the bungling, the cowardice, the heartlessness of the republicans had deprived the German people of its historic chance to become a unified community. In this sense, the Republic never won our love; it was a framework, a vacuum, ready to be filled by any force that was led by bold men.

The Youth Movement

The "youth movement," which I joined at the age of thirteen, pushed me beyond the comfortable hopes of the Democratic party. It had been in existence for more than a decade, had absorbed many streams of opinion, and had propelled many new waves of consciousness.

The *Wandervogel* (migratory bird) began before World War I, and at that time it was part of a general movement that encompassed the younger generation—a movement away from classicism and bourgeois values, from orthodoxy and hypocrisy, from intellectualism and rationalism, toward free life, free form, truth, the senses, romanticism, and irrationalism.

In contrast to political revolutions, which seek to change socioeconomic relations, our revolution wished to change the style of life: it wanted "life reform." It may not have achieved any tangible results. But all who were involved in the youth movement, either emotionally or intellectually, have felt that it significantly shaped their lives—for better or worse. Indeed, similar observations have been made by people as far apart as Karl August Wittfogel, the ex-Communist China expert, and Werner Heisenberg, the nuclear physicist.

Gustav Wyneken, defining the "Free German Youth" at its 1913 founding convention on Meissner Mountain, said: "Up to now, young people have been nothing but an appendage to the old generation, excluded from public life and restricted to passive learning. Now they begin to seek their own identity; they attempt to shape their own lives, independent of old people's indolent habits and of ugly conventions. We strive for a new way of life that responds to the nature of youth. Our aim is a new, noble youth culture."

Other leaders of the movement were Max Hodann, M.D., the promoter of sexual reform; Hans Paasche, the anti-imperialist writer who was assassinated; Professor Ernst Joel, who tried to politicize the youth movement; Hermann Popert, who successfully pledged us to scorn smoking and drinking; Walter Hammer, who pursued the Jacobin ideals of internationalism and republicanism; and Martin Buber, who translated mystical philosophy into humanitarian action.

I did not join the youth movement because I had thought about these ideas. I was recruited by sheer accident. Yet I fell in with the movement's spirit so well that I cannot imagine having engaged in any other course of development. To go hiking, I could have joined the equivalent of the Boy Scouts; to associate with similar people of my age, I could have chosen some Jewish community club; to express dissatisfaction with my family life, I could have given in to the Zionists' strong recruiting drive. To exercise my body, nothing would have been better suited than the numerous athletic and sports clubs. All these organizations had a purpose. The youth movement had no purpose, but was itself the purpose. That was its beauty. Here was a community which, to accept me, asked nothing but my surrender.

I became a devoted participant in this group experience even though I cared little for some of their activities: the mock-naive folk dances and the childish folk songs, few of which had so much as an interesting tune, the silly fairy tales from Africa and Polynesia whose mythology we did not understand, the romantic quest for quaint old buildings and smelly back alleys, the love for patriotic songs and blood-thirsty ballads about mercenaries in the Thirty Years War. But the long hikes during vacation, the great meetings around camp fires, the communal singing and dancing at rallies, the overnight sojourns in barns or youth hostels, the ritualistic "hail" greeting that distinguished the initiated, the comrade-ship that could be invoked any time, any place, from anyone whose attire indicated that he belonged, the sense of being part of the community of the elect—all this made the youth movement unique.

There was a decidedly "folkish" slant in all this: populist and romantically national, racial but not necessarily racist. To protest against fashionable jewelry, or to revive ancient handicrafts, members wore copper runes or imitations of old-German clasps. We celebrated the summer solstice and read Lagarde's *German Writings* or the cheap philosophy of Lang-

behn's *Rembrandt as Educator*, along with Werfel and Hesse.
Some were vegetarians or health faddists. Others revived folk
dancing or woodcraft or practiced a special way of writing
German script. Most abstained from smoking and drinking.
In one way or another, each of us was engaged in "body culture"; new forms of calisthenics were on the rise, and the
more radical among us engaged in nudism on Sundays. The
common denominator of all this was Rousseau's old battle
cry: "Back to nature!"

Yet it was Nietzsche who dominated our youth movement—though he was of the older generation. He had gone
mad, but his madness itself seemed to express the fundamental incompatibility between spirit and civilization. He had
fought the German philistines in the name of true German
culture; but that culture existed only in his ravings: a culture
which his *Übermensch* would create, a culture that would
transcend all preceding cultures because of its fundamental
trait—the abolition of good and evil.

In this context, an exegesis of his work is not germane; but
we knew what drew us to him. So far, all morality had consisted of injunctions which denied the human will, the human body, the instincts. Nietzsche had not only preached a
morality that recognized man, he also had the audacity to
write that no one before him had understood the nature of
good and evil—their basic identity and the irrelevance of ethical judgments. Hermann Hesse translated all this for us in
his *Demian* and developed a notion that was only implicit in
Nietzsche's thought: that the new morality was for the chosen community who, by definition, would be pure and devoted. Nietzsche himself could not evolve the idea of community because he was mainly concerned with his own
singularity as its prophet. But the next step would be for the
order of the elect to constitute itself through recognizing the
prophet and modeling itself after his image. This detail was
added by Stefan George, and Hans Blüher of the youth movement was right when he spoke of the "self-selection" by those
who would later recognize the Führer.

Nietzsche's secret: he spoke to our desire for "authentic-

ity." He made us believe that he was telling us something in
deepest confidence, and even that only by imagery and symbol. He addressed his reader as "thou" and consistently threw
out hints which he then immediately mystified by further
asking: "Hast thou understood?" Then he would complain
that no one else really understood the depth of his thought,
suggesting naturally that the reader had entered into a conspiracy with the author to fool the world and defy it. It flat-
tered many to be told that the multitude didn't understand
them. It was even more flattering to be told that they were
the true human beings in a world of automatons, that they
were nonconformist and profound in a world of conformism
and stupidity.

Nietzsche intoxicated us with his prophetic language, with
the dithyrambs which he had invented—or adapted from the
Greeks or the Bible—as a call to "him that hath ears." His
own self-selection was purely esthetic. He saw the new youth,
the children of the muses in opposition to the philistines; he
castigated the schools' pedantry, the worship of academic
education, the illusion of science—all those institutions that
translated into the shackling "culture" of our parents.

We were burdened by tradition and therefore welcomed his
attack on history; we were suffocated with education and
therefore hailed his vicious criticism of "educated philistines"; we despised materialism, skepticism, and cynicism,
and therefore thanked him for preaching a new faith. This
faith, to top it all off, had no specific content; instead, it asserted the right of youth. He told our parents to listen to us;
we were pure and sane, the world was rotten and unhealthy.
Nietzsche asked: Who will give the new generation life? And
he answered: No god and no man, but youth. Thus, he assigned to us a mission: to be fighters and dragon slayers, to
struggle toward a happier and more beautiful culture and humanity, to shake off all the senile ideas and pit a healthy
hatred against servile hypocrisy.

All groups, whether conservative or socialist, religious or
freethinking, sang the great song that united us: "As we stride,
side by side / and the old songs we sing / make the forest

ring / then we feel that we shall bring / the new age." The old songs and the new age—this ambiguity of romanticism defines the youth movement. We hated the present; most of all we hated the world of business and industry and our parents' social conventions.

But against this old reality we summoned not a new one but the old songs about a maiden's love or a soldier's farewell, the hum of the spinning wheel or the peasant's fear of savage marauders. Most of us believed that we were getting back to the earth, to simplicity and purity. Some went all the way and joined a farming or craftsmen's community (though very few could stick it out). The Zionists performed hakh-sharah—training for farm life in Palestine. The Socialist Youth, too, coined the slogan of "Community, love, and peace" with which it confronted the establishment's pettiness, meanness, jealousy, and hate.

The youth movement tried to shield us from a reality which after all we would have to face once we left school or university. We developed no means to change society. The movement was not just apolitical but antipolitical. There are still a few old-timers around who in their dotage continue to play the guitar, sing folk songs, and invite each other to a summer solstice fire; they are nothing but the caricature of a vital endeavor which they failed to transcend. No matter how nobly the youth movement helped to open my mind, there came a time when I had to enter the world of adults.

On balance, the youth movement was a romantic reaction against the mechanization and dehumanization of life as the industrial age was irresistibly approaching its maddest phase. But the utopian dream that youth can divorce itself from the given society, or that it can carry its noble aloofness into adult life, was brutally dispelled by the events that followed. In all candor, part of this was the youth movement's own fault. Instead of fighting for new institutions, or reform of the old, we left the world as it was and turned our backs on it. Instead of finding new life forms, we harked back to the old ones and persuaded ourselves that they had been good. Instead of seeking a new humanity, we pretended that a true commu-

nity could be resuscitated from the tribal past. A romanti-
cized view of the Middle Ages conincided with the philosophical and psychological fantasies of Ludwig Klages, Carl
Jung, and the cheap folk authors who tried to substitute ideologies for real solutions and racial community for human
solidarity. Although a good number of the early *Wandervogel*
members turned Communist, the movement's folk cult led the
majority to a nationalism that later became susceptible to Nazi
slogans.

It certainly would be a mistake to hold the youth movement and its folk cult directly responsible for the degenera-
tion of German nationalism into Nazism. Nothing could be
more alien to the youth movement's individualism and idealism than the plebeian dictatorship of a Hitler. But I cannot
agree with my friend Karl Otto Paetel, who has written that
no one ever touched by the spirit of the youth movement
turned Nazi. It is true that the youth *Bünde* later resisted in-
tegration into the Hitler Youth and continued, as long as possible, to practice their own way of life. They avoided the Hitler salute and sidestepped military pursuits. But, as would be
expected, they preferred doing their private thing to engag-
ing in political resistance. When called to the colors, they did
their duty as Germans. At least one of them made a bad record as commander of a concentration camp. Many died as
Hitler's army officers. A few survived and tried to regenerate
the old *Wandervogel* spirit under pathetically different conditions.

Sex and Politics

The youth movement cultivated the most contradictory
myths about the relationship between the sexes. On the one
hand, we prided ourselves on our free and open views of the
human body, but by declaring "eros" a sacred thing, we denied sex altogether. The relationship had to be sublimated on
such a high intellectual level that it generated more frustra-
tion than enjoyment. We could boast of having beautiful nude
meetings with girls' groups. But never were girls safer from

even a lustful look—although we berated each other for being "uptight" (verkrampft).

Homoerotic relationships were more openly acknowledged. Obviously homosexuals would be attracted by the "male group" nature of the movement, and some leaders approached younger boys. I have no doubt that there was an erotic element in my relationship with my leader, as well as later in my relationship, as a leader, with some of my boys and later again, as a teacher, with my class. Judging from the beautiful film, *Mädchen in Uniform*, the same may have been true of the girls.

From the beginning, the youth movement had assumed a flavor of all-male societies, an experience no mixed company was able to offer. It renewed the Greek conviction that a homoerotic attachment to an older comrade is part of a boy's education. I had a very close, intense, and beautiful friendship with two younger boys. One was Rudi Arndt, who was to play a courageous role in the resistance and who was to be murdered in a concentration camp. To the other I was so strongly attached that I could switch to heterosexual love only by a clever, if unconscious, transfer. His sister became my first girl friend, and this love remained chaste for a long time.

My discovery of sex coincided with my separation from the youth movement and conversion to socialism. The first experience I had of loving a girl was tortured and inhibited. Our clumsy experiments began in peasants' barns and contrasted starkly with the enlightened views we professed among friends. We supported all the liberal movements: free love, legal and free abortion, birth control, equality of the sexes, nudism, and legalized homosexual relations. We read Freud, and later we read Wilhelm Reich or went to lectures of pioneers like the sex researchers Dr. Magnus Hirschfeld and Dr. Hodann. We were older then and had outgrown the youth movement. But I could not help noticing that the people we met there were just as uptight as the teen-agers we had met in the youth movement.

This strange combination of eroticism and puritanism is perhaps typical of adolescence in my generation, or at least among the middle-class youth movement. One day, when the leader of my group felt threatened by a girl's love, he made us take an oath that we would always remain a boys' group. Another time he offered to resign because he felt he was "too interested in a girl." Years later, when I met him in London, he was still unmarried.

The preservation of the all-boy society was another facet of the idea of the youth community—an evasion of the urge to develop, to meet the other sex, to found a family, to raise children, to become a responsible citizen. This form of homosexuality was a sort of flight. There was altogether too much talk about sex in general and the morality from which we intended to be liberated, in particular. But the talk was not accompanied by the spontaneity we craved. I am told that the Socialist Youth held similar attitudes; they, too, were repelled by their parents' sexual mores.

I received a notion of proletarian love when I joined the Communist Youth at the age of eighteen. The main problems my new comrades faced were technical. They had no rooms where they could meet their friends in private, and they had little information about birth control. Many were frustrated and fervently believed that all such problems would automatically disappear under socialism. Sex had to be stolen furtively where the opportunity presented itself, and the ugliness of these occasions contributed to a sadly distorted sense of values: the liberated proletarians looked at sex with the eyes of the society from which they were trying to escape. They wanted more freedom, but they still believed that sex was ugly. Class-conscious workingmen watched over their daughters' virtue no less vigilantly than their employers; brothers expected their comrades to treat their sisters with more respect than they themselves showed their girl friends. Some vowed that, if they were to "defile" a girl, she should be middle class rather than one of their own; many a young man who went steady with a comrade remained chaste until shortly before his marriage, or expected the bride to be a virgin. I have known Communists who jilted girls because they had "yielded."

To tackle the second problem, Berlin's Socialist district administration had clinics, and it was easier to obtain information on birth control, or even an almost legal abortion. Many young Socialists and Communists believed that this was all that was needed to solve the "sexual question." Few realized that questions of women's rights, too, had to be answered if ever we hoped to alleviate what was then called "the biological tragedy of woman" and the "sexual anguish" (Sexualnot; today we would call it "sexual oppression") of youth. Two books with such titles made a great impression. From France came the slogan, "Mon corps est à moi" (My body belongs to me).

The mixed groups in the Communist and Socialist Youth offered a shelter for the meeting of boys and girls. Friendships naturally developed within the political and philosophical framework; this in turn gave the movement that inbred quality which almost made it a society within society. We distinguished between "comrades" and "bourgeois" not only by opinions but by life style and the company that was kept. Most unmarried couples in the Communist Youth stayed together for long periods, referred to each other as man and wife, and were accepted as such by the others. In this they were considerably ahead of other social strata. Only in the early 1930s (the time of the Depression) did "wild marriages" (common-law marriages) come to be recognized in all strata.

Prostitution is the ultimate exploitation, where the body itself is dehumanized and made into a commodity. This was pointed out by Moses Hess, an early friend and collaborator of Karl Marx, who had married a prostitute. Most comrades read Bebel's classic, Women Under Socialism. Unfortunately written in the ponderous German style, just the same it is probably unsurpassed to this day. Unlike the bourgeoisie, workers had a human understanding for prostitutes, but despised those who used them. We had a few prostitutes in the Berlin Communist Youth; if they were accepted with some measure of circumspection, it was only because they were too easily blackmailed by the police.

I don't believe that the 1920s were wilder than the previous generation. But what my father had done before his marriage was not supposed to be mentioned. After the war it could be admitted or even publicly discussed. The old hypocrisy was going, along with the "double standard." One of the few things in which the youth movement could claim success was the change in society's sexual attitudes. Middle-class girls were no longer supposed to be ignorant on their wedding nights, and sex relations became freer among peer groups, notably within the middle class.

Obviously, this improvement did not come at a single blow for the whole of society; qualifications are necessary. Middle-class girls were still brought up to be virtuous. And we still had the popular plot in movies and lowbrow novels: low-class girl meets upper-class man; they intrigue to get married, with respectable relatives acting as go-betweens; happy ending. The youth movement taught that middle-class marriages, especially those of the arranged sort, still the practice in my parents' youth, were nothing better than legal forms of prostitution.

Berlin was a city of fairs and conventions. It had its high society with its need for entertainment, but I believe that the huge supply of whores resulted from the economic situation rather than from increasing demand. In fact, I believe that the new morality of the youth movement and the changing morality of the middle class must have reduced the demand for them. Most of my classmates, and certainly all my friends, had their initiation into sex within their peer group, and they no longer depended on the "low company" that their fathers had kept.

At that time, Berlin had the reputation of being the vice capital of Europe. But we must not confuse vice with the new morality. The crowd in which I traveled was certainly as moral in its own way as the middle class; we had no traffic with the Babylonian marketplace that figured in sensational reportage. In the papers we read about an occasional sex murder, about white slavery, and homosexual scandals; indeed we used a most inappropriate occasion, the trial of a homosexual student for murder, as a pretext for holding a mass meeting which protested "The Sexual Oppression of Youth under Capitalism."

We knew that love and cocaine could be bought on the Kurfürstendamm not far from our own coffeehouses, or perhaps even at such places themselves. But when cartoons, pornographic novels, and protest literature referred to sin, they usually meant the fast life of high society. For most Berliners, the faith in petty-bourgeois virtue was still very solid; it was precisely this frustrated philistine whom Goebbels and Streicher aroused against the pagan libertinism of the bourgeoisie. The Nazis appealed to the same indignation that had animated the youth movement. One day during the Depression, I happened to refuse a dime to a beggar; the man began to shout the most obscene curses at me because he suspected that every Jew was wasting tax money on whores.

Portrait of a Christian

It is time to introduce my wife and her family. She was born in Vuga, Tanzania, which was then a German colony. Her father was a Lutheran missionary; on both parents' side there were several generations of ministers. Her father's faith was simple and liberal. He looked at Jesus as an exceptional human being, the last and greatest of the Prophets. He felt that Jewish monotheism was a great advance over paganism, but was sorry that the Jews had rejected the gospel of mercy. Christianity was a matter of higher morality rather than of higher doctrine. His goal was to bring the poor Negroes relief from the oppressive service of their many cruel gods, and to liberate them from the superstitious bondage to their medicine men, from the foolish taboos and obligations of their tribal religion. He may have felt, also, that the German missionary schools taught black children to read and write; that the German army taught black recruits a discipline they did not know naturally, and that German missionaries, educators,

and administrators could protect the Negroes from the merciless capitalistic exploitation that they suffered in the British colonies. (There were few things that excited public opinion in Germany as intensely as the Boer War.) Indeed these
imperial idealists tried to restrain the German plantation
owners who knew no limits to their ruthless exploitation of
the colonized country and its natives.

Had anyone called my father-in-law a colonialist, he would
have either rejected the epithet as slander or not understood
it. Nor would it have occurred to him that anything was
wrong with his patriarchical attitude to the natives. True, they
were children; but so were most of the Europeans, and all
needed the guidance of God's vicars. He believed in authority, and he felt that black people could not be entrusted with
high-level authority. Despite his liberal theology, and despite
the respect he felt for the Africans' singularity, he was a conservative and, like most Germans living abroad, enthusiastically nationalistic during the first world war.

After the war, with the German colonies lost, he had to
return to Germany and there he worked with a most remarkable group of dedicated Christians. They believed in poverty
and social work and practiced as much Christianity as was
possible within an un-Christian system. All the fine people
of that crowd whom I met were completely devoid of vanity,
never wanted anything for themselves, and always served
others. Though they were unusually naive about politics in
general, instinctively they knew evil when they saw it.

The village to which Pastor Rösler was assigned had a
rather conservative complexion. At the time I visited him and
his family, a problem had arisen. The church authorities, who
depended on the support of the government, had asked their
ministers to preach an appropriate sermon on Constitution
Day. This was anathema to the anti-republican peasants; on
the other hand, the old man wished to fulfill his duty toward
his superiors. The whole family looked with anxiety to Sunday. How would the pastor square the circle? Well, the texts
of Luther's Bible were clear: Everybody must obey the authorities, but a Christian's conscience was free, and the pres-

ent problem was just one instance of the Christian's two-edged position in the world.

The constitution was not the only problem the family had on that day. I was the other. Not only did I look Jewish, which might be odd enough in a minister's house, but when before dinner everyone began to clasp hands in preparation of saying grace, the pastor was suddenly moved to start the meal without a prayer—it may have been the only time in his life he did that. But apart from this difficulty, my appearance must have given offense. I wore a provocative shock of unruly hair, shorts, and a Russian-type shirt. For the peasants, having a Communist stay in their pastor's house was probably too much. Anyway, I was asked to leave, or rather, we were asked to leave together. They even gave us some money for travel expenses—probably unaware of how far their daughter by then had been estranged from their own moral code. I was amazed at the mixture of tolerance and ignorance.

The old pastor died a few years after the second world war, and I never saw him again after that first, unpleasant encounter. But I did receive a letter from him on April 1, 1933—a most significant date, and it was the most remarkable letter I have ever received. It was the day which the Nazis had set aside for one of their "spontaneous" anti-Jewish actions—the boycott of Jewish stores. S.A. (Sturm-Abteilung–Storm Troop) men were placed at the door of every store; crowds assembled to watch who would enter. The city trembled in expectation of disorderly attacks or plundering—which, interestingly, did not happen. On that day I received the following letter, which I can transcribe almost verbatim from memory:

Dear Mr. Pachter:
I have to undergo surgery which will deprive me of my remaining eye and I am using this last occasion to write a few letters I have meant to write for some time and which I cannot leave unwritten. I remember the day when you came to my house and I behaved very badly. Please understand that I was quite unprepared to see a Jew and a communist. It was too much for me then, but now I feel

ashamed, especially on this day of shame for Germany. I know how you must feel, and I am afraid that I must assume my share of responsibility for this. I hope that you can forgive me, and I pray that you come again to my house. You will receive a warm welcome. Yours very sincerely, Pastor Nathanael Rösler.

I showed this letter to my parents, who were deeply moved by it and handed it around to their friends. It was a source of great comfort to some small part of the Jewish community at a most tragic moment.

Mine had apparently not been the only letter the pastor wrote before he lost his eyesight. Another had gone to a church friend, who showed it to someone in the Department of Justice. This official had expressed admiration for the writer, whom he did not know. It so happened that a few days later this same official was handed the file of one Hedwig Rösler who had been arrested as an underground worker. He inquired and was told that she was the minister's daughter. Indeed the police had seized underground papers in her room and she was awaiting trial at the city prison. But at that time the Nazis had not yet taken over every office; it was still possible to use social connections to obtain the release of a prisoner; so Hedwig was released after a few days in jail.

My mother-in-law wrote us a letter on another infamous date, November 9, 1938, the "Reichskristallnacht," when the Nazis called on the populace "spontaneously" to smash all Jewish property that they could put their hands on. By that time we were living in Paris, and for fear that a Nazi censor might see her letter, Mrs. Rösler did not dare to say what she meant to say. Instead, she mentioned that her daughters had been rehearsing some arias, among them the beautiful duet from *Elijah,* and she added one short sentence in Kishambala—a Bantu dialect related to Swahili, but spoken only by a few thousand people: "Tizabulwa ni shoni." The text of the duet reads: "Zion spreadeth her hands for aid, and there is neither help nor comfort." The Kishambala sentence translates: "We are overwhelmed by shame."

After the war the old pastor, now completely blind, again

wrote to me and to my father, repeating his invitation to come back to Germany. Such were the people whose friends organized the Church Bearing Witness during the Nazi years. I have known others like them, similarly devoted and similarly unworldly, who were cruelly tortured in concentration camps.

PART II

The Communist Youth

Inspired by republicanism and the romanticism of the youth movement, I had no doubt that it would be possible to introduce a fully democratic society through militant action. But like the young Marx, I came to feel that this would have to be accomplished through a great act of purgation, a birth, an apocalyptic leap which would carry us from the realm of servitude and necessity into the realm of freedom and cooperation. It was the oppressed who would create this new world. I placed my faith in their virtue (disaffected members of my class often like to feel that the oppressed have no vices) and began to think about forms of political action.

The first real proletarian I came to know was Alice, my girl friend's close friend. She declared that we were rotten bourgeois, but that we might redeem ourselves by joining the Communist Youth. Although I lacked conviction, I thought it might be worth a try. At the first meeting I attended, I embarrassed Alice in her comrades' eyes by talking about Goethe. A comrade named Harras cut me short and said that the Communists had overcome their humanist phase and were now a militant, disciplined proletarian organization which did not give a damn for the classical writers. Another asked if the Communist Youth shouldn't do something about the schools; Harras told him that such minor problems would be resolved after the seizure of power. Right now, all that mattered was to recruit students and discipline them for the revolution.

I hated Harras, especially since Alice seemed to respect him, but I was also impressed by the self-assurance of this sturdy young worker who seemed to be as fully in possession of the true doctrine as a parish priest. The group apparently accepted his words as the authoritative interpretation of the General Will, and he made no secret of the source of his assurance: he was in communication with the higher reaches of the party, the General Staff of the revolution, who had all the relevant information.

Faced with this entirely new phenomenon—after all, I was a born nonbeliever—I realized that there were only two alternatives: leave, or accept everything. I soon learned that one does not contradict the speaker; if he provokes a discussion, it will only be to test the firmness of the group's faith. Yet I liked the people and wanted to be accepted by them. Alice was very popular, and through her I met many of the comrades in their miserable slum dwellings. They were strong and free, they had a kind of humor that did not exist in middle-class families, and they accepted me as a curiosity. They were not impressed by my education but felt moved to help me understand the many things a middle-class boy does not know. Although I was not quite sure that I belonged with Alice's group, I went out with them often; since my girl friend was seeking new company, there were additional reasons to immerse myself in the group's political work.

The meetings took place in an old, run-down apartment in the Alte Jakobsstrasse, in the southwest of Berlin, not far from the Vorwärts building. I went there regularly, trying to earn the confidence of those superior youngsters, for whom every problem had been solved by Marx and Lenin and who were so sure that they would transform the world. I made friends with some and won Alice's respect by working hard for the cause. The group went chanting in the streets every Sunday morning; we had to ring doorbells and explain political issues to disagreeable people while their even more dreadful kids or lovers were yelling and while nauseating smells poured forth through open doors. Yet I always came back with a respectable number of signatures for the release of some jailed comrade or with money for the Chinese revolution. After a year of this, Alice let me kiss her. But if there ever was the prospect of an affair, it was uttlerly destroyed by a political event—the purge of the left in the Communist International.

The leader of the German Communists at the time was Ruth Fischer, the daughter of a Jewish professor of philosophy in Vienna, who had first devoted herself to psychoanalysis and then forged a spectacular career in the Communist party. She was a fiery orator and had considerable personal charm. Party members loved her, but she represented the so-called left wing—the faction that had followed Zinoviev rather than Stalin. Her common-law husband, Arkadij Maslow, directed the Central Committee, but being Russian, he could not be elected to any office. He was quite intelligent, but an utterly cynical and unpleasant character. The German Communist party's transformation from a great libertarian movement into a disciplined cohort of Russian authoritarians was largely his work, but he erected his own gallows. When Stalin gained power in Moscow and decided to rid himself of his Russian rivals along with their friends abroad, all the German militants' love for Ruth Fischer was turned into contempt and hatred by the wave of a hand—a letter published in the party paper, *Red Flag*.

Cold-blooded as this change of the guard may have been, in essence it was the Communist party's necessary adjustment to the nonrevolutionary conditions of the period. The dictatorship in Russia was forced to make concessions to the peasants; in the West the Communists had to compete with the Social Democrats for the workers' votes. That meant devoting most of their efforts not to revolution but to trade-union affairs, parliamentary maneuvers, and other reform work.

I came to know Maslow and Ruth Fischer well. With their utterly negativistic turn of mind and pervasive political demagoguery, they were incapable of any such constructive policies. But given my romantic predilections, I had to side with "the left" or, as it soon was called, the ultra-left. After all, I had not joined the Communists in order to outdo the Social Democrats in "reformist" policies. I was not yet ready to abandon the pledge of confrontation, of bearing witness to a new world. At first, the majority of the Communist Youth were on the left, too. But soon, to my surprise, Harras and Alice, along with most of their friends, decided that one always stays with the party and ardently embraced the new line. Only a year before, in their eyes, my middle-class background had prevented me from abandoning my bourgeois reformist illusions; now that same middle-class ideology kept me from seeing that the workers wanted day-to-day reforms.

Nevertheless, I did not want to be separated from my comrades, and I disliked Ruth Fischer, who always made advances to young men. To avoid expulsion from the party, I therefore went to Freiburg, where the Communists were so weak that they needed every helper they could find. But I learned that dogmatism is a powerful force, not easy to escape. Ultimately, I was to be the most decisively influenced by those friends who most strongly combatted it.

Some Men to Emulate

When the first world war ended, one of its most important results was that the artist Hermann Struck married my aunt. That was how I came to meet this extraordinary, handsome, and noble man. He was orthodox, but his friends were socialists and bohemians. He had an enormous collection of modern art, but his own paintings were very traditional, even pre-impressionist, and he never drew a nude, though he liked to tell slightly risqué jokes. He was tolerant in great things and insufferably righteous in small ones. When on Sabbaths we visited him at his home, which was a half-hour's tramway ride from our house, we had to say that we had walked all the way, and he pretended to believe it. If he forgot to light the lamp on Friday night before sundown, he was too pious to strike a match, but did not mind inconveniencing his non-Jewish neighbors to do it for him. Once I asked, with the facetiousness of a thirteen-year-old rebel, if the Bible did not say that the law was meant for the "foreigner" as well; he rebuked me severely. His pat answer to questions of ritual and orthodoxy: One is not allowed to reason about such sacred matters.

Yet he encouraged my unorthodox reading and shocked my father by giving me Nietzsche's books to read. He was the only man in my family that I admired, and everybody seemed to revere him as a patriarch. Through his wide connections he was able to help hundreds, perhaps thousands, of people, and he never rejected any petitioner. On his door he had a sign saying: "I am very busy and have no time to gab about art and similar trifles."

In 1923 he built himself a house in Haifa and helped found the Jewish homeland. My aunt learned to run an orthodox household and a kosher kitchen. She also embraced Zionist politics, though she was probably the most liberal and most assimilated in our entire, vast family of faithful liberals and assimilators.

Through Hermann Struck I was introduced to Albert Einstein. He was then the saint of science, and I was aware of mutual visits between the Strucks and the Einsteins. I had asked my aunt if it would not be possible to obtain an autograph of Einstein, and one day, after consultation between the two wives I suppose, I was ordered, or rather honored, to present myself at the Einstein apartment, Hufelandstrasse 5, to collect my autograph. Mrs. Einstein opened the door and called: "Albert, an autograph!" The professor appeared—a tall man with an open face and a mane that made him look like a musician—holding a sheet of paper in his hand. He smiled kindly but disappeared right after giving me the paper. The whole, world-shaking encounter had taken about two minutes. I was so impressed that I did not read the autograph until I was back down in the street. Probably advised that I was a science buff, the great man had written: "Goodness and a strong character are better than intelligence and learning."

What he meant by that I learned on my second visit. Struck had made an etching of Einstein, and Einstein was supposed to sign about fifty prints of it. I was selected to take the folder to his house. This time Einstein himself opened the door, had me sit down, and announced that it would take some time;

meanwhile he would give me something to read. He slid his hand along his rows of books and pulled out a slim volume which, I gleefully thought, was about the size of his immortal work on relativity. When I opened it, however, it was Moszkovski's book of Jewish jokes, and to my embarrassment he had marked the ones that were a little on the salacious side. I was so excited that I did not remember a single one of the jokes I read and, on leaving, forgot my hat so that I had to go back and have the great man open the door for me once more. I stammered and must have been red all over. I was also furious because he kept calling me "little man." I was fourteen years old, after all.

At that time Einstein was a very controversial figure. Although the theory of relativity had been published well before the war, it was not until 1920 that it seemed to acquire philosophical significance in the public mind. The term "relativity" suggested an ideology of general doubt, of revolution. People who failed to understand what relativity meant in physics were heard to complain that "Einstein is relativizing everything." It was as if he were responsible for the postwar world, or indeed for the revolutions that were shaking or threatening it.

Now there is a profound connection between the philosophy of our time and the relativity principle. Long before Einstein, some great minds had learned that we must not take our impressions of the world and our modes of perception for granted.[1] Just as the revolution of the sixteenth century was accompanied by the insight that the earth orbits the sun, so the revolution of the twentieth century went with the insight that space and time form a continuum. And just as the reactionaries of their day pounced upon Galileo and Giordano Bruno, who supported the revolutionary Copernican concept, so the new reactionaries pounced upon Einstein. Mass meetings were called to explain or to refute his theory. Instead of leaving verification to scientific tests, anti-Semitic rowdies shouted insults at the scientist, or at science itself. Racist orators exclaimed that German innocence was in danger of being raped by Jewish sophistication, as though truth and falsehood depended on race, nationality, or religion rather than on certain measurements of the next total eclipse of the sun.

Some of the boys in my class were interested in science and particularly in astronomy. At that time I hoped that astrophysics would solve the philosophical problems bothering me. I believe that I started reading about astronomy when I was eleven; despite other interests, I have always kept informed about the latest theories on the origin of the universe. I read Kant's cosmological theory when I was fourteen, and even then I was impressed by the story of Laplace's answer to Napoleon. Asked by the emperor why his book on the origin of the universe never once mentioned the creator of the universe, he answered, "Sire, I have no need for this hypothesis." Self-contained systems have always held great fascination for me, whether in mechanics, in science, or in politics. I gave much thought to the possibility of a *perpetuum mobile;* the utopias I wrote at an early age were presented as closed systems where the nature of man had to fit in with society.

Ten years after my visit, I had another encounter with Einstein. The Communist party at the time ran an adult education program called the Marxist Workers' School, and Einstein agreed to give a lecture. Of course he would not discuss relativity but extemporize on his general philosophy. Some of us were intrigued by just such a prospect: to listen in to a great man's thinking process. I cannot say that his performance on this occasion was memorable—his *obiter dicta* in some compilers' anthologies are rather naive, I think—but even less edifying was the behavior of the audience. Strong in their Marxist schooling, the Communist workers boldly got up and told Einstein that his thinking was not sufficiently dialectical and that relativity was a bourgeois concept. It was then that he showed his great humanity. He patiently tried to correct what he said must be misunderstandings and endeavored to find merit in the most naive arguments. He was less indulgent with some Communist intellectuals whose harassments he obviously was not experiencing for the first time. It was clear that they did not understand scientific philosophy, that he did not understand sociology, and that neither knew what the other was talking about.

I shall now introduce a man who has had the greatest influence on my thinking, my career, and my political development—Karl Korsch. I first met him when he taught a course in Marxism at Berlin University. The lectures had been arranged by the Communist Students' Club, since Korsch was barred from all official teaching at German universities. Several years before, the left-wing government of Thuringia had imposed his professorship on the State University of Jena, where he taught labor law and Marxist philosophy. When the Independent Socialists merged with the Communists in 1920, he went along and was made munitions-supply director in the abortive uprising of 1921. Two years later the Social Democrats and Communists formed coalition governments in the states of Saxony and Thuringia; Korsch was made State Minister of Justice. But the federal government intervened with armed might to depose the revolutionary governments, and Korsch spent most of his ministerial days literally underground—in basements. In the 1924 elections, the Communists gave him a seat in the Reichstag to secure immunity for him; by agreement with the State University, he would continue to receive his salary provided he never set foot on the premises again.

This gave him leisure to write, teach, and advise unions on their bargaining rights. He was not a good speaker, and he could never organize his courses very well: he would go along, as if by free association, from one tangent to the next. But what associations! What tangents! I have learned more from one aside of Korsch's than from a whole course taught by academic teachers. He was most brilliant in those improvisations which reflected his wide reading in philosophy, anthropology, psychology, and sociology. In his hands, a mere introduction to a topic turned into a trip through the wisdom of the ages.

What fascinated me above all was not the encyclopedic

knowledge of the man, but his method. He did not seem to teach any specific subject but rather a way of thinking about issues. His digressions made sense because he showed us dimensions and connections that no textbook could accommodate in its systematic display of the material. In fact, his method reflected his doubt that there could be any fixed "system"—not even a Marxist system. Had anyone tried to take notes on his lectures, he would have needed three-dimensional sheets, but we all were too fascinated to take notes anyway.

There was one exception, however. That was Sidney Hook, who did not know enough German to understand everything. He sat next to me in a private course which Korsch gave in 1930, I believe; on his return to the United States, Hook published a reasonable account of Korsch's views on Marxism.

The Communists were unhappy about both the course and the man. Being dogmatists by nature, they could denounce capitalism only if they had a countersystem—and, moreover, a visible one, i.e., the Soviet Union. Korsch made no secret of his knowledge that all was not well in the homeland of socialism. Of course he was able to quote Lenin, chapter and verse, and begin another trip through the most sacred Marxist scriptures to show why the contradictions in Soviet development were philosophically necessary.

Most of his Communist audience could not stomach this any more than a Baptist audience can stomach a Christology by Kazantzakis. For Korsch, Marxism was not a closed system but a method whose development was wide open. This method was based on the dialectic first expounded by Hegel and then concretely employed by Marx, only to be beaten to death by Communist priests. After Korsch's lectures, no philosophical eunuch could tell me that dialectics was the Holy Triad of Thesis, Antithesis, and Synthesis; for there is no synthesis other than the one that carries the contradictions which will explode the system again. Dialectics can easily be frozen into a Byzantine game, but in the hands of a young Hegel, a Marx, or a Korsch, dialectical thinking can be the tool of revolution.

These ideas have been more amply developed by Korsch in

a small book, *Marxism and Philosophy*, which at the same
time deals with the relationship between Marxist ideology
and the actual class movement. At about the same time, Georg
Lukács failed to draw the revolutionary conclusions from his
acute theories; later he hid his sterility behind Leninist orthodoxy and a busy output of rigidly Marxist judgments on literature. Korsch, by contrast, was expelled from the Communist party. Unlike the Trotskyist and Leninist oppositions,
however, he did not think that one should either found a new,
purer Communist party or fight for readmission into Stalin's
party. He felt that orthodox communism was no longer a revolutionary proposition and that a future revolutionary situation would produce a new type of proletarian movement. In
expectation of that possibility, he had taken up contacts with
the "workers' opposition" in Russia and the syndicalists in
the West.

I was then in Freiburg, a little university town with a small
Communist party local. If I had any hope of influencing a few
people I had to pretend that the Communist party was capable of reforming itself. Disrupting it in Freiburg would serve
no purpose; Korsch himself had advised that I avoid expulsion. So I, confidently, wrote him an optimistic letter, boast-
ing of my success in being elected local leader on a platform
which I considered a tactical compromise. Instead of the expected pat on the back, I received a long and angry letter
chiding my opportunism and saying in effect: "If a young
man under twenty maneuvers around ideological honesty, he
may indeed go places." Since "going places" was the one
thing one was not supposed to strive for in politics, this judgment was devastating. From that moment on, I saw in Korsch
not only an intellectual and political leader but a moral leader
as well.

I have had many tactical disagreements with Korsch, and
later I came to a very different estimate of our political situation. At one time we fell out completely. But through all
these experiences, some of which were very unpleasant and
threw an unfavorable light on other aspects of his character,
I never lost my profound respect for his integrity and his in-

tellectual honesty. He was capable of highly flexible tactics and admitted compromises on matters of organization and coalition politics, but he would never conceal his opinion or theories.

It so happened that I received a similar lesson at the same time from a man who in every respect was the opposite of Korsch. Georg von Below, my professor of medieval history at Freiburg University, was a Prussian Junker and a monarchist, an enemy of any type of progress, to the point of ignoring women students in his classes. He hated the Republic and the bourgeoisie. But his research had led him to recognize the importance of autonomous guilds in the development of early urban culture. This finding was contrary to traditional teaching and to the ideology of his class, which attributed the rise of crafts to the initiative of aristocrats. Yet he fought valiantly for his view and for others on which he pledged his students not to compromise.

In another respect, too, he influenced my thinking. His specialty was constitutional law and economic history, which he saw as inextricably linked. He was continuously working on the borderline between history, law, economics, and sociology. His method of following his subject matter into new contexts became a model for me.

Incidentally, he was the only non-Marxist among my teachers who understood the romantic roots of Marxism. He himself was utterly unromantic. A fall from a horse had left him crippled as a young man and hence unsuited for the pursuits of his class. It was out of necessity that he became a great scholar.

Dr. Faustus and Erasmus

Many years later, in 1951, when I was living in the United States, I had occasion to remind Einstein, now at Princeton, of our acquaintance. I had written a biography of another great

scientist and innovator, the sixteenth-century Doctor Paracelsus, and I sent him the galleys. He answered with some flattering words, expressing interest in the stormy career of the
protagonist, and added: "I think it is difficult to penetrate
into the mind of a person so remote from us."

I had depicted Paracelsus not as a man who unerringly
marches toward a goal but as a deeply disturbed soul, searching rather than finding, striving rather than achieving; not as
a modern man embodying the Renaissance or the Reformation but as a genius from the waning Middle Ages, from a
time of trouble and crisis—a veritable Dr. Faustus. (Goethe,
before writing his *Faust*, had engaged in profound studies of
Paracelsus' approach to nature.)

Paracelsus' path ultimately did not lead to the modern
triumph of science. I did not even try to portray him as a
fellow deserving of any great sympathy. He was a boisterous,
vainglorious charlatan, forever confusing his extraordinary
intuitions into nature with the wild speculations of occult
science. But his loving embrace of the universe, his endeavor
to relate the microcosm to the macrocosm, his unstinting service to truth and to suffering humanity will always fascinate
those who strive for knowledge.

Even while deploring his errant search through darkness, I
made him my hero. I placed this Faustian character in opposition to the serene humanist Erasmus, his friend, patient, and
antagonist. It would not be easy to find a pair less felicitously
matched than these two: one all light, the other all darkness;
one well established, the other forever wandering astray; one
radiating clarity and wit, the other devoid of any sense of
humor and suffering from a distorted sense of reality.

Just the same, these two have some things in common, and
somehow I feel that, taken together, they represent the range
of my own potentialities. In a way my *Paracelsus*, subtitled
Magic Into Science, is my own autobiography. I can sympathize with both Paracelsus' longing for faith and Erasmus'
skepticism, Paracelsus' attempt to embrace a chaotic world
and Erasmus' insight that all science is concrete. Both had

connections with the heretical Left, but stayed aloof from the new orthodoxy of the Reformation.

There may have been other famous men I could have mentioned. But with these two I have lived through many years of intimate research. And although I cannot say I was directly influenced by either of them, they are closest to my heart.

Thomas Mann also was writing a *Doctor Faustus* when I wrote mine. I never met him, though I came to know his brother Heinrich in Paris and met his children—Klaus, Golo, Monika, and Erika—at various functions; none of the latter impressed me, and the influence Erika Mann exerted over her father as his political commissar or his spokeswoman was altogether negative. Yet I have heard Thomas Mann speak and lecture, I have read perhaps all his published works and have used them in my courses as the most significant, most intelligent, most perceptive documentation of our time. Still, I cannot count him among the greatest writers. I feel he is overpolished, overironical, and overcivilized. While he has explored just about every disease of our age, usually he has managed to empathize with it just a bit too much to be a true moralist. In *Buddenbrooks* he has caught the mood of the declining patriciate, but he has missed the world of the bourgeoisie.

In almost all of his works Thomas Mann expresses the artist's repugnance for the world of the burgher. Only in *Lotte in Weimar* (*The Beloved Returns*) does he treat the aging Goethe as the burgher who takes a jaundiced view of his youthful ideals. In *The Magic Mountain* the burgher is a windbag, the spokesman of totalitarian technocracy is a true intellectual; more important, all of society is described as decaying, and the only escape seems to be the war. Although by 1924, when *The Magic Mountain* appeared, Thomas Mann had been converted to democracy, he was still drawing on the philosophy of his wartime treatise, *Reflections of a Non-Political Man*, where he praised the struggle of German Kultur against Western civilization. And although Thomas Mann later became the most prominent of antifascist intellectuals, his ultimate political stance still shows him as the artist who remains censoriously aloof from middle-class society.

By contrast, both Paracelsus and Erasmus were protagonists of the middle classes. Despite their jibes at human foibles and philistine traditionalism, they exemplify the spirit of methodical striving which was the hallmark of the new age.

Goethe's Faust also strives—and, characteristically, he strives toward life. Thomas Mann's Faustus strives toward destruction. Perhaps his picture is more timely, but Goethe's conception is braver and has always been mine.

Studies and Antistudies

When I first majored in literature, it was for the love of writing and writers. But I soon found out that, in order to earn a license to teach German or English, one had to study Gothic, Old and Middle High German, Anglic, and Middle English. Fortunately I was interested in the history of language, but I had little ability to learn grammar; at exam time I barely made it. Later I was fascinated by combining linguistics with archeology, psychology, and philosophy, and I have pursued these studies on my own as an amateur. For language is the matrix in which we think, the depository of our culture. I follow current debates with rapture, and I still hope that the study of language will answer some questions on the nature of man.

In the field of literature, I found the scholarship of the time deplorably sterile and Byzantine. Searching for biographical data or tracing the "sources" of an idea rarely yielded insights into the working of an author's mind. Apparently my literature professors' ambitions were confined to catching one author with his pen in another's inkpot. Although it was fashionable to treat writing in the context of social conditions, most textbooks simply had a first chapter on the general history of the age and then never looked back to it again.

I was soon repulsed by these exercises, which would merely gather dust on library shelves, and transferred to psychology, hoping to find there the life that was sorely lacking in philology.

At Berlin University, I could not have wished to find a better Department of Psychology. The Gestalt school was represented by Wolfgang Köhler, Max Wertheimer, and Kurt Lewin, all inspiring teachers who would later make a significant impact in the United States. Philosophy of education was in the hands of Eduard Spranger, who owed his appointment to the Democratic Minister of Education. His holistic views were close to those of the Gestalt psychologists, but he was a Platonist and loathed Rousseau, the Enlightenment, and positivism. He followed the educational philosophy of the German classics, from Schiller to Fröbel, which emphasized the value of play and beauty in mankind's education and upbringing. The youth movement liked him because he held that the child's world and the adult's world are radically different and that learning consists in the process of letting the native genius mature. Education, therefore, had to start out "from the child's point of view" (*vom Kinde aus*). He quoted the Gestalt psychologist Kurt Koffka: "For the child there is only play— or, in a way, nothing is play."

My first girl friend, Walli, was a kindergarten teacher and got me wildly involved with the theory of education. She switched to the Montessori school, which taught that a child's mind must receive early training through "work." During the 1920s the two schools, Spranger's and Montessori's, feuded bitterly; but I could not see that their different verbalizations expressed a basic difference in attitude. The Fröbel school was older and therefore more apt to take the master's words too literally; the Montessori people were decidedly more open to quite new ideas. In Walli's nursery school, children were allowed to play train with the sacred blocks, while the Fröbel materials, designed to stimulate the imagination, had crystallized into rigid patterns. I suspect Fröbel's word "imagination" appealed to German romantics, while Montessori's "work" was dear to socialists. Korsch's wife, Hedda, was one of Maria Montessori's friends—but then, Mussolini too honored the dottoressa Montessori with a medal.

This was extracurricular for me, and so was the new interest in psychoanalysis which we pursued with great zeal. Here for the first time, it seemed to me, was a clue to man's mind. We had fervent discussions in a circle which Dr. Siegfried Bernfeld had assembled in Berlin. He tried to marry Marx and Freud—an attempt repeated ten years later by Dr. Wilhelm Reich with more fanfare and less success. Despite his efforts to introduce psychoanalysis into politics, Bernfeld convinced me that psychoanalysis can explain but not cure, ask pertinent questions but not solve the problems which modern society inflicts on man's psyche. Academically, the same problem presented itself in psychology that I had met in literature. What interested me was not taught; what was taught did not interest me.

This is where the archetypal Doctor Faustus story becomes relevant for the young scholars of my generation. The joys of learning were limited by the frustrations of new frontiers. Like the old magus, I had tried many academic disciplines and found that I knew less than before—because by now I had lost the illusion that through knowledge one can gain salvation. Philosophy did not provide the magic formula that would solve all the riddles. It still was up to man (to me, or to a group I was affiliated with, a class, or a nation) to determine mankind's destiny. In practical life, this meant action for public causes; in studies, it meant giving up the quest for universal laws and getting immersed in specific, living history. The study of history, to which I turned with lasting ardor, also had an added advantage: as a history of ideas it afforded me continued contact with the thinkers who had searched for systems.

In choosing teachers of history, I was rather lucky. At Berlin University I had two outstanding liberals, Friedrich Meinecke and Hermann Oncken—Meinecke a subtle spirit who studied great historical ideas such as sovereignty, cosmopolitanism, and the national state; Oncken an authority on diplomatic history. Both were concerned with the phenomenon of power and strove to domesticate that monster. When Hitler came to power, Oncken quickly published a book on Cromwell, with many warning allusions to the present. He was promptly forced to resign his chair. Meinecke held out with a few students and emerged after the second world war as a foremost critic of recent German history.

Addendum: In Oncken's seminar on the Organization of Peace, I met two people who were to influence my life. One was Hedwig Rösler, whom I was to marry ten years later in France. The other was Jürgen Tern, a friendly, levelheaded, and evenhanded fellow who at the time did not reveal the clout he was to wield after the war. He majored in economics and later joined the staff of a great economic weekly. He also had connections with the prestigious liberal daily, *Frankfurter Zeitung.* I must say that we were not very closely acquainted; but during the war, in New York, when I talked with my wife about the Oncken seminar, I said to her: "I bet Tern never turned Nazi." After the war, I was sent a bundle of German papers and discovered that Tern was the editor-in-chief of one of them—which meant that he had been cleared by the Allied occupation authorities. I was so happy— and not just because I had won my wager—that I immediately sent him a pound of coffee and some other things which the starved Germans badly missed. A correspondence ensued; he published some of my letters, then suggested that I write regularly for his paper. So I became the first German newspaper correspondent in New York after the war. Since money could not be transferred out of Germany then, this column had to be a hobby at first. Later, I asked the publisher to make payments to my wife's family, who were living in very dire straits in Tübingen. And thus, sideways, I slipped into a journalistic career.

But I have run ahead of my story. Let me return to the days of Weimar.

Laws of History

I studied history for a purpose: not to glean lessons in prof-
itable conduct for the statesman but to understand why and
how nations and classes act, to discover the driving forces
and, perhaps, to see what it all meant, whether God, or Hegel's World Spirit, or some inherent great law had designed
a plan of human evolution through the ages. I read Saint Au-
gustine, who had projected the vision of man's progress toward redemption—a promise transfigured by enthusiastic
prophets like Joachim da Fiore, Savonarola, and Thomas
Münzer into revolutionary ecstasies. In Tolstoy's *War and
Peace* I read that "the finger of God" was secretly guiding the
action of men who foolishly imagined that they made decisions. Above all, I read the great systems of Condorcet, Comte,
Hegel, and Marx who, despite their divergences, all agreed
on the basic premise of nineteenth-century philosophy: mankind was progressing from ignorance to knowledge, from superstition to reason, from fear to pride, from dependence to
self-determination, from primitive to complex relations, from
tyranny to democracy, from oppression to equality, from need
to freedom. Just as Darwin had shown how the higher animals developed from lower species, so mankind was irresistibly marching, despite occasional setbacks, toward a higher,
more perfect culture, toward self-redemption.

Most Western philosophers had accepted this great vision.
In the beginning of our century it still was a matter of course.
After World War I, however, a book appeared which denied
all this. Mankind had no history, Oswald Spengler said; only
civilizations have a history. They invariably live through a
period of rise followed by a period of decline. Spengler and
Arnold Toynbee defined two dozen such civilizations, each
of which had lived through its antiquity, its middle ages, and
its modern times, after which there had been a stagnation
characterized by mass culture and Caesarist governments.
Spengler predicted that ours would be an age of technocracy
and totalitarianism. The slant of his work was clearly reac-

tionary and antidemocratic. By saying that he saw the coming of the termite state, he prepared people to accept it. The sensational German title, *Der Untergang des Abendlandes* (which literally means "the Occident will perish"), was contributed by the publisher and probably made for the success of the book. It was the rage not only among students but above all among the educated middle class, whose demise he made palatable, or even perversely enjoyable, with the aid of a mystical *Kulturphilosophie.*

Science here was degraded into myth-making. Other writers followed, each claiming superior insight by virtue of race, blood, nationality, or mythological tradition. Although academic historians pointed out the numerous errors and misrepresentations in Spengler's book, they had no real answer to his theories as long as they believed that history was nothing but sound and fury, with no sense or direction. They accepted as "fate" whatever history might ordain and gave this defeatist view the noble name of historism. Fate, or destiny, was the word most often heard in discussions of history.

This was unacceptable to me. I had long debates with a lecturer at the History Department, one Dr. Horst Michael, who belonged to both the Rankean school of historical thought and the nationalist right. He wrote the speeches of Franz von Papen, who later played such a deplorable role in the rise of National Socialism. We would walk through Tiergarten park and test various ideas about the meaning of history; he also told me frankly about the plans of Hindenburg's circle to abolish the Republic. When the Nazis came to power, he did not wish to break off our friendship; but I had to meet him in odd places like the waiting room at the railway station. I would punish him for his cowardice by being at least an hour late, but he always waited patiently to tell me how bad things were. Being a soldier's son, he planned to seek shelter in the army. I don't know what happened to him during and after the war. I guess if we could meet again he would argue that the history of our time had confirmed his pessimistic view, and I would argue that, despite all our present worries, the world has moved toward more equality for more people, higher consciousness, and better control of our destinies, not to speak of living standards and medical services.

But certainly, even if this can be called progress, it cannot be the purpose of history to feed and clothe some poor people better. Something bigger and nobler was required to defeat the gospels of doom. Furiously I read Gibbon's *Decline and Fall of the Roman Empire* and Jacob Burckhardt's *Reflections on World History*, as well as other interpretations of history. A many-volume work by Karl Lamprecht had been hotly debated in the previous generation, and my teacher Georg von Below had criticized it. There seemed to be agreement that, after reaching a peak of energy, cultures tended to become hedonistic, or "sensate," in Pitirim Sorokin's language. They would then forget the virtues that made them great and lose faith in the old gods; other-worldly, enthusiastic cults would take over, and cultural activity would become stagnant. Some people even said that the law of history ran parallel to the second law of thermodynamics, which dooms the universe to a final standstill. Were we going to end, like other civilizations, under barbarian despotism in a society without history? My quest for historical laws was no vain game; it was a matter of survival. Of all the philosophers I read, only Marx had put the question exactly in these terms: a new understanding of historical progress must give meaning to the efforts of a revolutionary class to save civilization. I cannot say that I came to communism because I read Marx. I read Marx after I had become a Marxist. Nor do I think that the theory of surplus value or the law of capitalist accumulation could have converted me. I agree with Lukács that to be a Marxist one does not have to subscribe to any of Marx's economic doctrines; even at the time when I taught these doctrines I found them pedantic and disappointing. The economic equations that govern the business cycle can be expressed in terms of other theories and in fact have been expressed more effectively and more accurately by others. To illustrate complex growth processes, Marx used simple arithmetical examples—not even algebraic ones; any sophomore today could tell him that for such purposes one needs calculus.

Nor was I much happier with the so-called materialistic interpretation of history as it was outlined in most textbooks. One does not need Marx to see that economic interests have a decisive influence on political behavior. But it seems to me that laymen are much too eager to find sordid economic motives, or even to believe in a conspiracy of economic interests, to explain everything, from the Declaration of Independence to the assassination of Robert Kennedy. Marx never taught such nonsense; to those who attributed that kind of doctrine to him he replied: "I am not a Marxist." After all, the man who called to the workers to rebel against their economic conditions would hardly have told them that their thoughts and actions were determined by these conditions, or that socialism would come automatically, without their action. Of all the teachers of Marxism, Bertolt Brecht has best grasped the polemical, ironical point of so-called economic determinism; it is Peachum the capitalist in the *Threepenny Opera* who sings: "We would be good and not so tough, but the conditions are too rough."

Marx did say that technological development provides a challenge. He speaks not of individual interests but of broad classes that are propelled into historical action when society is in a state of crisis. The socioeconomic interests of a historical class tend to coincide with the next stage in mankind's development. Marx's theory of history provides the revolutionary class with the awareness that it is destined to save civilization by destroying its temporary shell, for all growth processes imply destruction of the old and birth of the new. In the courses I taught at evening schools, I always denied that Marx expected any automatic progress from capitalism to socialism. The question, rather, was whether capitalistic development would lead into the general marasmus of wars, civil wars, stagnation, and barbarism, or to a revolution that would put the actual producers of national wealth into control—a goal which modern technology has made both possible and necessary for the first time in history.

The next step in history, action for socialism, was the necessary conclusion of man's majestic progress. Marx thus preserved history by overcoming it, and overcame it by realizing it; Hegel scholars will readily recognize there the three meanings of *aufheben:* to preserve, to abolish, to raise. This was also the program of the young Marx with respect to philosophy: to realize philosophy by negating it, to overcome it by realizing it. The same program had been proclaimed by Goethe in his *Faust,* where constant striving is given a higher reward than the blessed possession of the truth. But the idea was really best expressed by Lessing: If God were to hold in his right hand the truth and in his left the eternal striving for it, I would embrace his left hand and exclaim: Father, give!

Ultra-Leftism

My academic studies at Freiburg left me enough time for politics. The town was very Catholic, and the Communist Youth local was quite small; in fact, it met in my room. I lived as an exchange student, which meant that the girl whose room I occupied lived in my father's house in Berlin. There she studied the piano and must have been very talented, since Arthur Schnabel agreed to teach her for free. While she was a credit to my parents, any hope my hosts might have placed in me were soon disappointed. They did not like my visitors. Especially when the visitor was a girl, the lady of the house always felt an urge to get linen from a closet in my room. She would not even knock at the door.

In another way, too, I brought disgrace to the house. The Communist party had no money to pay for advertising; hence during election campaigns we pasted our posters on the walls, clandestinely, at night. A very romantic way of being political. But once we were caught by the police and had to spend the rest of the night in jail. When the captain took down our names, trades, and addresses and my turn came, his jaw fell, and he put down his pen; he could only say that he had never expected to see this happen. The next day the whole town knew that there was a university student who had gone around putting up posters for the Communist party. My poor hosts—fabrics and ready-to-wear—feared that their store might be boycotted; a fellow student, who also was *au pair* and who had become a great asset to Freiburg's small Jewish community, informed me that I had created a calamity for these people. After all, didn't the traffic policeman deride me whenever I crossed his corner?

There were three Communist students in Freiburg beside me. One of them was to go to the Marx–Engels Archive in Moscow to help edit the sacred scriptures; the second was a Bulgarian; the third was Bauer, who had a strange, elitist attitude to the party. Personally he was a free-thinker; he read unorthodox magazines like *Die Aktion* and despised Lenin and Trotsky, along with all other dictators. But like Voltaire, he believed that the people needed some organization they could believe in even though the leaders, like priests, were allowed to aspire to a higher knowledge. In later years I was to meet this extraordinary man again and again. He became a scholar in the field of medical history; although he completed all the medical exams, he never wanted to treat a patient.

I had a different idea of party education and did my best in Freiburg to teach the unprepared proletarians the essentials of Marxist economics and sociology. In the process I became involved with one of the girls, who unfortunately was married to a very orthodox party member; the resulting conflict ended with my expulsion. I would not have lasted anyway, for the zealots in Berlin had found out about my connection with Korsch and reported my outrages to state headquarters. Disregarding the shortage of Communist poster-pasters in Freiburg, and setting aside a vote of confidence by the members, a party secretary came down to demand that I either revoke my Korschian heresies or be expelled.

I went back to Berlin to study with Arthur Rosenberg, a scholar ostracized by both the academic establishment and the Communist orthodoxy. As a lecturer in Greek and Roman history at Berlin University, he received only a per capita fee from his few students. He had no chance to advance in any department, and since he was not among the examiners, no student had to take his courses. His lectures were among the most interesting I ever attended; his books on the origins of the Weimar Republic, on Bolshevism, and on Democracy and Socialism are classics. Before others who became more famous, he showed the class character of ancient civilization. Later he was lecturer at Brooklyn College. I cherish the friendship he gave me, and I shall forever be grateful for his scholarly guidance.

But politically, I was on ice. Korsch rejected all proposals to found a new party; he held that in a nonrevolutionary period such an attempt could lead only to sectarianism. He told us to join larger organizations and there to work for more enlightened, long-range policies. He established contacts with certain Russian groups and with the revolutionary trade unions or the council movements that had flourished during the November revolution and still exerted some local influence in Berlin and in the Ruhr valley. Our most gratifying contacts, however, were with the Spanish syndicalists, who were to play such a great part in the Spanish revolution of 1936.

We published a small paper every two weeks that used current events to develop doctrinal points. We also met with other left-wing people in a group which called itself the Libertarian Socialists. Among its regular attendants were Alfred Döblin, the author of *Berlin Alexanderplatz*; Brecht; Augustin Souchy, the secretary of the Anarchist International; Orobon-Fernandez of the Spanish syndicalists; Manabandra Nat Roy, who had played revolutionary roles in India and China; Lehmann-Russbüldt the pacifist writer; Kurt Lewin the psychologist; Karl Liebknecht's brother Theodor, head of the rump Independent Socialist Party; Franz Pfemfert, editor of *Die Aktion*, and his wife Alexandra, who translated Trotsky's works; Arthur Rosenberg; the son of Hugo Preuss, who had formulated the Weimar Constitution; and Isaac Steinberg.

We had odd characters, too. There was Boris Ronninger, a Jew from Odessa, a genius and a polyhistor. His landlady let him room for free because she was afraid that some day people might point the finger at her for having evicted the second Einstein. He not only knew everything, he had everybody know that he knew better. Unfortunately, he was never able to organize his magnum opus, even though Emil Gumbel—the world-famous mathematician, pacifist, and civil-rights fighter—once locked him up in his house with orders to write it. His ingenuity remained occupied with the art of borrowing and conning. He was capable of calling me at midnight to say how wonderful my last article had been and ask for an immediate celebration. When we met, he would tear the article to shreds, eat a gigantic chicken dinner, and then borrow ten marks. Later he became a dignitary of the Church of England.

There also was "Wild Vasya," who had battled for the Bolsheviks in Moscow and then had been expelled from the party. By marrying the secretary of the German delegation to the Second World Congress, he was able to leave the Soviet Union. He proved as indomitable in the West as he had been in the East. I have seen him break up Communist meetings singlehandedly. The trouble was that at our meetings he defined democracy as his freedom to hold the floor indefinitely; not even the authority of Korsch, whom he worshiped, could silence him. We all loved him, though. His fierce revolutionary looks made him a marvelous extra in the jail-break movies which were the fashion. He also played himself in a film on the Russian Revolution. Like all our Russian friends, he was full of schemes to overthrow the Soviet government and a few others as well.

Another paranoic genius in our crowd was Adrien Turel. He imagined that technology was nothing but an immense uterus fantasy which males had invented to avenge themselves for women's ability to bear children. Then there was a young Lithuanian who had shot President Voldemaras, and a number of young Hungarians: Paul Partos who was to play a part in the Spanish revolution, and his friend André Friedmann, who later would become the most famous action photographer in World War II under the name of Robert Capa.

Isaac Steinberg was a most interesting and remarkable man, a true Russian saint with all the weaknesses of such men. His righteousness was insufferable, his goodness suffocating. He was People's Commissar for Justice in Lenin's first cabinet, but was soon outmaneuvered by Lenin's Cheka and proved unable to protect his comrades from persecution. He wrote a little book on his experiences as a commissar. It shows a certain respect, or perhaps awe, of Lenin's person and abilities, but it also shows the impossibility of being Lenin's ally without being crushed. His experience certainly matched his ethical view that one must never be the devil's ally. He envisaged the revolution as a beautiful cleansing of the people, where only the unjust would perish; he could never understand why revolutions bring forth terror organizations.

He truly believed in the trinity: God, justice, and socialism. The story went around that once he was late to a Soviet People's Commissars' meeting because he had been tardy with his morning prayer, tefillim and all. He was an anti-Zionist but helped found Jewish communal settlements in South America and thought of the Jews as a chosen people. He believed in "going to the people" but remained an aristocrat even when he was a pauper. Having worked with Lenin, he hated Marxism from the bottom of his heart. I recall giving a report on the prospects of revolution in India, using overwhelmingly negative statistics; Steinberg rose, indignant, his beautiful forehead furrowed in anger, and shouted at me: "But can't you see, young man, that a people there is suffering and Gandhi is arousing them to fight—not for your Marxist economic goals but for freedom and dignity?" When he was through with my report, no dog would have taken a bone from me.

I suppose that none of us could have been the ruthless sword of revolution. We saw our role differently; we saw ourselves as a check on injustice. We were for radical transformation of institutions, but also for goodwill toward people. We felt that only equality and democracy could justify a revolution. Unless the revolution brought freedom to all, and soon at that, it would be perverted in its own leaders' hands.

That was the lesson implied in all the historical revolutions we studied, and most of all in the Russian Revolution. We had all grown disillusioned with the Soviet Union. As long as Lenin lived, compromises were honestly admitted and the Party's ideology remained intact. We might have accepted even worse distortions of the Soviet state, but what we considered fatal was dishonesty. Bureaucracy was being passed off for socialism, tyranny for freedom, party dictatorship for the necessary road to a Communist society. If in the beginning the existence of the Soviet state had been an asset to the European working class, now it was an embarrassment and an obstruction. Since the Communists demanded complete allegiance to everything that came out of Russia, all issues became confused and lines were drawn between an Eastern and a Western orientation. It was at this time that Stalin devised the encirclement complex which has dominated Soviet foreign policy ever since—this was to be the subject of *Weltmacht Russland*, a book I wrote much later.

Sectarianism and Commitment

When one is a political animal, it is difficult to endure sectarian isolation. Since Korsch did not belong in that category, he looked with skeptical irony at my feeble attempts to proselytize. A few of my frantic endeavors might prove instructive. My sister and my dear friend Rudi Arndt had become involved in a group which called itself "The Black Gang," a name taken from the song celebrating the great German Peasant War of 1525; they also loved to sing pirate songs and, of course, the songs of the Red army, navy, and air force. The gang's leader was one Max Fürst, whom they all worshiped though I could never understand why. The real thinker was Hans Litten, a man of great sensitivity and talent which he loved to waste on trivia. At that time we were enemies since he wished to continue the youth movement in a more radicalized form and believed in the separateness of the Jewish people.

Tragically, it was he who in the end paid the highest price
for political engagement. As a lawyer for Communist militants he fought very effectively in the courts and once obtained a sensational acquittal; he also angered Hitler by calling him as a witness. In revenge the Nazis threw him into a
concentration camp and tortured him so cruelly that in the
end he took his life in order to escape the pain and the deg-
radation. Rudi Arndt, too, became a martyr; he was executed
for sabotage of the German army—undertaken on behalf of
the Communist party. Another close friend, Hilde Monte, was
apprehended on a clandestine mission into Germany during
the war.

Most of the group, indeed, turned to politics with a vengeance. They were all very enthusiastic and, largely upon my
urging, became militantly active on behalf of Communism.
But to my surprise they failed to see the difference between
the humanist communism which I preached and the Communist party. *Wenn schon, denn schon* is an untranslatable
German locution meaning: If you want to go, go all the way.
The ducklings I had hatched swam away, and many of them
soon became orthodox defenders of the CP line whatever it
might be. Some rose to positions in the party; some were able
to escape to Moscow from Nazi persecution; not all escaped
Stalin's purges. After the war the survivors returned to Germany as bosses in the German Democratic Republic—which
is the main reason why I dare not go there; in my ex-pupils'
eyes I am the worst of renegades.

Looking back at the episode, I must sadly admit that, although I could build a faction and split an organization, I
could not hold on to my proselytes. This has happened to me
several times, and I can only console myself with Max Weber's famous theorem that an ideology is not like a taxi which
one may order to stop at any corner. The moment people want
action, many of them will follow the cruder, more massive
organizations and their cruder slogans. I have found this to
be true on many occasions. Yet the corruption is not merely
ideological but very material too. Through common friends I
have learned that some of our former crowd have turned into

real party hacks and live apart from the people in the opulent government compound at Pankow. My shame is not that these former followers of mine became Communist officials but that they were not among those who, on later occasions, voiced opposition to the harsh regime in which they took part. Only one who marginally belonged to that circle defected after the bloody uprising of June 16, 1953. He was Heinz Brandt, a cousin of Erich Fromm, who wrote a book about his experiences.

The second level of my involvement at the time was proletarian. In the workers' suburb of Neukoelln, where everybody was either a Socialist or a Communist, those who did not take part directly in political organizations at least joined some workers' sports group, workers' chess club, or other front activity. Those who loved gang fights joined the "Young Red Front," a militia appealing to tough guys whom the Communist party vainly tried to keep out of trouble. On one occasion when the party prevented a rumble against the reactionary Steel Helmets (*Stahlhelm*), one such group got mad and split. Politically inexperienced and without guidance, they cast about for an ideology, and this was how I came to speak to them. I must have sounded radical enough, so they adopted me as their political adviser.

I had to give weekly reports on the situation and to produce a mimeographed sheet for them. But my reports got shorter and shorter as I noticed how eager they were to finish with the formalities and get to the main business of their meetings: drinking, singing, and dancing. The girls usually appeared only after my report. The paper also was too political, too ideological for their taste, and we let it die after a few issues. The great test of the group came on May 1, 1929, when the Communists battled the police in the street. My boys, of course, rushed into the fray and defended a barricade; I don't know where some of them had gotten guns. Fighting shoulder to shoulder with the Communists, they slowly began to drift back into the fold. I continued to see the few who still associated politics with some intellectual activity, but the group dissolved as an organization.

Then there was a third level of activity, which was more
suitable for me than the others. I became interested in teaching. Most Germans do not go to high school, but left-wing
and benevolent associations tried to quench their thirst for
knowledge through night schools or the so-called people's
universities. I joined such a school in a workers' district run
by a Christian socialist, Professor Friedrich Siegmund-
Schultze, who was well known also for his field work in social assistance, agrarian reform, and other humanitarian enterprises. There I built an audience for a course on Marxism
and met people who were unsectarian and unmilitant, but
who felt the need to identify with some cause. They were of
all ages and communicated well. The professor's assistant,
whose name I have forgotten, was a fine man of conservative
leanings who would do anything for the people though little
through them. When the Nazis came to power he said, almost
in the same words Dr. Michael had used, that the army would
be the only place to shelter him.

In this People's Academy I had the first taste of an occupation I would take up in New York many years later—adult
education. At the New School for Social Research I was to
find the same kind of mixed audiences: young people who
came to learn something, and middle-aged people looking for
a cause or trying to keep in touch with the world of ideas. It
goes without saying that I never taught any field for the sake
of knowledge as such but always connected it with the march
of ideas or with the opposition between idea and reality. In
this respect education is always a critical enterprise, com-
pelled to push open closed doors and ultimately promote
radical change.

PART III

Anti-Semitism

The revolution of 1918 and the peace treaties of 1919 sub-
jected eastern Europe to strong waves of migration and ex-

changes of population. Germans were expropriated or harassed in the areas given to Czechoslovakia, Poland, and Rumania. Jews, finding themselves without the Habsburg protection, or who were actually being attacked by anti-Semitic mobs in Poland and in the Ukraine, came to Germany in search of asylum and opportunity.

Our first reaction was humane solidarity. Our youth group established posts at the railway station to serve the refugees refreshments and to direct them to reception centers. Alas, we did not understand their Yiddish, we did not like their caftans, and we found their manners strange. These people in all their misery looked down on us who had so visibly forgotten our heritage. They had no intention of learning from us or taking our advice on Western rules of behavior. They continued to be a source of embarrassment for the German Jews; weren't they, in a current phrase, "creating anti-Semitism"? True enough, they wore the clothes our ancestors had shed a hundred years earlier, now considered symbols of inferiority. They "talked with their hands," which my classmates, either innocently or to tease me, knew how to imitate. They sold old clothes—what else could they do?—and thus seemed to question our respectability and prosperity. Their business ethics were not the most commendable, and this again tended to reflect on the reputation of all Jews. They lived crowded in a few narrow streets where they displayed the manners of eastern peoples whom all Germans, and especially German Jews, thought less "cultured."

Worst of all, when they were successful and emerged from their ghetto, they invaded spas and places of entertainment, flashed their jewelry, and in many ways made themselves conspicuous—a sin German Jews had learned to avoid. Having no social ties to the community, they were not inhibited about taking advantage of other people's needs. When inflation destroyed middle-class fortunes, houses could be bought for a song, and much property was mercilessly transferred into the hands of people whom the German middle class did not consider its equal. This resentment not only created anti-Semitism among gentiles, it also affected German Jews. We tried as hard as we possibly could to repudiate "eastern Jews," to disown any connection with them, to disqualify them, to show that we despised them perhaps even more than the gentiles did.

Especially repugnant seemed those who came from Galicia, the Polish part of the Habsburg empire, and from Ruthenia, now part of the Soviet Union. But the term "Galizianer" was extended to include all eastern Jews, except Lithuanians and Russians, most of whom were upper class and who constituted a sort of Jewish aristocracy. Among them were many who had fled from bolshevism. Their German and their manners were more correct; they found smoother ways to economic security in the West. Some of them whom I came to know well were Mensheviks (Social Democrats from whom Lenin's Bolsheviks had split), and they wielded considerable influence on the policies of the German Social Democrats— not always for the best. Their fanatical hatred for the Soviet state helped create a "cold war" orientation.

I also came in contact with members of the Polish Bund, a non-Zionist socialist party for Jews who could find no home in the corrupt Polish Socialist party or in the underground Communist party. These people were not narrow and fanatical like the Zionists or the Communists; they presented a deeply humane socialism with a personal and populist touch. Although I could understand their Yiddish only with difficulty and disagreed with their philosophy, I found much to admire in their attitude. But they obviously lived in a different age. Like my friend Isaac Steinberg, they were biblical socialists for whom solidarity with their own tribe was the most natural thing and concern for the rest of mankind an extension of the law by which they lived.

The question of anti-Semitism has given rise to an academic industry. There are learned books and scores of statistics that have sought to analyze the problem. Some of these books emphasize the continuity of anti-Semitism in Germany from the time of Martin Luther to that of Hitler. A major proponent of this view was Erich Fromm, the well-known psychoanalyst and a friend with whom I hate to disagree. An-

other is George Mosse, a historian whose family owned a great
newspaper concern in Berlin and who considers Nazism just
one episode in the unending struggle between Germans and
Jews.

The question must be asked differently, however. Anti-
Semitism has appeared in many countries at various times
under special conditions of psychological, political, and
economic stress. Anti-Semitism is a matter of time, place, and
class. In high school I had most in common with a student
who was a youth leader and who believed in Nazi ideology.
Later he found a job with Goebbels, but he was not anti-Semitic. On the other hand, most of us despised two lower-class,
beer-drinking boys who, even at that time, were members of
the Bismarck Youth, a decidedly anti-Semitic, reactionary
youth organization. Those who were involved in Nazi politics never made a secret of it in my presence. One of them
openly showed his hostile feelings to me and to all Jews.
Others, who also were politically active on the right, assured
me that they objected "only to eastern Jews." Some candidly
stated that there were too many Jews in the government or in
the professions to which most of them aspired, and particularly in show business.

Later, at the university, I encountered anti-Semitism in a
more palpable form. Fellow students in the history and literature departments were reticent and uncooperative; occasionally I found my seat taken, as if by accident, or met overt
hostility from perfect strangers. Some professors converted
their lectures into Nazi agitation, though they did not harass
me personally.

In small towns, Jews may have felt that they were sitting
on a powder keg. Jewish country doctors, Jewish cattle deal-
ers, Jewish lawyers, Jewish department store owners were not
popular. In big cities Jews did not have to notice such hostility, either because they were better integrated or because they
could fall back socially on their own associations. Apart from
religious organizations, there were Jewish lodges, Jewish patriotic organizations, the Zionists, and also a separate Jewish
youth movement, itself split many ways. But there was no

official segregation as at that time existed in the United States. I was shocked, coming to this country in 1941, to find that certain beaches were closed to me; such a thing never existed in Germany before the Nazis. Only the islands of Sylt and Borkum, in the North Sea, were known to be frequented by anti-Semitic mobs, and decent people stayed away.

In the backward areas, like the Bavarian Alps, anti-Semitism was an outflow of religious bigotry. The crucifixion story, the periodical performances of the Passion Play at Oberammergau, the allegation of ritual murder, but above all simple ignorance created suspicion. I had to convince my classmates that we were not speaking Hebrew at home, that I was not hiding something strange and terrible, that not all Jews were either capitalists or Bolsheviks, and that we were not controlled by a central directorate like the Elders of Zion.

It is necessary to distinguish between religious, social, and political anti-Semitism. Socially, the Jews were segregated in their own clubs and lodges; it was rare for them to rise in the big banks, in the steel and machine industries, the army, or the diplomatic service. Few dared to buy land and farm it, for in the countryside one depends upon the neighbors' goodwill. But none of that need lead to political anti-Semitism as it did in France during the Dreyfus affair, in Austria under the Vienna mayor Karl Lueger, or in Poland under the colonels' regime. In Germany, the anti-Semitic and racist parties had never polled many votes before the Great Depression. Moreover, although Jews were not particularly welcome in the German Nationalist or Center parties, neither of them had an anti-Semitic plank in its platform except for the vague assertion that they wanted "a Christian state."

Anti-Semitism was political or quasi-political at the universities where student organizations were lobbying for a *numerus clausus* (a Jewish quota). It was political among the youth organizations that excluded Jews, such as the "Young Germans" and the Bismarck Youth. But up to September 1930, no one believed that a party which was programmatically anti-Semitic could become a major force in Germany. That year, when Hitler achieved his great Reichstag victory, it was a shock to many people. Suddenly it was revealed how out-of-touch they were with the temper of their country. Probably it shouldn't have been such a shock; the tide had been rising for some time.

Prosperity and Depression

By the middle twenties, the Republic had grown stable and prosperous. The revolutionary threat of 1923 had been turned away; big business had joined the government in the person of Chancellor Stresemann; Germany received ample credits from the United States, which it used to build up a modern industrial plant and the most advanced municipal institutions. When I traveled abroad, I could see that our school buildings, our public baths, our plumbing were better than those in the countries that had won the war. Germany had become the most modern country in Europe and had overtaken all except the United States in industrial output and living standards. Moreover, the average German's way of life was changing rapidly. Electric home appliances, radios, elevators, central heating, running hot water became available for people with medium incomes. Former luxuries turned into conveniences or even necessities.

For a few years, prosperity seemed to reconcile the reactionary classes with the Republic. Civil servants enjoyed stability, farmers enjoyed protective tariffs. When further American credits depended upon acceptance of a new plan to repay Germany's war debts, the nationalists, who as a matter of principle opposed all reparations, provided enough yes votes to carry the necessary legislation. Their paramilitary veterans' league, the Stahlhelm, declared that it would cooperate "within the framework of the present system." The handful of irreconcilable hatemongers had to go further to the right— to Hitler, who was then considered a mere crank.

Admittedly, all this was based on the assumption that overseas markets would expand. But no one did anything to develop them. In fact, business did not even develop our domestic market. While labor economists clamored for a wider and fairer distribution of purchasing power, the trade unions contented themselves with demanding modest pay raises; they offered no plan to smooth the business cycle.

However, industrialists now accepted the social changes the revolution had wrought. They did business with the Russian Communists; they sat down with trade union representatives to bargain and sign collective contracts; they accepted at least some parts of the youth revolution's style and mores. Fashions that had seemed to threaten the most solemn traditions of family life were being absorbed and domesticated. Men wore long hair (originally called "storm brush") and wide, horn-rimmed eyeglasses to look like artists or movie tycoons; women used lipstick and cut their hair short while some even smoked in public. Hemlines first showed the ankle, then the calf, eventually the knee. Everybody discarded hats. Conservative waistlines were painfully trimmed to athletic youthfulness. Sunlamps manufactured a healthy-looking tan for those who were too busy to take a day off on the beach. Women started going to universities and occupying business positions formerly reserved for men. The flapper and the career girl were accepted; social relations between the sexes became freer. Along with the corset, many taboos were to fall. The "roaring twenties" came riding on a wave of prosperity and social freedom in Germany, too.

For a while, the boom fed on itself. Quotations were rising on the stock exchange, and people thought they were rich; everybody was promoting some investment scheme; more installations, houses, and factories were built in anticipation of rising consumer demands. But when that demand failed to come forth, the manufacturers found that they had the capacity to produce more goods than they could sell. The party was over all too soon. I still remember the silly phrase of an American president: "When people lose their jobs, unemployment results." But behind the stupidity of the words there is a truth: Unemployment was the *totality* of misery, the inability of the *system* to feed its citizens. When one man is unemployed, there is cause for charity and sympathy; when thousands are unemployed, there is cause for political action. But the conventional economists' wisdom was: Let's wait until the system has cured itself—as though this were a fever that would disappear naturally.

The Social Democratic party claimed that it was "the doctor at the sickbed of capitalism," but it prescribed no medicine. The Communist party gloated that the patient was dying. The establishment papers took their cue from Emile Coué (a psychotherapist, famous at the time, who urged people to tell themselves every morning the equivalent of: "Day by day, in every way, I am getting better and better") and implored everyone to help build "confidence." The desperate ones proposed war: against the Western archenemy, against the Soviet Union, no matter. The papers also were full of millionaires jumping out of skyscrapers and of mighty ones caught with their hands in the community chest. One particular sensation was the suicide of Ivar Kreuger, who had built an industrial empire on his monopoly in matches; my friend Helmut Wickel had written a half-admiring, half-denunciatory book about him entitled *A Nothing Conquers the World*. One day Kreuger was found in a Paris hotel room, buried under fake securities with which he had tried to shore up his power. It was almost irrefutable proof that the system was disintegrating. Surely, had Karl Marx risen from his grave to be told that one-fifth of all union members were unemployed, he would have exclaimed: "This means civil war! The revolution must be on its way!"

Rumblings on the Right

Throughout the 1920s, nearly everyone I knew condemned "the system," though not all agreed upon what the system was; some meant capitalism, others meant the Republic. Those on the right—and that included the majority of the students—saw the Republic as a symbol of Germany's humiliation; they found proof of Germany's corruption in the many scandals, abuses, and malfunctions of the system.

Above all, their hostility was aroused by the new elites. Having long been used to government by the "well-born," the people were not inclined to take orders from workers, craftsmen, and petty officials. The term "bureaucrat" now took on the meaning of a know-nothing who spends his time annoying honest businessmen, a clock-watcher, a schemer who does not deserve to have power and who abuses it. The word "boss" (Bonze—originally a Japanese priest) defined the petty tyrant who uses and misuses power in his party or trade union.

Schoolboys sang: "And even if they spread caviar on our boot soles, we won't let Ebert rule us." The middle class whispered little jokes about Ebert and Scheidemann and their difficulties in acquiring aristocratic manners. Mrs. Ebert was supposed to have told Mrs. Scheidemann that she was serving peas at a state dinner; Mrs. Scheidemann replied: "That's very awkward; peas always roll off my knife."

But this was not all! Murder was the weapon of the right. They killed Rosa Luxemburg and Karl Liebknecht. They killed the Socialist Prime Minister of Bavaria Kurt Eisner; the Independents' leader Hugo Haase; the Socialist representative Karl Gareis; the Catholic leader Matthias Erzberger, author of the Reichstag resolution that led to the armistice of 1918, as well as Walther Rathenau, the industrialist and foreign minister who resolutely insisted that Germany pay the reparations she had undertaken to pay. According to an official estimate of the Minister of Justice, rightists committed 354 murders between 1919 and 1923 alone.

Perhaps even worse than the murderous banditry was the judicial harassment of the left. The judges usually let the right-wing terrorists go free or slapped their wrists gently, but handed severe prison sentences to republican militants for trifling offenses. Justice was not just peeking out from under her blindfold, she was committing outrages with her eyes wide open. The victims were Communists, Socialists, and republicans—but, above all, people who had denounced the army or uncovered its illegal dealings: its clandestine rearmament in contravention to the Versailles Treaty, its collaboration with the rightist organizations, its secret operations in Russia.

Of course anti-Semitism was another line of attack. Labor leaders, Communists, republican statesmen, the "traitors" who had signed the Versailles Treaty, profiteers who exploited the German people—they all were supposed to be Jews who either lined their own pockets or worked for a world Zionist conspiracy to ruin the nation. Novels were written to denounce the defilement of German virgins by Jewish sex fiends; Karl Kraus—a Jew himself—criticized Jewish journalists for debasing the German language. Horror stories illustrated the eternal war between the knightly German soul and the commercial Jewish spirit—a notion that received its philosophical elaboration in Ludwig Klages' Der Geist als Widersacher der Seele (The Intellect as the Soul's Antagonist). The most notorious of these concoctions—the alleged Protocols of the Elders of Zion—had served first the French and then the Russian racists; despite irrefutable proof that it was a forgery, the Protocols came to serve the purposes of German reaction.

Yet there were no riotous outbreaks against Jews until the Nazi government explicitly ordered them. Instead, there was something different: organized Nazi terror against all opponents. During the two years before Hitler's rise to power, 53 people died in street battles or as a result of political assaults. The Nazi's victims could have been republicans, Communists, Socialists, or simple citizens who spoke out. Among them, there were probably some Jews. But the point is that these assaults were not directed against the Jews per se, but rather against those who attempted to resist the Nazis and so unconsciously identified with "the Jew."

The Republic Totters

From the start, the Nazis had been organized as a paramilitary organization. They tried to dominate the streets; they would establish a strong post at a corner beerhouse and then enlarge their area to the next corner, crowding republicans and Communists from their meeting places. They also staged provocative parades through streets where they did not have a single friend. If they were attacked, the police appeared and suppressed anti-Nazi violence; if they were not attacked, they trumpeted the cowardice of the republicans.

People soon did not dare speak disrespectfully of the Nazis for fear of being denounced and beaten up by hoodlums. Once it was no longer deemed reprehensible to associate with Nazis, people decided to join those who seemed to be winning. Moreover, for an unemployed young man there were material and psychological advantages in joining the storm troopers. He would get a uniform and boots, a military cap and a dagger; he would learn to use a pistol. That changed him into a man. Up to then he had been a bum whom nobody wanted or respected; Hitler gave him a soldier's self-respect. Whenever he beat up somebody, Goebbels would announce in streamer headlines that once again the brave storm troopers had defeated Germany's enemies.

By contrast, the boys of the Republican Defense League (Reichsbanner) never got recognition from their party. They complained to the editor of *Vorwärts* (the Social Democratic party paper) that, at best, there might be a half dozen lines, somewhere on an inside page, saying that at such and such a place Nazis had had a brawl with "persons of different persuasion." The editor explained that republicans wished to conduct a dignified campaign and therefore could not boast when they had won in a gang fight. The boys got discouraged and disgusted for want of active support. They were risking their bones for the party; at least they expected to be recognized for the heroes they were. When they protected the places where refined revolutionaries like Kurt Tucholsky spoke in public, they received no thanks, for their organization was not supposed to be "the weapon of the barbarians," as our song proclaimed so proudly.

At the *Vorwärts*, however, newspaper reports about Nazi brawls with "persons of different persuasion" were carefully collected in a big scrapbook; when the scrapbook was full, it was solemnly taken to Chancellor Brüning with a request to do something about the violence. Since I had business in the *Vorwärts* archive, I watched the whole episode, from its inception, with skeptical interest. When the party secretary left for the Chancellery with his scrapbook, I told him; "He will take it, assure you that it will be studied by the Minister of Justice, and you will never hear about it again." I was wrong. The chancellor gave the scrapbook right back: "These are just newspaper clippings; I cannot act on unofficial information."

My point is that the Republic was not defended militantly and that its defenders were discouraged by the republican authorities. By contrast, its enemies used deliberate terror and received official support. From the beginning, the army was not at the service of the constitution. When in 1920 monarchist officers started a putsch—the Kapp Putsch, which would ultimately be toppled by a general strike—the chief of staff told President Ebert: "Reichswehr will not shoot at Reichswehr." Three years later, at the time of Hitler's Beer Hall Putsch, the same chief of staff, General Hans von Seeckt, had the nerve to tell the president: "The Reichswehr stands behind me."

When Hindenburg became president, the army had its own foreign policy and supported clandestine organizations. Hindenburg's friend, General Kurt von Schleicher, soon became the Republic's kingmaker; he decided who should be chief of staff, defense minister, and even chancellor. His economic aim was to free Germany from the reparations burden; his political aim was to free the government from parliamentary control; his military aim was to restore German power through an alliance with Russia. The first aim was achieved when the President of the United States, Herbert Hoover, granted a moratorium on all war debts. The second nearly occurred when Schleicher made Heinrich Brüning, a Roman Catholic monarchist with an iron will, Chancellor. Brüning and Hindenburg dissolved the Reichstag and ruled by decree. New elections were held on September 14, 1930, and the response was astounding: Nazi representation soared from a dozen to 107 deputies, with the Communists winning 77 and the Social Democrats 143 seats. Since no working majority was possible, Brüning went on ruling by decree. But in 1932 Hindenburg was reelected with the support of all the bourgeois parties as well as the Social Democrats. Brusquely, he dismissed his former ally and appointed his friend, Papen, as chancellor. Although he had even less support than Brüning, Papen was able to depose the Prussian government, which was still in the hands of the Weimar Coalition. The consternation which this act caused led to Papen's dismissal and his replacement by Schleicher. But with the Nazi tide on the rise, in January 1933, Hindenburg was reluctantly forced to withdraw his support and name as chancellor, Adolf Hitler.

A Critical Choice

On May 1, 1929, the Communists forced a showdown. One year earlier, they had declared that the Social Democrats were the "main enemy" and started a concerted campaign with the Nazis to overthrow the Republic. So, when the traditional May Day parade of the Berlin labor organizations was banned—for fear of violence—by the Social Democratic police chief, the Communists defied the ban and demonstrated. I was among those who got their share of truncheon blows; I had to go to an eye clinic for repairs. From that day, it was indeed hard for any champion of civil rights to forgive the Social Democrats.

But Trotsky understood the problem. In his trenchant style, he declared: "When I am assailed by two guys, and one has a club and the other has a gun, I try to get rid of the gunman first." One can criticize liberalism but still recognize its merits and defend it against reaction. Any other attitude is ultimately undialectical. But six months after the May Day demonstration, the Communists increased their vote at the expense of the Social Democrats. Unfortunately, it was a Pyrrhic victory. There was never any militant, unified action to defend the constitution, nor to develop radical policies to overcome the Depression, nor to oppose the new "presidential government" that would culminate in the rise of Hitler.

What to do? It was not the time to stand on the sidelines. It would have been easy for me to join up with the great number of honest young workers who were leaving the Social Democratic party in disgust over its policies and compromises. A regional opposition group had grown out of the old left in Saxony, where the tradition of Rosa Luxemburg was lingering strongly. There was a revolt among the Young Socialists in Berlin and elsewhere. They all desired a more determined, more leftist, more ideological policy, more class war and less parliamentary maneuvering, more militancy and fewer compromises, and above all, a clearer orientation toward the old Marxian prognosis that the Great Depression must be the final crisis of capitalism. I certainly liked this line.

The Social Democratic presidium provided an additional reason for me to support these people. In a vain attempt to stifle their criticism, it expelled them over a petty point of bylaw violation, as brutally and insensitively as the Bolsheviks were periodically purging their party. It was natural for those whom the Social Democratic party had expelled to the left, and those whom the Communist party had expelled at various turns of its line, to seek cooperation and eventually a merger. This was the origin of the SAP (Socialist Workers' party) in Germany, whose most important spokesman was Paul Frölich, and of the POUM (Partido Obrero de Unificación Marxista) in Spain, with which I came to be associated later.

Participating in those adumbrations of a Marxist renaissance I met many people whose paths I had crossed before or was to cross again and again. There was my old friend Bauer from Freiburg, still commenting sarcastically on the people he was trying to lead; there was Joseph Dünner, who had left the Communist party with Paul Levi, as well as some younger followers of Rosa Luxemburg.

Outstanding among them was Arkadij Gurland, of a Moscow menshevik family, who at the time was editor of the Social Democratic daily in Chemnitz (a heavily industrial town in Saxony). He was vastly talented and well liked in the party, but he had little taste for action. Brilliant in giving a theoretical explanation of any problem, he was unable to reach practical conclusions. His doctoral dissertation, attempting to restate Marx's view of dictatorship, is a typical example of his working method. Instead of answering the burning question whether Marx would have supported Lenin's formula of the dictatorship of the proletariat, he held that Marx merely had sociologically characterized some states as dictatorships of the bourgeoisie, to which the reverse would be equally sociological descriptions of the dictatorship of the proletariat—which left the reader wondering whether Marx had ever said anything about the form of the revolutionary state. It was almost inevitable that Gurland should edit a biweekly magazine, *Marxist Tribune*, which would polemicize on a very high level and attract contributions from notable persons but would prove politically ineffective.

Soon enough it became clear to me that splinter groupings or parties such as the Socialist Workers' party lacked the resources, organization, and working-class support necessary to provide a real alternative at a moment of crisis. Thus, with great reluctance, I decided to join the Social Democrats. The majority of my friends were on the ultra-left. Some dismissed my decision with cynicism, others met it with dismay, and still others understood my choice. But, though debates raged over the choices of people like me, only with Korsch were my differences at once purely tactical and fundamentally profound. For in his view we were not facing a catastrophe; at the worst, Hitler presented the kind of tactical problem that Trotsky had recognized. For Korsch, the criterion of a good decision was whether it increased the consciousness of the workers and their autonomous activity. He was not one to defend institutions such as the Republic. He was waiting for the masses to get up and fight fascism; he did not expect that the Republic would do that. On the other hand, he had told his followers that they must be active in some mass party, and some of them hoped to prod these mass parties into action.

This, we felt, was exactly what Rosa Luxemburg had done

in the prewar days. She had been an effective and loyal organizer for the SPD whose policies she was denouncing as too soft at the same time and almost in the same breath. If the term "dialectics" as it is used by revolutionary Marxists ever had any meaning, it was here: to use the militant defense of the Republic as a lever to gain power for the workers' organizations and to impose measures that also would overcome the crisis of capitalism by abolishing its institutions. This is how I and many of my friends then interpreted the teachings of the great masters of Marxism.

The Social Democratic Party

My idea was that it would be sufficient to radicalize the old Social Democratic party, give it the right ideas, and renew the Marxist spirit of class war. Some of the younger leaders had the same feeling; they pleaded for "activism" and dynamic leadership. Carlo Mierendorff was a fascinating speaker who ignited the will to resistance. He and Julius Leber injected the language of the youth movement into our propaganda. They often spoke against the materialism of bourgeois society which was responsible not only for unemployment among the workers but for the alienation of young people as well. They also emphasized that Social Democrats were not antinational, and in many other ways addressed themselves to those strata whom the Marxists never reached—peasants, students, small shopkeepers. Above all, they found inspiring new symbols of militancy and encouraged the Republican Defense League to increase its activities. Also, they were in close contact with the religious socialists who clustered around the radical theologian Paul Tillich.

Others in this group, such as Adolf Löwe and Eduard Heimann, attempted to adjust socialist planning to the possibilities of the market economy well before Oscar Lange systematized his idea of "market socialism." Last, I have to mention the most promising member of this group—Kurt Schumacher. In the Nazi time, he would become an inspiration to his fellow concentration camp inmates; after the war, he emerged as a living martyr and as the leader of the Social Democratic party. I may not have agreed with many of his later political prescriptions, but Schumacher was a charismatic figure who retained an almost mystical sense of mission. He was a fighter and a comrade of deep humanity.

They were an extraordinarily talented lot. But the group was caught in a double bind. On the one hand, their attempts to lure a desperate middle stratum (*Mittelstand*) into the Social Democratic party could not compete with the dogmatism of the fascists, who better understood the hatred those social strata felt for the Republic and for all the progressive values associated with it. On the other hand, this group's militancy as well as the coherence of its innovative program put the youngsters at odds with a party leadership that had grown old and rigid.

This last point became immediately clear when I attended my first party meeting. There were some elderly citizens, sincere in their traditional convictions, but unable to do much about them. They listened politely to a speaker who had been sent from the central office and who patiently explained the presidium's policy on some aspect of world politics, or maybe even some subject of a more general educational value. Then, sipping their beer and smoking their cheap cigars or (since during the Depression that was even cheaper) pipes, they discussed organizational matters affecting the district and felt important in contributing their share to the public interest. Occasionally they were able to refer needy comrades to the district's City Hall, since ours was a "red" district. For the rest of the evening they played cards, and I soon learned that proficiency in their favorite game, Skat, was as essential as doing the little chores that had been discussed. There was little call for debate, or rather, it was predicted and tolerated that Comrade so-and-so would make a little speech for the opposition platform, to which others would reply by reciting the day's editorial in the *Vorwärts*.

This happened every Wednesday, as had been the custom since Bebel's time, and it was obvious that these meetings had the primary function of manipulating party opinion in favor of the presidium. There were few women and fewer people under thirty, and the entire show lacked any trace of militancy. Any hope of reforming the party "from the bottom up" waned with the experience of actual party life. It was not a problem of the party's ideology, or even of the right policies, but rather a socio-organizational problem. The party's structure did not permit the kind of militancy that might have saved the Republic; the presidium knew that, or perhaps felt it in its bones.

The Death of the Republic

Historians will forever wonder whether the Weimar Republic might have been saved. Following the landslide election of September 1930, some suggested that it was necessary to let Brüning's cabinet fall and allow a new rightist majority to form a government that would include the Nazis. Because the Depression was only just beginning, these leftists believed that such a cabinet would contrive its own ruin; the Nazis would then be exposed as the stooges of monopoly capitalism which orthodox Communist theory said they were. In such a scenario, another possibility was that the left wing of the Nazi party might split off—as indeed some radical factions did in 1932. At any rate, the right would fail on its own; the workers' parties could sit back in opposition and await their turn.

No one can tell whether the parties of reaction would have allowed such a transfer to take place. Where the Nazis gained cabinet posts, they used them ruthlessly to subvert the constitution and to purge the civil service and police. When Papen became chancellor, he deposed the republican government of Prussia and thereby gained power over the single best organized defense of the Republic, the Prussian police. Before yielding power again to a left-wing government, the conspirators around Hindenburg probably would have put an end to the Republic by a coup d'état. They tolerated the weak

Brüning cabinet only because it depended entirely on the president's benevolence.

Paradoxically, the republicans also tolerated Brüning, though for the opposite reason. As long as he seemed to derive his powers from the Reichstag rather than from the president, a semblance of parliamentary legitimacy was maintained, and so was the legal basis for a republican and Social Democratic comeback. The alternative to Brüning was civil war, and for that the working class was unprepared. The rising unemployment figures had radicalized only the workers' phraseology, not their determination; in fact the working class was demoralized, and its parties did nothing to unite the proletariat against the common enemy. Rather, the two parties fought each other. The Social Democratic leaders feared an alliance with the Communists as much as a coup from the right, and the Communists, whipped by Stalin into a frenzy of nihilism, did not mind Nazi victories as long as they were at the expense of the Social Democrats. The Communists actually went as far as to join a Nazi-instigated referendum against the Prussian government and to support a Nazi-led strike against the Berlin subways. In both cases the workers repudiated the perverse alliance between extreme right and extreme left; but when Papen staged his coup against the Prussian state government, they did not lift a finger to defend it.

With hindsight, we may say today that no policy could have had more disastrous results than the one which the Social Democrats pursued. They trusted Brüning, who only thought to destroy them—we know that now, after the posthumous publication of his shameful diaries. The Social Democrats did not even impose conditions for their support, such as a ban on Nazi uniforms or a generous pump-priming program to overcome the Depression. But anyone who has ever made a crisis decision must sympathize with their dilemma. To oppose Brüning meant to risk the downfall of either the Republic or of the party and trade unions as they were then constituted.

The role of the Communist party was more wanton. Many

Karl Radek, international Communist leader and journalist. In 1919 Walther Rathenau "went to see Lenin's emissary, Karl Radek, in a Berlin prison to find out whether a national war of liberation might not be fought under the flag of social revolution."

Rosa Luxemburg.
She thought of war as "the preordained outgrowth of the capitalistic system." "The seizure of power, she said, 'cannot be accomplished in one blow. It must be a progression of acts by which power is achieved on each level, one after the other.' "

Wandervogel group (1911). "The youth movement had no purpose but was itself the purpose."   *Archiv für Kunst und Geschichte, Berlin*

Scene from the unforgettable *Mädchen in Uniform.* "Middle-class girls were still brought up to be virtuous."

Museum of Modern Art/Film Stills Archive

Albert Einstein. "Mrs. Einstein opened the door and called: 'Albert, an autograph!' "

Karl Korsch. "A man who has had the greatest influence on my thinking, my career, and my political development."

The Brandenburg Gate, by Ernst Ludwig Kirchner. "Berlin, for those who knew it, was four million hard-working citizens."

Nationalgalerie Staatliche Museen,
Preussischer Kulturbesitz, Berlin;
PHOTO: *Jörg P. Anders*

Weidenfeld & Nicolson, London; PHOTO: John R. Freeman

From *Simplicissimus,* satirical weekly. Cartoon by Olaf Gulbransson. The late Social Democratic leader, August Bebel, looks at the Socialist party split into factions. Heading: The new Socialist Party. His voice from Beyond says: "For me there are no socialists any longer, there are only splinter parties." (Gulbransson is recalling the kaiser's much-quoted declaration: "For Me there are no parties any more, there are only Germans.")

The exotic Josephine Baker. "Hemlines first showed the ankle, then the calf, eventually the knee."

Friedrichstrasse, **by George Grosz.** "George Grosz in his cartoons mercilessly exposed the vulgarity of the . . . urban middle class."

Weimar Marketplace. "By convening the Constituent Assembly in Goethe's old town, the founding fathers were seeking a symbol."

comrades recognized that the "social fascist" thesis, which identified the Social Democrats as "twin brothers" of the Nazis, was nonsense. In fact, everyone who was in a position to know has said that in 1925 Stalin personally intervened to countermand the Popular Front strategy of German Communists who had proposed that the party support a moderate candidate in the presidential elections; the separate Communist candidacy, instead, assured the electoral victory of Hindenburg and the Republic's enemies.

The Communists learned nothing from their mistake, nor could they. By 1926, the party had become a tool of Russian foreign policy. The line was set in Moscow; those who criticized it were expelled. With the victory of "socialism in one country," the consolidation of power by Stalin, and his famous "left turn" of 1919—which was left in name only—the insularity of the Communist movement and its total obedience to the Soviet Union was solidified.

Any possibility of a "reformist" alliance with the Social Democrats became illusory. And dogma came to the aid of this ill-starred position. "After Hitler, Us!"—so ran the slogan. Rather than maintain the Republic, which at least guaranteed the possibility for Communist organization, the party followed a "revolutionary" course. It meant to bring down the Republic and preserve its own organizational discipline for a seizure of power, whose "inevitability" was guaranteed by the Comintern's ideological priests. The victory never came; what followed was only the tragedy of a nation.

To my mind, the only alternative to Nazism was the concerted militant action of the left. Given the shortsighted pragmatism of the Social Democrats and the willful blindness of the Communists, such an action would probably have been impossible in the Germany of the late 1920s and early 1930s. In the Popular Front policy practiced in France and Spain, perhaps something was learned from the mistakes of the past. But not enough. This horrible combination of vacillation and orthodoxy is still with us; as long as it remains entrenched, a radical socialist course can neither be formulated nor followed.

My Republic of Weimar

It is not a mere nostalgic fantasy which now glorifies the years of the Weimar Republic with the halo of a Periclean age. Few periods in history have seen a similar outpouring of genius in the arts and sciences; few periods have seen such lively debates on ideas and ideals or such spirited participation of all citizens in the battles over the common weal. Few governments have given their citizens similar liberty to criticize or even revile them, to ridicule society and to strive for goals that transcend the existing system. It was an extraordinary age of contrasts and of dynamic development; even its most severe critics were part of the scene. Did not Plato, the partisan of aristocratic Sparta, belong to democratic Athens as Brecht, the partisan of Soviet Russia, belonged to the Weimar Republic?

By convening the Constituent Assembly in Goethe's old town, the founding fathers were seeking a symbol that denied Potsdam, the birthplace of militaristic Prussia. But their choice also suggested a tradition of classical staidness that had no meaning to anyone but high-school teachers. The political, cultural, and economic capital of the Republic was Berlin, the city of greatest atmosphere and sweep, of adventure and creativeness, the city of the new elites and of bohemian liberty, the city of partisanship and debate.

Berlin shared the fate of all big cities of antiquity in that some prophets of doom denounced her sinful life, her distractions, her shallowness. The great Babylonian whore of the Western world had once been Paris, now she was Berlin. Some severe judges have attributed the downfall of the Republic to the laxity of its morals. One eager historian has described Berlin as a meeting place of "Comintern agents, Dadaist poets, expressionist painters, anarchist philosophers, sex researchers, vegetarians, Esperanto prophets, freeloaders, courtesans, homosexuals, drug addicts, nude dancers, black

marketeers, embezzlers, and professional criminals."[2] O.K.; a
few prototypes of all these species exist in every big city. The
trouble with the description is that these people never met,
and never constituted, the public that was Berlin. They lived
on the fringe or in the interstices of society. One could easily
add a dozen more ingredients: pimps, the jovial crime Mafia
(*Ringvereine*), sadistic schoolteachers, carousing university
students, armless acrobats, nagging civil servants, sex cultists, nudists, Christian Scientists, Ahurō Mazdāo worshipers, corrupt city officials, anthroposophists, etc., and one
would still not have exhausted the supply of oddballs who
happened to live in Berlin and still did not constitute "Berlin."

Berlin, for those who knew it, was four million hard-working citizens endowed with a special kind of humor, half *gemütlich* and half ironical, addicted to a special beer, and heirs
to an inimitable language which cries out for being used in
slightly off-color lyrics, in a spoof on some establishment, or
in self-persiflage. Berlin, in the natives' fond but slightly un-
believing phrase the "Athens-on-the-Spree," had wit and
verve, satire and avant-garde theater, famous cabarets and
coffeehouses, mass meetings and street brawls. It was a unique
mixture of irreverence, hope, and exhibitionism. Sentimental
humor and cheekiness were typical of the famous Berliner
loudmouth. Fritzi Massary sang: "I am a respectable woman,
I know when to stop." Claire Waldoff sang of the "little
man's" or "little woman's" love; if you listen carefully, inside the swashbuckling heavy in some of these songs there is
a soft-hearted petty-bourgeois.

Which is the real Berlin? That of the pimps and pushers,
or that of the mass demonstrations on the large plaza before
the Old Palace? That of tourist guides and newspaper col-
umns, or that of workers and shopgirls? That of sterile scholars and their staid magazines, or that of the avant-garde theater and lively critics? When you speak of Munich, you do not
confuse the *Oktoberfest* with *Schwabing*, or the *Feldherrn-
halle* with the *Pinakothek*. In Berlin, too, you could find all

these things—separately. That which was new, sensational, modern, and progressive was one part of it, and definitely things were happening every day.

Whether you were a direct participant in those happenings or heard about them from others, you always felt you were a witness of a great time. At least someone you knew had been there, whether "there" was the first performance of a new Brecht play or a daring show of the Tiller Girls, Jimmy Walker's visit or the Seven-Day bicycle race, a brawl between Nazis and Communists, the *Presseball* or the Schmeling-Sharkey championship fight. Berlin was swarming with talented young people aspiring to be writers, actors, statesmen, champions; they all seemed to know about each other and to add up to a great fair of ideas and movements. Some of these people fancied themselves as the new bohemia and displayed their connection with the underworld or the demi-monde, or with celebrities in the arts and especially in the movie industry, of which Berlin by now pretended to be the capital.

There also were those who never made it, the dropouts and free-loaders. Many would-be bohemians never made history or finished a novel. Yet it is they whose antics have given Berlin the name of a loose city. To listen to their stories, you might think all Berlin was engaged in wild parties, collective sex, harebrained schemes to instantly get rich and famous, or drunk and dissolute. The truth is that I lived in Berlin for twenty-six years without ever visiting a Haller Revue or Femina, the equivalent of the Copacabana; neither my friends nor our parents would have known where to find the places of vice, let alone have participated in orgies. The truth is also that those writers, actors, and performers who got anywhere lived rather sober lives in modest rooms rented from middle-class widows; they worked very hard to survive, performed odd jobs, or went hungry.

Isherwood and Pitigrilli have described Berlin's seamy side; but the people in that milieu were outsiders and déclassé. The pimp and the profligate were different from the *Three-penny Opera* déclassé, who symbolized all of society. Forty years later, after viewing the movie *Cabaret* based on Isher-

wood's story, I wondered how much of it was typical. To my
great regret, Americans must have thought that this was Berlin. Watching the film, one does not understand where the
Nazis came from or, even worse, one gets the idea that these
interesting foreigners and Jews with whom one sympathizes
are surrounded by hostile, gross, crude natives who are only
waiting for a chance to unleash the terror. Berlin, however,
was republican to the last and had a Socialist–Communist
majority.

Nor should the tragic fate of the Republic be seen as a punishment for the exuberance of the 1920s. Going through the
memoirs of some famous people who had access to high society, such as Oskar Maria Graf, Carl Zuckmayer, Ludwig
Marcuse, I get the impression that they all were writing about
the same nude party, the same one-legged prostitute, the same
supplier of cocaine. Had Isherwood just once, upon leaving
his boarding house, turned left instead of right, he might have
found a Berlin different from the one which began on Nollen-
dorfplatz (where Sally Bowles' now famous pension stood)
and extended along the fashionable Tauentzienstrasse and
Kurfürstendamm. There also were the world-renowned gathering places of bohemia: Romanisches Café, Lunte, Zuntz, Café
des Westens (called Café Grössenwahn), Kaffeeplantage—
whose patrons, of course, included fewer bohemians than
camp-followers and voyeurs.

And there were the more radical critics of this society: Erwin Piscator had his revolutionary theater precisely on Nol-
lendorfplatz, and at the other end of Kurfürstendamm was
the satirical Kabarett der Komiker, a cabaret that was quite
different from Sally Bowles's. It practiced "cultural bolshevism" and gave a forum to all who looked at life under the
Republic with a sarcastic eye or found amusement in the
mores of the age. For its audience it gathered both the moralists who felt that this criticism was bitterly serious, and the
enlightened bourgeoisie which liked to laugh at its own foibles and to make fun of its—aptly called civil—servants.

Just as Beaumarchais's *Marriage of Figaro* was staged before the aristocrats at Louis XVI's court, so Berlin's cultural

elite was amused by Brecht's *Threepenny Opera* with Kurt
Weill's endearingly singable tunes. We were all excited by
its sham-revolutionary bite, as we were by the strange jazz
musicians brought over from America, or by the savagely
brilliant colors which Nolde splashed on his canvases. It was
the exuberance of a generation that found so many means to
express its despair and so many problems to express despair
about. Many new plays by Pirandello, Bruckner, Schnitzler,
and Shaw dealt seriously with predicaments of the modern
world; others did the same thing in a facetious mood, and
neither proposed to overthrow the system. Traditionalists invariably labeled as "cultural bolshevism" any deviation from
prewar, Wilhelminian tastes. Indeed, as Ossietzky put the
matter: "When Kokoschka paints a sunset in colors never seen
in Farther Pomerania . . . that is *Kulturbolschewismus.*"

But neither were all intellectuals left-wing nor were the left-
wingers all that left. They easily blended with the establishment and in fact were part of it. The muck-raking Kabarett
der Komiker was owned by the Mosse family, publishers of
two establishmentarian newspapers, and when we applauded
the new Russian movies we were moved by their art as much
as by any political appeal.

Culture and business, theater and administration mixed on
solemn or relaxed occasions, and then one could see that culture was itself part of the establishment. I have a photo which
shows General von Seeckt, the chief of staff, with Gerhart
Hauptmann, author of *The Weavers*, in a theater box. (I have
forgotten whether they meant to honor the army or to legitimize art.) I have another, showing Heinrich Mann, the most
leftish of the acknowledged writers, with Chancellor Gustav
Stresemann at the Presseball. This ball, and the one that took
place in the Reimann graphic design school, were the most
coveted occasions at which to be seen while having fun.

I mention all this merely because some writers have presented Weimar society as deeply polarized and the left-wing
intellectuals as totally isolated in their principled criticism.
Neither was actually the case. Left-wing and right-wing poets
spoke to each other as poets and addressed each other as

"Meister." Politicians of right and left parties met in the Reichstag restaurant and addressed each other as "Herr Kollege." Rowohlt published Communist and Nazi authors—even an assassin like Ernst von Salomon. A man might easily belong to a number of crowds with widely differing aims, some overlapping and others contradictory. But then, Weimar culture was as contradictory as everything else in my world.

I have often thought about my ambivalent attitude to the Weimar Republic, and I must explain it. On the one hand, I was clearly in opposition—not just to the ruling parties but to the entire "system"; on the other hand, this system was the one that gave life to all our opposition. Monarchists and fascists might attack its most fundamental principles; we on the left criticized it for not living up to these very principles. Communists and left-wing intellectuals often condemned the "capitalistic republic" and especially its continued betrayal of republican policies, its continued employment of monarchist judges and army officers, its class justice, its denial of equality. But I parted company with friends who well-nigh rejoiced whenever once again some terrible event, like the killing of thirty-three demonstrators on May 1, 1929, "unmasked" the Republic as bourgeois and the Social Democrats as spineless. I could not agree with friends who voted against the Prussian coalition government or joined a Nazi strike against the moderate trade-union leadership. Their attitude was worse than suicidal; it was deeply immoral and opportunistic—if not simply dictated by Stalin. Just as they had at the time of the Hindenburg election in 1925, the Russian and the German Communists were collaborating to undermine the German Republic.

This is not just a postmortem on a policy that failed. Rather, it is a matter of historical justice to say that, for all its shortcomings, the Weimar Republic was one of the freest states that ever existed, that it afforded the working classes greater opportunities for collective improvement than any other European state at that time, and that its cultural life was determined by progressive minds more effectively than at any other time in German history.

There was Berlin, bubbling over with new ideas and new activities. There was, in Frankfurt, the famous Institute for Social Research. There was the avant-garde theater and there was the youth movement. There were societies of all sorts, promoting knowledge and science, religion and superstition, sports and dance. There were political movements, right and left, extremist and conservative and moderate. Weimar was the coexistence of all this: the pluralism, the tolerance, the opportunity to choose and to proselytize. It was precisely this critical edge which made the cultural and political life of the Republic so exciting and which gave this whole period its complexion.

Ultimately, there is no "Weimar," there is only the spirit that can be grasped from its contradictions. These contradictions created the most open and lively of all the systems I have ever known—including that of the United States—which tragically led to the most barbaric regime known to man. That is the strangest contradiction of all.

[2]
Expressionism and Café Culture

ACH generation has its own way of voicing protest and acting it out. At the end of the nineteenth century, the naturalist rebels—Gerhart Hauptmann, Bruno Wille, Wilhelm Bölsche, and other friends—had established their exile ten miles outside of Berlin, near Müggelsee, a lake that was the end point for the Sunday excursions of city dwellers.[1] Some of that generation had studied abroad and known the coffeehouses in Paris or Rome, but they did not transfer the coffeehouse cult to Germany. Although some writers, like other people, had their *Stammtisch*,[2] this was not the "life of bohemia."

The next generation was that of *art nouveau*, called *Jugendstil* by the Germans. It was an urban rebellion, and its center was the artists' quarter of Munich, Schwabing. Around the turn of the century it was Germany's answer to the Left Bank. Here were the artists' cafés, the studios, the editorial offices of the satirical weekly *Simplicissimus* and of the exuberant magazine *Jugend* (Youth) which gave its name to the flowing, decorative style. The literary youth movement of that generation was led by Arno Holz, Frank Wedekind, Richard Dehmel, Johannes Schlaf, and others who looked up to Nietzsche, Oscar Wilde, and Walt Whitman. In his monograph on *Die Bohème* (Stuttgart, 1968), Helmut Kreuzer describes it as "informal groups living or gathering in artist or

Reprinted with permission from Stephen Eric Bronner and Douglas Kellner, eds., *Passion and Rebellion: The Expressionist Heritage* (South Hadley, Mass.: J. F. Bergin, 1982).

student quarters of large cities, meeting in public places like cafés, bookstores, and galleries, or in studios and editorial offices." Their life style more or less deliberately displayed their contempt of conventionality, authority, and middle-class values; their expressions, in art and writing, defied traditional wisdom and academic respectability.

As their enemies saw them, they were especially antagonistic to philistine notions of family, property, and career. Averse to materialism and to profit, this particular generation also practiced and preached sexual liberation and "life reform." Among its friends was the Viennese architect Adolf Loos, who had started the "Truth in Living" movement. However, not all bohemians were "life reformers." Some dressed like dandies (Sternheim, Benn), or even wore a monocle (Rudolf Leonhard) or a red vest (Roda Roda); others were extravagant (Else Lasker-Schüler), deliberately sloppy (John Höxter), or hirsute (Erich Mühsam).

"Nature" and "Truth" were the slogans which these artists contrasted with the pushy, materialistic bourgeoisie of the new empire, with its stuffy, hypocritical Kultur and its academic art. Yet, Schwabing was really an epicenter of the new Reich. Its hand-me-down materialism appeared slightly dated, its opposition to the nouveau-riche imperialism of Wilhelm II a mere offshoot of the local resistance against Prussian predominance, or of the good old days' resentment against the twentieth century. Munich was rapidly falling behind. When Gottfried Benn's *Morgue* appeared, *Zwiebelfisch*, once *the* avant-garde paper, wrote: "A person who goes mad used to see white mice dancing. Modern Berlin has gone him one better; it sees rats."

The Munich natives were condescendingly referred to as *Hiasl* (boors); they cordially retaliated by calling the Schwabing crowd *Schlawiner*, which may have been telescoped from *schlappe Wiener*, "sloppy Viennese," since many bohemians had come from the Austrian monarchy and its Slav (Bohemian!) provinces—maybe also because they needed haircuts and did not do much except debate all day long.[3] In the early days of the century, the Munich crowd still included, apart

from the painters, many names that were to become significant—Heinrich Mann, Leonhard Frank, Gustav Meyrink, Klabund (Alfred Henschke); also the *Simplicissimus* cartoonists
Olaf Gulbransson and Henri Bing, the future Dadaist Hugo
Ball, and Erich Mühsam.

Nevertheless, the writers who were to become identified
with Expressionism soon left for Berlin: the true contemporary opposition had to locate itself where the new bourgeoisie met with the new licentiousness. Geography here becomes significant, and we have to pinpoint the location. At
the eastern end of Unter den Linden was the Royal Palace; to
its north, east, and south extended "working Berlin," the
throbbing city with its middle classes whom the artists despised, and its laboring masses whom they ignored—good old,
conservative, and progressive Berlin with its traditional virtues and vices. At the western end of Unter den Linden, beyond the Brandenburg Gate and Potsdamer Platz, where the
Wall runs today, began *das feine Berlin* with its civil-servant
and banker families—the distinguished "Old West."

But the city expanded further west. New, modern houses
with electric lighting, elevators, and central heating were built
for the new bourgeoisie between the suburbs of Charlottenburg and Wilmersdorf (still outside the city limits). This was
the "New West," fashionable and luxurious, stretching along
the new artery, Tauentzienstrasse and Kurfürstendamm. Three
literary reminders: it was here that Effi Briest took residence
in a new building; here that Christopher Isherwood strolled
in search of adventure; and here, of course, that Joséphin Pé-
ladan and Pitigrilli (the immoralists idolized in the 1920s)
learned about cocaine. A strong contingent of Jewish
bourgeoisie and the beginnings of an entertainment industry
added spice to the area. At the far end of Kurfürstendamm
was Lunapark, an amusement center where bohemians used
to spend more time than their biographers would care to admit.

At the entrance of Kurfürstendamm, Kaiser Wilhelm II had
built the monstrous Memorial Church (Kaiser-Wilhelm-Ge-
dächtniskirche), in whose shadow were the Romanisches Café

(so called because of its round-arched arcades), a busy station of the cross-town metropolitan railway, a modern department store, and the zoo. By day, nursemaids walked their wards here to see the animals; by night, streetwalkers paraded their charms in this new neighborhood where the strutting new establishment displayed its wealth and its mores. Soon the philistines too were going to have their Saturday night excursions to "see the artists."

For here, at the corner of Kurfürstendamm and Joachimsthaler Strasse, was the Café des Westens which poets, painters, and actors made their hangout. Ernst von Wolzogen used to come here after performances of his modernistic *Bunte Bühne*; here Herwarth Walden founded his Association for the Arts—Verein für Kunst—which promoted Expressionist painters. His first wife, the ethereal and rhapsodical Else Lasker-Schüler, served as muse for the round table and as the galleon figure for the art shows. During the day, the café was occupied by earnest young men who were quietly reading, writing, or drawing; conversation was discouraged. But in the evening it filled up with characters sporting flowing locks and artists' cravats; the place was noisy with ardent discussions as new ideas were tried out, new enemies denounced, new votaries converted.

"It was the café of my friends and of my critics, also of my first affair," wrote Ernst Blass, the Dadaist. "What I was participating in, with anguish, was a literary movement, a crusade against the philistine . . . against the lack of feeling, against obtuseness and sterility, against traditionalism. In the café the soul was appreciated. The café was an institution to educate artists, a tough school of which I am still proud, a sanctuary, a parliament without parliamentary abuses. The timid learned to speak. We learned to be aware of what was really close to our hearts. It was an education to be truthful to our feelings." (Abridged translation.)

The artists' contempt for the philistine, the *Spiesser*, was fully reciprocated. If the café was an attraction to the sightseers, the respectable middle class of the neighborhood was unhappy about its invasion by undesirable elements. Some papers asked whether the "swamp" was to be permitted in their midst.[4] Berlin was "the city with the heart of asphalt," indeed, as Else Lasker-Schüler had written. But the café remained, to protest against the cruelty, the loneliness, the vacuity of Berlin. The ground floor of the Café des Westens was a large room furnished with a number of small white marble tables. Glass plates covered those on which an idle draftsman had doodled a design or a painting. On the second floor there were chess and billiard tables. As German cafés must, this one also displayed a half dozen daily papers. Most bohemians read only the *Feuilleton*, where they and their friends expected to be published, reviewed, or at least talked about. Some drama critics, like Alfred Kerr, Herbert Ihering, and Bruno Engel were friendly to modern ideas. Anyway, to get all the news of goings-on in the literary world, one had to read all the papers. This was one important function of the café. To understand the rest, a few sociological details must be considered.

Most of the young artists, poets, writers, and critics came from well-to-do families which insisted that they attend the university. This was the age when grants or stipends were virtually unknown; nor did one work one's way through college. Young academics had to be supported by their fathers until a good many years after graduation. Also, in contrast to the present generation of rebels, few then majored in literature or history, for the cultural rebellion was directed precisely against—and was provoked by—the academic sterility of scholarship and the oppressive high-school teaching in these areas. Most studied law or medicine as a solid foundation for future income. They would not think of selling their pen (none used a typewriter yet). Also, publishers and theater producers considered avant-garde writing a work of honor and love that need not pay, or be paid for. Thus, Johannes R. Becher received a monthly check of 150 marks from his father,[5] even when he was recognized as an up-and-coming poet and was doing editorial work for the publisher Heinrich Bachmair. Only the established writers of the previous generation, like Hauptmann, Thomas Mann, Hofmannsthal, and other protégés of S. Fischer (the prestigious publishing house) could support themselves by their trade, and they were duly disparaged by the young rebels. These rebels had to live either with their rich parents—as some did even after marrying, naturally, in the "New West"—or in miserable furnished rooms.

And here two pieces of information should be kept in mind. The Berlin apartment, as viewers of *Cabaret* may have noticed, was laid out so that visitors had to pass through the parlor, where a zealous landlady (or parent) kept watch over the tenant's (or childs) virginity. "Storm-free pads," with direct access to the staircase, were rare and expensive. For company in the evening, therefore, a young man had nothing but the café. Living arrangements were largely responsible for the mores of the age. But hardly any book discusses prostitution in terms of the geographical conditions of family living.

Then too, the mornings in every household were dedicated to the ritual of housecleaning, for which purpose men were supposed to vacate the premises. What was there but the café? Even if intellectuals had not been afflicted with the neurosis known to them as *Budenangst,* phobia of the pad, they would have fled the uncongenial home and sought refuge among fellow sufferers. Proximity to—and aversion against—the father's house, dependence and liberation from it, determined the significance of the café as the locus of the counterculture.[6]

The café was a home away from home, a sanctuary from the world's paltriness, a working place, a meeting place for friends, a safe shelter from alienation. *Geborgensein,* being nestled, was a subject which at the time began to interest psychologists and philosophers. In 1914, *Die Aktion* published a poem by Yvan Goll entitled "Café":

> All the fellow humans in the city
> but dusty, pale lanterns
> reflecting alien light
> But here I found friends . . . .
> like music
> what they say
> radiates over the rustling of the cyclopes' city.

The six lines omitted compare the friends to the woods and to the animals, in the spirit of the Expressionist painter Franz Marc.

"We could do without nearly everything, except coffee and the café," said Ferdinand Hardekopf, who has been called the king of Expressionism. But the coffeehouse was more than company (*Anschluss*, Becher's term). One met not only with friends but with first readers and helpful critics, editors, sponsors, and even mentors. The café was the "launching pad," as Else Lasker-Schüler said, not only in the material sense but in a deeply intellectual sense too: "our best place to learn what is new," Stefan Zweig recalled; and Wolfgang Goetz confessed that the café was "a school that taught us to see, to know, to think."

Paul Cassirer, whose gallery launched the Expressionist painters in Berlin, once advised a lady, perhaps with tongue in cheek, to send her son to the café for six months in lieu of the university. For those who were seeking initiation, the café was an academy; for those who already belonged, it was "a fair" (*unsere Börse*, as Else Lasker-Schüler put the matter). New clubs and magazines were planned and founded, new *Richtungen* (tendencies) and fantastic new names for them were invented—*Neopathetiker, Neorhetoriker, Aeternist*— while roommates and sexual partners were swapped. It was a veritable game of musical chairs, a constant hustling and bustling. Everyone knew everyone else. And although individuals often ideologically realigned themselves, split with one another, sat at different tables, or refused even to speak, they all participated in one great comradeship: the community of those who had rejected the philistines, laughed at their Kultur, transcended their morality, and knew that they were *die Kommenden*, the coming generation to whom the future belonged.[7]

"We were possessed. In cafés, in the streets and squares, in our studios we were marching constantly, driving ourselves to express the inexpressible,"[8] Johannes R. Becher was to write in his memoirs, which otherwise are by no means uncritical of the young rebels' exuberance but convincingly testify that exuberance was their most genuine product. Perhaps this assertiveness, this sense of extraordinary assurance, earned them the epithet *Grössenwahn*, which in the Berlin idiom sounds somewhat more mocking than "megalomania" or "delusion of grandeur." The artists and their writer friends have charged that the term was coined by some Babbits who hated them. But the bohemians accepted it, and to my ear it has the self-flattering ring of an intellectual's self-irony. Anyway, whatever the origin of the term, aficionados fondly referred to the Café des Westens in Berlin and to the Café Stefanie in Munich as "Café Grössenwahn."

These two places were populated largely by the same kind of people, or even by the same perambulating, ubiquitous individuals. Among them was Peter Hille, whom Else Lasker-Schüler called "the Good Lord"; poor John Höxter, who financed an expensive habit by being witty for half an hour in front of some curious nabob; the ugly, dwarfish poet Jakob van Hoddis, whose real name was Davidsohn; the chess-playing, uninhibitedly abrasive anarchist Erich Mühsam—and many, many more whose description would require a wealth of adjectives. Traveling poets and artists, too, were immediately introduced to these coffeehouses, there to be discovered and accepted as comrades-in-arms and invited to give readings and shows. The arrivals of Kokoschka and Werfel were such great occasions.

No other café was ever honored by the title "megalomania" except the Romanisches, which inherited it after 1921 when the Café des Westens had closed and bohemia was no longer a coherent crowd.[9] The Romanisches always had more voyeurs than artists; perhaps guests, some of whom had once belonged to *Grössenwahn*, now famous, would occasionally return to visit their former haunt. Although cavernous, the Romanisches never achieved the atmosphere of creative poverty and conviviality of the older café. That distinction, in the later 1920s, fell to a smaller place further down the Kurfürstendamm called Die Lunte because its owner, a short, squat lady who gave credit to artists, was forever chewing a cigar end, a *Lunte*.

Café des Westens and Stefanie were by no means the only bohemian gathering places. In Berlin, after his separation from Else Lasker-Schüler, Herwarth Walden held court for a while at the more distinguished Café Josty on Potsdamer Platz; other circles were fathered in the Café Austria and in Dalbellis Weinstube. The publisher and writer Munkepunke (Alfred Richard Meyer) had a luncheon table at a place code-named Paris, and a weekly table in Wilmersdorf in the Biberbau. Among his friends were Oskar Kanehl, Gottfried Benn, René Schickele, Rudolf Leonhard, Max Herrmann-Neisse. But it is characteristic of memoirs of the period that these same names should also turn up on many other lists.

In Leipzig, the publisher Ernst Rowohlt had his luncheon table at Wilhelms Weinstube and passed his evenings at the Kaffeebaum, where visitors admired his boisterous humor and drinking capacity. He loved conviviality and was always accompanied by his faithful adviser Kurt Pinthus, future editor of the famous anthology *Menschheitsdämmerung* (Twilight of Mankind). Their work, which was most decisive in winning public acceptance for new authors, could easily be imagined without any coffeehouse connection, but of course they depended on communication with the *Grössenwahn* crowd in Berlin and Munich, and especially with Max Brod's circle in Prague (Kafka, Werfel, Haas, Weltsch). When Kurt Wolff split with Rowohlt, however, he did quite well without frequenting coffeehouses.

Leipzig was the center of the book industry, and writers in search of a publisher were always in abundance. But no circle was permanent, and no intellectual center of the modern movement could develop in that industrial city. Munich also had publishers who were interested in modern writing: Langen, Beck, Piper, Bonsels (himself a poet). But, as I said, Schwabing's great time was drawing to an end in the second decade of the century. With that, the crowds separated. The new establishment of the *Jugend* and *Simplicissimus* magazines met at the remote Torgelstube in near-exclusivity. Franz Jung, forever envious of success, referred to recognized writers as "Torgelstube types." Bohemians who tried to retain the

image of the Parisian artist still gathered at Stefanie (There-
sien- and Amalien-Strasse), or across the street at the Café
Bauer. There they met Franz Blei, an excellent mentor for the
younger artists and an editor-founder of many little magazines. Another center of attraction was the adventurous psychoanalyst Dr. Otto Gross, whose mysterious relationship with
the Richthofen sisters has been uncovered only recently.[10]

The Blue Rider group stayed in Munich. But the painters
who had constituted Die Brücke in Dresden had good reason
to transfer their studios to the capital. I have already indicated why "the scent of Berlin," praised in a contemporary
hit song, might have been most stimulating and why, in particular, the border area between the New West and the Old
provided the audience for a new avant-garde that was no
longer bohemian in any romantic, nostalgic, or even artistic
way. Here was the most modern bourgeoisie and its critical,
disgusted sons; here were the new vices of a disintegrating
society; here was the searing self-doubt of the entire Kultur
business, the total rejection of society.

This becomes clear when we compare the Grössenwahn
crowd with other critics and opponents of the empire and its
culture. Basically, the Wilhelminian establishment was being
attacked by two kinds of opposition—that of the pub and that
of the café. The socialists carried their agitation to the places
where the workers would drink their beer and play their
games of cards. Their meeting halls, obviously, were in the
north, east, and south of the city. Their counter-kaiser had
been August Bebel, the beloved leader of the Social Democratic party, who however ruled his party like a patriarch and
who was anxious to appear respectable in the reactionary
government's eyes. His immediate aim was to bring the
masses more material comforts. To the artists, this meant
making everyone into a Spiesser and perpetuating Spiesser-
tum (Babbittry). Although some socialist leaders also preached
a new morality, socialism did nothing to promote a cultural
revolution.[11] Richard Dehmel and Franz Pfemfert were the
only ones who thought of combining the politics of socialism
with the anti-politics of art (Gerhart Hauptmann had forgot-

ten that once he hoped to do so). A few others were interested in both radical politics and radical art—like Paul Levi, later on the leader of the Communist party—but took pains to keep their crowds separated.

The literary naturalist of the preceding generation had pointed the finger, exhorted society to remedy its abuses, analyzed people's reactions, and offered them better mores with greater insights. The new generation of artists was not interested in improvements, nor in changes or revolutions that would only substitute new rulers and new rules for the old ones. Their purpose was to abolish society, not to improve it; to expose the hypocrisy of bourgeois Kultur, not to ennoble it. The genteel culture had reached its apex, inevitably to be followed by its doom; the artists' job was to announce, not to avert, a cataclysmic overthrow of the existing society.

Someone had called the coffeehouse a "waiting room"—presumably thinking of a career. The guests, as in a story by Conrad or Kafka, however, were waiting for a quite different event. Voluptuously, they visualized the destruction of Sodom and Gomorrah. The poet Jakob van Hoddis gained acclaim with an apocalyptic fantasy:

> The philistine's hat blows from his pointed head,
> the storm is here, the sea is rising . . .

His colleagues recognized this as bold, new language; they admired even more highly a similar poem entitled "War" by Georg Heym. When he read it to a large crowd at the Café Austria in 1911, they heard him predict in stark, hammering words an end with a bang. We must be careful not to read it, with hindsight, as a forerunner of the antiwar poetry that came much later. It was a horror poem meaning to convey the sense of crisis and apocalypse, of that cultural doom which Heym welcomed no matter what might bring it on. Shortly before his tragic death in 1912, he wrote in his diary: "If only one were to start a war, even an unjust one! This peace is so rotten, oily, and filthy." How close life and death were connected for these Young Werthers is inadvertently re-

vealed by Becher's "We were so seized with this lust of living that we would not have hesitated to shoot ourselves
should this our life turn out to have been less than life-size."

Heym drowned at the age of twenty-five, trying to prevent
a friend from committing suicide—but perhaps it was a double suicide. They were deeply mourned, for everybody loved
and admired Heym as a standard-bearer. In appearance, the
handsome, blond Heym was the opposite of van Hoddis; but
they shared this sense of catastrophe, as did many of their
friends. Walter Hasenclever's first play was called *Nirvana—
A Critique of Life*; Oskar Baum, who was blind, wrote *Existence on the Brink*. The closer Europe came to world war, the
shriller sounded the voices of despair among these radical
writers. No way out, no compromise, no hiding place. When
Kurt Wolff started publishing a series of books by new authors, he could think of no better title for it than *Der jüngste
Tag* (Day of Judgment); each volume sold for 80 pfennigs.

Franz Pfemfert printed Heym's and van Hoddis' poems in
his magazine *Der Demokrat*. His increasingly strident tone
led to a break with his publisher, and in 1911 he was forced
to start his own journal, *Die Aktion*. The title, which would
scarcely have been possible a year earlier, was conceived in
bed according to Alexandra Ramm, his wife and permanent
assistant. Pfemfert was interested in politics, or rather anti-
politics (he eventually was to lead a syndicalist group) and
did not commit himself to the Expressionist program. But he
published Expressionist drawings and woodcuts regularly and
exclusively, employing *Grössenwahn* artists as a rule; thus he
provided outlets for Expressionist poets, prose writers, and
critics. His table at the "Café Grössenwahn" included Carl
Einstein (married to Alexandra's sister), van Hoddis, Anselm
Ruest (Ernst Salomon), Ludwig Rubiner (the most decidedly
political of these writers), Max Oppenheimer (whose cartoons were signed Mopp), Mynona (Salomon Friedländer),
Heym, and Kurt Hiller. Moreover, he published Gottfried
Benn, Alfred Lichtenstein, Oskar Kanehl, Else Lasker-Schüler, Ernst Stadler, Franz Jung, Claire and Yvan Goll, Johannes
R. Becher, Walther Rilla, Erwin Piscator (the future stage di-

rector), Karl Liebknecht, Rosa Luxemburg,[12] and Charles Péguy on matters of political interest.[13] His courage and his insight were greatly admired, although he was irritable and
given to sharp attacks on renegade friends. He was not on
speaking terms with Herwarth Walden, although both were
using the same café, publishing the same authors, and generally pulling in the same direction.

Herwarth Walden (Georg Levin) must have been a man of
extraordinary qualities as friend, editor, and adviser. He had
a knack for discovering and developing talents and, which is
rare, he was able to keep their loyalty. Many have testified,
after his tragic disappearance in Stalin's purges, how much
they learned from him and how great his influence had been
in the *Grössenwahn* circles. He founded, published, edited,
merged, and revived more little magazines than anyone else,
shading them a little to the left or to the right by giving the
floor here to Mühsam, there to Dehmel, quarreling with sponsors and getting fired by outraged publishers until finally, in
1909, he decided to start his own weekly, *Der Sturm* (Tempest), whose title was taken from one of Else's poems. His
aim was to provide a forum for unknown, unrecognized writers, for untraditional art and new values. His friends and con-
tributors included the gamut of Expressionist creators: Alfred
Döblin, Heinrich Mann, Ferdinand Hardekopf, Alfred Mom-
bert, Peter Hille, Walter Mehring, and Adolf Loos, who had
built the "house without eyebrows."

Der Sturm arranged readings of new poetry and prose, exhibitions of Expressionist painters, and happenings. In 1912
Marinetti was invited to open its show; he went at it with his
notorious sense of notoriety, flinging manifestos from a taxi
and shouting: "Down with galleries! Burn the libraries!" until the police stopped him. There was a yearly Sturm-Ball; the
one held in the last year before the war was styled Revolu-
tionsball, and everyone had to appear in a symbolic or historical costume. Of course this was nothing but a bohemian
masquerade, but the name announced a change of climate.
Walden had once placed art above all: "Art is inhuman, one
must sacrifice humans for it"; at that time it was Pfemfert

who felt that art must serve the revolution. Later their roles were reversed; Pfemfert stayed independent of Lenin.

The third personality we must mention as part of the Expressionist coffeehouse scene was Kurt Hiller (poets called him "the doctor"), who in the 1920s was to become the major editorial writer of *Die Weltbühne,* the political organ of radical intellectuals (mostly Jewish) who could not decide between the Socialist and the Communist parties. Hiller was credited with having the sharpest intelligence and the most polished style. In 1909 he had split away from a literary society to found his own New Club (Der neue Verein), exclusively devoted to contemporary works, which met weekly in the Nollendorf Kasino, Kleist-Strasse—a ten-minutes' stroll from the Café des Westens. But soon he found himself overrun by younger members led by Georg Heym; they split over Heym's Nietzschean antirationalism, and Hiller started a new club, Das Gnu. A gnu is a ruminant, looking half bull and half antelope—which seems an apt description of the Neopathetisches Kabarett and the neopathetic poetry it was supposed to serve (the term apparently was invented by Stefan Zweig and was used before "Expressionism" came to prevail).

Hiller was one of those exciting people who turn up in everyone's memoirs but who do not leave a lasting mark. His table at the "Café Grössenwahn" was always attended by admiring adolescents, and he openly fought for his rights as a homosexual. He had many friends and was able to enlist practically all the prominent guests for his cabarets and readings. These were so well attended that he had to hire the large hall of the Café Austria in Potsdamer Strasse. There, Heym and van Hoddis read their epochal poems, Werfel was a visitor, and Hasenclever had his strident play, *The Son,* performed shortly before the war.

For the sake of fairness rather than completeness, we must add here a list of persons whose circles and activities overlapped with those most intimately involved in *Grössenwahn.* Above all, no history of Expressionism could be written without mentioning the work of Paul Cassirer as both owner of the gallery and publisher first of *Pan*, then of *Die weissen Blätter*. His editors were Wilhelm Herzog and René Schickele. The gallery was also used for readings of *Der Sturm*, *Die Aktion*, and Gnu groups. And credit should be given to the stage director Karlheinz Martin, whose *Tribüne* in Charlottenburg was the first theater-in-the-round and staged, among other experimental and Expressionist plays, Toller's *Wandlung*. An earlier theatrical venture was *Das junge Deutschland*, which could give only closed performances for invited guests. Max Reinhardt, however, generously placed his Deutsches Theater at its disposal.

We have seen that the coffeehouse culture was intimately related to the notable Expressionists' other activities: their clubs, shows, readings, exhibitions, cabarets, balls, papers, and book-publishing ventures. It was basically the same crowd that provided the various audiences for papers and happenings, and no matter how many factions they formed, they were constantly drifting around each other.

The interpretation, however, gets rather complicated when the participants' sidelines are treated on the same level as the major phenomenon, the counterculture. A *Stammtisch* is not coffeehouse culture. Not every publisher who held a table at some restaurant made a contribution to that culture. On the contrary, it can be shown that some went to Josty or to Paris in order to avoid their colleagues from *Grössenwahn*. Likewise, Expressionist readings took place at the Café Sezession and elsewhere; this was a matter of convenience which is remarkable only if public readings are considered essentially different from private readings in a sponsor's house. Private readings were extremely rare, however; in the four years that preceded World War I Expressionism had gone public and become a public affair. New magazines were being founded almost every month. René Schickele's *Die weissen Blätter* (under Cassirer's imprint) was perhaps the best publication of the era; Ernst Blass's *Argonauten* was drifting rapidly toward the right, while others proclaimed in their titles that they were veering to the radical left. *Freie Strasse* (Open Road), edited by Franz Jung; *Revolution*, edited by Hugo Ball,

Richard Huelsenbeck, and Franz Jung; *Kain* (*Cain*—Journal for Humanity), edited by Erich Mühsam; and *Neue Jugend* (New Youth), edited by Wieland Herzfelde, are examples.

The war put only a temporary end to these activities. Many of the papers emigrated to Switzerland, and their staffs reopened coffeehouse life in Zurich's Café de la Terrasse and Café Odéon; Dadaism was born in the Cabaret Voltaire. Even more than Expressionism, Dada had this coffeehouse character—the character of total nihilistic opposition. And, as was natural at that time, it was even more profoundly disillusioned with mankind.

The war paralyzed and decimated the bohemian movement, split it, and politicized it. The high point of "Café Grössenwahn" came when someone broke out in an enthusiastic cheer for the sinking of the *Lusitania* and Leonhard Frank sent him to the floor with a box on the ear. But *Der Sturm* stopped publishing, *Die weissen Blätter* went to Switzerland, and Pfemfert, to maintain his paper as a means of communication, made the intellectual sacrifice of self-censorship. Instead of political news and comment he reprinted the silliest items from the patriotic press, hoping that the knowing would understand. The reality of the war soon taught futurists and apocalyptics that their destructive enthusiasm had been, to put it mildly, misplaced and that Expressionism was no substitute for political action. Except in the safety of Switzerland, the coffeehouse counterculture could never again be the mold of revolution; nor could art and poetry be its form of realization. Confronting the catastrophe it had announced, the Expressionist *Geist* proved itself bankrupt. It would, however, cause many tremors in the cultural field, producing a wealth of artistic creations which are still to be appropriated.

The Intellectuals and the State
of Weimar

LOOKING back at ancient Athens or the first German republic, one is tempted to say that the cultural elite speaks
most contemptuously of those states that give it the
greatest freedom—and a glance at the contemporary scene in
the United States might confirm that impression. Strangely
enough, the intelligentsia, ostensibly committed to freedom,
usually rejects the liberal state and craves one that is more
structured or more communal: a state in which intellectuals
would have their assigned role. But in proclaiming their opposition, these dreamers stamp their own spirit on their age
and state; in our memory Athens now glows with the halo of
Socrates, whom she condemned to death. Our pious image of
the Periclean Age omits the slavery, the misery, and the imperialism of the first democracy but glorifies its intellectual
legacy, its beauty, and its humanity. In a similar vein, the
legend of Weimar's intelligentsia has grown like ivy over the
fallen pillars of the Weimar state. But that state—which today
is still the object of historiographical opprobrium—may one
day share the fame of its world-renowned citizens; posterity
may revise the judgment of those contemporaries who attributed all the glory of Weimar to its adversaries and all the
infamy to the Republic.

Reprinted with permission from *Social Research* (Summer 1972).

Prima facie, intellectuals had no need to feel alienated in the Weimar Republic; they were honored and well paid. As academic persons or teachers, they enjoyed the security and status of the civil service. In a society which still measured a man's value by his title, they were Herr Direktor, Herr Geheimrat, Herr Redakteur, Herr Architekt, Herr Rechtsanwalt, Herr Professor; anybody who wielded a pen expected to be addressed at least as Herr Doktor. Newspapers, magazines, and book publishers provided an abundant market for every style, taste, and shade of opinion; Germany was one of the few countries where a writer could live by his craft. The states and cities supported opera and theater; there were prizes for poetry, drama, and novels; there were academies of science, of belles-lettres, and of the arts. Press balls and art balls, where everybody who was anybody mingled with the mighty, were almost state affairs, while those who wished to differ or dissent had their own respective *Gemeinde,* cult, or secession. Virtually no one risked being harmed for professing unpopular views.[1] On the contrary, even the strangest belief found some group to maintain a publishing venture.

By all ordinary standards, the intellectuals ought to have been "gruntled." If they were disgruntled, part of the reason was precisely the diversity of interests which forced writers and creators to compete in an open market. The Republic had issued the slogan, "Gangway for talent," but the intellectuals would have preferred to be administrators of cultural goods, a priesthood of established truths rather than dowsers searching for hidden gold mines. Intellectual life was as pluralistic as politics and business, and the most common complaint was that the Republic was nothing but an arena for contending interest groups.

German intellectuals could never approve of a republic that defined politics as "who gets what." In their tradition, politics was an exalted realm where *Geist* had to inform *Macht.* Friedrich Meinecke, the liberal historian who rallied to the Republic, taught that each state must have *its* "reason."[2] G. F. W. Hegel had taught that the state is "the realization of the Ethical Idea" and a manifestation of the "Objective Spirit."

In such a state, the intellectuals saw themselves as *der allgemeine Stand*,[3] comparable to the guardians in Plato's *Republic*—a work, incidentally, which is entitled *Der Staat* in the German translation. It was discussed in the upper high-school classes; and those graduating were invariably addressed as the nation's future leaders. They knew, of course, Friedrich Schiller's couplet: "Es soll der Sänger mit dem König gehen; sie beide wohnen auf der Menschheit Höhen."[4] (Let the bard walk with the king; they both live on the summits of humanity.)

Schiller's views on history and beauty, which had dominated German middle-class thinking throughout the nineteenth century, still had a decisive and fatal influence on German intellectuals of the Weimar period. Freedom, he sang, exists "only in the realm of dreams." Realization of these dreams now was being projected onto faraway countries or the long-past age of German glory. To some, *Geist* had again become *Macht* in Soviet Russia; others fondly sought a return to the Reich (which means both kingdom and empire), where *Geist* and *Macht* had seemingly been fused. But now, "dead was the nation whose gods had died" (Ein Volk ist tot, wenn seine Götter tot sind), as Stefan George had said in *Das neue Reich* (1928). Indeed, when Thomas Mann announced his conversion to the Republic, he did not accept its (admittedly ugly) reality of 1922, but recommended to it "the politics of Novalis," which was to "make politics poetical." True, the Republic needed an idea, but it did not need a spook (*Geist* meaning both spirit and ghost).

The ideological superstructure did not simply and automatically follow changes in social structure, it also produced reactions of its own. The intellectuals resented the change in their social status and were bewildered by the sudden lack of structure in the state. Their alienation from the rest of society expressed itself in dreams of elitist gardens. Hugo von Hofmannsthal wrote *Der Turm* (1925), while the Stefan George cult degenerated into fantasies flirting with Moeller van den Bruck's notions of *The Third Reich*. It is true that *Der Turm* (The Tower) is usually interpreted as a symbol of the "soul" which a merciless "world" is threatening to deprive of its "mythical ground." But why then did the poet choose for his symbol the fantasy of absolute monarchical rule? Obviously, not only did it represent his value scheme but he took for granted that others would recognize this order as the natural, better one. Similar observations can be made on the allegedly otherworldly poetry of Rilke and George; the "inner self" always seems constructed upon the model of the hierarchical state in the "outer" world. The students understood the implicit message.

Others renewed the ideology of the Teutonic Order, and Ortega y Gasset's pamphlet *The Revolt of the Masses* (1925) was a best seller. As social life was being democratized, the idea of fixed estates (*Stände*) was gaining ground in the academy.[5] Hence the paradox: The one class that more than any other claimed to live by its wits was bitterly resentful when the Republic told it to do just that.

Unexpectedly, this elitism did not remain restricted to the Right. Similar contempt for "mass democracy" was expressed by Professor Leonard Nelson, leader of the International Socialist Combat League (ISK), and by the Socialist Youth leader Hendrik de Man.[6] A steady stream of invective against the "booboisie" came from the poisoned pen of "the Austrian Mencken," Karl Kraus, head of another cult, who declared in his weekly *Die Fackel* that he could not live in a "republic of hairdressers, postal clerks, and salesmen." It is even more surprising to find the same tone in the weekly which many considered the purest clarion of the left intellectuals, *Die Weltbühne*. There Kurt Hiller complained that the Republic was governed by "bumpkin rule" (*Pachulkokratie*); his colleague Kurt Tucholsky denounced the Republican Defense League (*Reichsbanner*) for being too straight, too "organized," and lacking in style and idealism.[7] To Ludwig Marcuse, the Republic was *ein geistloser Staat*. Likewise, when the Social Democratic party adopted a new "revisionist" program at its Heidelberg congress in 1925, *Die Weltbühne* asked indignantly whether the program could not, at least, be "radically revisionist." What it missed most was style, bearing (*Haltung*), nobility.

Intellectuals right and left were contemptuous of the bourgeoisie, as they had been, indeed, since the medieval squabbles between town and gown. Otto Dix in his paintings and George Grosz in his cartoons mercilessly exposed the vulgarity of the republican leadership and the urban middle class. The sight of them might have provoked anyone under thirty to exclaim, like one of Peter Gay's interviewees: "And for that we were supposed to mount the barricades?"[8] It did not occur to us then that we might defend the Republic *against* Grosz's models. For in our view the fault lay with the Weimar state itself—which had neither *Macht* nor *Geist;* we rejoiced at its demise instead of using democratic militancy to fill the Republic with *Geist*—a dialectical operation which, for instance, Spanish anarchists understood better than German philosophers. To the latter, the barricade was only a metaphor.

Being short on power, the Republic tried to be long on *Geist.* At its cradle stood the most eminent thinkers of their generation: Max Weber, the father of modern sociology, and Ernst Troeltsch, the philosopher of culture;[9] the economists Franz Oppenheimer and Rudolf Hilferding; the novelists Alfred Döblin and Heinrich Mann; the poets and playwrights Richard Dehmel, Gerhart Hauptmann, Fritz von Unruh. The new state repudiated the imperial flag and made every effort to become another Athens. The Constitutional Assembly was convened in Goethe's town, Weimar. At the suggestion of Friedrich Naumann, the charismatic leader of social liberalism, several *Länder* adopted the name "People's State" (*Volksstaat*) instead of "Republic." The constitution, drafted by the distinguished teacher of constitutional law, Hugo Preuss, was inspired by the noble model of 1848–49.

To some extent, all of Weimar culture was an elegy on that aborted revolution—either a renunciation of the prewar

Expressionist impulses or a frenetic attempt to retain them
after the revolution had spent itself. It was difficult to understand that the revolution had not been the beginning of
something new but the end of the prewar movement. René
König could therefore say that "the 1920s were over before
they had a chance to begin."[10] The left, paradoxically, cultivated nostalgic memories of the bohemian revolt in the beginning of the century.

While the bourgeois republic failed to actualize what its
predecessors had been unable to obtain seventy years earlier,
the republican intelligentsia still hankered after Freiligrath's
and Herwegh's ideals of democracy. Kurt Eisner headed a
leftist government in Bavaria; after his murder the anarchists
and Independent Socialists, under the leadership of writers
such as Toller, Traven, Landauer, Mühsam, and Silvio Gesell,
proclaimed a Soviet republic in Munich. They celebrated festivals of liberation but were unable to govern, or to organize
their defense. The Communists deposed them, only to be
bloodily suppressed by counterrevolutionary troops. Landauer was murdered, Toller sent to jail. A modern playwright, Tankred Dorst, has used Toller's own reports to show
that Toller mistook the revolution for an Expressionist happening.

Writers, stage directors, cabaret singers, satirists, and others, in their turn, mistook happenings for the revolution. The
stage seemed to be the world once again, and wonderfully
daring productions opened a new view on the world for eager young audiences.[11] In poetry, this was the era of Oh
Mensch lyricism[12] and Expressionism. It was followed by
Dada—"a radical young artistic intelligentsia's fanfare that
was supposed to blow bourgeois society away."[13] To be sure,
much of the revolutionary emotion was not a new beginning
but the echo of prewar upheavals. Magazines such as Der
Sturm and Die Aktion hardly needed to change their tone.
But they were no longer underground.

Just as the revolution had an esthetic quality, so esthetics
took on a revolutionary quality. Obviously, neither could last
very long. The reality of the bourgeois republic was class war,

bargaining, compromise, but not even in its intentions was it poetic. Whether the poets thought they were revolutionary or the revolutionaries thought they were poets, neither could cope with politics. The barricades are for one day; only on Delacroix's brilliant canvas does that statuesque, light-gowned goddess of freedom continue forever to brandish her tricolor, urging the masses on and on to further action. Thomas Mann spoke of "*bellezza* radicals" in referring to those orators and enthusiasts who wanted the revolution pure, beautiful, and terrible. They saw themselves as the new Lafayettes and Carnots. They longed for new symbols of power and stronger manifestations of the new *Geist*. Like Marx in 1848, they would have liked to declare war on the old regime, which for many was represented by the Versailles Treaty and the powers of the materialist West.

What they had in mind can perhaps be deduced from a similar venture in Budapest. There a tiny group of Marxist intellectuals was able to seize power in the name of national honor. They abolished the middle class by closing all shops, declared war on Czechoslovakia and Rumania, ruled by terror for a few weeks—and after their defeat came to Germany, where these intellectuals wielded enormous influence on the flowering of the "Weimar spirit." Georg Lukács brought a radicalized Hegel with him; Anna Seghers (married to a Hungarian sociologist) wrote the only communist novels in the German language where partisan inspiration did not stifle poetic imagination; Ladislaus Moholy-Nagy taught "dynamic constructivism"; Karl Mannheim introduced "sociology of knowledge" and assured intellectuals that they were "freely floating" above the class bias to which all other minds were subject while Frederick Antal revolutionized art criticism. The rest of them—from their other place of refuge, Moscow—directed the German Communist party.

The transfugees from the K.u.K. monarchy, who knew how to quote from the German classics most eloquently, often exhibited the "Weimar spirit" with the truthfulness of caricature. After all, they lived in that state of alienation which by now had become the problem of all writers and artists.[14]

Among the knowing, Kafka was acquiring his strange fame; his message, "We are all prisoners,"[15] was understood after the revolution had been aborted. The exiles of 1919 who strove to perpetuate their position of departure throughout the 1920s thus symbolized the situation of the left in Weimar and anticipated their fate as exiles a decade later.

I shall show later why the Weimar writers could not be "contemporaneous,"[16] and took their stand "outside" the Republic.[17] The intellectuals always hated the burgher and never meant to be "inside" the bourgeois state, except as guests. But in a tragic sense they became outsiders again in 1933 when a barbaric regime declared modern literature and science to be "alien." At that point an interesting inversion occurred. In retrospect, and seen from the vantage point of exile, whatever had been great and valuable in Weimar politics and letters seemed to have been leftist, critical, *kulturbolschewistisch,* Jewish. Lion Feuchtwanger, on arriving in Hollywood, declared that all German literature was in exile;[18] by inference, those in exile were German literature, and German literature was based on a tradition of leftism. It was here in exile, in the coffeehouses of Prague and Paris, at the Institute for Social Research and the New School for Social Research in New York, in the small "colonies" of refugee writers on the Côte d'Azur and the American West Coast, that the myth of the "Weimar intellectuals" was created. The writers in exile became a moving force in the international mobilization of culture against fascism and lent enthusiastic help to the Popular Front. They were highly visible at the International Writers' Congress at the Paris Mutualité in 1935 and cheered the edict of the Communist International at its Seventh World Congress, that the proletariat must "inherit classical bourgeois culture."

In pursuance of this strategic change, the Communists now created audiences for exiled writers, infiltrated reputable publishing houses in Paris, Zurich, Amsterdam, and Stockholm and financed others, appropriated German literature, and quickly acquired a monopoly on labeling this writer as "progressive," that one as "reactionary," etc.[19]

The left line in letters now sought to divide artists and

thinkers into "reactionaries" and "progressives." On the one hand, there were those who sought to develop the democratic and humanistic values and ideals of the bourgeoisie; on the other hand, there were those who prevented the further development of these same values and ideals. In this way, a critical view of Weimar society could be linked up with a positive evaluation of its progressive forces. Especially to younger refugees, this vision provided a rationale for their existence. Alienated in foreign countries, they now were able to remember a spiritual home; to reconquer it, they could summon the aid of the world's people of good faith. The idea of the "Weimar intellectuals" was thus projected backward from the Popular Front period as both a banner and a wish. Amidst the hell that threatened to become the future, it was comforting to believe in a past that had been paradise. If Hegel said that it must be night when the owl of Minerva spreads its wings, one might add that the night of the 1930s produced the light of the 1920s.

It would be a mistake, however, to confine the term "Weimar intellectuals" to this group of the leftish-inclined, fellow travelers, and emigrants. We can speak of a republican establishment of the arts, letters, and sciences, with its academies, universities, respected publishing houses, newspaper *feuilletons*, exhibitions, theaters, and museums, where people of divergent persuasions were not enemies but merely rivals. Between them, antagonistic coexistence reigned over a wide gamut of personalities, tastes, and convictions. Presiding over this establishment were Walter von Molo, a nationalistic hack writer now happily forgotten; Thomas Mann, who had once propagated imperialism in the guise of the nonpolitical man (*der Unpolitische*) and who now promulgated uncommittedness in the guise of republicanism; and finally, Gerhart Hauptmann, the one-time radical who was now wallowing in romantic eclecticism. As a sort of poet laureate, he composed prologues for republican festivals, and later performed the same service for Hitler.

In the political world and among social thinkers, the Republic found itself isolated after the first few years. Of the founding fathers, Naumann, Max Weber, and Troeltsch died; Walther Rathenau and Matthias Erzberger were assassinated. Hugo Preuss, having failed to disestablish Prussia, was neither nominated for election nor renamed minister, and although many cabinet members after him had academic titles, only two or three can be called intellectuals.[20] Nor did the Reichstag debates produce great ideas, and great orators were few and far between.[21]

Weimar politics was the domain of politicians, not of philosophers. The great intellectuals who rallied to the Republic—such as Meinecke, Hermann Oncken, Ernst Cassirer, Ernst Robert Curtius, Max Scheler, Eduard Spranger—did not engage in party politics and were mostly right-wing liberals. The bulk of the academic intelligentsia, with the exception of the few who had been imposed on faculties by a Socialist state government, were conservative, reactionary, or even Nazi-oriented. Hans Kelsen was the only one to engage in debate with the nationalist ideology-makers; Radbruch, as Minister of Justice was unable to have Ludendorff convicted of participation in the Kapp Putsch; Redslob, as *Reichskunstwart*, the Reich's art curator, tried vainly to give the Republic visual symbols. Arnold Brecht's memoirs are a moving testimony to the loneliness surrounding the defenders of the Republic. In the field of social policies, Hilferding developed a theory of "political wage," but his party failed to act on it and, instead, adopted an ideology of *Wirtschaftsdemokratie* (economic democracy), misappropriated by one Dr. Naphtali from Sidney and Beatrice Webb's *Industrial Democracy*. While the left and the far left were quarreling over the proper interpretation of Marx's teaching on the business cycle or on proletarian dictatorship, the democratic center had no theory of the state and not even much of an ideology. In the crisis of democracy, the intellectuals fell back on the civil service idea of authority, backed by the monarchists Hindenburg and Brüning.

In 1931, under the Brüning government and with the Nazis at the door, Karl Jaspers published a small volume, *Die geistige Situation der Zeit*, as volume 1000 of Göschen's popular-science series. He warned that utopianism and fanaticism are merely two forms of failure to "grasp the political—a task so high humanly that few can be expected to be equal to it" (p. 87). He recommended some vague form of "authority" and resignation to the "consciousness of a state-bound fate" (*staatliches Schicksalsbewusstsein*, p. 90). The poverty of democratic thought contrasts with the fertility of the right in producing both concrete, practicable theories and captivating ideologies. Hans Freyer, Carl Schmitt-Dorotič, Oswald Spengler, and Ernst Jünger prepared the ideological tools for a "revolution from the right."

There may, however, be a more profound reason for the Republic's failure to attract the intellectuals and to develop a state consciousness of its own. The literature of the age reveals an increasing interest in psychology and a general retreat from political thought. "Privatization of the mind" was just another aspect of the alienation problem that occupied the intellectuals' consciences. Psychology and anthropology became the foremost sciences of the age; the novel went psychological or existentialist. Much of this literature deliberately repudiated the burgher, both *qua* bourgeois and *qua* citoyen, and concerned itself solely with the plight of the individual. But while this trend was truly European, the German authors had a special knack of turning every Young Werther's sorrows into charges against society. Thus, in his bestseller, *The Maurizius Case*, Jakob Wassermann's young Etzel Andergast painfully discovered the hypocritical scaffolding on which his father the judge had built his life, while Franz Werfel boldly entitled a novel, *Not the Murderer, the Victim is Guilty.*

Lukács is certainly wrong when he suggests that Thomas Mann was "in search of the bourgeois man." On the contrary, his novels allow the reader to share vicariously in the experience of alienation; reputations in the literary establishment were built not on conformity but on confessions of anomie. This had been a long time coming but was now receiving recognition: the erstwhile bohemians now became academicians.

Obviously, members of the academies had to have established their reputations well before the first world war. The writers Thomas Mann, Gerhart Hauptmann, Bernhard Kellermann, Jakob Wassermann, Alfred Döblin, Heinrich Mann, Georg Kaiser, Carl Sternheim; the poets Rainer Maria Rilke, Stefan George; the painters Kandinsky, Nolde, Liebermann, Corinth, Kokoschka, Schmidt-Rottluff, Kirchner; the sculptors Kolbe, Lehmbruck, Barlach; the physicists Planck, Einstein, Nernst; the philosophers Vaihinger, Husserl, Scheler, Cohen, Rickert; the composers Schönberg, Alban Berg, Hindemith; the social scientists Max and Alfred Weber, Dilthey, Sombart, Gumplowicz, Oppenheimer—to name only a few—had done their most significant work earlier in the century and actually belong to the period of decadence and Expressionism rather then to the Weimar period, which their illustrious but waning presences could illuminate but no longer shape. Thus, Peter Gay found it necessary to attribute much of the "Weimar spirit" to the generation of its "fathers."

On the other hand, a number of creators whose names today are intimately connected with the image of Weimar were known then only to a rather narrow group of pioneers, or did their best and most significant work after they had left their homeland—in exile. This group includes some of the most noteworthy writers, artists, and thinkers: Robert Musil, Hermann Broch, Nelly Sachs, Walter Benjamin, Manès Sperber, Arthur Koestler, even Bert Brecht; the group around the Frankfurt Institute for Social Research, notably Erich Fromm, Theodor W. Adorno, Herbert Marcuse; among many others also E. Voegelin, Leo Strauss, Rudolf Arnheim, Siegfried Kracauer. They often represent the "spirit of Weimar" better than some whose most creative period actually was during the 1920s.

Moreover, many names which became the signature of the Weimar period proper were not unknown before the first world war. Thus, Bruno E. Werner, in his superb eulogy of the Weimar literature,[22] notes that as a high-school student and a soldier in the first world war, he read Kafka, Döblin, Sternheim, Benn, Musil, Meyrink, Heinrich Mann, Kaiser, Edschmid, Schickele, Heym, Trakl. His extreme youth may have prevented him from including Franz Werfel, Heinrich Lersch, Walter Hasenclever, Fritz von Unruh, Klabund, and Leonhard Frank or Oskar Loerke, who at the time influenced many young poets. All these authors had been acclaimed or had performed successfully before 1914.

A case could be made for placing the caesura of modern culture not in any year around 1918 but at the beginning of the century. The attack on Western middle-class culture, the rebellion of *Geist* against materialism, the critique of all traditional values, the liberation of the senses—all these traits of "Weimar" thought and art had been present and fully developed long before World War I. Neither in savagery nor in brilliancy were these works often to be surpassed during the decade that followed. Heinrich Mann did not write anything better after the war than *Professor Unrath* (1905) and *Der Untertan* (1911). In these novels, he was attacking Wilhelminian society.[23] In republican times his criticism was no longer fundamental. Like Werfel, Meinecke, and other writers, he now saw politics as a tragedy and no longer expected the state to be just. "A state based on truth and justice could not exist for a single day," he wrote in *Die Weltbühne*. Ideals were still to be fought for, but their realization could be expected only in the realm of dreams.

Likewise, the materialism that Stefan George denounced was of the imperialist age. But what, early in the century, had seemed to be a concerted protest of all poets and writers against the established bourgeoisie now split up into a number of small establishments. Each writer, poet, or thinker had his own *Gemeinde* (following; literally, congregation) or cult, and from Theosophists to Wagnerians, from "Georgiasts" to positivists, from the various youth movement groups to Expressionists and the cultural Trotskyists, all could coexist in a pluralism of sects each of which constituted a small counterestablishment. While the intellectuals resented this cloisonné arrangement, it permitted them to live in a society from which they claimed to be alienated—to be its civil servants or academicians while warning others to beware of its blandishments.

In his own ironical way, Thomas Mann has pleaded indulgence for the artist's antics and at the same time repudiated any idea of seriousness: "An artist is a fellow who is no good at anything serious or useful; he desires to be free to perform his antics but will do nothing for the state or may even be subversive; incidentally, he also is profoundly childish, inclined to exaggerate, and even a little seedy. Society should treat him with quiet contempt. . . . He refuses to work for a civilizing or political purpose, to improve the world, etc. It is not fair to scold him for that. A work of art may have moral consequences, but one must not hold the artist responsible for them or ask him to have such intentions."

Indeed, if Marinetti could be hailed in Italy as a fascist writer, if Céline could be cheered in France as a pioneer of letters, it is hard to see why Emil Nolde and Gottfried Benn, who both thought they were Nazis, should have been rebuffed by Hitler. The totalitarian mind, however, utterly deficient in a sense of humor, cannot allow, or even admit to the existence of, any private dream realm. The republican establishment consists of, and almost requires, a variety of private cults, provided they coexist with and within society.

These assumptions, however, could not be maintained when society itself came apart, when styles and ideologies fastened themselves to various political parties and deep class conflicts tore the pluralistic Republic to pieces. The metaphors did not stay in Schiller's realm of beautiful appearances but were mistaken for political realities. Esthetic differences were escalated into ideological irreconcilabilities. We must therefore return once again to the committed writers of the right and left to determine the nature and extent of their commitment.

Considering the writer's position in the Republic, it is hard to understand why the image of the "Weimar intellectuals" in the popular mind should still be that of an impetuous crowd of insurgents criticizing and debunking the manners of the Republic, deeply alienated and disgusted with its politics, and militantly carrying the flag of revolution at the head of the proletarian masses who were being held down by the police clubs of the Social Democratic government.[24] In actual fact, the Weimar intellectuals were generally the most satisfied rebels in history. Some went beyond tickling the bourgeois; but what they justly criticized was exactly what the establishment itself found unpalatable in the Republic. Proletarians could not afford to pay for seats at *The Threepenny Opera*; the socialist "People's Theater" in Berlin never performed a Brecht work. The banter of Erich Kästner, Brecht, even of George Grosz, was as tolerable to the liberal bourgeoisie as, say, Dick Gregory is to New York Jews. Mack the Knife was fun; Kurt Weill's melodies emasculated whatever bite Brecht's caricature of Peachum might have held. The *Weltbühne* writers denounced reactionary courts and power-hungry militarists, both remnants of the previous regime. This ability of the mature bourgeoisie to laugh at its own system passed for subversive radicalism. In all newspapers the *feuilleton* editor was more radical than the political editorialist.

Much of the literature dealing with contemporary social and political themes—say, Eric Reger's reportage novels on Adenauer's rule in Cologne or Hans Fallada's *Little Man, What Now?*, a world hit in 1932—is read today only for historical interest. Most war novels are forgotten, too. Some exceptions are, on the patriotic side, the crystalline language of Ernst Jünger's *Storm of Steel* (1920) and, on the pacifist side, Arnold Zweig's *The Case of Sergeant Grischa* (1927) and Ludwig Renn's sober *War* (1928). The worldwide best seller, *All Quiet on the Western Front* (1928), though, had never been intended to be an antiwar novel; its author had no further ambition than to write honest reportage—which it is. But since its publisher was the great Jewish house of Ullstein, the Nazis declared the fatherland's honor offended, and demonstrations against the movie made it a *cause célèbre*. A similar fate befell Carl Zuckmayer's play, *Der fröhliche Weinberg* (The Merry Vineyard, 1925), an earthy comedy that was intended as pure fun but became a scandal when the Nazis needed a "cause." Nor was the cheeky Berlin comedienne, Claire Waldoff, really offensive except to the most squeamish provincial ears. Schnitzler was no more daring than Wedekind had been, but since he was still alive, the prigs denounced him as pornographic. Both were really great moralists of pre-Weimar vintage. Quite generally speaking, social criticism in republican times hit hardest the abuses of militarism, the late war, the servility of *Beamte* and *Spiesser*—all vices of the preceding era.

The title of Theodor Plievier's novel, *The Kaiser Goes, the Generals Remain* (1932), expresses the cause of the lag. Unfortunately it was still necessary to attack the abuses and dangers of imperial culture and institutions because they were still felt as shackles on the Republic. The double appearance, in 1930, of a play by Zuckmayer and a novel by Wilhelm Schäfer called *The Captain of Köpenick*, based on a true event in Wilhelminian Germany, confirms this deplorable state of affairs. Likewise, both Hermann Hesse's *Demian* (1919), the book appropriated by the youth movement, and Thomas Mann's *The Magic Mountain* (1924) drew heavily on the experience and vocabulary of the prewar debate and actually end with the first world war.

Authors who were truly contemporary were not immediately successful. Kafka, Robert Musil, and Hermann Broch, all outsiders, have acquired higher significance only in our own generation. An exception was Alfred Döblin, whose *Berlin Alexanderplatz* (1930) and *Giganten* (1932), almost alone in Weimar literature, combine modern imagination with a merciless observation of the modern world.

For a limited audience, Bert Brecht's didactic plays and poems put imagination deliberately into the service of the cause; though he did not join the Communist party, he was always at its service. Party members were Erich Weinert, Johannes R. Becher, Anna Seghers, and Friedrich Wolf. Although they dealt with contemporary material, they were not contemporary in any real sense. They looked at the world of 1929 from the aspect of what had been missed in 1919, or of the contrast between the German misery and the splendid Soviet reality. No one, neither left writers nor left politicians, seemed to care about people who needed new goals in a time of great distress. Brecht's movie *Kuhle Wampe* (1932) and some new ventures of Vienna's Socialist Youth were isolated attempts; the chance to mobilize a humanitarian protest during the Depression was missed by the left.

Nor could the lacunae be filled by the following two curious occurrences. In the early 1930s, Max Horkheimer and Herbert Marcuse turned the program of the Frankfurt Institute for Social Research away from social and economic theory and toward *Kulturkritik*. At the same time, J. P. Mayer and S. Landshut discovered in the SPD archives a manuscript of the young Marx which they felt set a new goal for the socialist movement: to liberate, not the proletarian from unemployment but man from alienation.[25] At that moment, such a return to "German socialism" was even less helpful than the Communists' more orthodox Marxist exegeses, and was promptly hailed by people like Werner Sombart and Hendrik de Man. Indeed, Proudhon already had complained that the intellectuals had substituted love for revolution while Hegel had mocked the Germans for "operating inside their skulls."

In contrast to the theoretical dearth on the left, one must admit a considerable body of impressive works on the conservative and totalitarian side. Having mentioned the political theories of Spengler, Freyer, and Carl Schmitt, we may add ideology makers like Ernst Jünger (*Der Arbeiter, Herrschaft und Gestalt,* 1932) and the medievalists Othmar Spann and Edgar Salin. The quality of right-wing novels may, in the judgment of posterity, be inferior to the best of the left, but during the 1920s they achieved larger printings. This was most obviously true of low-brow and popular-entertainment literature—thrillers, war novels, sentimental love stories—and other escape literature.[26] Leaving aside the blood-and-soil enthusiasts, a good number of reputable writers, including academicians, glorified the monarchical past, the German nation, war, and militarism, or slandered the "Western spirit" and the Weimar system. Such were the Stefan George followers Rudolf Alexander Schröder, Ernst Bertram, and Rudolf Borchardt; Paul Ernst (*Der Zusammenbruch des Idealismus,*

The Collapse of Idealism, 1919); Arthur Moeller van den Bruck (*Das Dritte Reich*, 1923); Gustav Frenssen (*Der Glaube der Nordmark*, 1936); Hanns Johst (*Schlageter*, 1932); Walter von Molo (*Fridericus*, 1924 ff., inspiring a number of movies with Otto Gebühr creating a national hero); Erwin Guido Kolbenheyer (*Paracelsus*); Ernst von Salomon, a terrorist posing as a writer; Rudolf Binding (*Opfergang*); Edwin Erich Dwinger (*Deutsche Passion*); Werner Bergengruen (*Herzog Karl der Kühne*); Hans Grimm (*Volk ohne Raum*—a story set in a former German colony—giving the Nazis a stirring slogan).

We must include the considerable distribution of such older works of German nationalism as Lagarde's *Deutsche Schriften*, Langbehn's *Der Rembrandtdeutsche*,[27] Walter Flex's war novel, *Der Wanderer zwischen beiden Welten*, and Rainer Maria Rilke's *Die Weise von Liebe und Tod des Cornets Christoph Rilke* (both especially loved by the youth movement), as well as the political poetry of Agnes Miegel and other poets better known and better loved for their more esoteric meanings. We must further add the myth-oriented psychology of Ernst Krieck and Ludwig Klages, the historical works of Dietrich Schäfer and Ernst Kantorowicz, the racist propaganda of the Goethe scholar Gustav Roethe, Hans Günther's race doctrines, and the hate against the Republic which ran through the academic establishment, culminating in Heidegger's dedication of Freiburg University: Give "knowledge service" (*Wissensdienst*) to the Nazi state.

Academic people, in particular, looked back to pre-republican days when Germany was powerful and respected throughout the world. High-school teachers were generally reactionary; university professors often used the teaching of literature, history, or the social sciences to propagate antidemocratic thought. Publishing houses and magazines promoting racist and nationalistic ideas, not to speak of low-brow entertainment, were numerous and well-financed.[28]

The aims of conservative intellectuals were mostly determined by the word "anti": They were anti-illuminist, antiliberal, anti-Semitic, antisocialist, anti-intellectual, antidemocratic, antiparliamentarian, anti-industrial—in a word, "anti" everything that had happened since 1789. They even wanted to re-agrarianize Germany (Sombart's word: *auflanden*, 1935), and some proposed to stop the industrial revolution—that is, if they stooped to mention such mundane matters as industry, commerce, money, finance, and work at all. Most German intellectuals simply were above this. Rilke asserted, in a famous line, that "poverty is a great radiance from within."

But we must differentiate between genuine conservatives, whom the Nazis rightly called reactionaries, and nihilists like Spengler, Moeller, Heidegger, and Jünger, whom the Bolsheviks rightly called "petty-bourgeois gone wild" (*wildgewordene Kleinbürger*). They raved about the revolution but they meant apocalypse. Moeller van den Bruck felt that "a great nation can hope for no more magnificent end than to perish in a world war," overwhelmed by a coalition of all other nations.[29] Under certain circumstances, the left played along with the right extremists. Thus, Karl Radek sought support from German nationalists in 1923 and read an unusual obituary to the Enlarged Executive Committee of the Communist International: a eulogy for Leo Schlageter, a nationalist terrorist shot by French occupation officers in the Ruhr. Kurt Tucholsky at one point found that higher morality he missed so much in German republicans in, of all groups, the *Camelots du Roi*.

The confusion could be further illuminated by a list of intellectuals who changed over from the extreme right to the extreme left and vice versa, even as they did in other countries (e.g., Georges Sorel supported both Mussolini and Lenin). There also were the "National Bolshevists" on the left and the "Left people on the Right" who tried to combine nationalism with populism, socialism, or even Communism. And finally there were some—fewer than in France though—who would applaud any strong action or gesture likely either to antagonize the burgher or to stir him out of his lethargy.

Of course it was only a minority, on the right and on the left, that propagated nihilistic, futuristic, Dadaist, or surrealist politics. But there were more who felt that such poetry might serve as a substitute for a policy. Their Sorelian cult of actionism was married to a dreamy faith in the mysterious Orient, which they wanted either to conquer or to be conquered by. All these national-bolshevist groups shared an ardent advocacy of *Ostorientierung*—not to be confused with Willy Brandt's *Ostpolitik*, a policy of accommodation with the Soviet Union—i.e., an alliance of all the "proletarian nations," the losers of the last war, the victims of imperialism, "to free them from Western rule."[30]

It would be nice if Professors Deak and Schorske were correct in claiming that the *Weltbühne* authors were distinguished from the National Bolshevists by their "Western orientation." Unfortunately, this was not so. *Die Weltbühne* published diatribes by Heinz Pol against the Kellogg Pact and by Gilbeaux against Locarno. Nor is it true that these intellectuals found Communism incompatible with their idea of liberty. *Die Weltbühne* often published Communist authors; Kurt Hiller called on the readers to vote Communist—to be sure, only to ask for a "broad coalition" after the election; consistency was not his forte. Intellectuals are notorious for being mavericks in general; if, therefore, some failed to find permanent homes in the Communist and Nazi parties, that does not prove that they were averse to totalitarianism. Some *Weltbühne* writers believed that the Third Republic was the true heir of the Great French Revolution, others believed that the Communists were. But their esthetic, basically pre-World War I view of politics committed them to a totally false image of Jacobinism and made them irrelevant to the situation of the Weimar Republic—even when their criticism was relevant.

Having said that the Weimar intellectuals were neither as influential as their enemies have charged, nor as leftist as memory imagines them, that their "spirit" had been fully grown long before the 1920s began and came to flower long after the decade ended, I now suggest that the intellectual universe of the Republic was not primarily defined by Germans. What would Weimar culture have been without Rilke's translations from French poetry? What would German dance have become without Isadora Duncan or Anna Pavlova? Every new volume of *The Forsyte Saga* was a literary event in Germany. Bernard Shaw had become a German author for all practical purposes; Upton Sinclair sold more copies in Germany than in the United States. Germans were as thrilled by Edgar Wallace as Englishmen, not to mention the Wild West, which was every schoolboy's dream. We looked at Tom Mix movies, adored Mary Pickford, danced first the Hiawatha, then the Charleston, and listened enraptured to Dixieland, which we mistakenly called jazz.

On all levels, this culture was international. The world literature, from Hamsun to Dostoevsky, was ours; even our nationalists stole their ideas either from the East or from the West. Moeller van den Bruck got the *Third Reich* myth from the Pan-Slavs—he translated Dostoevsky; Ernst Jünger never acknowledged his debt to Charles Maurras and the French integralists. Döblin, a better writer and a better man than Jünger, did give James Joyce credit for the style and structure of *Berlin Alexanderplatz*. Fischer's *Neue Rundschau* exchanged essays and authors with *La Nouvelle Revue Française*. One saw political implications in Charlie Chaplin movies, Mickey Mouse, *Potemkin*, and René Clair. Pirandello was a frequent guest at Munich and Berlin festivals. Anatole France, Maxim Gorky, Jaroslav Hašek, and Upton Sinclair provided political ideologies for the German left.

Eclecticism made cultural life exciting. Exotic cults captured the European imagination. Josephine Baker and Al Jolson were lionized. Klabund and Brecht in their parables spoke Chinese; Hermann Hesse and Waldemar Bonsels had their protagonists go to India. Rabindranath Tagore toured Europe and was exalted in Germany. The middle-class, middle-brow faddists' curiosity left no foreign culture unravished. There was a Bahai temple in Berlin. Buddhism, Hinduism, drug fetishism were fashionable; Japanese prints graced the walls of cultured households. For anyone craving spiritual bread there was always the mysterious Orient—and more recently, of course, from Soviet Russia a new faith.

I have already mentioned the enormous contribution Vienna had made to "Weimar culture," and now I must say that Weimar itself, the little town in Thüringen, always remained a provincial backwater. The real hustle and bustle in business, culture, politics, and amusement was in swinging Berlin. We all took part in its *perpetuum mobile* at meetings, debates, parties, balls, festivals, productions. Weimar or Berlin: No one cared any more about the place that gave this republic its name because the spirit of its commotion (*Betrieb*) could be experienced only in the capital. Nor, to tell the truth, did anyone care about "intellectuals." The true representatives of the age were not its writers but its showmen: Erwin Piscator, Max Reinhardt, Leopold Jessner, Fritz Lang. Perhaps the Weimar Republic was not a Periclean Age after all but the age of Marlene Dietrich. We were not great innovators, we were innovators on a small scale. We did not generate the great idea that might have led us out of the impasse in our social, economic, and political plight. Far from "freely floating," the intellectuals were being floated and coaxed and pushed. We were a generation of first-class mediocrities; never had there been so many brilliant failures, so many excellent second-raters—wonderful people like Zuckmayer as well as dreadful ones like Benn. We did not suffer, we were not alienated. Each of us lived in his crowd and had his audience; each was a priest of some cult or a functionary of some church. In no period of German literature or art were creative spirits so well adjusted to their environment, audiences so eager to accept whatever artists presented as the latest chic of their own sensibilities.

For indeed, variety, an urgent sense of change, of transition, and of crisis were the very conditions of success. In ever-accelerating rounds, literary fashions crowded each other. Excitement was found not just in the ever more sensational content but in the very fact of rapid change. Hermann Hesse may not have been unfair when he charged that modern German literature had too many "journalistic elements"; indeed, the novel of reportage and of social significance was much in demand. The manufacture, distribution through mass media, and consumption of artistic and semi-artistic products was a veritable fair, a market obeying its own laws. Art, literature, even philosophy had to join this dance. Few of us knew then that it was the death dance of democracy. Too many resented the fact that the Republic was not meant for dancing. If Weimar was Periclean, then it was so in the sense that the original Periclean Age, too, was a time of mortal crisis.

VIRTUOSOS

[4]
Friedrich Meinecke and the Tragedy of German Liberalism

To understand things of value, you must gaze calmly into the abyss of history.

—Johann Gottfried von Herder

That good may come from evil is not proof of Reason's cunning but of its impotence.

—Friedrich Meinecke

WHEN the Free University of Berlin was founded in 1948, the natural choice for its rector was, despite his eighty-six years, Friedrich Meinecke, professor emeritus of modern history and for forty years editor of the professional historical journal *Historische Zeitschrift* (HZ). He was author of three monumental works: *Cosmopolitanism and the National State, The Idea of Reason of State,* and *The Origin of Historismus*—the latter term referring to the school of German historians whose undisputed leader he was.[1]

But it was not his achievement as a scholar that recommended Meinecke; it was his political background. He had been a liberal almost all his long life among a faculty that was mostly reactionary and nationalistic; he had opposed the kaiser's warlike policies and had helped in the founding of the Republic. Hitler had deprived him of both his academic position and his editorship. He had spent the Nazi period in

Reprinted with permission from *Salmagundi* (Winter 1979).

"internal exile," had kept close contacts with Resistance leaders, and after the war had emerged with a small but searing book, The German Catastrophe,[2] which candidly discussed the fatal forces—not just the practical mistakes—that had driven Germany into the abyss.

More recently, however, both Meinecke's credentials as a liberal and the merits of Historismus have come under attack.[3] His ideas were found to diverge from the Western concepts of freedom and of liberalism. Iggers says of Historismus: "The great theoretical questions that are man's legitimate scientific concerns remain unanswered." Although historians are not usually expected to answer philosophical questions, Meinecke and his friend Ernst Troeltsch had indeed tried to find metaphysical foundations for the German liberal conscience. Today, however, we study their texts not for any truth they might have revealed; to us they are indicators of their Zeitgeist and barometers of the forces they represented. In this study I shall use the crisis of Historismus as a key to the understanding of the crisis of German liberalism. There is good reason to examine this "attitude to life" (as Meinecke called Historismus) because after twenty-five years of eclipse it is experiencing a revival in Germany.

Since the term Historismus will occur frequently, I need to explain why I retain this ugly coining instead of following those who are using "historicism." Unfortunately, Benedetto Croce and Karl Popper have preempted the latter term for the Hegelian view that history is a perennial progression toward a predetermined goal and each period is a stage on the way to the next "higher" one. Historismus is the diametrically opposed view: that "all periods are equally close to God" (Leopold von Ranke). Although both historicism and Historismus deny any eternal nature of man and are both hostile to biological views of history, they differ in two important respects: historicism sees all human history as one and as subject to universally valid laws of development, applicable to all nations alike; Historismus stresses the unique individuality of each historical formation and assumes that each nation, each period, each individual lives under its own star—"the law by which thou first wert formed" (Goethe). Historismus means that "everything is in constant flux and that the flux brings to the fore ever new formations" (Meinecke).[4]

Part I will give the general outline of Meinecke's attitudes to history and politics, from deluded optimism in the beginning of this century to the disillusionment in the two world wars: "The Demon Ignored." Part II surveys Meinecke's life as a liberal, his fight against the forces that threatened his conception of the state: "The Demon Without." Part III is an analysis of Reason of State: "The Demon Within." Part IV is a critique of Historismus: "The Demon Triumphant."

I. The Demon Ignored

The prestigious *Historische Zeitschrift* (HZ) began its hundredth volume, in 1908, with a thoughtful essay by its editor, Friedrich Meinecke. In it he questioned the conventional claim that scientific methods can lead the historian to an objective view of "what really happened" (Ranke's famous formula). He contended that history could be written only in the context of a concrete nation and state, hence it had to be informed by a philosophy, or even by a temperament. Sixteen years later, in his introduction to a new edition of Ranke's *Political Dialogue*, he stated: "A subtle connection exists between the work of the statesman and the work of the historian"; while the latter must not allow partisanship to becloud his research, "the true nature of the events will disclose itself only to him who experiences them and empathizes with them. . . . No history of any value has been written that was not inspired by a will to act."[5] Even the selection of one's topic is influenced by one's interest or, at least, preferences; against Max Weber's well-known theorem of value-free scholarship Meinecke retorted: each cultural achievement is "a breakthrough, a revelation of the spiritual into the causal nexus," hence it "could not be recorded without a lively feeling for the values it reveals."[6]

An example of this kind of commitment was the first of the

three great works that made Meinecke's name: *Cosmopolitanism and the National State*, which introduced a new subject and a new method into historiography. Its preface declared: "My book is based on the conviction that German historiography, without abandoning the valuable tradition of its methods, must rise to a freer vision and find contact with the great powers of political and cultural life; without prejudice to its own aims and purposes, it should engage more boldly in philosophy and politics." The book was one of the first in a new field—intellectual history *(Geistesgeschichte)*; or, perhaps more precisely, it used the development of an idea, in this case "nationhood," as a key to the understanding of a decisive turn in German history: the transformation of a *Kulturnation* into a *Staatsnation*.

This development had been described by others as the victory of Prussia over the Great-German ambitions of the 1848 revolution, as the unification of Germany, as the triumph of Bismarck, etc. Meinecke went back to the time of the Napoleonic wars, which the Germans remember as their "Wars of Liberation" or "The German Uprising" (1812–1814). He studied the ideas that had animated its leaders and found that German patriotism had grown out of the fertile soil of the eighteenth-century Enlightenment, its humanitarian, cosmopolitan spirit. This was in opposition to the schoolroom teaching that the German nation had rejected Western humanitarianism and embraced Bismarck's blood-and-iron philosophy instead. Like Humboldt and Fichte, Meinecke always differentiated between patriotism and nationalism; the latter he thought vulgar. His achievement, hailed by the reviewers as a work of art, was to show the emergence of the new Reich in a twofold mirror: the cunning of the statesman reflected the birth of a new *Geist*, and that *Geist* embodied the emergence of a new state. To a jubilant generation of German students before World War I, Meinecke gave the message that power could be ennobled and that German history offered to idealists a vision of transcendental values—the state as a thing of highest cultural virtue! No legitimate state without *Geist*.

The message cut both ways. On the one hand it idealized the existing state and gave liberals an excuse to cooperate with it, as indeed they had been doing then for forty years; on the other hand, it suggested that the state must live up to the ideals that had been imputed to its origins. Was this just a pious hope? In the political articles Meinecke wrote at that time for the daily press—for he practiced the involvement he preached, and but for a speech defect might have run for a Reichstag seat—he attacked the state for which his book claimed such a splendid philosophy. Not only did the emperor's foreign policy seem perilous and reckless, the very structure of government was at fault: elite positions were held by an aristocracy that no longer brought forth leaders but pursued petty agrarian interests; in two-thirds of the country the majority did not have equal voting rights; on the eastern estates the farmhands were living in semiservitude, and in the rest of the country workers were considered "enemies of the state."

Nevertheless, the book resounded with chords of harmony. Thanks to the above-quoted *Geist*, the commands of Christian ethics were living in beautiful symbiosis with the demands of power policy, just as the liberal middle class was prospering in harness with the semifeudal state.[7] If Alexander Pope said, "Whatever is, is right," and Hegel said, "What is real, is rational," Historismus proclaimed that "What has been growing must go on growing" or, as Meinecke was to express it later, "Out of the realm of that which is and which will be, there constantly emerges . . . the notion of what ought to be and must be"[8]—a dangerous philosophy which, as we shall see, may lead to acceptance of all historical *faits accomplis*.

How can criticism of the Wilhelminian state be reconciled with the warm support Meinecke's philosophy offered it? This may not be understood, he replies, by outsiders who try to fathom the nature of the Reich with extraneous yardsticks: "Humanitarian enlightenment had been ethical, so had romanticism; both had a common enemy that was, to their way of thinking, unethical: the power state of the ancien régime. Both chided as blind power lust *what is in the nature of the state itself.* They moralized from the outside instead of trying to understand the state from the inside. They failed to notice that ethics had two aspects: one universal and one individual, concrete aspect. From the individual aspect, the apparent immorality of the state's power-political egoism can be morally justified. For *that which springs from the innermost essence of a natural being cannot be immoral."* [9]

This last sentence has often been cited as a horrid example of German political Darwinism. It is indeed characteristic of the school of Historismus, but it is by no means isolated in the literature of the first decade of this century. It springs from the *Lebensphilosophie* of Wilhelm Dilthey (who was Meinecke's teacher), from the Vitalism of Hans Driesch, from the pragmatism of William James, from Henri Bergson's élan vital and *évolution créatrice,* and from George Bernard Shaw's philosophy of life. Meinecke applied their ideas to the life of states, dealing with the nation-state as with an individual in quest of self-fulfillment. The idea was expressed in a book by Rudolf Kjellén, *The State as an Organism,* [10] and it must be distinguished on the one hand from Treitschke's "right of the stronger," on the other from Hegel's interpretation of the state as "the reality of the moral idea." Meinecke had rejected both concepts—Treitschke's because it was vulgar and biological, Hegel's because it placed the state at the service of an idea or of the progress of history. What he had in mind was the understanding of the state as a living, developing organism which followed the command of its "inner law." Goethe had bequeathed to Historismus the theory: You are bound to follow "the law by which thou first wert formed. Sibyls said so and prophets: Nor time nor power ever will destroy wrought form that vividly develops." [11]

This is how we must read *Cosmopolitanism.* The liberals had formulated their aspirations in the Wars of Liberation, had failed to realize them in the 1848 revolution, and therefore could not oppose Bismarck when he achieved German unity in his own way. After 1866, when he defeated reactionary Austria and launched Germany on her path to world power, it became sheer sectarian dogmatism to persist in sterile opposition. The fruit of German unity might have been ill-gotten, but it tasted just as sweet. Historismus always sanctions the results of the power struggle. Although the end may not justify the means, evil means do not invalidate the goal once it has been reached. Thus the Liberals teamed up with Bismarck's state, changing their name to National-Liberals.

This was Meinecke's position in 1907. Thirty-three years later, he was faced with a similar dilemma. Hitler had defeated France and threatened to unite Europe under the swastika banner. Meinecke then wrote to a historian friend: "I need not tell you that I have followed the recent [German victories] with pride, joy, and deep emotion. But those who until recently were in opposition have it less easy than the Liberals in 1866. We may wish to, but we cannot, yet. . . . Light and shadow are so distributed that the shadow does not yet appear as belonging to the light. It almost seems as though the motive power of the great and necessary revolutions stemmed from the demonic, evil part of human nature rather than from the good part."[12]

The demonic! In the earlier work, the state had been all *Geist;* in that complacent age before the world wars, the contest of many individual state personalities had appeared as almost a quadrille danced in the sweet harmonies of European culture. Even their rivalries had been seen as revelations of "a higher human order striving for individuality, self-determination, and power."[13] War itself hardly changed the relations between equals.

Now, with the advent of mob nationalism, these assumptions could no longer be made. Hitler had no respect for other nations' integrity and sovereignty, let alone for their unity; he acknowledged no limitations to power; he represented no *Geist* but only barbarism. Meinecke saw the nature of the beast, and his historical tools, he found, were no longer sufficient to deal with it. The book he wrote under the Nazi Reich, the voluminous *Origins of Historismus,* was a tired retreat from history to estheticism—not a surrender to the demonic forces but a declaration of bankruptcy. Liberalism, as we shall see, had no answer to Hitler. Only after the fall of the Third Reich, only after the victories had been followed by disaster, did Meinecke look back, as an old man, on the history he had helped to explain and shape, and acknowledged that the "demon" had been present at the very beginning: "In the brilliance of [Bismarck's] achievement we were not sufficiently aware of the hidden darkness . . . where the disease might set in later," and "it is in the very nature of [the state] that something demonic may leap up at any given moment and seize control of the ruling authorities."[14] Note the different tone in which the "nature of the state" is referred to here and in *Cosmopolitanism*. Historismus no longer was able to justify "whatever springs from innermost nature." The German nation stood accused of having produced, from its innermost nature, the monster of Nazism.

To anticipate the end of our story: in his last work—which certainly did not pretend to reach the level of scholarship to which its author had been accustomed—Meinecke tried above all to give his countrymen confidence that their history did not altogether condemn them but held out some "hope"— which is the last word of the book. He tried to show that Hitler was an extraneous, barbaric irruption into German history, not an organic outgrowth of that history. At the same time, the wisdom of his old age had taught him that "the power of the state ever and again acts as an end in itself. The historian . . . recognizing reality . . . perceives the tragic contrast between that reality and the ideal. Tragic indeed is the history he will have to write."[15]

In his last lecture, "Ranke and Burckhardt," he also conceded for the first time that Burckhardt might have been right in asserting that the state is evil by its very nature and that culture, which alone guarantees the nation's survival, should now be seen as standing outside the state (although by then, 1946, Germany had no state). In a review of Spengler's second volume he says: "It is understandable but in the last resort unsatisfactory to insist on the dualism in man. This leads to systems which tear history apart into genuine and inauthentic, sunny and shaded sides. . . . True knowledge will always strive, like Goethe, for the ultimate unity of things."[16]

We shall now follow in greater detail the pilgrimage of this historian from a position of optimistic monism to one of tragic dualism.

II. The Demon Without

Friedrich Meinecke was born in 1862 at Salzwedel, a small Prussian town where his father served as a petty official. He grew up amidst the victory celebrations of 1864, 1866, and 1870/71—happy, brief wars that led to the unification of Germany under Bismarck and to the rapid rise of the Reich to world power. The father's house was conservative, pietistic, and patriotic. Meinecke's university teachers also earned the name of "the Prussian school of history," and it was under their wing that he obtained first a position at the Secret State Archive and later as assistant editor of *Historische Zeitschrift* (HZ). There he gained the gratitude of traditional historians by warding off the onslaught of insurgents who tried to introduce psychosociological methods, recognized the importance of economic history, and suggested a progression in the history of civilization.

Meinecke, who soon became editor, was never interested in the history of civilization. He found it a somehow unworthy subject, "nothing but a colorful picture book of mores . . . and material factors of external life, down to eating and drinking habits. This petty-bourgeois, pleasure-seeking interest in the history of civilization has been awakened decisively by Voltaire."[17]

The main issue, however, was causality—whether history obeys any laws—a question to which Meinecke was to return often. He rejected all determinism, even attempts at systematizing in history. He praised Ranke for "not enclosing life in the mortuary of definitions." Only in the socioeconomic mass processes does a blind law of causality prevail; ideas, religion, the arts and the sciences are freely created. Mediating between the two extremes—body and soul, matter and spirit—

is the realm of the political, which participates in both: it freely creates forms but it must work through material interests; its impulses come from great individuals, but they must find material forces to lead and to mould. Political history studies the unfolding "wrought forms" (Goethe) or "God's thoughts" (Ranke) or "historical individualities" (Meinecke). These, and the ideas about them, are the proper study of history.

For the same reason, the *HZ* fought valiantly against positivism, Marxism, Hegelianism, and all other attempts to find "laws" in history—Lamprecht, Spengler, and Toynbee. It is true that in defense of professionalism the *HZ* also warded off the attacks of Stefan George's school and of other myth makers. But the Nazis were not altogether wrong when they charged, thirty years later, that the common people never appeared in the pages of either the *HZ* or of Meinecke's works. We must label him a traditionalist working at the center of the establishment. His first work was a rather conventional two-volume *Life of Field Marshal Hermann von Boyen* (1896–99). Boyen was a reformer during the Wars of Liberation, the creator of a people's army, a Kantian, a hero, and a model for Meinecke's own political development.

Religious doubts had led to estrangement from the father, but Meinecke's first steps into politics were still guided by his Christian heritage. He followed the court chaplain Adolf Stoecker, an anti-Semitic demagogue who hoped to win the workers over to the monarchy but who found only middle-class and aristocratic sponsors. Meinecke accepted the Christian Social party's principle of national community but became disgusted with its vulgarity and passed over to the Progressive party. There he found a congenial group of brilliant intellectuals: Max Weber, the father of German sociology; Hugo Preuss, who was to write the Weimar Constitution; Theodor Heuss, who was to be the first president of the Bonn Republic; the historian Walter Goetz, whom the Nazis were to deprive of his chair, and Ernst Troeltsch, the liberal theologian turned sociologist; above all Pastor Friedrich Naumann, who tried to transform political liberalism into social liberalism and the empire into a social monarchy.

The Progressive party was opposed to the Prussian caste system; it aimed to crack the power of the Junker class, to break up the big estates in the east, and to replace the aristocratic form of government by modern, more democratic selection procedures. Although it was not opposed to imperialism, it became increasingly worried by the kaiser's erratic course in foreign policy, his blustering provocations, his perilous challenge to British sea power. However, Naumann's Mitteleuropa design should not be mistaken for a forerunner of the Common Market; it was an intelligent alternative to militarism. Meinecke interpreted it to say: "Our imperialism should be federative rather than expansionist." He was unemotionally modern. To Pan-German fretting over the emergence of Slav states in the Balkans he answered that their policies would have to be guided by interests of the region, not by racial emotions and, he added: "Race theories have wreaked enough havoc in science; they could produce worse delusions in politics."[18]

Meinecke was then teaching at Strasbourg and Freiburg, in the freer atmosphere of southern liberalism, and in close contact with the Baden school of neo-Kantian philosophers, who also were liberals. He concurred with their well-known distinction between natural and cultural sciences: the former seek universal or general laws while the latter deal with phenomena that are not repeatable, hence can be neither predicted nor used to test a law. The "cultural sciences" (*Geisteswissenschaften*) are also concerned with values. For both these reasons Meinecke concluded that history was not "science" in the sense of the natural sciences. But far from being less than a science, history thereby becomes free to be more than a science and to follow its value-oriented concerns, relating the "higher" purposes to the pursuits of statesmen and state thinkers. In this conception, the historian is able to create the saga of his nation even while observing the strictest rule of scholarly research.

It was in these happy years that Meinecke wrote his optimistic *Cosmopolitanism*, hoping that national community, the reconciliation of power with the whole nation, including the workers, could yet be realized.

That day seemed to have come in August 1914, when the war fever swept the peoples of Europe, when the soldiers marched happily to the front and promised the girls that they would be home by Christmas with presents. The workers, who so long had stood aloof from the national community, now joined enthusiastically in the defense of the fatherland. On August 4, the Social Democrats in the Reichstag voted the kaiser's war appropriations unanimously. In his memoir Meinecke remembers that "this was one of the most beautiful days of my life"; [19] he also joined other professors and writers (like Thomas Mann) in explaining to the world that this was a war of *Geist* against materialistic rapacity. When Entente propagandists retorted that the Germans, not content with aspiring to world domination, also claimed a monopoly on *Geist*, friend Troeltsch asked back: "Why should the Germans not fight for their right to be different?" Meinecke endorsed this sentiment, but he also hoped that the war, like the Wars of Liberation a hundred years earlier, would become a war of German renewal.

He admonished the kaiser's government not to lose the beautiful momentum. Now, while the Germans were winning, was the time to enlarge the Reichstag's responsibilities, to abolish the discriminatory three-class suffrage in Prussia and the Junker domination in government. New and more capable elites were growing out of the middle classes and even from the workers' ranks.

As a historian, Meinecke also offered this lesson from the past: a fair and honorable peace must be negotiated, leaving no *ressentiments* and no *irredentas* that would endanger the postwar peace. He was distressed by the unrestrained chauvinism the war had unleashed, and especially by the Pan-Germans, who sought extensive annexations and German domination over Europe. Their misuse of great German names of the past provoked Meinecke to charge: "They imitate the mannerisms of these idols; of their inner pathos they know nothing. They emulate their firebrand extravaganzas but ignore the political-philosophical conceptions from which their heroic will had sprung and which were diametrically opposite to the dilettante nationalism of our contemporary racists. Humanity was then the springboard of patriotism. . . . They read Fichte's *Address to the German Nation* but they lack the humanist background that is the true source of national policy."[20]

Still more courage was required to tell an academic audience that the much-heralded contrast between the Germanic and the Latin spirit existed only in the viewer's eye.[21] Even so, Meinecke's own peace aims look moderate only when compared with the Pan-German program. Instead of annexing Belgium, he merely wished to reduce it to a satellite state; he proposed to annex Baltic Kurland; from England's and France's colonial empire he wanted to take only enough to connect Germany's possessions in East and West Africa. Although he knew, earlier than most Germans, that any chance to win the war had been lost in its first months, he expected the German troops to hold out on French territory to the last day.

Patriotism had always narrowed the minds of German liberals. Nevertheless, when Meinecke moved to Berlin, he helped found the League for Freedom and Fatherland as a counterbalance to the Pan-German League and worked on the Peace Resolution of the Reichstag majority. Rightists later were to charge that the German armies has been "unbeaten in the field" but were "stabbed in the back" by defeatists, traitors, and Jews. The right also charged that by signing the Versailles Treaty, which all Germans held to be unfair, the left had espoused the Entente's thesis of Germany's war guilt. As we have seen, this latter charge contained a grain of truth: liberals like Meinecke felt that German diplomacy under the kaiser had missed opportunities to appease England, and Social Democrats were convinced that the kaiser bore a major share of responsibility for the outbreak of World War I. These were very important issues for both German politics and German historiography. And it is necessary to ascertain which position Meinecke and, under his editorship, the HZ took on both questions.

The HZ frequently polemicized against the Entente thesis of Germany's war guilt, but it never tried to disarm the rightists' double charge that the republican parties had ended the war too soon and signed the war guilt clause without need. All through the 1920s, the HZ failed to call the kaiser's regime to account for starting the war, losing it, and not telling the German people the truth about it.

Meinecke made a subtle attempt to mention the subject in the book he had begun to write during the war. He refers to the famous chapter in the Discorsi (I, 53) where Machiavelli discusses "ignominy": it will always be difficult to explain to the nationalistic mob a decision that seems to be cowardly; while demagogues recklessly clamor for confrontation policies, the statesman must have the courage to accept ignominy if it is necessary to save the country. Then Meinecke goes on: "The most powerful statement [on raison d'état] is found at the end of Discorsi (III, 41). It must have sounded in the ear of a certain great statesman during the [First] World War: that one may save the fatherland con ignominia. 'When the question is how to save the fatherland, one should not hesitate.' "[22]

Like all his colleagues, Meinecke thought little of the masses, especially where foreign policy was concerned. Since he saw the state, above all, as an entity rivaling other states, his concern for democratization was motivated less by a demand for justice than by the need to integrate the workers in the national enterprise. His politics were patrician; his historical thinking was informed by a strong desire for continuity. He often asserted that his philosophy was comprehensible only to an "elite of highly cultured men" and would do little good to the fainthearted.

When the revolution occurred on November 9, 1918, Meinecke did not immediately accept it. But he saw that the monarchy could not be brought back, that the republic was the only institutional framework in which the Reich could survive.

Like Stresemann and Rathenau, he was a *Vernunftrepubli-kaner*, a pragmatic republican. He helped to convert the Progressive party into a Democratic party; he supported the concept of a "broad coalition" comprising the moderate middle-class parties and the Social Democrats. He was active in the campaign against Hindenburg (1925), but in the early 1930s he supported President Hindenburg's project to strengthen the presidency. Instead of the unstable party government, he would have liked to see a *Vertrauensdiktatur*, a trusteeship dictatorship which, of course, was to prevent the Nazis from mobilizing the mob.

The Republic's foreign policy also could profit from a critique of the blunders committed by the previous regime. Meinecke therefore studied the failure of *The Anglo-German Rapprochement 1890–1901* and advised the Republic to seek "means other than the old power politics."[23] Meinecke's political intent was immediately recognized, and the book was severely attacked by nationalist historians like Gerhard Ritter and Otto Westphal (who called Meinecke "the Locarno historian," alluding to the treaty of 1925 that reconciled Germany and the Western powers; ludicrously East German historians now echo this charge).

It also fell to Meinecke's lot to defend the Republic against anti-Semitic slander, especially the charge that "alien elements" and upstarts had been favored by the revolution. In 1926 he told an academic audience:

> It is true that some strata of our population, which only now have obtained the opportunity to be integrated into the nation's life, have not yet acquired all traditions of our national life. That their life should be alloyed with cosmopolitan ideas is quite legitimate and relates to our ideal of humanity which the nationalistic strata have lost. Let me admit that there have been episodes of disloyalty vis-à-vis the old regime—reactions against its misdeeds. Our left-wing press, which generally strives to preserve our national values, shows once in a while—if I may be candid—some Jewish *ressentiment*. These are infantile disorders in the process of a development that will integrate those strata that so far had been kept outside the state.[24]

Jews, however, were only one of the new strata that had recently gained access to public life. The revolution of November 1918 brought recognition to the new masses; politics became a game of parliamentary parties. Instead of the dream of national community, there was pluralism; the nationalization of the masses had resulted in what Hendrik de Man was to call "massification (Vermassung) of the nation" and Ortega y Gasset The Revolt of the Masses. Politics was no longer the preserve of an elite that might be inspired by an idea, but had to address itself to the interests of economic groups and to the passions of the mob. New forces became active in world history, and the alternatives open to a German policy were all equally distasteful. "We have to choose between the capitalist-imperialist order that enslaves us, and the federative-socialist order that contrasts with all our traditions," wrote friend Otto Hintze to Troeltsch. Meinecke was deeply worried about the loss of that authority which he always associated with Kultur. In a review of Jacob Burckhardt's letters he recalled the master's criticism of the "terrible simplifiers" and continued: "He saw the coming of the terrible authority that was to save us from disrespectful democracy. This was the deep conflict in his nature, which hated power as evil but knew that without it no higher culture is possible" (HZ 1923).

The war experience had cast much doubt on the prewar years' harmonious outlook and had brought Meinecke closer to Burckhardt's pessimistic, dualistic philosophy. The mobilization of the masses had changed the nature of warfare. Militarism, nationalism, and capitalism now formed a fatal triumvirate that threatened to engulf Western civilization. All these new developments, to which was added the powerlessness of the Reich, forced Meinecke to rethink his assumptions. He could no longer presuppose any preestablished harmony between power and spirit, and while he was not prepared to abandon the Rankean faith in the ethical value of the state, he also had to admit that Historismus opened the door to subjectivist, hedonist, relativist ethics or at least to a pluralism that looked much less appealing than Ranke's "joyous variety of state personalities." Troeltsch spoke of the "crisis of Historismus" and wrote a heavy volume, Problems of Historismus, which Meinecke reviewed in HZ (1923).

Both friends were apprehensive of the "abyss of relativism," of an "anarchy of values" that plagued the Western world, and both were looking for ways to bridge the chasm between *ethos* and *kratos*. But, a hundred years after Hegel, they no longer found the bridge in any "cunning of history" that might force the ideal and the real to converge in infinity: "All is individuality, each follows its own private law, everything has a right to life, everything is relative, everything flows—give me a point in space to stand on!"[25]

III. The Demon Within

Meinecke gave his own answer to the crisis in the major work he had begun to write during the war: *The Idea of Raison d'Etat in Modern History*. It is a work of doubt and ambiguity, bearing the scars of many ideological battles. Its theme is the problematic of power—not simply "Machiavellism" as the title of the translation would indicate.

If once the state had appeared as the most noble embodiment of a nation's awareness of eternal values,[26] now it is seen as acting under physical constraints; no matter how high the purpose of some men may be, the very structure of the state makes it prone to lapses into baseness. "It is a frightful fact of history that we cannot hope to achieve radical morality in that [highest] community which comprises all other human communities" (p. 12). Worse, the historian often is bewildered by immoral forces which nevertheless bring forth desirable results. Although moralizing history is still widely practiced, scholarly history "is obliged to accept the uncomfortable fact—disturbing, nay shocking though it be—that nature and reason are not as easy to distinguish as friend and foe" (p. 9).

When we clearly realize that in the life of states the noble and the mean are inextricably intertwined, then Meinecke's definition of Reason of State will not sound surprising. He calls it "the bridge" between the power impulse and moral responsibility.[27] *Kratos* and *ethos* together build the state, and each state must seek its particular reason of state; no general rule of conduct can be spelled out for all rulers—which follows from the basic tenet of Historismus and its rejection of all "moralizing history."

As a study of techniques of statecraft, Machiavellism therefore is of little interest to Meinecke; its problems "belong in the realm of nature, with ants and bees" (p. 7), its answers are based on mere "cunning," and the underlying morality is strictly utilitarian. Should a prince keep treaties? Yes, if he wishes to build confidence. Must he always keep treaties? Not when the state's survival is at stake. The criteria of conduct are found along an axis from prudence to recklessness, or from practicality to impracticality.

But a Christian prince must think not only of his credibility down here; he must also consider his credit account in the afterlife. A formidable bookkeeper, called conscience, tells him to temper the immoderation that lurks in every act of state and to fight the "demon" of *pleonexia* (cupidity): "Next to hunting and loving, pleonexia is the most powerful elemental impulse in man" (p. 4). Considered rightly, this ethics is prudential too, and the anguish of a prince who sins for the good of the state still does not yield us a political ethics. The decision whether he will remember Hell is still subjective, a matter of his conscience alone. Just the same, and notwithstanding Machiavelli, statesmen do recognize a second axis which guides their conduct; it runs from the permissible to the impermissible, and statesmen write memoirs to persuade posterity that their aims were pure. Few are as cynical as Frederick the Great, who introduced his *Histoire de mon temps* by saying: "I hope that posterity will distinguish between the philosopher in me and the ruler, the respectable man and the politician."[28]

But Meinecke wishes to liberate us from this frame of reference and to steer us toward an intrinsic understanding of power. The subtle method he uses to lure his reader away from the "moralistic" to the historical approach is characteristic of Historismus at its fascinating best. In the beginning, Meinecke reports, Frederick justified his wanton war for Silesia by saying that he had his subjects' best interests in mind—a feeble argument, and Meinecke readily admits that the Silesians were not happier after being conquered. When the war lasted seven years, moreover, Frederick's argument no longer sounded credible, and he shifted it ever so slightly: "Rulers are the slaves of their resources; the interest of the *state* is their law." In a new edition of his early work, *Anti-Macchiavel*, he made a similar change. Instead of "The king is the first servant of his *people*," it now read: "The king is the first servant of the *state*." Meinecke comments shrewdly:

> "At first sight the earlier draft may strike one as more modern. . . . But in fact 'people' then stood for mere population, subjects, not for any real nation. . . . The term was purely humanitarian and rational-istic. Frederick's transition from 'people' to 'state' indicates a move-ment in the direction of modern thought, toward the national state. . . . The ability to understand such entities is a characteristic of the modern mind. . . . It was Frederick's state that first created the fixed and definite form with which it became possible for a mere population to be welded into a nation with its own vital will. (p. 308)

Presumably, the Silesians need not be happy but they ought to be proud that they provided the opportunity for Prussia to become a big power. Later, Meinecke even introduces a He-gelian argument to bolster Frederick's claim: "He laid the foundations of a state that would eventually be constitu-tional" (p. 309). Providential history is anathema to Historis-mus; but to celebrate certain heroes, the function of Hegel's World Spirit is taken over by a new notion of Reason of State which diverges sharply from the ordinary meaning of Ma-chiavellism. By no means is everything permitted to every state. Where the state fails to fulfill an ideal, it cannot invoke any "reason" of state to justify its sheer lust for power. Thus Meinecke treats the Renaissance *condottieri,* from whose maxims after all Machiavelli abstracted his theories, with ut-ter contempt. What does great credit to Frederick is but petty selfishness in the case of those Italian princelings: "Their im-pure, petty means hardly concealed their powerlessness. Their states had no real nobility; their *ragione di stato* could not justify power from an idealistic point of view" (p. 91). What they were lacking, obviously, was that specific Geist that gives a state an identity and welds its people into a nation: "Ragione di stato was not yet seen as the public welfare. . . . The state was still incomplete, its power and authority had not yet reached the dignity of being self-evident" (p. 123).

One should expect that from here a historian pursuing the march of the national idea would be led to notions such as "general will," "commonweal," or "public happiness." Strangely enough, The Idea of Reason of State does not mention these terms at all, nor does it discuss their authors. For all we learn from Meinecke, neither Rousseau nor Cromwell, neither the French nor the American Revolution (not to mention Marx or Lenin) produced any political theory.[29] The reason for this omission was not simple German provincialism. Meinecke was striving for a positive view of the state; for him the revolutionary state embodied all that the state should not be—the instrument of the masses, expression of the passions, the "demonic." Such states hardly deserved the name, and their ethics were lower than that of a condottiere. He could not concede to them a reason of state. He never tires of telling us that Geist, a noble idea, must inspire the state, or else it is left to the demon.[30] I am afraid his bias here is one of class and of political orientation. Such partisanship violates a principle of Historismus: that no historical formation and no individual Geist is to be preferred, or dubbed "higher"; that all are alike in value. Yet in practice both Ranke and Meinecke freely used the predicates "higher" and "lower," and they did not recognize any Geist of which they disapproved.

Nevertheless, Meinecke's selection of those states that have Geist, and those that don't, does not seem quite so arbitrary. The demon is known by the fact that its behavior is uncontrolled and the power drive is unchecked. Geist, by contrast, is where the state sets itself limited goals. We already have encountered praise for a statesman who took ignominy upon himself to save the fatherland.

Most revealing is the laudatio for Bismarck. To Meinecke he represented "the most sublime and successful synthesis between the old *raison d'état* of the cabinets and the new popular forces. . . . With Machiavellian ruthlessness and acute calculation of power resources, he created the German state, but the same calculation also enabled him to see the limits of Germany's power. An intimate connection here exists between his temperate foreign policy after 1871 and his suppression of parliamentary and democratic tendencies. He was deeply convinced that responsibility to parliaments made it difficult to avoid risky policies."[31] In the concluding chapter Meinecke touches again on this subject of mass nationalism, of the passions of popular parties, of the need for the statesman to fight the "Machiavellism of the masses." Referring to the Ruhr occupation by France in 1923, he denounces "the modern forces of militarism, nationalism, and capitalism, which stand behind France's *raison d'état*" (p. 423)—all known to be insatiable.

This ties in with a second line of thought which provides the woof to the warp of his argument throughout *The Idea of Reason of State*. In Meinecke's mind the ideas of democracy and revolution were closely enmeshed with the Enlightenment of the eighteenth century, and this in turn had been identified with the "shallow French mind." During World War I German intellectuals, led by Thomas Mann, had sounded the clarion of a cultural revolution against Western ways of thought. Historismus was counted upon to show the deepest understanding of the cause in dispute; for the root evil of contemporary Western culture was its tradition of Natural Law—the doctrine that had come down from the ancient Stoa through the philosophy of the Christian Middle Ages to the Enlightenment; it had led to the idea of the social contract, to pacifism, and eventually to positivism and Marxism. Its basic flaw was the assumption that reason is one, and that its conclusions are applicable to all situations and all people alike. It was responsible for pluralism and egalitarianism, for the idea of progress in history, and for the moralistic approach to *raison d'état*. It produced "the naive illusion that one can distinguish between just and unjust wars,"[32] and it paid no respect to outstanding individuals like Frederick the

Great and Bismarck, or to lofty state conceptions like theirs. Can they really be judged by the same standards of morality that are rightly invoked against a Cola di Rienzo, a Robespierre? The "generalizing" approach left no room for the contemplation of that which was unique; its abstract principles suppressed that which had grown organically.

Second, the rationalist approach is mechanistic and does not lead to an understanding of natural, organic bodies like the state. An example of the pernicious contract theory is Hobbes' *Leviathan*. Strong though Hobbes would make his state, essentially it is no different from the "liberal nightwatchman state." Put together mechanically for purely utilitarian purposes, it is not a life form to which people can become attached emotionally. "Hobbes' Leviathan has no soul."[33]

Reason of State can be understood and vindicated only from the vantage point of Historismus, which conceives the state as "a life that springs from an original tendency, from an inner movement";[34] the history of the idea of Reason of State is the story of the development of this approach. Moreover, the way Meinecke has written the story, the idea really emerged in a continuous polemic against social contract theory, and its real history is the battle of German Historismus against French rationalism, a world-historical battle not just between two conceptions of politics but between two political cultures—the one starting from community and constituting the state as its soul, the other starting from the individual and constituting the state by contract. "The fundamental shortcoming of Western thought was that it had no grasp of the real state and could not affect the statesman deeply. It did not prevent the modern hypertrophy of Machiavellism, and it resulted either in confused complaints and doctrinaire postulates, or in hypocrisy and cant."[35]

Only where power is seen as the life element of the state, only where historical reality is grasped, can Reason of State be understood and used. Since each state must find its particular Reason of State, the problem of ethics has been shifted from philosophy to history, or from a judgment applying general principles to a judgment sizing up a particular historical entity.

We might elucidate this idea further by differentiating it from others that look similar. Hegel had "legitimized the bastard" with the device of the "cunning of Reason," and he placed state power at the service of a higher idea. He combined ruthless realism in regard to particular state action with a transcendent view of world history: "The filth of reality that surrounded the philosopher did not besmirch him" (pp. 350 and 368). Ranke had criticized Hegel, but in his own practice he totally identified the statesman's conduct with the development of the state personality; he saw the finger of God in all manifestations of history and "tended to set aside the elemental motives. . . . His optimistic outlook hid the murky side of the power struggle from him" (pp. 388f.). But at the same time he opened the door to a relativistic view that had an explanation for everything, and after him came Treitschke, Nietzsche, and "the sinister host" of Darwinians, naturalists and chauvinists who "used the predicate 'moral' rather lightly" to justify immoral acts (pp. 407–8). Cautiously, Meinecke warned the Germans that their vitalist theories, their blind acceptance of all state power as "moral," had put them in the wrong. He criticized Treitschke for justifying war as a moral necessity. "German historical thought tends to excuse and idealize power politics on the ground of superior morality. Thus, despite all reservations that were made, it pointed to a crudely naturalistic ethics of force."[36]

From here on Meinecke's argument became dialectical—or perhaps it merely zigzagged: if power was seen as the essence of state, self-preservation took precedence over moral obligations, and a state striving for power did not act morally but in the elemental sphere. "It is possible for this power drive to be moral—if it serves moral qualities—but even then it does not lose its natural character" (p. 407). The line which Meinecke draws is so fine that being on the side of decency may become a matter of personal character rather than of precepts of conduct (p. 409). Meinecke saw a "sinister line going from Machiavelli to nationalism," but he treated "this error . . .

with respect" (p. 410). For these forces which Meinecke fears
are the same forces he must use to build his state. They are
destructive when they are not mastered by Reason of State,
but they cannot be repudiated. The whole point of Historismus is that the higher purposes of power are inseparably tied
to the vital forces and interests. Without the unremitting
power drives of some groups of men, mankind would not
have reached the stage of state-building, and would still be
without those higher forms of organization that make culture
possible.[37] The Hegelian vision of "stages," which Historismus rejects in other contexts, becomes essential here, not as
a theodicy but as a reminder that evil forces are a *necessary*
part of history. War, too, "can never be banished from the
earth because it is inseparably tied to the nature of the
state."[38] Elsewhere, he quotes Adam Ferguson: "Without the
jealousy of nations and the practice of war, civil society would
not have found its form," and adds: "This remark points to a
new age . . . that gives the state its due place."[39]

Throughout the book, a constant dialectical development
has taken place: the demon, who must provide the driving
force for cultural achievement, also may destroy it; Reason of
State must both tame and develop the demon. They are engaged in unrelenting struggle. Toward the end of *Machiavellism*, therefore, only the plaint remains: "In history there
are too many things in which God and the Devil are intertwined. One of the most important is Reason of State. . . .
The historian can never tire of gazing into it." Likewise, in
his essay "Causalities and Values," Meinecke remarked:
"What is most shocking is to discover an intimate link of
causality between the biological and the ethical spheres: that
great, beautiful cultural values often originate in mean, un-
clean causes, working up from night and the deep, so that it
sometimes looks as if God were working through the Devil to
realize himself."[40]

The fight between good and evil, which Historismus had
claimed to transcend, had been reproduced *inside* Reason of
State. Meinecke may have thought that the "moralizing" approach to Machiavellism could be waved aside by the magic
wand of history. But the historians were in a position some-

what similar to the psychologists: they had driven out the superstitious belief in the Devil only to find the Id inside the personality structure. So the ideal may no longer fight the evil forces from "outside," but it must now fight them inside. The very last word of *Machiavellism*, therefore, is the tearful ambiguity: "The statesman should always carry God and the State in his heart, or else he may be overpowered by the demon (whom he cannot shake off completely anyway)."

Clearly, no abyss has been bridged, no dichotomy has been transcended; history has not superseded philosophy; the two horns of the dilemma are as visible as before; a liberal's conscience still faces Machiavellism, and the liberal political theory is more bewildered than before it was stated so bravely and succinctly. Meinecke frankly acknowledged that historians had no answer to relativistic ethics. "Historical thinking, . . . which perhaps is the only remaining key to the understanding of man, dissolves everything into flowing life, threatening to lose the firm hold on one's own condition and to leave us with a skeptical relativism."[41]

To escape from the dualism, Meinecke refined his three-tier model by relating it to three kinds of causality:

—On the lowest level, nature is ruled by the blind laws of "mechanical causality" or "external necessity." Here effect is always equivalent to its cause, and all creation is languishing in the servitude of this our animal heritage. (This is the neo-Kantian heritage.)

—On the middle level, "organic causes" (also called biological or teleological causes) rule "individualities" (which may be persons, groups, classes, states, churches, or other institutions). Obedient to "internal necessity," each follows its star, its entelechy, or "destiny" (*Schicksal*, a key word in German philosophy through the first half of this century, means not accident but metaphysical necessity). Effect here may transcend its cause—as development or transformation. (This is Dilthey's and vitalism's contribution.)

—The highest realm is occupied by pure ideas and values. Here causality is creative morally, spiritually, or artistically. It is truly free; it alone, therefore, is "historical." For "cultural history alone is history," it alone creates "singular spiritual values: historical individualities." Not surprisingly, "Historical individuals are those that have a tendency toward the good, the true, and the beautiful."[42] (This may be the influence of Eduard Spranger, to whom Meinecke was close.)

Such astounding formulations might have landed Meinecke in some form of Platonism. But as yet, in this "second period," he had no intention of dismissing as irrelevant all the history he loved—"where the clashing of the mundanely crude forces of political life awakens individual ideas which struggle for realization"—and he declined to say "whether the state itself or Plato's idea of it is the higher value."[43] For he knows that, to realize themselves, the highest values have to descend into the arena of the middle tier, mix with nature, and become tainted with causality. He is too much of a historian to enjoy for long the contemplation of pure values. To do that, he treats them as "individualities." Thus we find "the Prussian idea," used not as a metaphor but as a reality. Even the admiring Walther Hofer explains that with Meinecke one can never tell whether an idea is a general principle or a life force, an ideal or an instinct; and Johan Huizinga poked fun at the German disease of "historical anthropomorphism": collective entities are reified and seem to act as though they were persons. Meinecke was quite aware of the danger this entailed when others, e.g., Treitschke or Spengler, used such techniques:

> Moral responsibility is not concentrated in one individual but must be borne by the collective, although it can act only through individuals. . . . Where collective purposes are at stake, the moral sense is weakened; the agent takes the view that 'the business' requires acts that an individual might not take upon himself. . . . Actions for supra-individual purposes have a tendency toward matter-of-factness, and at the same time a frightful tendency toward cold heartlessness. We do not say this for sentimental reasons but to demonstrate the tragic nature of historical life.[44]

When he wrote this, Meinecke did not know that twenty years later the German nation would have to answer the charge of "collective guilt." As a historian he had seen that to act means to incur guilt, but neither he nor Troeltsch mentions "original sin" in this context. What they see is man's private conscience pitted against *Schicksal*—the inevitable collusion of the "high" with the "low." In each individual case the mixture had to be evaluated differently. Thus he resented Voltaire's description of the base motives in Frederick the Great's policies and stressed their "spiritual" tendency. But idealistic historiography cannot evade this dilemma, either to suppress the seamy side of its heroes or to sanctify it.

There is a deep philosophical calamity hidden in this moral dilemma, at least for one so intimately connected with the tradition of German idealism. The historical individuality— state, party, or person—must represent a universal principle, or rather must embody it as the tragic hero does in a drama. Unless the general and the particular, the idea and the interest, freedom and necessity, creativity and causality meet in the movement of this individuality, history loses its meaning. In his important book, *Geschichtschreibung und Weltanschauung*, Professor Walther Hofer has made a heroic effort to square all the categories for Meinecke, but he can do that only at the expense of history: the living, acting subject of history disappears when the idea is to be saved, and the idea is beclouded whenever the state individuality appears in all its dimensions.

IV. The Demon Triumphant

The problem, then, is to live with the contradiction in full awareness of its irreconcilability. Both Troeltsch and Meinecke have often resorted to the word "tragic" to describe either the human condition as they saw it or the philosophy on which they had to settle. "Both the ideas of identity and of individuality—those two supreme and fruitful ideas of the modern German mind—showed the inner tragic, two-edged quality of all great historical ideas and forces."[45]

"Tragic realism" also was the prevailing style of German

literature during the Weimar Republic, and tragic was indeed the fate of the liberals, who vainly tried to imbue that republic with the *Geist* of classical Weimar.

Meinecke recommended to the republicans, as great models of German statesmen, Frederick the Great and Bismarck. He did not mention any more the heroes of his first books, the reformers of 1814 whom he knew so well: Humboldt, Stein, Hardenberg, nor the liberals of the 1848 revolution. Did liberalism generate no heroes, no ideas, no conception of the state?

Meinecke's style seems to exclude a definite stand. Everything is "yes–but," "no–however," "on the one hand—on the other," "both this—and its opposite." His subtle ambiguities, the fugatos of argument and counterargument chasing each other, the ritardandos, the anguish—all that liberal philosophizing seems weak in comparison with the robust certainties of the Catholics, agrarians, and conservatives on the one hand, the Communists on the other, and looks like mere literature next to the nuts-and-bolts approach of the positivist school. His Hamlet nature is vulnerable to the irrationalist attack from the nationalist right and to the rationalist assault from the left.

The liberal bourgeoisie was not armed ideologically when the demon struck. *Machiavellism* went to press when Hitler staged his Beer Hall putsch; it appeared in the same year as Thomas Mann's *Magic Mountain,* and indeed there is much that the two authors and their books have in common: the same ambiguity, the same wrestling with the ever-present demon, the same efforts to grapple with the problems of a liberal conscience.[46] The similarity becomes frightening a few years later when we see the historian and the novelist alike turn away from the uncomfortable political problems that inspired their works of 1924, and seek refuge in estheticism and a secondhand humanism.

Meinecke's third great work, begun in the late 1920s and published in 1937 under the Nazi regime, inaugurates his "third period." It is a deeply contemplative, but ambiguous book because of the circumstances under which it appeared.

Origin of Historismus investigates a series of eighteenth-century writers and evaluates each according to the percentage of rationalism and of Historismus that can be detected. But the series breaks up abruptly with Herder, and surprisingly the last 150 (out of 600) pages are devoted to Goethe, although Goethe admittedly did not care for history and had little to say about it.[47] (At the same time Thomas Mann was writing *Lotte in Weimar* (*The Beloved Returns*) and *Joseph and His Brothers*, and Hermann Hesse, after the searing *Steppenwolf*, the dream story *Narcissus and Goldmund—Death and the Lover*). After having been told that history is the only road to the understanding of man, we are given the advice to flee from history into the realm of humanist reflections, from public virtue to private serenity.

Were the early 1930s the time to abandon contemporary themes? Here, precisely, is the trouble with the book. Meinecke, just like Thomas Mann, chose to exalt the humanism of Goethe, and no one can doubt that a few years later this was a courageous thing to do. (Georg Lukács, interestingly, applied the same strategy in Moscow.) For Meinecke, however, this meant shifting the battlefield from political philosophy to culture. He did not confront the barbarians at all but turned his back on history. What had seemed an odd misuse of philosophical language in the "Causalities" essay (see text to note 42) is suddenly seen as the way out: only cultural history is history; the relationship between political and cultural history is broken. Where the development of the National State idea had been based on a substratum—the German Reich—and the development of the Reason of State idea still could be grafted on a development of European history, the development of Historismus had turned into the *Lebensphilosophie* of given individuals. History, instead of being made concrete, was estheticized.

The liberal bourgeoisie had once embraced a straightforward materialism, tempered by residual Christianity. The resulting tensions, however, had become intolerable for a large part of the middle class by the turn of the century; their materialism degenerated into biological, racial, or Nietzschean

naturalism, or else evaporated into mysticism. The more refined and educated strata of the upper middle class, on the
contrary, strove to maintain the continuity with the classical
period of German idealism, especially with its worship of the
personality. Historismus, as Meinecke had rightly said, was no
theory of history. It was a personal philosophy, an attitude to
life—but not a weapon, in time of need, against the barbarians.

How inadequate Meinecke's approach was at this juncture
can best be gauged from the boorish attack on him in, of all
places, the old *Historische Zeitschrift* (HZ). "Capitalist bourgeois society has produced a capitalist bourgeois historiography," wrote the Nazi professor Walter Frank; ridiculing "the
Hamlet-like pallor that hung over his declining culture," he
asked jeeringly whether "Meinecke's patriotism is strong
enough to abandon Western civilization in exchange for German hegemony in Europe."[48]

More subtle but no less severe, the Marxist historian Eckhart Kehr alluded to Meinecke's pet image—that he was in-
viting his reader to walk a mountain ridge (*Gratwanderung*,
as he calls it in his preface to *Origin of Historismus*): "The
superiority feeling of mountain climbers is highly developed
in German intellectual historians. . . . They concern themselves with things that have little practical significance. They
shy away from ideas that have revolutionized the world. Democracy, socialism, bolshevism are taboo. . . . Even those
who are republicans or democrats are conservative." Intellectual history, as seen by Kehr, is "a way out for the dis-
oriented bourgeoisie; it gives them the temporary feeling of
exaltation, of ranging on a high mountain."[49]

In going back to the "origins" of Historismus, Meinecke
evaded precisely those problems into which Historismus had
led, the "crisis" which Troeltsch and he had discussed ten
years earlier. Having written a book about the "evil side of
power [whose] excesses have been accepted all too lightly,"
having recognized that the core concept of Historismus, individuality, "might be used to justify the excesses of power
politics,"[50] he now limited the scope of his book so that he

did not have to comment on the responsibility of Historismus for that which followed. Only in two passages does he digress for a dig at "the real-political snobbism of some younger historians who think they have learned from Bismarck how to overcome obstacles," and at "the biological-morphological manner of Kjellén" (whose geopolitics had become a Nazi ideology).[51]

A third, no less serious criticism concerns an increasingly strident nationalism in Meinecke's style. He introduces Historismus as "the great German movement. . . . The German *Geist* here accomplished its second great feat after the Reformation."[52] Its coming, he had previously declared, was "the greatest revolution in thought which the West has experienced. The belief in the absolute validity and uniformity of reason, which had ruled until then, was now destroyed and replaced by the insight that reason manifests itself in a variety of forms. . . . This richer and more profound image of the world" was not simply a concern for professional historians but "a new vision of life."[53] With a certain animosity he represents the older view, that of Enlightenment and of rationalism, as "Western" or, more specifically, as "French," and instead of describing it as a manifestation of a European *Zeitgeist*, again and again he sets it up as a target for the "German" intellectual uprising.

Such a treatment not only flies in the face of all teaching of Historismus, it is also poor history. Germans were as much enthralled with the philosophy of the Enlightenment as Westerners, and Western writers—philosophers, historians, poets, novelists, and critics—were as deeply involved in the romantic reaction against the Enlightenment as Germany's Storm and Stress writers. To be sure, Meinecke gives due credit to Shaftesbury, Montesquieu, and above all to Edmund Burke; but Rousseau gets less than a page, Tocqueville is not mentioned at all, and when Meinecke has to admit, ever so grudgingly, Voltaire's immense merits for historiography, he cannot help adding: "However, the irrational profundity of the soul was unknown to him."[54] Montesquieu, likewise, gets a bad mark for ignoring "the incomprehensible."

The nationalistic bias becomes ludicrous when Vico has to be included among the insurgents. A Latin and a man of the Enlightenment, yet aware of irrational motives—how to get around this? We remember that the book appeared when Hitler and Mussolini were forming an axis; hence, Meinecke can comment: "Germans and Italians have a greater ability than the French to overcome intellectualistic inhibitions and to think from the totality of the soul." [55]

The truth is that notions such as *Zeitgeist*, national spirit, genius, etc., had been formed in the eighteenth century and helped to bring history back from the reporting of "what really happened" to the art of creating a national myth. Historismus became an ideology. But this artistic, inspirational, and almost mythical conception of history now was declared to be the highest achievement of *Geist* ever, erected as the model others must strive to emulate, or used as a yardstick by which other nations' cultures were to be measured. As an egregious monument to this exquisite culture, the book on Historismus seems to say to Germans of present and future generations as well as to observers abroad: Our present state may look ugly, our present rulers may be barbarians. But no one can take away our Kultur. A future Germany will be built on this Kultur, even though today it can exist only in the rarefied atmosphere of classical *Bildung*.

For unfortunately, the conception of Kultur which Meinecke offers in *Origin of Historismus* is drained of all sociological and political significance. It is personalist and humanist; it is contemplative rather than activist; it preserves an unpolitical sphere for the individual but it no longer places the individual into the stream of history. For all the rewarding insights and delightful speculations it offers, the book escapes into the realm of beautiful appearances, where Friedrich Schiller had located the German freedom. It is an eloquent, often moving testament of a bygone period, but it seems to accept its own time with resignation. Meinecke seems to be hibernating, dreaming a beautiful dream. Gottfried Benn, the Expressionist poet, in the postwar poem "Quartär," also compared the present age with "one of God's dreams," but only to point to its ephemeral nature: "a joke of the old spiderman."

Nevertheless, and despite all these causes for criticism, in at least one respect *The Origin of Historismus* will serve Meinecke's reputation in the West. While in earlier writings he had rarely defended the individual against the state, here he is frankly individualistic. He also used the centenary of Treitschke, in 1934, to pit his liberal individualism against the nationalist state worshipers who also invoked his authority.[56] This was not quite new for him. At the end of World War I, he had told an audience of army officers: "If we don't wish to impoverish ourselves, we must not allow one type of personality to disappear: the man whose horizon grows wider as he confronts history, and who achieves the infinity of a spirituality that is both mild and strong in facing all that is human";[57] and in the essay on "Causalities and Values" he simply takes this for granted: "Next to the elevation of one's moral and spiritual personality, the greatest challenge to man's ethical capacity is the moralization and spiritualization of the state."[58]

Meinecke had never deified the state like Hegel, and he had become critical of Ranke's attempt to see the state as God's work. But he had hoped to "spiritualize" and to "moralize" it—and failed. More and more he now saw "shadows" in the real world; the demonic had triumphed, and the spiritual had no choice but to retreat into that natural abode where humanism could be practiced in books. In thus retreating, Meinecke failed to see that he was retreating from Historismus itself, which had been created precisely to reconcile the historian's and scholar's contemplative mood with the active life of the state.

When Meinecke published the book, he knew that the days of Historismus were numbered. As a *Weltanschauung* it looked backwards; as a tool of political analysis it failed. Without a fight, the middle-class republic succumbed to Hitler because liberalism lacked the idea that could have been opposed to him. Its *raison d'état* had foundered in Hindenburg's antechamber; its nationalism was swayed by Hitler's ability to outbid any demagogue.

Hitler's successes in foreign policy silenced all opposition. Who could condemn the Anschluss? The "liberation" of the Sudeten Germans, the destruction of Czechoslovakia, the victories in Poland, Norway, and France placed liberals before an agonizing choice. Meinecke's letters of the war years, though nothing that he published, betray a nationalist bias and little sensitivity to the crimes of German aggression.

After Hitler's fall, Meinecke asked whether National Socialism did not perhaps have a place in history. After all, the two great movements of the nineteenth century tended to merge in Nazi ideology: "individualizing nationalism and confederative socialism." The idea was splendid, but Hitler had only used it as an ideology for his personal power drive. The state had run berserk; its evil side had been cut loose from Reason of State.

Was this really all that needed to be said about Nazism?

After World War II, when Meinecke felt called upon to give meaning to German history, Historismus was unable to provide guidance. The German catastrophe was also the catastrophe of German historiography. Meinecke had to recognize that he had failed to see how much evil there had been in Bismarck's state and, in fact, in all states. That the German state was as evil as all others was less painful to admit than that it had incurred more guilt than they.

The question an honest historian now had to answer was whether Hitler was an aberration, an alien element, or a more or less genuine fruit of German history.[59] Meinecke saw both the continuity and the disruption; he clearly stated: "The Third Reich was the greatest misfortune that the German people have suffered throughout their existence; it was also their greatest shame."[60] Yet he repeats almost verbatim his profession of faith of forty years earlier: "Can anything that awakens a great nation be condemned as an inclination to go the wrong way?"[61] Germany's way was not an *Irrweg* but an *Unglücksweg*—not a path taken in error but a path of sorrows.

The German catastrophe had come about through a series of unfortunate accidents: Hindenburg's senility, the blindness of the military, the rapacity of the Junker caste, the mistaken romanticism of the youth movement; but in Meinecke's book there was no theory of Nazism. Hitler simply fell under the category of "evil."

Increasingly in these last works, Meinecke used the language of mysticism into which he had lapsed on earlier occasions whenever he was out of his depth. To save himself from the dilemma between causality and *Geist*, he leapt into the "vertical" dimension—a simile at best which explains nothing. This language is pervasive in the second half of *Historismus* and in the late essays. Whenever problems are intractable, we are referred to intuition as a judge of last resort. Whenever we catch one of Meinecke's heroes—Ranke, Bismarck, Frederick the Great—in a contradiction, we are told to "divine" the solution. Whenever ethical problems threaten to require metaphysical coordinates, we are led to the slippery *Urgrund*, the primeval ground, of the soul.

Although Meinecke was no churchgoer and believed in no personal God, religion was the soil from which his philosophy grew, and Christianity was the ground from which he criticized Hitler. If his conscience was the unerring guide of his judgments, this was possible because he was drawing on a stock of reverence that had been accumulated in German idealism for centuries. We can believe his assurance that by recognizing the fact of "value relativity" he did not mean to endorse relativistic ethics. But what he can justly claim for himself he cannot make binding for others. He has no message for an age which can no longer draw on that same reservoir of religious convictions. Moreover, we can see how contemplation increasingly took the place of engagement in his writings: more and more he came to recognize the overweening power of the anonymous forces and of necessity. What is left for the individual who wishes to assert his integrity is to withdraw into Kultur (like the despised Voltaire to cultivate his garden, or like the ambiguous Machiavelli to read his beloved classics).

At the end of *The German Catastrophe*, his advice to his compatriots is "to form Goethe circles." What he once said of Treitschke may apply to Meinecke himself: "In spite of his dangerous theory, he possessed a high sense of responsibility, for he was a deeply moral man."[62]

[5]
Walther Rathenau: Musil's Arnheim or Mann's Naphta?

EARLY in the 1920s, nationalist louts were chanting in the streets of Berlin: "Kill Walther Rathenau, that god-forsaken Jewish pig!" On June 24, 1922, three of these fanatics assassinated him in his open car, one day after an ex-minister of the former kaiser had told the Reichstag that Rathenau had sold Germany to dark international powers. Indeed, as foreign minister of the Weimar Republic, he had signed the famous Rapallo Treaty, inaugurating what today is called *Ostpolitik* (and what was then attacked with the same intensity and vilification). He had also tried to convince the Germans that they must pay reparations to regain the confidence of their former World War I enemies. Moreover, he had said during that war: "Should Kaiser Wilhelm return victorious through the Brandenburg Gate [in Berlin], world history would lose its meaning." And worse, he had written: "Four hundred persons of wealth and power, who all know each other and communicate with each other, hold in their hands the fate of the planet"—words which German nationalists quoted as the cynical admission, by an insider, that the mysterious "Elders of Zion" had indeed conspired to destroy Germany, as charged in their propaganda.[1]

All of this should have made Walther Rathenau a martyr of the left, or at any rate a symbol of republican virtues. But after a flurry of indignation, a one-hour general strike, and a

Reprinted with permission from *The Boston University Journal* (1978), no. 3.

state funeral, he was soon forgotten. No monument graces a public park in Germany, no foundation supports worthy causes in his name, his writings have not been republished; and although some of them—notably *A Critique of Our Age* and *Of Things to Come*—have proved prophetic about post-industrial society, his name is generally not included in the galaxy of brilliant intellectuals who make the Weimar period so fascinating a subject for posterity.[2]

The intellectual community, notably those on the left who otherwise are very sensitive to the Weimar scene, have been turned against Rathenau by a novel that appeared only seven years after the heinous assassination to assassinate Rathenau a second time—in his character, or rather its caricature.

Robert Musil never made it a secret that Rathenau was the model for Dr. Arnheim, the counter-hero in his unfinished masterpiece, *Der Mann ohne Eigenschaften* (*The Man Without Qualities*). Nor did contemporary critics have the slightest doubt as to who was the brilliant talker and schemer described as "a mixture of wit, business, luxuries, and erudition . . . intolerable to the highest degree [to the author's protagonist, anyway], . . . a man who was able to talk with each person in his or her own language." Indeed, Rathenau's admiring aide, von Moellendorf, had said: "He was like an element that can amalgamate with any other."[3] Of Dr. Arnheim, Musil says: "He could talk molecular physics, mysticism, and pigeon shooting"—no wonder, for Rathenau held a Ph.D. in physics and pursued the study of Jewish mystics so ardently that he learned Hebrew for the purpose. More sardonically, Musil continues: "Bergson's philosophy applied to the price of coal—imagine the depressing effect on a businessmen's meeting. Success was inevitable since the man sounded so mysteriously impressive." The initiated could almost hear Rathenau speaking; René Schickele, the novelist, had quipped: "Rathenau goes from raw materials to Christ."[4] Also, Rathenau had been accused so often of plagiarizing Bergson that he felt it necessary to deny any affinity with the philosopher who, by origin and attitude, was indeed related to him.

Musil's dependence on his model often goes to embarrassing details. Thus, Rathenau explains the persistence of what
he calls "national character" by using a simile: In a fountain,
the shape of the jet remains the same while the individual
drops of water change every fraction of a second. In the novel,
Dr. Arnheim shows his brilliance by using a similar simile:
A marching column of soldiers retains its shape while different individuals are passing by. Hans Mayer, the critic, once
asked Musil whether Rathenau, a tall man, used to put his
arm around his interlocutor's shoulder, as Dr. Arnheim does
in the novel.[5] Musil, he reports, "grew pale with anger and
answered: 'Yes, and imagine, he did it to me, too.' " What
irked Musil is revealed in a diary entry as early as January
11, 1914:

> Dr. W. Rathenau—a wonderful English suit. Ash-grey with dark
> stripes framed by small white eyelets. Easy, warm fabric and yet infi-
> nitely soft. Fascinatingly arched chest and sides all the way down.
> Somewhat negroid in the skull. Brow and front skull form a spheric
> segment, then the skull rises towards its back. The line from the chin
> to the farthest point back forms a 45° angle with the horizon. Small,
> boldly curved nose, lips bent apart. I don't know what Hannibal looked
> like, but I had to think of him. He likes to say: My dear doctor, and
> grabs your arm in an intimate way. He is accustomed to be the center
> of the discussion. He is doctrinaire, but always the gentleman. If you
> raise an objection, he will readily agree: I grant you that but . . . He
> says, *and here I get the idea of the financier in the hotel scene:* By
> calculating you achieve nothing in business; you can lick a man once,
> but next time around he'll remember and lick you. You can influence
> people only if you have intuition; you must be a visionary and forget
> your purpose.[6] (My italics)

This is indeed the character, not in one scene, but as the
evil spirit in the book, the seducer and project-maker who
mixes metaphysics with business, a man with infinite powers
of persuasion yet ultimately a fake. To understand the function that Musil assigned to Dr. Arnheim it must be remembered that *The Man Without Qualities* is to *War and Peace*
what Picasso's *Déjeuner sur l'herbe* is to Manet's. Diotima is
as much Austria as Natasha is Russia; she is defended by a
Kutusov-like Count Leinsdorf, and the title hero bears a striking resemblance to Pierre Bezukhov. Austria's good old ways

are being threatened by the intrusion of the Prussian Jew, with his imperialist schemes and his modernistic manners. Musil certainly holds no brief for the easy-going and traditionalist bureaucracy of old Austria, but his most savage satire is reserved for the pushy bourgeoisie, its ideologies, its mixture of financial with metaphysical speculation, its hypocritical denial of capitalistic reality. Some of this seems to be lifted right out of Rathenau's works; Arnheim says: "Reason alone is no guide to morality, or to politics for that matter. . . . Men who have done great things always loved poetry, music, discipline, chivalry . . . such men alone succeed."

We are in the world of Richard Wagner devotees: music, poetry, chivalry are no longer ideals in their own right but proofs of the will to power. The bourgeoisie is not content to serve customers; it aspires to participate in the "higher things," or even claims that business has metaphysical foundations or that a good metaphysical conscience is good for business. Indeed, if Rathenau's works were to be summarized in one sentence, they would have to be characterized as one continued effort to cleanse business of its dirty selfishness and to ennoble it with transcendental aims.

Rathenau came from a liberal, emancipated, and assimilated Jewish family. His father, Emil, had parlayed a small engineering shop into the multimillion-multinational General Electric Corporation. He was a disciplinarian, a hard-driving and anxiety-driven businessman with a no-nonsense philosophy. He held romantic reveries to be tolerable in his wife and his mother, but utterly impermissible for the talented son who was to inherit the firm. Since their temperaments were incompatible, young Walther was banished to a provincial branch factory where he could both "prove himself" and pursue his artistic hobbies. He did both with a vengeance. At thirty he had been so successful that he was able to retire; he had also begun to publish poetry, aphorisms, and essays which proclaimed his rejection of everything his father stood for. He was critical of the prevailing business ethics, of the confining Jewish middle-class mentality, and of its political liberalism.

Yet Rathenau was no bohemian, and although he associated with modern writers and painters (Liebermann was his cousin; his circle included Wedekind, Hauptmann, Buber, Dehmel, and Hugo von Hofmannsthal), his own taste ran to the conservative, classical style. His protest writings were conceived in the nostalgic fashion of the turn-of-the-century idealists—the refined writers of *Die Tat* and other publications of the Diederichs Verlag. Even before Max Weber analyzed the "Protestant work ethic," Rathenau identified the materialistic ethics of business with his father's religion, and he attacked the calculating rationality of purpose-oriented, "soulless" commercialism which in the public mind was associated with "Jewishness." The idealistic, soulful pursuits, by contrast, were seen in the Teutonic traditions from the medieval knights down to the Prussian state. An essay of his in Harden's *Zukunft*, entitled "Hear, O Israel" (1893), appealed to Jews in Germany to divest themselves of dirty materialism and to imbibe the spirit of German idealism.[7]

In his major philosophical work, which appeared in 1913, *Zur Mechanik des Geistes* (On the Mechanics of the Mind), and in his earlier aphorisms Rathenau distinguished between the Soul, which is free of purpose and therefore generous and courageous, and Reason (*Verstand*, which others also called Understanding), which is purpose-oriented and subject to anxiety. Consequently, there are Courageous Men on the one side, and Fearful Men who are also the Practical Men on the other. The latter know only business and become responsible for the "loss of the soul," the mechanization and alienation, the many sicknesses of the age.

The theme of alienation, which at the time was being discussed by philosophers like Simmel, Lask, Dilthey, Weber, and Lukács, stayed with Rathenau to the end of his life. In one of his last essays, *Von kommenden Dingen*, he still asks, What is Purpose? and answers: "Something never to be attained, never to be known; a dimly perceived complex of security, property, life, honor, and power. . . . Driven by these chimeras, man strays from one unreality to another. This is what he calls living, working, creating. A curse and a blessing bequeathed to those he loves."

There is no doubt that his forever-worrying father was the target when Rathenau expressed utter distaste for the *Zweckmensch*—the man who lives for nothing but purposes and for whom "everything turns into a means: things, people, nature, even God. But even when he achieves his purpose, he remains poor and unhappy."

All of this is strangely similar to the anti-Semitic literature of the day, and not surprisingly Rathenau summarized the alienation process as "de-Teutonization." He was clearly under the influence of Julius Langbehn and one gets the impression, from his diary entries, that Nietzsche's "blond beasts" owe their metaphysical capacities to God, whereas others can only work to acquire them. It is also known that Rathenau looked up with affection to fair-haired men; one such, to whom he wrote in the rare "thou" form, was the founder of a eugenic league and had the delicacy regularly to send him copies of viciously racist attacks on his person. It is almost pathetic today to read Rathenau's answers, in which he pleads with his friend to admit that a Jew can become a good German, through worthy acts.[8]

In reviewing Rathenau's book, *On the Mechanics of the Mind*, Musil wrote sarcastically: "He uses metaphysics as a substitute for nobility" (which, the reader was to understand, the author lacks or covets). To him, Rathenau was the bore who covered his vacuity with witticisms, his lack of taste with extravagance, his insecurity with feverish planning, his insensitivity by supporting symbolist poets, his coldness by associating with everybody, his rapacity by raving about the soul—in short, the second-generation Jew who, having made his pile, now tries to muscle into refined society, to be a Maecenas, or even to penetrate into the holiest of holies—writing poetry and philosophy. Academic critics also have rejected Rathenau's efforts as unoriginal and unprofessional, and have noted that he was unaware of what their likes had said, or disdained to say, about similar subjects.

Although Rathenau's book contains many shrewd observations, it rarely rises above the level of "popular science for the highbrow" of the early century. But it points to serious, highly topical problems which the author was to take up in later pamphlets: *Zur Kritik der Zeit* (A Critique of Our Age) and *Von kommenden Dingen* (Of Things To Come). In the earlier work, he had apparently not been familiar with the analyses of bureaucracy and of alienation by Max Weber, Georg Simmel, Emil Lask, and others, and therefore had been forced to use the language of the utopian socialists, who often confused capitalism with usury and with Jewish trade. In the later works he quoted the sociologists who had denounced the trend toward the "termite state," the total rationality, the seamless community of production and business, the rule by purpose-oriented organization men. Like Marx he saw these developments as necessary consequences of capitalistic rationality: the abstract, calculable, infinitely divisible and flexible, exchangeable and functional character of the division of labor. The organization of mass production had revolutionized man's relationship with his environment, taken the soul out of production, destroyed free creativity, and substituted for it specialization and mass culture. This erosion, moreover, had already affected noneconomic institutions, above all the state: from a sacred, religious, organic institution it had been turned into a mere administration, the soulless instrument of economic necessity.

This is the language of J. G. Fichte or of the German youth movement, and undoubtedly it contains many elements on which the Nazi ideologists were to build their myth of German regeneration (with this difference that Rathenau says "soul" where they say "blood"). But Rathenau differed from these romantic protests in an important respect. Like Marx he knew that one cannot turn the wheel of history backwards; capitalism had to be accepted and overcome. It could not be bypassed, ignored, or abolished. If Rathenau's critique of capitalism was not altogether original and not couched in professional jargon, it was remarkable through the position of its author, a confirmed believer in the system's beneficial effects—he called it "eu-plutism"—and a successful practitioner of its potentialities, which he was soon to develop in both practice and theory.

For Walther Rathenau was neither a Rimbaud nor a Thomas Buddenbrook; he could not enjoy the contemplative life which he envied. A reconciliation with his father made it possible for him to join the firm as a director in charge of electric installations abroad; association with a banking firm, the Berliner Handelsgesellschaft, gave rise to one of those conglomerates whose tentacles extended over many industries in Europe and America. At forty, Rathenau was a tycoon, holding over sixty directorates in companies at home and elsewhere, and manipulating a financial–industrial empire extending over three continents. Long since had he passed from a producer's function to the more fascinating operations of corporate financing and organization, and he also wrote about the new features of developing capitalism which his penetrating mind now discerned:

> Electricity is not an industry but a complex. It creates new demands, controls new industries, penetrates all spheres of life from lighting to power to traffic to the use of new, concentrated machinery.
>
> Older industries used to produce articles that consumers wanted, perhaps combining nature's materials in new ways but ultimately leaving the choice to the consumer. Manufacturing industries have developed new techniques but essentially continued what the old handicrafts had done, with characteristic improvements. A new field of industry has been opened with electro-mechanics. It will transform a large part of modern life and of our way of doing business. Production no longer is directed to the consumers' needs; rather, these are created, or even are imposed, by the producer.

He further described the new forms of industrial organization, the new uses of money and credit; he not only recognized the possibilities of trust capitalism but pointed out its political implications.[9] He announced the obsolescence of the private employer and foresaw the benefits of planning. All of this may not have been totally new or original, but Rathenau admitted these developments before any other man of his background and persuasion gave them even a thought. He published his ideas in expensive editions, which did not make him popular with men of his status.

Probably Musil saw correctly that Rathenau's views, supported no doubt by his wit and charm, his knowledge and usefulness, had opened the doors of the highest society to him. His diaries show an almost uninterrupted stream of conferences with diplomats and ministers. It was quite unusual for a Jew to be admitted to court, to be able to buy a palace that once had belonged to the royal family, and to receive there the visit of the kaiser in person (the chair whereon the imperial posterior had rested was afterwards cordoned off against profanation by any common arse, and the diary notes carefully the jokes the kaiser told). Although Rathenau was highly critical of the kaiser's policies and character—and said so courageously in public and private on many occasions—he remained loyal to him and defended him even after the revolution.

Came the war, the imperial Jew was the only German to see that it could not be won with old methods. He saw that it was to be a total war, an economic war which required regulating the supply of raw materials, rationing food and consumer goods, organizing the manufacture of arms and ammunition. After lobbying in the proper places, he was given an office in the War Ministry to organize Germany's war economy. The office was immediately walled off from the strategic services, not so much as a safety measure but to immunize the military from the civilians—imagine a Jew in the imperial office! He formed so-called war corporations, which enlisted private business into a mobilization plan, and worked happily with General Ludendorff, one of the few commoner generals and a strategic genius, who also was a proponent of "total mobilization." Later they fell out over the imposition of unrestricted submarine warfare, which Rathenau thought a great mistake. In oblique articles he then attacked the reckless war-aims propaganda of the Pan-German annexionists, the mindless strategy of the military leaders, and their refusal to tell the German people the truth about their poor prospects of victory.

His efforts to persuade the Germans that they had to seek a negotiated peace ended in his total isolation from the government, and yet he did not join the forces on the left which by then were demanding such a peace. Rathenau called for a *levée en masse*, a Jacobin war, a guerrilla force of the whole nation against the harsh terms of the armistice.

Here is the crucial break in Rathenau's thinking. The wartime experience had taught him that the old Prussian Junker class was no longer capable of leading the nation and that private enterprise, unaided by planning authorities, was no longer able to feed and outfit the nation in times of crisis. The traditional middle classes had not shown the political maturity and foresight that would be needed to recruit and train a new class of leaders. Like others of his generation, Rathenau looked to the young army officers who had shown courage and merit; he appealed "to the Youth of Germany," in the glowing terminology of revolutionary warfare, and he went to see Lenin's emissary, Karl Radek, in a Berlin prison, to find out whether a national war of liberation might not be fought under the flag of social revolution. He bombarded the ministries with memoranda showing how a Spartan regime of national defense might be imposed; he calculated the minimum on which a German family might be asked to exist. (Later, Spengler would publish similar fantasies under the label of "Prussian Socialism.")

To form a real community of the nation, these sacrifices would have to be shared by all alike. All classes must be abolished. Advancement was to be earned; rewards would be in terms of honor. "If we wish to be one nation, we cannot have proletarians. The will to nationhood is incompatible with the caste system. He who wants German men cannot want German proletarians." He denounced the "walls of glass" that prevented the social rise of those who had neither education nor property. He proposed nationalization of monopolistic enterprises and distribution of responsibility among all those who participated in production. Workers must have an incentive to be interested in their jobs and must share in the administration of the business. On the other hand, the profit incentive was no longer necessary for management, since in the modern corporation ownership had been separated from management functions anyway.

In calling for industrial democracy (*wirtschaftliche Selbstverwaltung*), Rathenau trusted that "moral incentives cannot produce more loafers in a planned society than there are involuntary unemployed under free enterprise." These moral incentives were "responsibility" and "solidarity," the consciousness of service to the nation. Leadership, he dreamed, should come from merit rather than from wealth; therefore, inherited wealth should be taxed away, and all luxuries that drew on the nation's resources should be forbidden. Consumption was to be declared "a public affair."

In all this, however, Rathenau was not motivated by egalitarian convictions. He was rather an elitist and a technocrat. But he was concerned that inequality in education might waste valuable brain power. Nor was he a republican emotionally; on the contrary, he jibed that "under parliamentary government every lobbyist for the laxative industry is a Demosthenes." But he felt that parliament provided a good school of politics for the middle class, and he looked forward to the formation of a "National Economic Council" where the many interest groups might be represented (such a third chamber was actually created in the Weimar Constitution). "The purely political state is an obsolete notion. It has lost its supremacy." Even more obsolete, of course, was the old European liberalism of the middle class; it had created no great state. Indeed, so disappointing did Rathenau find the performance of his own class in the dire crisis of leadership that, shortly after the collapse of the empire, he had a brief fling with bolshevism and cultivated the company of Marxists like Rudolf Hilferding, editor of the left-socialist *Freiheit*.[10] He said he had "the feeling that I am the vehicle of a revolution which overthrows the gods of the pre-1914 world—

the world to which I belong." While even left-wing socialists proposed to pay compensation to expropriated shareholders, Rathenau advocated socialization without compensation.

From romantic nationalism to social imperialism to total mobilization to Jacobinism. What we see here is not the bewilderment of the man Rathenau who happened to be a Jew and a Prussian, but the birth of that unique phenomenon that flourished briefly during the German revolution of 1918–1919, before the Weimar Republic consolidated itself—national-bolshevism.[11] It is the intellectual source of Nasserism and Fidelismo as well as many other manifestations of modern authoritarianism. It was one of the potentialities of the German revolution that remained unfulfilled, and the loss of that opportunity resulted in the pathetic aftermath, the chauvinist-racist-populist movements that broke down in Hitler's Beer Hall Putsch, 1923, but were resurrected later in the rise of Fascist and Nazi power.

It is utterly mistaken to interpret this Jacobin response to the 1919 situation as the ideology of big business. For proof one has to go no further than to Rathenau's great adversary, the steel and shipping tycoon Hugo Stinnes, who financed the right-wing parties and pursued an old-fashioned nationalist–conservative policy of obstruction against the Republic's domestic and foreign policies. Rathenau himself abandoned his Jacobin stance very soon, hailed Noske as the great savior of the Republic from bolshevist chaos, and helped to found the Democratic party, which counted among its luminaries Max Weber, Hugo Preuss, Ernst Troeltsch, Friedrich Naumann, Fritz von Unruh, and other intellectuals; it was conceived as a party of radical reform but soon, to Rathenau's regret, became the party of the liberal middle class.

As minister for reconstruction and reparations, and then as foreign minister, Rathenau abandoned nationalism and became the foremost spokesman of the so-called fulfillment policy (accepting the harsh terms of the Versailles Treaty), which was to lead Germany back into the family of nations. Realism had once again overcome the romantic reveries in Rathenau.

But little did his assassins know how close he had been to their own illusions.

The greatest monument to that Jacobin-totalitarian phase of German history is to be found not in Rathenau's works but in two books by Thomas Mann. The first, *Reflections of a Non-Political Man*, was written during the war. It expressed more clearly than Rathenau ever did the mystical sources of his nationalism; it was the perfect complement to Rathenau's ideas on total mobilization. But strangely, the two men never seem to have communicated with each other. Later on, Thomas Mann repudiated the book and bought up all remaining copies. He used its ideas as evidence, however, in a more reflective work which weighed both the rational-liberal and the mystic-totalitarian potentialities of German history: *The Magic Mountain*.

It must be counted as a great loss to world literature that Thomas Mann never met Rathenau, and that instead he used, as model for the Naphta character, that pale Marxist philosopher, Georg Lukács. Or, to put it another way, the mind boggles with anticipated and frustrated delights at the idea that, instead of the satirist Robert Musil, the creator of *Felix Krull, Confidence Man*, might have taken hold of the character of Rathenau. Instead of the fanatical Jesuit, a sinister shadow hovering over Europe, Naphta would be a full-bodied Renaissance businessman, an achiever and speculator, a worthy opponent not of the doctrinaire Settembrini but of the fat Mynheer Peeperkorn; *The Magic Mountain* might then have become the masterpiece it just missed being by a hair. In creating Naphta, Thomas Mann forgot that he was really a humorist; but those traits in Rathenau's character that provoked Musil's satire might have suggested to Thomas Mann the vulnerability of the totalitarian—which the novel fails to show. He was himself sympathetic to Rathenau's approach, as becomes evident in his oft-quoted remark that "a pact between the conservative idea of culture and the revolutionary concept of socialization, between Greece and Moscow, a meeting between Marx and Hölderlin would be good for Germany."

This was precisely Walther Rathenau's idea of the "people's state." The question for the historian is not whether he affected this attitude but whether it was capable of being sustained by the nation for any length of time; whether the Reichstag was to be a stock exchange for the lobbyists of various class and group interests, or the forum for the constitution of "the general will," and whether the new republic would be able to speak in the name of the nation. Many, including Paul Levi, held it possible, at the time, to advance the social revolution by conducting a national campaign against the Versailles Treaty. Rathenau's friend (and biographer) Kessler dabbled in a conspiracy to overthrow the Weimar Coalition and to install a strong government of nationalist civil servants, headed by the then foreign minister, later ambassador to Moscow, Count Brockdorff-Rantzau, who wished to keep open the alternative of a pro-Russian, anti-Western policy.

In such a government of National Mobilization, had Rathenau not been persona non grata with the Independents, he would have been the natural candidate for the Ministry of Economic Affairs. But the whole scheme foundered anyway because the Independents were committed to peace and the German people were in no mood to fight against the Versailles powers, or to surrender power to a Soviet government. In 1919, most Germans knew that the realistic alternatives were either occupation by the Western powers, or fulfillment of the treaty. But the parties of the right decided to let the left-and-center coalition take the blame for signing the treaty, and then to monopolize and exploit the campaign against its fulfillment. The leaders of this campaign were the steel and shipping tycoon Stinnes, the press and movie tycoon Hugenberg, the former Minister of the Interior Helfferich, and the floor leader of the German Nationalist Party, Hergt. They used the unpopularity of the treaty, and the humiliation of the German nation which it spelled out, to discredit the Republic and to vilify its leaders. This seed of hatred was to grow into a harvest of assassinations and conspiracies.

In the beginning, Rathenau was far away from the events. His name was tainted by his role in organizing the war economy and his association with prewar imperialism. He had even been on a list of war criminals because of his involvement in the use of Belgians in German munitions factories. When the first Socialization Commission was nominated, the Independents vetoed his participation (he was invited later on, into the second Commission); he failed to win a seat as a candidate of the Democratic Party in a hostile district and when his name was mentioned, among many others, as a possible candidate for the presidency, the Reichstag minutes record "Laughter on the Right." Though at heart a monarchist, he had been a critic of those policies which the right now was nostalgically committed to defend.[12] He had also convinced himself that the Versailles Treaty could not be resisted head-on but had to be eroded by proving that the attempt to fulfill it would lead to disaster.

He did not think that the revolution had brought any essential changes to the structure of German society, and he had a low opinion of its leaders. Contemptuous remarks like "Only the personnel has changed" and "We are governed by punks" were widely reported. In spite of that, he was asked, and agreed, to serve as minister for reconstruction and to conduct the negotiations on Germany's reparations debt. And despite his serious doubts about the wisdom of taking such a responsibility,[13] he could not resist when he was offered the post of foreign minister. A hot wave of anti-Semitic propaganda was the immediate result; racist speakers foamed against the "Jew republic," the "stab in the back," and the international conspiracy against Germany.

On August 26, 1921, right-wing extremists shot and killed Matthias Erzberger, the (Catholic) Center deputy, who had once been an imperialist but in April 1917 had drafted the Reichstag's "Peace Resolution" and in November 1918 had been the one to sign the Armistice. Early in 1922, a priest came to see Chancellor Joseph Wirth and revealed that one of his penitents had confessed that "Rathenau is the next on the list." Rathenau also received threatening letters and never left the house without a revolver in his pocket. But he could not stand being accompanied everywhere by a secret-service man, and he refused to change his routine of driving to the office in an open car. He went to the World Economic Conference at Genoa in April/May 1922, concluded the Rapallo Treaty with Russia, and was murdered on June 24, 1922.

He was murdered not because of what he stood for but because of what he was—for being Jewish, that "quality" which he had tried so fervently to repudiate but which forced itself on his life even in the midst of social "success." When once, at Court, Frau von Hindenburg had suggested to him that he might go into politics or the diplomatic service he had blurted out, rather indiscreetly: "You forget that I am a Jew, and that is impossible." When he gave the fatherland the service without which it could not have sustained the war effort even through one winter, he was snubbed so offensively that he left the job to be finished by his second-in-command. He endured all and was ready to serve again when he was needed. And most certainly, despite his disclaimers that he did not need the people, he needed to be needed, to prove that they needed him. But the significance of his life did not reside in the psychology of this person, or in the reaction of this Jewish character to his German environment, but in his intellectual development, in his ability to become a mirror of his age.

Granted that Rathenau was all that Musil attributed to Dr. Arnheim, the novelist's arrogance did not reside so much in his omission of the redeeming features. After all, as a sovereign writer he did not have to show his hero's other side— his self-laceration and suffering, his martyrdom, his touching traits of caring, of sacrifice and sense of duty. But in his hatred Musil failed to grasp the historical dimension of Rathenau's life as a symbol of an alternative course of German destiny— the Jacobin republic. Musil's concern was to reveal the hollowness of the bourgeoisie and of its cultural pretensions. To reverse Hannah Arendt's phrase, he thought that banality itself is the evil; he failed to see Naphta. Thomas Mann, by contrast, thought of evil as a spiritual power and therefore made Naphta fascinating and almost respectable. He did not see that both Settembrini and Naphta were windbags and that the real forces that were determining Germany's destiny then were of a different nature: that the problem of her political destiny did not derive from her preoccupation with death but from her chosen form of life. Musil must have felt that he had asked the wrong question in the first volume, for he never finished the second—how could he, seeing Dr. Arnheim as his neighbor in their common exile fleeing from the followers of Naphta? That both could have been reflections of Rathenau was Germany's true tragedy.

But apart from the question of generosity, the relationship between Arnheim and Rathenau raises a question of propriety. Naphta was obviously a composite figure with whom both totalitarians of the right and of the left could identify. Thomas Mann did not identify the model either but left it to doctoral candidates to find out, so that Lukács was able to shrug the question off: "So what, if he used my nose?" The relationship between Rathenau and Arnheim was so explicit from the beginning that an uninformed reader might attribute all of Arnheim's utterances to Rathenau. And here one must ask: Granted that the satirist was free to attack the type which Rathenau–Arnheim personified for him, was he not under some moral obligation at least to protect Rathenau's memory from charges of which he was not guilty?

I have shown that Rathenau's problem was the cleavage between dirty, purpose-oriented business and purpose-free beauty or duty. But Arnheim's failing is just the opposite. He constantly confounds the two worlds. He gives God the good advice to "build the millennium on sound business principles and to delegate its management to an experienced merchant who also should be equipped with an education in philosophy." Musil's linguistic devices unmask Arnheim as lacking taste. He speaks the language of American advertising: "Homer and Christ have never been equaled, not to speak of being bested," and to make the point absolutely clear he adds: "Yes, Homer and Rosegger [an Austrian writer of cute short stories in dialect] are solid reading matter." When he mentions Goethe, he never fails to say, "the great Goethe," as though his recognition of greatness were adding to his own stature.

But greatness, Arnheim feels, can be achieved in any field and by any kind of skill, writing as well as tennis or photography; even a race horse is called "a genius." This can be so because in our age quantity has been substituted for quality. The caricatured Dr. Arnheim muses with Simmel: "Moral wealth is a sibling of money wealth. . . . Morality has put logic in the place of the soul: Logic presupposes moral values. If moral goods were not repeatable, we could not prescribe moral behavior. This quality of being repeatable, which relates morality to reason, is also the property of money." Arnheim uses the language of measuring and weighing even to express delicate matters of the soul: "A responsible person will not spend his spiritual capital but only the interest if he wishes to make a gift of his soul. In this soulless age, a man must husband his soul to save it for the proper day when he will take it out of the strongbox."

This is caricature. Musil's technique consists in lifting an idea or argument from Rathenau's context to show that it is not only dishonest and muddled but actually reflects and justifies the reality it pretends to criticize or avoid. For indeed, Rathenau remained a technocrat who did his share, in both business and government, to create those "soulless instruments of rational necessity" which he deplored in his writings. Musil, wondering how mystical raptures and shrewd business sense could cohabit in the same mind, was obviously angered by Rathenau's disinclination to draw any radical conclusions from his sharp insights. Having chosen the life of an outsider for himself, he resented the man who had opted for success. This has earned him the admiration of the New Left thirty years after his death, and has helped prevent historians from seeing Rathenau in the Weimar setting.

[6]

On Re-Reading Hermann Hesse

WHY did a rock group call itself Steppenwolf? Why not Moby Dick? The first answer came, the other day, from a young taxi driver in New York who had a pocket edition of *Demian* next to him on his seat. He is studying German at college and was told to read Hermann Hesse; he feels Hesse is like J. D. Salinger. I am rather intrigued: Hermann Hesse was the poet of our youth, back in Berlin during the turbulent 1920s. We read him aloud and we worshiped him like a prophet. He was our living romantic poet when we were under twenty and the century was in its twenties. But what can a New York taxi driver do with Hermann Hesse in the 1960s?

Other students, I find, also have been told to compare him with Salinger. But their teachers did not tell them how to transpose the German mood of the 1920s into the American mood of the 1960s. Both Hesse and Salinger tell young people that the straight world does not understand them; both convey the feeling of being crushed by the claims of a world they fear. But Hesse compensates for the loneliness by asserting that he knows of another world, a dream world which belongs to poetic souls only; Salinger knows no such world.

In other words, Hesse was a romantic, Salinger is not. Moreover, Hesse deliberately reminded his readers of those first German romantics who flourished a hundred years before him. He imitated their language, their titles, the moods

Reprinted with permission from *Salmagundi* (Spring 1970).

they created; he rewrote, re-created for us the romantic age because we were having a renaissance of the romantic and of the gothic anyway. In reviewing these themes and re-creating these poetic images Hesse was our contemporary. But what in the world is he, of all people, re-creating for American youth in the sixties and seventies? Why a Hermann Hesse renaissance?

I must confess that I was not just confused but also a little jealous, as if I had suddenly run into my first girl as someone else's wife. Hesse seemed to belong to us and to no one else, and even though we progressed far beyond him, even if we did not like his later works, even if we had not thought of him lately, there was something so sacred about the Hesse cult that it seemed impossible for anybody else to understand, let alone appropriate him. I think I owe the reader this warning: what follows is the angry fruit of prejudice; but I still think it worth my while and his to write it down—if only to sort out my own feelings and come to grips with my past.

Obviously, it was first necessary to buy the translations. What a torture to inflict such rubbish on anyone! Like certain French wines, German romantics don't travel. The English of the translations I have seen is abominable; it is unfaithful to the literal text; it is incapable of rendering the mood; it misses the point almost entirely. When Hermann Hesse writes *bürgerlich* he does not mean *bourgeois* but "square," "philistine," "middle-class"; and when a woman has *merkwürdige, tiefbraune Augen* he does not mean "remarkable dark brown eyes," for *merkwürdig* is the word which the romantics use to describe dozens of wondrous maidens' mysterious eyes, none of which they would have referred to as "remarkable." I am not caviling; I simply mean to say that it cannot be the poetry of Hesse's language that attracts young people in America. For that poetry does not come through in the translations; and even if it did come through for the learned reader, how should the uninitiated understand the allusions to Spitzweg's and Richter's drawings in a word like *bürgerlich*? Or in the words *fromm* and *das Frommsein*, which simply have not been translated if the words "religious" and "religion" have to do?

But it is not all the translator's fault. Can one really write and read, taste and understand, in our day and age, a sentence like "Oh, how sharp was the bitter taste of spring on my tongue"? It was corny even when it was first written, and I am angry at myself to discover that I was not aware then how corny it was. This observation, of course, should prompt me to compare my own feelings then with those of the present generation. If they fail to see that it is trite then, after all, they may feel as we did about Hermann Hesse: that it really did not matter how bad his prose was and how poor his poetry. What mattered was that one could *feel*. In Hesse we saw a man who stood out against his time and age, a character like his Steppenwolf, shamefully aware of his own participation in the world of the burgher and also aware that he could transcend it. Yes; I have reread Hesse in German and I am now sure that he was a poor writer, that when he did not know how to say it he expressed it with preciousness, that his romanticism was affected, a pose, a device, an unclever attempt to conceal his inadequacies. He could not construct a story. No indeed, he was not a story-teller to begin with; his people don't come to life, they remain puppets or silhouettes from whose mouths the words that should characterize them hang like draperies on gothic church windows.

My simile says nothing against Hermann Hesse; it may be high praise indeed. He always used the story to make a point; he invented characters to make them say what he intended to say. He never thought of the characters and the story first.

Yet I am angry at myself because I notice all this now. It did not bother me then and it probably does not bother the young people today. They like *Demian* not because they would ever recognize him should he be their schoolmate, but because he seems to know something about things which other people don't know or don't admit. They like the idea of Steppenwolf though they probably would have no respect for him should he be their teacher. They may agree with him,

but it is impossible to see him, to believe in him. On reread-
ing *Steppenwolf* I find that this is hardly a novel but rather a
psychoanalytical tract. Yet I also recollect, like old friends,
all the many things that attracted me when I was sixteen. It
begins—how embarrassing for Hesse and for me—with the
suitable stage props: the young Nietzschean adept, the mysterious stranger who, one divines, has a great secret to hide
and is suffering a great deal. Besides Nietzsche, the right
names have been evoked before the novel is beyond page 10:
Buddha, Goethe, Gandhi, Michelangelo's *Night* (those of us
who did not have a reproduction of his *Adam* over their bed
certainly had *The Night*); Jean Paul and Novalis, the two great
German romantics whom we loved. The hero's name, Haller,
is that of a forgotten Swiss poet, a contemporary of Rousseau's, who composed an enormous poem, "The Alps." How
the hell should my taxi driver in New York have known all
this? For us, of course, those names indicated what was to
come and with whom we should identify.

And we were neither mistaken nor misled. Soon we were
told how those great seers had been prettified and castrated
by the school teachers, converted into classics whose bust
any burgher could place on his mantelpiece to feel that he,
too, could communicate with things eternal. How we rejoiced then in this masterful diatribe against our humanist
education, against the drabness of classes and the petty ty-
rants who dissected the most beautiful poetry! How the author understood our yearning to be one with the great ones
without having to count their meter, to worship their genius
without using them as a treasury of useful quotations! Going
further, Hesse criticized the conventional wisdom and its
purveyors, puritanical morality and its confessors; in *Demian*
he firmly established the students' solidarity against teachers
and parents. We loved him because he understood us.

He also understood that we were a suicidal generation. Demian is fatally wounded in the war. No one can measure the
deep honesty of Hermann Hesse, a pacifist and expatriate
since World War I, who nevertheless found it necessary to let
his hero, our hero, volunteer to die for the fatherland; but he

Friedrich Meinecke. "A liberal almost all his long life among a faculty that was mostly reactionary and nationalistic."

Walther Rathenau, foreign minister of the Weimar Republic. Assassinated by nationalist fanatics, he was a victim of character assassination in Musil's *Der Mann ohne Eigenschaften*.

Robert Musil could not understand "how mystical raptures and shrewd business sense could cohabit in the same mind."

Hermann Hesse. "Why did a rock group call itself 'Steppenwolf'?"

Hermann Struck, self-portrait. "When the first world war ended, one of the most important results was that the artist Hermann Struck married my aunt."

Martin Heidegger. "How could this reticent metaphysician . . . march with the plebeian Brownshirts?"

Adolf Hitler. "Heidegger apparently assumed that there was some basic affinity between his philosophy and Hitler's mission which would enable the Führer to turn philosophy into practice."

The Bettmann Archives

Bertolt Brecht. Lotte Lenya, actress wife of the composer Kurt Weill, standing in front of a poster of Brecht. "Bertolt Brecht was an ironical author who liked to conceal his meaning while provoking the reader to find his own answer."

Karl Otto Paetel. "After all, it took courage to attack Hitler in front of two hundred storm troopers."

Erich Mühsam.
". . . the chess-playing, uninhibitedly
abrasive anarchist, Erich Mühsam."

understood something his present-day followers have not understood: the war was not our parents, as Jules Renard said—the war was us. Steppenwolf is driven to suicide precisely because he is a superior being, or rather because the conflict between everyday *bürgerlich* life and the life of the spirit becomes unbearable; this causes him to seek out danger and to expose himself to suffering. His aim is not to make life more perfect, as the squares would, but to liberate himself from it by "going back to Mother Earth, to God the Universe" (*das All,* poorly translated as "the all").

There is a good deal of Wagnerian Götterdämmerung in all this, and we believed in it—that's why Hitler could capture so many from the old youth movement. But Hermann Hesse did not believe in it, he took it back; he was afraid of the truth he had uncovered and he saw that it was dangerous to let Steppenwolf loose. Hesse's criticism was double-edged. The bourgeois seeks preservation, not abandon; he prefers peace to being possessed, convenience to liberty, comfort to pleasure, law to force—but the genius does not know whether his abandon will lead him to God or to the Devil, whether he is a saint or a criminal. Moreover, this Nietzschean Superman is quickly shown to be quite a bourgeois himself. The God he sought, Abraxas, had to be the god of good and evil, Yahweh and Satan. The Nietzschean Superman was not to know good and evil but only his fate, or rather his entelechy. In *Demian* it is called destiny; in *Steppenwolf* it is the law of the senses, a Freudian pleasure principle.

Now it is the curse of German literature that it has to discover "the senses" about every thirty years. But Hesse never shows the senses at work. He only relates that they are at work, or that someone dreams they are. He mentions "unimaginable, frightful, deathly love plays," but he never allows the reader to feel, to see, or to experience love. His "arts" are very cerebral when he speaks of love. But, strangely, he does give us a full description when it comes to war, to the art of destruction, and he does bring home its wantonness. For us the lesson was clear, while it does not seem to be clear to his new followers. Hesse said in so many words: We can-

not go back to innocence, we must go through this hell that
is ours. Americans could have learned the same lesson from
Thomas Wolfe: You can't go home again. It is strange that
America's youth today should misunderstand Hesse to say
that one can and must go home.

Hesse rejected the destruction of the self as well as its attempts to lose itself in "trips" and other drug experiences. In
our time it was cocaine, in the sixties it was LSD. Marijuana
was not known to us or to Hermann Hesse, but the medical
inoffensiveness of pot is not the issue. The issue was, for
Hesse, whether we are permitted to run away, and the verdict
was a clear no, although it does not follow from all his stories. He saw the problem of modern living as a judgment on
human nature; he considered us condemned to live, but free
to consider life a dream—maybe a bad one—and to laugh at
it. The most impressive part of his philosophy is his faith in
our ability to overcome the curse of existence by humor; in
that respect he was close to Thomas Mann. But I must confess that at the time we were rather impervious to this part of
his confession. We were as deadly serious, grave and grim as
our successors of the sixties, and the only thing we really
have in common with them is the utter lack of a sense of
humor.

Hesse did not really have a sense of humor either, he only
saw that he needed it. His attempts at humor were pitiful;
what would our revered Jean Paul have made of the mirror
game at the end of Steppenwolf! It is a humorous situation
to see oneself completely taken apart into a hundred little
pieces and put together again in different ways; but at that
time we only understood Hesse to say that modern man is
devoid of real substance. The desperate relativism of Hermann Hesse was inaccessible to our generation of protesters
because we, like Steppenwolf, wanted to have our full substance recognized as a valid alternative to the Establishment.
Hesse, in all his endings, says exactly the opposite. He says
that man can be a hundred different things at the same time;
that there is no dichotomy between Steppenwolf and the Establishment, or youth and age, or good and evil; that each

man can re-arrange his personality by putting the pieces together in different ways—and consider it all a game. In his
old age he reiterated this faith in *The Glass Bead Game.*

We have sensed that such a faith leads to madness unless
it is combined with mysticism and astrology. As is well
known, Hesse inclined to both, and the youth movement of
the sixties has just discovered astrology. We inclined to mysticism, which was one of the attractions of *Demian,* but we
did not and could not accept or even understand Hesse's theory that man is a game. Perhaps it was Hesse's good luck that
he was such a poor story teller and that he never brought the
game off as a story; thus we could misinterpret him to say
that the Establishment is the game. Many of us, then, believed in something much worse—Destiny.

I suppose this is a German vice—to shrug off responsibility by referring to some dark force that commands our Destiny. It was the philosophy that prepared German youth for
Hitler. It is not in Hesse, nor in Nietzsche, but both of them
could be misunderstood to support such views. Especially if
one misunderstands the unhappy endings of Hesse's stories,
one might get the idea that man must accept his fate and
submit to what has been destined for him. To correct such a
view we should remember the context in which Hesse wrote.
To put it bluntly, he wrote against us, against our tendency
to withdraw into a "youth land," against his own humanism
and his tendency to withdraw into the land of poetry and
mysticism, or into Hindu philosophy, a fad at the time. He
taught involvement not in any particular cause or on any particular side, although he had his own causes, but involvement in contemporary issues. Like Thomas Mann, he despised the burghers most for representing a world to which
one cannot go home any more, for the false sense of security,
for the illusions and hypocrisies about the realities of life
which they taught their children. But he had even greater
scorn for those who were *bürgerlich* at one remove—the
humanists and cultists who pretended that the ideal side of
middle-class values could be preserved without acknowledg-
ing their ugly side; the hypocrites who lived off middle-class

culture and pretended to be above it. He constantly fought against culture heroes, but alas, like Nietzsche, he had the bad luck to become one himself.

But was it bad luck? Can it be an accident that two different generations in two different countries have misunderstood an author so thoroughly? Was he not guilty of seducing us first? Though at heart a humanist, he rejected the culture that had been built on humanist values; though as intellectual as the great classical writers, he renounced their reliance on man's intellective capacities, and he opened the way for the great succession of anti-intellectualist writing, for the great retreat from the technocratic twentieth into some utopian century where magic would provide for the material and spiritual needs of mankind. Above all, I think we were attracted by his message that the age of individualism had passed and some new community was called for. It was not his fault that others interpreted this new community as the community of the trenches, the suppression of the individual, the cult of the state. Here you have the Hermann Hesse of my youth—we had better put him on the shelf of poisonous books, next to Zarathustra.

[7]

Reflections on a Relative

HERMANN Struck was born a hundred years ago in
Berlin of a wealthy, orthodox family. He was known
not only as one of the finest draftsmen of his generation but as a leading Zionist before World War I and as an
early settler in Haifa, then Palestine. He was the friend of
many celebrities whose portraits he drew—preferably on copper plates so that they could be reproduced as etchings.
Among them were Theodor Herzl, Albert Einstein, Hermann
Cohen the philosopher, Max Reinhardt the stage director,
Richard Dehmel the poet, August Bebel the labor leader, Arnold Zweig, and many other Weimar intellectuals. He was
most famous, however, for his portraits of Jewish types from
all countries—Eastern Jews and Sephardic Jews, Jewish merchants and Jewish craftsmen, Jewish dock workers in Salo-
nika and halutzim in Palestine, Yemenites both Arab and
Jewish, rabbis and peddlers and beggars on the Lower East
Side of New York, and especially working Jews.

The models came from two sources or occasions. One was
his extensive traveling. In each country he found picturesque
types as part of the landscape. In these early wanderings he
had not yet come into his own as a painter. Although he was
sufficiently famous to have a one-man show in New York, his
drawings were rather traditional in the academic German
manner.

It was quite a different experience, however, when fate, or

Reprinted with permission from *Forward* (New York), August 3, 1980.

rather history, took him to Poland and Lithuania. In 1914 the war broke out and the Germans soon occupied a large part of certain Baltic countries which then belonged to Russia. The kaiser planned to win for himself the crown of those countries and therefore he wooed their populations. One minority that certainly had no love for the czar was the Jews, and it was hoped that they would help the Germans to pry Poland away from Russia. Thus the commanding general, Erich Ludendorff, addressed an appeal to them in Yiddish: "Tsu meine lieben Jidn in Paulen," assuring them of the benevolence of his all-high monarch. To advise him on Jewish affairs, or today we might say as a public relations officer, he also called on Hermann Struck as a man well known in the Jewish community and of orthodox persuasion.

The whole scheme was full of ironies, for Ludendorff did not know that Struck was a Social Democrat who did not care a hoot whether the Germans won the war. But of course, being drafted and equipped with an officer's rank, Struck could not refuse to serve. But there was one condition: if Ludendorff really wanted an orthodox Jew, he must provide him with kosher food in the officers' mess. Struck's job made it necessary for him to eat with the staff, and he dined kosher at the general's table to the end of the war. He had, of course, a good many opportunities to alleviate the plight of Jews in the occupied areas, but what he did to win the war history does not report.

Something else, however, happened to him. He discovered Eastern Jews, their mores, their speech, their physiognomies, their gait, their folklore, their worries. For the first time he drew Jews not because they were interesting or romantic or picturesque, but as Jews who were part of a people. He studied their faces furiously, and fifty-two of the most significant portraits have been collected in a book which is now a collector's item: *Das ostjüdische Antlitz*, with a text by Arnold Zweig.

It is a deeply moving story. Here is a man who had been a leading Zionist and had worked for the Jewish people all his adult life, a man who had visited congresses and had been employed in important missions; yet it was only in his fortieth year that he discovered the Jewish soul, and among people whose education and style of life had been so very different from his. It is fair to say that up to that time Hermann Struck had been a German painter who also had Jewish concerns and occasionally used Jewish subjects. Although he signed his works with his Hebrew name, Hayim-Aron ben David, the drawings he had brought back from his first trip to Palestine had not been different in quality from the many landscapes he had drawn in Holland, England, Scandinavia, Germany, and Italy. Now came these totally different testimonials of the Jewish soul in Poland and Lithuania, simple and sensitive. A simultaneous collection of a hundred portraits representing prisoners of war—all races drawn from colonial regiments with the picturesque uniforms and colorful headdresses of Afghans, Singhs, Bashkirs, Somalis, etc.— seems interested mainly in the superficial aspects of these types. The difference is striking.

After the war, Struck married and built a house in Haifa which at that time, of course, was under the British mandate administration. Here again he lived in two worlds. On the one hand he was deeply involved in the development of the country; that was still the time when a visitor was told the story of every tree that had grown. Struck knew (and, naturally, drew) the High Commissioners and gained so much credit with the British officers that later, when they tried to stop the Jewish immigration, he was able to secure certificates for refugees in distress. The conflict between the desperate Jews who tried to find asylum for more refugees, and the English who tried to protect the Arabs' interests, changed his views of Zionism. Originally his Mizrachi philosophy did not call for the creation of a state; he was happy to have a British passport. But when I saw him for the last time, shortly before the outbreak of World War II, he declared that the Jews needed the power of the state to make Palestine over into their own home. He did not live to see the fulfillment of this dream, for he died in 1944, in the midst of turbulent events that changed the nature of the Jewish question and the face of Zionism.

The other development that came from Struck's emigration to Palestine belongs in the history of art. The country opened for him a world of color he had not explored before. To that point, he had not done much painting in oil, but then he perfected the technique—so much so that the National Gallery in Berlin sought two of the bright, sun-flooded views of the Holy Land. Unfortunately, however, this springtime of creativity was to be brief. Either the painter's powers were waning or his humanitarian and political activities absorbed too much of his energies. Anyway, the fact is that the output of his last years is less abundant and less exciting than the earlier work. A few aquas give moving testimony of his love of the country, but it must be said that in these mediums he did not achieve the mastery which art historians have recognized in his etchings. The fine, sensitive line, the sharp definition of a profile which this medium permits, the sheer craftsmanship which delights the collector, they all have assured his etchings a steady place at art auctions, even though the name is not familiar to a wider audience. Especially his landscapes are highly appreciated.

In all this, Struck was not a modern painter. His contemporaries went through post-Impressionism, Expressionism, Futurism, Cubism, and other modern styles. Although he owned many paintings by avant-garde artists, he never tried their styles himself. Nor did he follow his friend Marc Chagall in inventing a fabulous Jewish mythology, or his friend Louis Corinth in devising new forms. He could patiently explain to laymen why he saw beauty in the modernist creations, but he stuck to his own austere, conservative style. As a craftsman of the burin (he also was the author of a classic textbook on the art of etching), he probably felt that his art showed to best advantage in this medium.

Among older Jewish painters, his closest friends were Max Liebermann, who also lived in Berlin, and old Josef Israëls, whom he visited often in Amsterdam. Struck and Israëls, who was very much concerned with the fate of the Jewish people, shared many interests, but there also was another attraction in Amsterdam. Struck considered Rembrandt the greatest painter of all times. He studied his work very carefully and did research on his life. His secret wish was to prove that Rembrandt had been a Jew.

[8]

Heidegger and Hitler

The Incompatibility of *Geist* and Politics

THE philosophical genius who died on May 26, 1976, at the age of eighty-seven, nearly a recluse in his Black Forest abode and nearly silent for twenty years, has offered the world as many riddles as he proposed to solve. An elitist who kept aloof from the crowd, he nevertheless assumed the pose of a prophet. His subject was the most abstract and esoteric of all philosophical problems, pure Being—which he was so anxious to distinguish from being (*sein*) that he used the archaic spelling *Seyn* (Beeing); yet he unleashed a worldwide movement, vulgarly called Existentialism—only to repudiate it. A fascinating teacher who kept his disciples' loyalty beyond all disagreements, he nevertheless complained that he had never been really understood. He never completed a book (even his major work appeared as Part I, never to be followed by Part II). But the planned edition of his collected works will comprise eighty volumes, and scholars from all continents have contributed to the *Festschriften* presented to him on his seventieth and eightieth birthdays, while literally shelves of books are being written about the question of what Heidegger really meant or whether he meant anything at all. His style is so original and impenetrable that some praise it as the adequate instrument of expressing the

Reprinted with permission from *The Boston University Journal* (1976), no. 3.

deepest thoughts, while others dismiss it as a hoax invented to mask mere emptiness.

But I shall not try to expound here the significance of Heidegger's philosophy, nor speculate on the social causes that made it a fad. My concern is a strange episode in his career: his joining the Nazi Party in 1933, in conjunction with his assumption of the rectorate (the academic presidency) of Freiburg University. The question is: how could this reticent metaphysician, who had preached the inwardness of noble souls, march with the plebeian Brownshirts? Did he commit the crime that has been called "the treason of the clerks"? Was it simple opportunism? Or was the philosopher presumptious enough to think he could succeed with Hitler where his eminent predecessor, Plato, had failed with the Tyrant of Syracuse, Dionysius the Younger?

There was this difference, however. Plato wanted to teach the tyrant (as Diderot hoped to teach Catherine the Great—with equally disastrous results). Heidegger apparently assumed that there was already some basic affinity between his philosophy and Hitler's mission which would enable the Führer to turn philosophy into practice—the dream of every philosopher, which makes his political mistakes so much more culpable than the butcher's or the baker's.

For indeed, although philosophers have often cultivated the image of being absent-minded or above the ways of the world, actually they have never been reluctant to tell statesmen what they should do and, moreover, what politics is all about. A baker or a butcher can make a mistake in politics. Even a poet has license to be wrong. We have forgiven Balzac that he was a royalist and Dostoevsky that he was a staunch anti-Semite, anti-Catholic, and Pan-Slavist. Somehow we are able to separate the man from his writing, and the politically naive citizen from the insightful observer of the human scene. But can a philosopher afford to be wrong? Especially one who, like Heidegger, has taught us to "live authentically," to look down on the vulgar dealings of the crowd, to break out of the banality of everyday politics?

In trying to answer this question, I shall examine Heidegger's political philosophy and its relationship to his metaphysics, for in fact he had never been a philosopher standing aloof and preaching detachment from the affairs of the world. Or perhaps I should say more cautiously: the effect, back in the 1920s, which Heidegger's philosophy had on my generation was precisely "engagement." I remember the fascinating experience of reading *Being and Time* when it appeared in 1927. Conventional philosophers told us to park our emotions and prejudices at the checkroom outside their lecture halls; in particular, Heidegger's (and my) teacher, Husserl, introduced new devices to make sure that everything we knew from prior experience was "bracketed" when we analyzed pure ideas. Here, however, was a philosopher who told us that man does not think with his head alone but with his whole person. "The philosophizing 'I' is not an unconcerned eye," writes Professor Otto Pöggeler in his tribute to Heidegger's eightieth birthday. "It is a person who is concerned with various practical affairs, must live with other human beings, has a conscience, is always faced with the problem of death, worries and fears; he is a man in a situation." Man was once again the measure of all things. In this respect Heidegger's appeal was comparable to that of Marx and of Nietzsche—as well as of Dilthey, who also had approached philosophy from the angle of "life" and society.

Where Heidegger was different, again, was in this: others treated philosophy as an outflow of life (and some Marxists, as is well known, even as a mere reflection of economic relations); Heidegger claimed that his philosophy held the key to life. Or, again, since he has repudiated any suggestion that he was writing an ethics, I should say cautiously: this is what students of my generation read in (or into) Heidegger. If they read too much into it, the question is: was this perhaps the master's fault? Did not his language suggest that his philosophy was aimed at an ethics and, in particular, at a political ethics?

In fact, he has answered that question himself by his action. I was not a bit surprised when I heard of Heidegger's line-up with the Nazi government. I had never considered him a metaphysician standing aloof. He had been running around with extremist groups, and when Ernst Cassirer, the neo-Kantian rector of Hamburg University, had an academic disputation with Heidegger, Cassirer came home with the impression that his opponent either was anti-Semitic or was surrounded by anti-Semites. To be fair, I hasten to add that I have not found a word about Jews, or race, in any of Heidegger's writings. Also, a younger philosopher at Freiburg discounted Heidegger's Nazi friends with words like: "Oh he does that [associate with Nazis] to please his wife; they amuse him." Finally, during Heidegger's tenure as rector, no anti-Semitic demonstrations were allowed at the university; nor were any books burned at Freiburg.

It is time, however, to state the bare facts of the case. In March 1933 Hitler achieved power—legally, but in an election held under conditions of growing terror. In April, the Social Democratic rector of Freiburg University was forced to resign, and in a tumultuous session the faculty elected Heidegger to be his successor, on the not unreasonable assumption that he was the one most likely to get along with the new authorities, especially Dr. Goebbels, Hitler's cultural warden. The Nazi students gave the new rector an ovation and wrote in their newspaper, "We have always counted him as one of our own."

Heidegger's inaugural speech responded to the political climate of the day, but it was printed under the title, "The Self-Assertion of the German University."[1] Heidegger's defenders have read this as a warning to the Nazis to respect the independence of Academe. That this was not so will be seen when we analyze the speech and its sequel—an appeal by the new rector to the students to join Hitler's Labor Service. The climate of the day itself refutes the more amiable interpretation. Far from not interfering with the university, Goebbels meant to give the Nazi students and professors a free hand. It must be remembered that only five percent of the German population was attending, or had ever attended, an institution of higher learning, and that the majority of the students and teachers at these elite schools were militantly sympathetic to the "Government of National Uprising." Goebbels could grant the students a rather free constitution which tied them closely to the Nazi party but acknowledged their freedom from traditional curricula—the freedom to nazify the university. A true Nazi rector, Ernst Krieck, about whom more will be heard presently, said in his inaugural speech: "The new student law affirms the students' victory after a long fight for the renewal of the university." He expressed his confidence that in the new state the university would fulfill a new function springing from the new spirit of its teachers and students: "Intellectual freedom does not depend on any law, but the teacher's freedom must be grounded deeply in his character; he must confront the adversary powers militantly from the center of his conscience." (All translations are mine.)

With this in mind we shall be able to evaluate Heidegger's speech to students and faculty. He began by celebrating the Nazi ideal of education. Not content to define the role of the university as "forming the leaders and guardians of German destiny," he also rejoiced that, happily, "the much-vaunted academic freedom is being expelled from the German universities; it was unauthentic; it meant freedom to do as one pleased." From the advocate of "authenticity" this may sound surprising. What, in Heidegger's philosophy, is authentic freedom? Heidegger's answer was: "Labor service, military service, science service." In thus equating the work of the university with that in factories and army barracks, he remarked that studying should "no longer be a matter of choosing a profession but a service to the nation," and he concluded by misquoting a dictum of Plato's: "All greatness stands in storm." (The translation in my copy of The Republic says: "All great enterprises are fraught with danger." Heidegger used a word that would be interpreted not as "tempest" but as "assault." His language was always carefully ambiguous.)

That same year, Heidegger campaigned for Hitler's plebiscite approving Germany's withdrawal from the League of Nations. In explaining the vote, he said that it did not mean the mere approval of a tactical decision in foreign policy but, more important, that it was a vote "for the Führer and the movement that follows him unconditionally." When the Führer, embodiment of the National Will, gives expression to the call of destiny, no one can resist: "Whether we want it or not, at the moment [of crisis] the Führer alone is the present and future of German reality and its law."

Complementing this gibberish, Nazi ideologists went out of their way to exalt Heidegger's philosophy as the true expression of Hitler's politics. One, Professor Hans Naumann, claimed that Heidegger's major work, *Being and Time*, was a cyphered guide through Valhalla, the abode of the Teutonic gods; another praised Heidegger's impenetrable language for restoring the old Germanic myths and teaching the Germans to think mythically. (We shall discuss later whether the philosopher can be held responsible for such followers.)

Mutual admiration and chumminess, however, lasted less than a year. Heidegger disregarded a party order to fire one Professor Wolf, a meritorious teacher of political theory. Wolf had criticized the work of Carl Schmitt, then the foremost academic apologist of totalitarian dictatorship. Moreover, Heidegger himself had given offense to two powerful Nazi ideologists who were his rivals in the field of philosophy and who may have envied his fame or suspected him of unorthodoxy. One was Alfred Bäumler, official interpreter of Nietzsche and new rector of Berlin University; through his close identification with the Nietzsche Archive he had access to Hitler. The other was an early Nazi and pseudo-philosopher, Ernst Krieck, a peddler of blood-and-soil fantasies, who had become rector at Frankfurt University. It is hard to see where Krieck should have differed doctrinally from Heidegger; he had been using Heidegger's mythological language, though admittedly rather ineptly. Now he found his rival's philosophy too Jewish, too humanist, too personal, not sufficiently totalitarian and racist.

There followed intrigues in which the metaphysician was no match for the philosophical commissars, and after a mere ten months Heidegger resigned from the rectorship. Thereafter, he became openly critical of Hitler's cronies; in his lectures he attacked Bäumler's interpretation of Nietzsche, and referred to Krieck's philosophy as "not consistent with the great National Socialist movement." His classes then were supervised; he was prevented from traveling; near the end of the war he was sent into a labor regiment, where he got a taste of the "service" he had recommended to his students.

Bäumler had good reason to be annoyed. If Heidegger's close reading of Nietzsche was correct, then that great iconoclast could not be a forerunner of Hitler—a preposterous claim anyway. Nietzsche was elitist, antidemocratic, antihumanitarian, antirationalistic—but not for a moment would he ever have contemplated "using" Hitler or associating with him. He was, to use Heidegger's term, "an authentic man." Hitler was the opposite, and Heidegger's "mistake" was his failure to see that. His defenders plead that this may happen to anybody.

A man who preaches authenticity to others must not make the same mistake as the butcher and baker. Less than others can he allow himself to run with the crowd. When Heidegger praised the Führer, made speeches on his behalf, mouthed Nazi slogans about German Destiny, he displayed the behavior he had so eloquently described as "unauthentic." He must have discovered this soon, for his philosophy demanded personal decisions whereas the Nazi state had prejudged every issue. But even if Heidegger tried to hush the difference, the Nazis had to bring it to his attention. The totalitarian state does not allow any citizen to accept its rule in silence and to collaborate quietly. It demands constant assent, positive identification; it does not permit a man to compromise, to obey grudgingly. It requires a man's enthusiastic loyalty, or forces him to lie. Even the bootlicking Schmitt did not sound convincing and got the boot. Heidegger could not lie.

On the face of it, Krieck was right, too, and thereby Heidegger can be acquitted of the charge of anti-Semitism, except for the ambiguities of 1933. Had not his great work *Being and Time* been influenced by, and dedicated to, Edmund Husserl, the Jewish father of Phenomenology? Had not his numerous Jewish students kept faith with him? Among them, to name only those who have taught in this country, were Hans Jonas, Hannah Arendt, Herbert Marcuse, Walter Kaufmann, Karl Löwith, William Barrett, Werner Marx—some of whom went out of their way later on to defend Heidegger against those who insisted that "once a Nazi, always a Nazi." To make things more complicated, however, Heidegger seemed to confirm that axiom; he has never repudiated or even admitted his mistake of 1933, leaving his friends with the weak riposte: Can't a man make a mistake?

They will readily admit that it was "a great mistake," but continue to claim that it was a mistake "merely" about Hitler's person and the character of the Nazi party. A very strange excuse. Not even the proverbially absent-minded German professor of philosophy could be ignorant of the noisy Brownshirts in his classroom, or of the vulgar propaganda Dr. Goebbels was dinning into everybody's ears—plain rabble-rousing anti-Semitism, or primitive chauvinism. But we must not forget the conditions of the time. Depression and national humiliation had disaffected the middle class from the Republic. Many people on the right saw the Nazi antics as a mere circus. Their clever idea was to "use" Hitler for the purposes of a "conservative revolution" and then to dismiss him. When the cynical plan failed and the clown made himself master, one deceived deceiver, Hermann Rauschning, wrote an indignant book about The Revolution of Nihilism. Others had contributed important ideas to the Nazi philosophy, and yet were rebuffed, most striking among them Stefan George and Oswald Spengler. Both found that they had hatched monsters, and fled in horror, keeping their reputations reasonably intact. Yet their share of the guilt is part of the confusion typical of the intellectual ambiance of the 1930s.

This, however, is not the kind of mistake Heidegger could be charged with. For him, as for Nietzsche, nihilism was the disease that must provide its own remedy. He was truly inside that cultural revolution which had begun with Nietzsche.

Expressionism and futurism produced artists and writers who wanted to explode the "lies of humanism." Like Marinetti, the great Expressionist painter Emil Nolde was a confirmed nationalist and an anti-Semite as well. He greeted the Nazi regime with fervor and could never understand why it had no use for him and his art; as is well known, Goebbels forbade him to paint, despite his protestations of loyalty. Even worse was the disappointment of Germany's great Expressionist poet Gottfried Benn, likewise a man of the right and a conscious "Prussian." He felt that the Nazis were bound to assign to Expressionist artists the task of creating a culture of appropriate attitudes. He was rebuffed but stayed in Germany, grumbling and writing for posterity.

Did Heidegger, too, expect that the Nazis would realize his philosophy? And was his illusion founded any better than Benn's? Was his own fight against traditional philosophy in any way related to the Nazi fight against humanism? A man who can write, "The truth is not for everybody, only for the strong," certainly is no humanist in the accepted sense of the term. Even after the defeat of the Third Reich (when opportunists were trying to ingratiate themselves with the Allies by professions of humanism), Heidegger, always an honest man, continued to declare that humanism must be overcome. Does this make him a Nazi?

Ernst Jünger, to whom Heidegger has dedicated a book, once said: "I may not be able to recognize my enemy when I see him, but I recognize him by his voice." Anyone with an ear for the German language knows what Jünger, himself a great stylist, was speaking of. There lived, during the 1920s and early 1930s, a group of authors in many fields whose choice of words and use of syntax made them known as antihumanist, antirationalist, antidemocratic prophets of a new elitist belief, a new militaristic attitude, a new discipline. During the war, I published a collection of such expressions, *Nazi-Deutsch*, and quite independently Victor Klemperer, inside Germany, collected instances of murdered German (we had no knowledge of each other's existence); Dolf Sternberger and others also clandestinely wrote the *Dictionary of the*

Monster. (After the war it appeared in the *Frankfurt Hefte;*
Adorno's *Jargon of Authenticity* amplified the argument sociologically.) Among prime examples we used Jünger, Heidegger, the "blood-and-soil" authors, the playwright Hanns
Johst, Erwin Kolbenheyer, Krieck, writings of the youth
movement and of Nazi propagandists. All these authors use
military terms in contexts where they are not called for, and
confuse concrete with metaphysical references.

I have called this language and its authors "proto-Fascist."
They all repudiate the enlightenment of the past two hundred
years. Thus, Ludwig Klages published a book entitled *The
Intellect as Antagonist of the Soul;* Heidegger has coined,
"The most stubborn enemy of thinking is Reason"; Jünger
has confessed, "The best answer to the betrayal of life by intellect (*Geist*) would be the betrayal of Intellect by Intellect,and one of the great joys of this age is to participate in
this work of destruction."

Professor Robert Minder of the Collège de France has shown
that Heidegger's language in his political year was indistinguishable from that of his rival Krieck. Professor Paul
Hühnerfeld of Hamburg University complains, "Existence,
Anxiety, Worry, Death are man's lot . . . real life is life-unto-
death, exertion; fate is full of heaviness, unrelieved by the
slightest sense of humor . . . by God, it's a very German image of man that Heidegger teaches." But there were German
professors, like Nietzsche, who emphasized life! Heidegger's
concern with death, his coining "Being-unto-death," is not
German but fascist and echoed by all the proto-Nazi authors
in their worship of sacrifice. I must confess that my suspicion
of Heidegger's politics was first aroused when I realized this
bleakness in his philosophical outlook, this feeling of unrelieved, ineluctable catastrophe, which was so characteristic
of proto-Fascist feeling in the 1920s.

Heidegger, who also exalts sacrifice, especially frowns on
those who think of death as a danger that might be averted;
they "minimize death by trying to manipulate it; in being-
unto-death, by contrast, the expectation must be understood
unmitigated, must be trained [*ausgebildet:* Heidegger loves

military terms], and in the proper attitude must be endured [ausgehalten; the 'stick it out' of World War I]." That is to say, in the typically antihumanist manner of the Nazis, Death should not be faced reflectively but accepted in the way of a soldier, as fate.

Heidegger's language is usually rather abstract—for Heidegger is still concerned with pure being—and difficult; but suddenly, ever so often, we come across hard, concrete words that we know well from the political vocabulary. These words often stick out like a piece of fabric in a Dadaist painting, or they are emotional and value-laden in a way one does not expect to find in philosophical books. Thus, when Heidegger comes to speak of Mr. Everyman, he uses the German word *durchschnittlich* in a way which gives it the meaning of "mediocre" rather than "average," and he coins a new word, *das Man,* which in German sounds contemptuous, referring to Slavonic subhumans who don't know how to use the proper article.

When David Riesman, in *The Lonely Crowd,* analyzed the mass mind, he used the term "other-directed"—not very flattering, but a precise, technical term, not an epithet. Heidegger, by contrast, has fun with the common man. He finds him incapable of "speech," capable only of "chatter"; unable to ask questions, but "nosey"; deficient in character, but sensationalist; above all, "unauthentic," which is largely due to his being-with-others. This massive mediocrity is always envious of anybody who is "outstanding"; it easily agrees on what is acceptable and what is not. "Overnight, anything original is leveled down; anything won in hard fight is made common; every secret loses its power. This worry (*Sorge*— one of Heidegger's existential words) of the mediocre reveals an essential trait of [mankind] which I call the leveling down of all possibilities of being."

The tendency of modern democratic societies to make people more equal is: presented as characteristic of all urban communities (Nazi ideologists have always played the sturdy peasant against vile city decadence); vilified by epithets in the cheapest manner of the beer-hall demagogue who tries to flatter his audience at the expense of the "mass" outside; tied to some metaphysical calamity (*Einebnung aller Seinsmöglichkeiten*).

Unfortunately mythical language (as discussed in Ernst Cassirer's *Myth of the State*) is also the secret of Heidegger's fascinating and persuasive method. He is not an elitist, in the rational manner of Carl Schmitt or Pareto, with whom it might be possible to debate the advantages and disadvantages of this and that political system. He puts those who disagree with his point of view into a class of not-quite-human brutes characterized by a metaphysical defect; to debate with them would not be worth his while. They are unauthentic, as an existential fact. Unfortunately, most of humanity has been in this sorry state for the last two thousand years, and only to the few who understand Nietzsche has it been given to be authentic in the midst of an unauthentic world.

Heidegger wants to crush and to stir us. Like the contemporary disciples of Kierkegaard, for whom he has the highest praise, he makes it clear that our doom must be total before we can be resurrected. When he speaks about the excesses in technology, the faith in science, the shallow consumer culture, he will dub these manifestations of modern capitalism "Americanism" and duly condemn "Americanization," as do a majority of Europeans. But he will explain that these are not just some defects that might be repaired piecemeal but are symptoms of our total alienation from "the ground of being," of our "fallenness" and "loss of being."

One might assume that such a pessimistic view of man's state might lead to religion, or perhaps to mysticism, or at least to a very personalist desire to turn inward. To many critics, indeed, Heidegger's philosophy was nothing but a warmed-over version of German neoromanticism, which became popular during the 1920s. But there were those militant words, which seemed to promise a "breakthrough," a "decision." *Being and Time* had an apocalyptic ring. In a truly dialectical turn, man, totally alienated, unauthentic and Americanized, would have to touch his "ground of being" to become an authentic man. Vague as this seemed, it was clear that the turn would be revolutionary, or rather that the authenticity of the turn would be known by its total and revolutionary character. "Resoluteness is the ground of authenticity."

This still left unresolved the riddle of the "ground of being." More vulgar Nazi writers offered answers from the vocabulary of blood-and-soil, the German soul, the race, the blood. Although Heidegger was deeply attached to his native Black Forest and its folklore he could not, as a philosopher, ascribe metaphysical significance to any of these terms. But he liked to quote a letter by Rainer Maria Rilke in which the poet complained, "For our grandfathers a house, a fountain, even a dress, a coat, still had something infinitely trustworthy. Almost every thing was the depository of something human. Today, coming from America, empty and indifferent things, pseudo-things, trompe l'oeil of life are collecting. . . . A house in the American sense, a fruit from over there, has nothing in common with a house or fruit in which the hopes and thoughts of our ancestors have dwelled."[2]

This "dwelling of the ancestors" has a special significance for Heidegger. He believed that the people must stay where the gods had their temples and where their customs were respected. When he came to Marburg University, he made a point of wearing his native folk dress, and he rejected an honorable call to Berlin, the great Babylon, on the ground that he did not belong there. Like the German romantics, he deplored the loss of original harmony which came about when people abandoned their "ground of being," strove for technical inventions, material enjoyment, power over nature and other men, and, accordingly, adopted an alienating metaphysics that opposed man to nature, man to man. This had first happened at about the time of Plato; and ever since, mankind has strayed in the desert of false philosophy.

Strangely, these criticisms of our culture go back to Jewish authors like Mare and Bergson, but Heidegger found them with an antihumanist twist in the works of Ernst Jünger. This talented but perverse writer had been a soldier of fortune, had become fascinated with the machinelike bestiality of the battles in World War I, and called for "total mobilization." In 1930, he published a devastating book, *The Worker*, from which Heidegger borrowed his ideas on labor service. They both believed that the new technology had produced the totally soulless, mindless, and even sexless "type" who was just doing his duty like a soldier, the counterpart to the Men of Will and Power who, however unknowing, immerse themselves in this very same destiny, where *Geist* becomes indistinguishable from labor: "So-called intellectual labor is labor because it is deeply imbedded in the necessity of the historical being of our people. . . . There is only one German condition of life: the estate of labor, whose will has been formed in the National Socialist German Workers' Party."[3]

But the distinction thus conferred on labor seems dubious: "The human who has been a rational animal, which means a worker, now must drift through the ravaged lands. Labor today reaches the metaphysical rank of the objectification of all things. . . . The decline accomplishes itself in the breakdown of the world, which has been characterized by metaphysics, and in the devastation of the world which is its result. The breakdown and the devastation find the fulfillment they deserve when metaphysical man, the rational animal, is put in his place as a beast of burden."

Neither the thought nor the metaphor are new in German ideology. One thinks of Nietzsche's cry, "The desert is growing!" and of Max Weber's "world robbed of its magic." So far Heidegger is in the tradition of German romanticism. What is new is the poignancy and urgency of his call for a reversal, and his belief that he has found the instrument of this necessary and deeply metaphysical revolution: "The works that are being peddled about nowadays as the philosophy of National Socialism," he exclaimed in 1935, desperately trying to refute Krieck's nostalgic interpretation of Nazi philosophy, "have nothing whatever to do with the inner truth and greatness of this movement (namely the encounter between global technology and modern man)."[4] It is characteristic of the man

Heidegger that he published the piece, written in 1935, unchanged in 1953.

In a frequently repeated metaphor, Heidegger describes Europe as caught "in a great pincers, squeezed between Russia on one side and America on the other. From a metaphysical point of view, Russia and America are the same; the same dreary technological frenzy, the same unrestricted organization of the average man. . . . the farthermost corner of the globe has been conquered by technology and opened to economic exploitation; . . . time has ceased to be anything other than velocity, instantaneousness, and simultaneity . . . a boxer is regarded as a nation's great man; . . . mass meetings attended by millions are looked on as a triumph—then . . . a question still haunts us like a specter: What for?—Whither?—And what then?" And again: "We are caught in a pincers. Situated in the center, our nation incurs the severest pressure. It is the nation with the most neighbors and hence the most endangered. With all this, it is *the most metaphysical of nations."* [5]

To regain the authentic life, obviously, people must adopt a philosophy that will put them in contact once again with these truths, and at the same time make that revolutionary leap onto their own ground of being. He who founds the city in this spirit, therefore, reveals the Truth—not any particular truth but THE Truth. This will be the greatest breakthrough, breakup, and departure (*Aufbruch*); we are in the midst of the Nazi vocabulary, which in the rectorate speech comes through with fanfare: "This departure is a rupture!" He sounds the tocsin of the national revolution, for the Führer's resoluteness is making the German people authentic again.

The scheme is a cheap imitation of Marxian dialectics. Just as the proletariat, at the point of starvation but already representing the totality of productive forces, will have no choice but to launch the socialist revolution, so the German people will overturn its unauthentic existence at the point of its greatest distress and when the "worker" technology and metaphysics have fulfilled their time.

It is now clear what Heidegger's "mistake" was in 1933. He believed that an apocalyptic revolution was in the making. He saw this revolution embodied in his Nazi students. They correctly interpreted Heidegger's philosophy when they thought of National Socialism as the German nation's return to its roots while at the same time philosophy was turning away from its two-thousand-year aberration. Instead, Hitler revealed himself as a small-time, power-hungry tyrant. Apparently, Heidegger had telescoped something he held metaphysically necessary into something that was happening in 1933, a cosmic event into a national celebration. He had also made a mistake no philosopher should ever make: he extrapolated a philosophical or religious thought which concerned the individual and his relation to the world upon a political event which concerned a national collective. When Heidegger's dream about Hitler collapsed, his theorizing quickly returned to the level at which the problems appear in the form of personal queries addressed to that divinity in whom Heidegger, born a Catholic, could no longer believe.

My purpose has been to show that Heidegger's political aberration was not accidental but flowed from his philosophy and from his character. I have also shown that his idea of National Socialism was more profound than Hitler's and that his temporary support of Hitler's movement may indeed, from his own point of view, have been an error. But like Peer Gynt, the proto-Nazis were responsible for their "fantasied sins" and must answer for the monsters which they fathered on the true barbarians. As Stephen Bronner has argued, no philosophy is without ideological consequences for political practice,[6] and while no philosopher is immune to interpretation, some lend themselves to demagogic extrapolations and others do not.

Be that as it may, Heidegger disdained to excuse or exculpate himself, and his experience with power haunted him for the rest of his life. When the war was over, in 1945, the Allies deprived him of his chair; a cloud settled over his relationship with colleagues and former students, who admired his achievements as a philosopher but failed to understand his silence on the important issue of the philosopher's political responsibility. Meanwhile books have been written both attacking and defending or excusing Heidegger's political episode, with no encouragement from the master. For the rest of his life, he remained a philosopher of Existence.

Brecht's Personal Politics

I HAVE been asked to tell what I know about Bertolt Brecht's personal attitudes to the political questions of his time. Let me state in advance that I find it difficult to comply for two reasons—one external, the other intrinsic. Bert Brecht was an ironical author who liked to conceal his meaning while provoking the reader to find his own answer. In personal conversation he also preferred asking questions to giving answers; moreover, he found many situations so complex that humor was the only appropriate approach; and since humor always starts out from the proposition that before the court of history what is right today may be wrong tomorrow, it was often hard to predict on which side he would come down in the practical, everyday politics of the left.

The second difficulty was that Brecht shared with many other persons of his stature the habit of using people. This appears very clearly, though unintentionally, in the memoirs of Fritz Sternberg and others who boast that they had some influence on Brecht's intellectual development. Having been in the position of an apprentice, I am painfully aware that when Brecht asked me a question it was not to receive instruction from me, but either to educate me or to be challenged by my stupidity. Moreover, it was clear at all times that Brecht did not approve of my critical attitude to the Communist party or the Soviet Union. We avoided the subject whenever possible, and he compartmentalized his ambi-

Reprinted with permission from *Telos* (Summer 1980).

ances—keeping his party friends away from Karl Korsch and
me. Because of these limitations, I shall speak as little as possible from personal experience, and as much as possible from
public sources.

To understand why the poet Bertolt Brecht had to die in
East Germany, one must first comprehend how serious, how
deadly serious he felt about the reform of poetry and the
theater. When the soldiers came back from World War I, no
one was expressing their nausea, their disgust, their contempt of the middle-class reality into which they were supposed to integrate. Not the Expressionists, who greeted those
hardened and disillusioned trench dogs with the illusionist
effusions of *Oh Mensch* lyricism. Nor, of course, the dispens-
ers of traditional, classical German culture, the Ph.D.s who
directed middle-class taste back to the "culinary" consumption of cultural goods, the esthetic hypocrites and the hired
phrase-mongers who knew how to conjure up a magic mountain for money but did not speak of things that mattered (I
am merely paraphrasing; Brecht had a lifelong feud with
Thomas Mann).[1] What the new generation needed was a
theater that showed it like it was in a language like the one
that was spoken. Gottfried Benn, Ernst Jünger, Georg Kaiser,
Alfred Döblin, Bertolt Brecht, Arnolt Bronnen, and Heinrich
Mann provided that new language, and each in his own way
expressed his impatience with the old framework of thought.[2]
Most were uninterested in social reform or republican politics, nor did they care to analyze the middle-class individual's psyche; in fact, Goethe's great ideal, personality, had
disappeared in the trenches, and just when the Republic tried
to revive that ideal, inflation wiped out its material base,
middle-class property.

They all hated the *burgher* who had impersonated German
culture for a hundred and fifty years. Some of them also expressed their revulsion through some kind of political radicalism—of either the extreme right or the extreme left. But
even they were antipolitical rather than political: they considered reforms mere deceptions to make an intolerable status quo look tolerable. They expected the Republic to crum-

ble and did their best to push what was tottering, to desecrate what was holy, to debunk what seemed certain. Their politics were based on anarchist nihilism or elitist contempt: dreams of chaos and terror—Jünger's chiseled nightmares of the militaristic beehive, Benn's fantasy of a Führer acting out the Expressionist cataclysm, Bronnen's bloody version of a totally dehumanized man (for some years he was Brecht's closest friend, and Brecht staged his *Parricide*; later, to spite his Jewish stepfather, Bronnen joined the Nazis). It is simply not true that those who had been wounded by the front experience had to go to the Left. Brecht's gruesome *Legend of the Dead Soldier* may today look like a pacifist poem; but when we compare it with his other poems of that time, it is clear that he was interested in the gory images suggested by war, just as in 1774 Gottfried August Bürger had used the awesome fantasy of the dead soldier calling for his sweetheart. Reviewing later his poems of the 1920s, Brecht judged that they showed "bourgeois decadence." His poetry, he noted 1940 in his diary, *Arbeitsjournal (AJ)*,[3] then had reached "that degree of dehumanization that Marx saw in the proletariat, and at the same time the very hopelessness that raised Marx's hope. Most deal with decline; the poems follow our perishing society into its downfall. Beauty establishes itself on wrecks; the shreds are dainty; the sublime wallows in the dust; senselessness is hailed as liberation. The poet does not even identify with himself any longer" (*AJ*, 8/20/40).

In these early poems and plays Brecht poses as a cynic. His attitude to the world is one of brutal detachment, but he betrays an impish pleasure in following the antics of rogues and the lusty schemes of cheats, thieves, murderers, pimps and whores, vagabonds, and other rejects of society. His was the world of circus folk and bohemians; his patron saints were Arthur Rimbaud and Frank Wedekind.

What distinguished him from others who carried no less chaos in their souls were two things, both of which point to his later commitment. One was his ability to find the precise words that characterized this world, without necessarily speaking for it or on its behalf. Second, he was interested in these misfits only because they seemed to reveal some truths by which the respectable people also lived. The Chicago gangsters, the Soho underworld fell afoul of rules that merely concealed society's own crimes; they were both more amusing and more honest. But Brecht longed for rules that would take from them the stigma of contempt, and for some order that would liberate all from hypocrisy. Even much later, he referred to socialism by the code word, "the great order."

For basically, Brecht was a puritan, and the critics who admonished him to overcome his chaos were appealing to a responsive mind. In all this he resembled George Grosz. Through his art he meant to hold a mirror up to men, forcing them to see themselves as they were. His socialism did not grow out of the pity he felt for the poor or out of solidarity with the disinherited, or even out of his rebellious instinct, but out of his need for a better order. The status quo forced people to be hypocritical and to live by cheating their fellow man. This is how he saw capitalism. And this is especially how he saw America, the foremost country of free enterprise: a brutal, chaotic war for survival, each against all, with no holds barred, and tycoons whose morals were no better than those of thieves. In the Jungle of the Cities; Saint Joan of the Stockyards; Mahagonny: These images of an America he had not yet seen were validated by Hollywood when he came to live there ten years later. The parasitical, not the productive, side of capitalism is also the object of his scorn in The Threepenny Opera; again, the representatives of capitalism are underworld characters. When he equates prostitution with exploitation, he does not think that he speaks metaphorically. Pimps and beggar kings expound the wisdom of capitalist philosophy: "Eating comes first, then comes morality"; "We would be good and not so tough, but the conditions are too rough."

All of this was fun, however; the audience did not recognize the ruling class in those beggar kings (and that's why Brecht had to bring out the bitterness in The Threepenny Novel five years later). Alfred Kerr, admittedly not a wholly impartial judge, wrote that the original Beggar's Opera by John

Gay had attacked the society of his time much harder than Brecht; Theodor Adorno criticized Kurt Weill for writing songs that could all too easily be whistled like hit songs and were indeed so used with the bravado of people who proclaimed it as their philosophy that "For this world we live in, no man is bad enough," or who thought that the songs expressed the poet's own philosophy.

Some even thought that the songs were meant to expound Marx's economic interpretation of history as Brecht understood it. Nothing could have been further from his intention. By putting them into Peachum's mouth, Brecht was denouncing these views. Those who misunderstood him may have been unfamiliar with his new technique of theatrical demonstration, and therefore I may have to say a few words on his famous "estrangement effect."[4]

Precisely because Brecht did not identify with his ruffians, he had to prevent the spectator, too, from being carried away. He always placed some device—even if only a crier or a billboard announcing the scene—between spectator and actor; or he had a chorus address the spectator and ask him to judge the question. He kept reminding the audience of the fact that the actors were merely demonstrating and that it must not emphathize with, or root for, any of them. Consequently, the catharsis that Aristotelian dramaturgy demanded in the last act was deferred to the discussion that should take place after the play.[5] Pirandello had triumphantly introduced this style in 1921 with Six Characters in Search of an Author, which Brecht must have seen either in Berlin or in Munich.

Incidentally, Pirandello also had been concerned with the problem that bothered the German Expressionists: vanishing individuality.[6] His characters never know who they are. In A Man's a Man, Brecht showed how a man can be assembled and disassembled. Pirandello thought of life as a perpetual buffoonery: "We constantly create illusions about ourselves which from time to time have to be destroyed. My art is full of compassion for all who deceive themselves."

Understandably, Brecht's eulogists are reluctant to admit the double debt he owes to this "fascist" author. But it is surprising that they describe the "estrangement" devices as an instrument of Brecht's Marxist art after his conversion to communism. It is true that he began to use the term "estrangement" in 1930 (and in German it happens to sound very similar to a much-abused Marxian term which, however, was little known then: "alienation"). The technique had preceded its name, though. It could have been suggested to Brecht by the pre-Soviet director Vsevolod Meyerhold or through his own experience with the cabaret in Munich. It is clearly present in *A Man's a Man* of 1926, when Brecht was not yet a Marxist, and later on it was used by writers such as Friedrich Dürrenmatt and Max Frisch, neither of whom is a Marxist. Moreover, Communist critics have always been critical of these Brechtian devices in the theater, no matter how well they may be suited for agitprop groups.

Chronologically, then, we have established the following sequence. In his first phase, Brecht is the angry young man who gives voice to his generation's frustrations; he is a bohemian nihilist who shouts his contempt of the bourgeoisie from the stage. In his second period he is mastering his chaos through a new technique, the art of estrangement, which exposes, demonstrates, and denounces. But the outcasts are no longer his spokesmen; they exhibit the skewed order of the world. Brecht subjects himself and his audience to the discipline of the epic theater's analyzing technique. In his theoretical notes he begins to identify Aristotelian dramaturgy with the sentimentalism of bourgeois audiences. He eschews emotionalism and he teaches his actors to refrain from the effusions and gesticulations that still were the rule of the German and Russian stages.

With this, we enter into Brecht's third phase—the Marxist criticism of classical German literature. Brecht is not content to reject the famous German *Bildung:* he now unmasks its function, which is to deny the cruelty of life. In *Saint Joan of the Stockyards,* Brecht lampoons Schiller's *Maid of Orleans* and puts well-known quotations from Faust, or bowdlerized versions thereof, into the mouths of bourgeois while they conclude their most odious deals.[7] Unlike the rogues of the

Threepenny Opera, they no longer profess a materialistic philosophy but precisely the hand-me-down highmindedness which the German middle class tried so hard to maintain despite war, inflation and, now, Depression. The play, written mostly in the first Depression year, obviously owed much to George Bernard Shaw's *Saint Joan* and *Major Barbara*, and it gave a strong Marxist answer to Fritz Lang's famous movie *Metropolis*. Brecht held false idealism responsible for the acceptance of Nazi ideology, and he considered his materialist stage technique an appropriate antidote.

It is from this position that Marxist insights opened themselves to Brecht. He tells us that in writing *Saint Joan* he found it necessary to know how the Chicago commodity exchange operated, and looking for an answer in Marx's *Kapital*, he came upon answers to much broader questions. The Great Depression was knocking at the door, too, and Brecht had found a willing mentor in Fritz Sternberg, who was a *Weltbühne* contributor and had written a book on imperialism for the Frankfurt Institute for Social Research. But more important was Marxism as a critique of bourgeois ideology, and in this respect the decisive encounter was with Karl Korsch, author of *Marxism and Philosophy*, in 1929. Korsch had been expelled from the Communist party in 1926, and he used to meet with other dissidents to the left of the Communist party at the Café Adler in Berlin. Brecht and Alfred Döblin went there occasionally in 1930, but saw Korsch privately more often; probably Brecht met Sidney Hook there. Brecht did not really study Marxian economics, but was interested in Marxian dialectics. This was Korsch's specialty, and he also was alive to Brecht's concerns with developing a modern esthetics—much in contrast to the Party intellectuals, who had more and more fallen into a sterile Stalinist orthodoxy.[8]

But I must make a few reservations here. Brecht also saw many party Communists. With Wieland Herzfelde, John Heartfield, George Grosz, Hanns Eisler he shared artistic interests. In 1930 his friend, mentor, and sponsor Lion Feuchtwanger published a novel, *Success*, one of whose characters, a certain Pröckl, bears Brecht's features. Of him, another

character says: "You have been taken in by communism because from birth you have had no social instincts. What for
others is a matter of routine throws you when it is novel.
Poor man, you cannot empathize with people; you cannot
have sympathy with others; that's why you look for artificial
communication. Moreover, you are a puritan, you lack the
ability to have fun, and you have no charity."[9]

That may be unfair. But whoever knew Brecht was struck
indeed by his pose of coolness; as he had exhibited a cynical
hedonism in the first period, so now he painted his communism in the grey colors of sheer rationalism.

He also saw communism as a military, or perhaps Jesuitic
operation. In the oratorio he wrote with Eisler, The Measures
Taken, four Communists have been sent on a secret mission
into a foreign country. The youngest of them, however, com-
mits indiscretions: He takes pity on a toiling girl and lightens
her work for her, thus weakening her urge to rebel; he dis-
agrees with a merchant who expounds his exploiter's philosophy to him, instead of enlisting his help for a party under-
taking; finally he takes his mask off and leads workers into a
premature uprising, thus endangering the entire mission. His
comrades decide to kill him, and the chorus agrees with them.
Marxists might object that this is not the way a mass party
operates. Even under Stalin the Communist party was never
such a caricature. With just a few words changed, the Nazis
might produce the entire oratorio as a justification of their
Fehme murders.[10]

But Brecht's oratorio is concerned with politics only on the
surface; its real concern is the extinction of the individual. A
few months earlier, Brecht had written two didactic plays,
The Yes-Sayer and The Flyers, with very similar plots and
argument, except that the travelers are not emissaries of a
political party but in the first schoolboys and in the second a
group of crashed airmen. In either play a sick person must
consent to be abandoned. The theme is the overcoming of
individual pride, or even life, for the sake of the whole.
Brecht, who had shown his toughness first in the guise of
nihilism, now showed it in the disciplined form of commu-

nism. The theme of doing evil for the sake of good never left him throughout his life. It will appear later on in *The Good Woman of Setzuan* and in a deeply moving poem, "To Those Born Later":

> You who will emerge from the flood
> In which we have gone under,
> Remember
> When you speak of our failings
> The dark time too
> Which you have escaped. . . .
>
> [For we know only too well:]
> Hatred, even of meanness
> Contorts the features.
> Anger, even against injustice
> Makes the voice hoarse. Oh, we
> Who wanted to prepare the ground for friendliness
> Could not ourselves be friendly.
>
> But you, when the time comes at last
> That man is a helper to man,
> Think of us
> With forbearance.[11]

The Measures Taken opens the fourth phase: Brecht's total commitment to the party. The oratorio is not only ultra-Leninist in its conception of the party; it also condemns the leftish views Trotsky then held about the Chinese Revolution, and approves of the measure Stalin had taken against him—expelling him from the party in 1927 and from the country in 1929. At the time this procedure was called "liquidation" in Comintern language, but in 1930 dissidents were not yet shot.

Brecht the nihilist, who had despairingly doubted that there was anything stable in the world, had found a home that was stable. Some may detect a similar ambivalence between the anarchist and the disciplinarian in Jean-Jacques Rousseau. Obviously, Brecht's yearning could not be satisfied by the subtle and volatile Marxism of Korsch or the literary mysticism of Walter Benjamin; although he continued to see both of them, he also made fun of them. Like many others, he needed the hefty, self-assured Marxism-Leninism of the Communist party, the faith of an order rather than the self-critical analysis of intellectuals like himself. He despised intellectuals, and where his enemy was he knew all too well: in a world so full of doubts he could not doubt his own doubt. He rather accepted orthodoxy and discipline even in their most abstruse and ridiculous forms. He could declare in all seriousness that manufactured figurines showing Lenin in famous poses (pointing, writing, standing with his hands in his pockets) "are the most significant sculptures which the most progressive country in the world has produced." [12] He could be utterly offended that in the Swiss press "it is absolutely forbidden to write that freedom rules in the Soviet Union; whoever tries to plead for objectivity is called an agent of Stalin" (AJ, 8/19/42).

I once saw on his table Lenin's *Materialism and Empiriocriticism*, which was written against Machism—a subject Lenin surely did not understand and with which he dealt for purely factional intra-party reasons. I said: "Brecht, you don't have to waste your time; if you want to keep your respect for Lenin, don't read it." He grew very angry and put me in my place: "If it was worth Lenin's while to write it, it must be worth my time to read it." He had a totally reverential attitude to the sacred writings of Marx, Engels, Lenin, and Stalin, whom he always called "the classics," and even to the encyclicals of the sacred councils of the Comintern. After Hitler had come to power, I suggested that a discussion of the causes of our defeat was the first requirement for a comeback; he pointed to a resolution of the Central Committee which called the collapse of the labor movement an orderly retreat, and said: "How can we have suffered a defeat if we did not even fight?" Such sophistries were common when it was necessary to save the party's face.

Would a man do so much, and more, for a party to which he did not belong? Brecht denied under oath that he ever was a member, and that may well be true in a technical sense. [13] Like Arthur Koestler and other writers who might be more useful in their capacity of fellow travelers, he may have been asked to avoid formal membership. But his collaborator and companion, Grete Steffin, a member of long standing, was also his political commissar.

I come now to the fifth period, that of exile. To many refugees, even those who were not Communists, the Soviet Union appeared as the strongest and most reliable opponent of Hitler. To a man like Benjamin it was sacrilegious even to doubt the wisdom or sincerity of Stalin. Brecht's diaries reflect the struggle between Benjamin and Korsch for Brecht's soul. Brecht at the time had difficulties with the party, especially with the Communist culture popes in Moscow—Andrei Zhdanov, Alfred Kurella, and Georg Lukács, who were committed to "socialist realism" and who rejected Brecht's epic theater. A brief visit to Moscow had convinced Brecht that these people were very middle-class sentimentalists and that his archenemy Stanislavsky ruled the stage. He took residence in Denmark. When war overtook him in Scandinavia, he traveled, all the way through Siberia, to Hollywood, the Babylon of capitalist sinfulness, rather than stay in the Fatherland of the Workers.

Moreover, like Korsch, Brecht was not happy with the Popular Front tactics adopted by the Comintern in 1934. In his view, it blurred class confrontation and raised illusions among the workers. At the great Writers' Congress in the Paris Mutualité, 1935, which was supposed to enlist democratic intellectuals in the common cause, he read an appeal to overthrow capitalism first, after which Nazism would disappear of itself. He needed to see the world in black and white: on one side decadent, corrupt capitalism with its two helpers, the Social Democrats and the Fascists; on the other side the Soviet Union, virtue, and the workers of the world.

This had been the Communist party's view until 1934, and it had been responsible for the disastrous disunity of the left that facilitated Hitler's rise to power. When the Comintern finally, at its Seventh World Congress, abandoned this pernicious theory and the Soviet Union sought an alliance with France, Brecht held on to the view that fascism was nothing but a running dog of capitalism. Comparing the Nazi system with traditional capitalism, he found the former only "relatively worse" and in certain respects he even admired its greater efficiency and its "radicalism" which pleased him better than Social Democratic reform policies: "The Hitler regime is self-reliant capitalism; its policies are radical. Hitler's criticism of the Social Democrats and of the Frankfurt School is excellent."

In his ridiculous play, The Resistible Rise of Arturo Ui, he tries to show that nothing distinguishes gangsters, capitalists, and Nazis from each other.[14] Other plays of the exile period, too, suffer from Brecht's inability to differentiate between democratic and fascist methods of control. The most he will admit is that "the one conceals the violent aspects of the economy, the other conceals the economic nature of violence" (AJ, 12/15/40). This dogmatic Leninism carried over into the postwar period, when he opined that "to de-Nazify the Germans one will have to de-bourgeoisify them," a view which caused him to side with the East against the West Germans.

Some good plays present needless difficulties for the viewer because of a conflict between the author's healthy dramatic instincts and the shallow sociology he feels obliged to work into the drama. Thus Mother Courage, which appears as a moving exaltation of vitality in a suffering woman, was meant to show the insensitivity of a capitalist hawker; the Thirty Years War, of which the play shows an episode, was "the first capitalistic war," he explained.[15] He thought war, in particular "this war is the finest flower of capitalism so far, its last word, its purified, best version" (AJ, 4/14/41). And remembering that Lenin had rejected the notion of war guilt in 1914, he denied that Hitler was to blame for starting the war in 1939 any more than was "capitalism." Reading my essay on the structure of the German war economy, he almost triumphantly exclaimed: "It shows that the trusts have gained the upper hand over the state" (AJ, 8/28/43). When England was fighting its lonely battle against the rising tide of totalitarianism, he commented that they were only quarreling about the spoils (AJ, 12/15/40). A report on the American economy, dating back to pre-Pearl Harbor conditions, elicited the following confused, but highly significant speculations foreshadowing postwar theories of convergence: "The similarities between the two great movements, fascism and bolshevism, emerge better than their dissimilarities: planned economies, authoritarian states, all-powerful parties, both in parliaments and in civil military formations, the revolutionary forms, the hierarchies, the police systems, the propaganda methods, the myths, the waves of terror. The difference is, however, that this centralization is carried out by different classes." And he adds: "Perhaps the fascist counterrevolution can *erledigen* (in the double sense [of terminating and completing]) that dark phase which might embarrass the proletariat. All that can be done better by corporations than by soviets" (*AJ*, 10/27/41). Similar thoughts are expressed on reading Souvarine's book on Stalin (*AJ*, 7/19/43) and again after the war (*AJ*, 1/26/49). This shows that he was quite aware of the "dark" side of the dictatorship of the proletariat.

Brecht's relationship with the party in those years of comparative isolation can best be gauged from two of his most personal works. One is the moving "Legend of the Origin of the Book Tao-Tê-Ching on Lao-Tzu's Road into Exile," in which the emigrating sage writes down, at the request of a customs man, the essence of his wisdom: that the soft will overcome the hard.

1

Once he was seventy and getting brittle
Quiet retirement seemed the teacher's due.
In his country goodness had been weakening a little
And the wickedness was gaining ground anew.
So he buckled on his shoe.

2

And he packed up what he would be needing:
Not much. But enough to travel light.
Items like the book that he was always reading
And the pipe he used to smoke at night.
Bread as much as he thought right.

3

Gladly looked back on his valley, then forgot it
As he turned to take the mountain track.

And the ox was glad of the fresh grass it spotted
Munching, with the old man on its back
Happy that the pace was slack.

4

Four days out among the rocks, a barrier
Where a customs man made them report.
"What valuables have you to declare here?"
And the boy leading the ox explained: "The old man taught."
Nothing at all, in short.

5

Then the man, in cheerful disposition
Asked again: "How did he make out, pray?"
Said the boy: "He learnt how quite soft water, by attrition
Over the years will grind strong rocks away.
In other words, that hardness must lose the day."

6

Then the boy tugged at the ox to get it started
Anxious to move on, for it was late.
But as they disappeared behind a fir tree which they skirted
Something suddenly began to agitate
The man, who shouted: "Hey, you! Wait!

7

"What was that you said about the water?"
Old man pauses: "Do you want to know?"
Man replies: "I'm not at all important,
Who wins or loses interests me, though.
If you've found out, say so.

8

"Write it down. Dictate it to your boy there.
Once you've gone, who can we find out from?
There are pen and ink for your employ here
And a supper we can share; this is my home.
It's a bargain: come!"

9

Turning round, the old man looks in sorrow
At the man. Worn tunic. Got no shoes.
And his forehead just a single furrow.
Ah, no winner this he's talking to.
And he softly says: "You too?"

10

Snubbing of politely put suggestions
Seems to be unheard of by the old.
For the old man said: "Those who ask questions
Deserve answers." Then the boy: "What's more, it's turning cold."
"Right. Then get my bed unrolled."

11
Stiffly from his ox the sage dismounted.
Seven days he wrote there with his friend.
And the man brought them their meals (and all the smugglers were
    astounded
At what seemed this sudden lenient trend).
And then came the end.
12
And the boy handed over what they'd written—
Eighty-one sayings—early one day.
And they thanked the man for the alms he'd given,
Went round that fir and climbed the rocky way.
Who was so polite as they?
13
But the honor should not be restricted
To the sage whose name is clearly writ.
For a wise man's wisdom needs to be extracted.
So the customs man deserves his bit.
It was he who called for it.[16]

The play *Galileo* is another clue to Brecht's personal politics. It shows how the great scientist does not dare to defy
the church but secretly continues to pursue his studies. Asked
whether he meant to say that Galilei's recantation was a tactical maneuver intended to permit him to write the two great
dialogues, Brecht said: "No, the man is craven." Privately he
said that it would have been better for Galilei not to recant,
confident that someone would discover the foundations of
physics anyway. But he did not put that opinion into the
play.[17] For despite his difficulties, he needed the party more
than ever. The deeper reason was revealed to me in one
memorable conversation.

I went to see him about the Moscow trials. We were at a
crisis point in the Popular Front and at the height of the
Spanish Civil War, in which the Soviet Union was heavily
engaged. The trials, in this situation, were extremely embarrassing to the left, and I said to Brecht: "You are one of the
few people who might be listened to in Moscow; could you
not speak up?" His answer was amazing. He said: "In fifty
years people will have forgotten Stalin; but I want Brecht's
plays still to be performed then, and therefore I must stay

with the Party." So that was it! At the time I did not know
that Brecht had in his desk drawer the autobiographical stories of Herr Keuner, whom he describes as "without back-
bone. I of all people must outlive violence."[18] He also, at
about the same time, showed Benjamin a poem in which Stalin was compared to an ox that does much useful work and
therefore is given special food.[19] He liked to call Stalin "the
useful one."[20]

Brecht was convinced that communism would emerge as
the heir of European culture, and he wanted to be there to
share the future. He could not bear missing the bus of history. Therefore he had to be with Stalin when Stalin was in
the driver's seat. He had learned the lesson of historical inevitability all too well, far beyond his mentors' intentions. When
Korsch pointed out to him how Stalin discredited the cause
of socialism, he answered that one must distinguish between
government and society. Like Trotsky at the time, he felt that
Stalin would disappear and that socialism would remain; the
defense of the Soviet Union, therefore, had priority.

He defended Stalin's mock trials in public in his book of
political aphorisms,[21] though in private he mourned the disappearance of his friends, the actress Carola Neher (AJ, 1/39)
and the poet Sergei Tretyakov, his translator.[22] He continued
to see some dissidents who had not made their peace with
Western democracy. But in parables and arguments he kept
repeating to them his fundamental conviction that freedom is
not an eternal value but a petty-bourgeois prejudice.[23] Productivity is everything; Stalin's personality cult is explained
as a deliberate device to increase productivity (Me-ti, p. 89).
Like a new Machiavelli, he asserted that in all history "the
most beneficial institutions were created by crooks, while not
a few virtuous people stood in the way of progress" (p. 127).
Later, when Bruno Bettelheim published his observations on
the concentration camp, Brecht's diary burst out: "Interesting: the vanishing of individuality. . . . Such descriptions
should interest liberals who hold on to the notion of personality and who protest against the suppression of personal
freedom in the Soviet Union" (AJ, 9/20/44).

The analysis of the Stalin regime which Brecht confided to his diary, and even to *Me-ti* for publication at a later date, differed in nothing from Trotsky's: a regime that had begun as a revolutionary dictatorship but had fallen into the hands of bureaucrats. Yet, he refused to draw Trotsky's conclusions, and in *Me-ti*, he sided with Stalin even while admitting to Benjamin that the time to withdraw confidence had not come—yet.[24]

His confidence in the Soviet Union did receive a severe shock when Stalin allied himself with Hitler. His diary notes that Erika Mann, another political commissar, expects the Soviet Union to intervene on the side of the Western powers; it gives off a pained scream when instead the Russian hyena takes her share of murdered Poland; but then it consoles him almost jubilantly: "Hitler's war aim has been taken away from him. The Red Army marches into Europe" (*AJ*, 9/19/39). Nevertheless, he is disappointed that Stalin does not conduct the war as a revolutionary war, calling upon the peoples to rise; instead of creating soviets he uses Pan-Slav propaganda, Brecht notes scornfully. In winter, as Stalin invades Finland, Brecht wonders "whether the loss of sympathy among the world proletariat is worth the military advantages" (*AJ*, 12/24/39). Loss of sympathy! Brecht transforms an act of intellectual treason into a tactical mistake. Stalin still enjoys his "critical support"—but Brecht prefers to sit out the war in America.

After the war, Brecht went to East Germany, not without prudently arranging for Austrian citizenship and assigning the rights to all his past and future works to a West German publisher. The East German government, following a shrewd pattern throughout the satellite empire, spent considerable sums to attract writers and artists and to keep them happy. Non-communists like Arnold Zweig and Rudolf Leonhard went to live in East Berlin; they received comfortable villas at a time when workers had no coal to heat their homes. Brecht was given a lavish budget to organize a theater, the Berlin Ensemble, which became one of the foremost acting companies of the postwar period. Obviously, it had to produce "epic theater" for a reason that transcended his theory of art or—if one prefers—for a reason that lies at the heart of the theory.

For Brecht could have had no illusions about the regime they were installing in East Berlin. Even before he went there, he had jotted in his diary: "Since we had no revolution, we may have to incorporate the Russian model—I think [of it] with shuddering" (AJ, 12/26/47). He knew, and hated, the new culture czars: Johannes R. Becher, Willi Bredel, and Alfred Kurella; besides being Stalinists, they were also nationalistic—an abomination to Brecht. It is a miracle that the inevitable frictions between him and the Moscow-trained stalwarts did not end in a public showdown; but both sides avoided it—the others because they knew that Brecht was their greatest cultural asset, and he because he hoped, through the institution of the epic theater and the young actors and playwrights whom he trained, to plant a time bomb: a theater that would not allow its audience to settle down in complacent conformity but would force it to think, to debate, to scrutinize reality, eventually to take its rightful place in the building of socialism.

He went deliberately into the position of the sage who wrote the book Tao-Tê-Ching. One parable in the book Me-ti, which was published many years after Brecht's death, exemplifies this. A painter has sold to peasants a picture [illustrating Brecht's poem Lob des Lernens (In Praise of Learning)] which they did not like but bought because they felt sorry for him. Asked why they still had it, they replied: "The picture is as obtrusive as the painter. It hangs there and talks. It would yell if it were to be removed. It seems to fight. It is even intolerant and challenges the other pictures." [25]

When the East German workers grew impatient with the regime and in June 1953 rose against arbitrarily imposed work rules, Brecht did not openly support them but lent his public support to the government, while pleading behind the scenes that "workers who demonstrated in justifiable dissatisfaction [should] not be placed on the same footing as the provocateurs" and that "the errors committed on all sides" should be honestly debated. [26] He was impatient with the East German workers who failed to understand "the people's state in the form of dictatorship." But at the same time, he wished that the dictatorship would engage the workers in a dialogue and explain itself.

Later he wrote two poems, which were included in his "works" only after his death. The first says:

> After the uprising of the 17th June
> The Secretary of the Writers' Union
> Had leaflets distributed in the Stalinallee
> Stating that the people
> Had forfeited the confidence of the government
> And could win it back only
> By redoubled efforts. Would it not be easier
> In that case for the government
> To dissolve the people
> And elect another?[27]

But the other poem objects to the exploitation of his difficulties by jeering Westerners:

> Softly, my dear fellows . . .
>
> The Judas kiss for the artists follows
> Hard on the Judas kiss for the workers.
> The arsonist with his bottle of petrol
> Sneaks up grinning to
> The Academy of Arts. . . .
> Even the narrowest minds
> In which peace is harbored
> Are more welcome to the arts than the art lover
> Who is also a friend of the art of war.[28]

Brecht spoke up for greater freedom of artistic expression; dissenters like Professor Wolfgang Harich counted him as a friend. He also continued to visit Korsch whenever the latter was in West Berlin.[29] But he would not have received the Stalin Prize for Peace in 1955 had not the Soviet authorities been convinced of his absolute loyalty. He steadfastly denied that he was "sitting between two stools"; but to one visitor he remarked, jokingly, that the chair he was sitting on was

shaky.[30] He died before the Hungarian revolution could put
his loyalty to another test. My guess is that he would not
have gone West the way some of his colleagues did after the
new betrayal of socialist principles; for he had gone East when
he had fewer illusions about the regime than they. And he
honestly believed that the Western democracies, and in particular the West German government under Adenauer, were
inciting subversion in the East in anticipation of that war
which Stalin had averted so long. Brecht saw the cold war
mongers mostly in the West.

But here was also a source of disagreement with his comrades in East Germany. From his earliest utterances he had
been an opponent of war, of militarism, of nationalism in all
its manifestations. He was deeply committed to peace, and
while not averse to the use of violence in a revolution, he
was profoundly worried by the prospect that socialism would
defeat capitalism not by revolution but by war. He looked
with suspicion and anger at the revival of militarism in East
Germany, at the nationalistic spirit propagated by some of his
writer colleagues in East Berlin, at Bredel's and Becher's
blood-and-soil lyrics, at the deliberate cultivation in East Germany of the heroic Prussian traditions. War and the spirit of
war were for Brecht manifestations of that world that he had
set out to overcome.

Brecht was forced (or persuaded) to omit from a new edition of the *Home Breviary* a poem which speaks in unflattering terms of the Red Army, and to change the ending of *The
Trial of Lucullus* from a pacifist to an anti-Western meaning.
The collaboration between him and the East German authorities was uneasy, but we cannot doubt that both sides felt it
was productive. Brecht considered himself a soldier of the
revolution, and for him as a Marxist that was indissolubly
tied to the Eastern system of planned economy. He looked
with contempt at intellectuals who left because they felt
righteous about the failings of that system. He knew that he
was not a socialist writer and had no hope of participating in
that socialist future still lying beyond present expectations.
He was, according to his own definition (*AJ*, 8/5/40), a bour-

geois writer who had made the proletariat's cause his own. Their common aim was to "wipe all proletarian features from the face of humanity." He knew that the actual proletarians were far from seeing this goal; they had left him in the lurch badly in 1945 when they failed to use the advance of the Russian armies to start a revolution of their own. They had failed him in June 1953, when they followed demagogues, but on that occasion he confesses to have seen "the only force of the future." This was three years before his death. His last word was hope.

Requiem for a National Bolshevist

OF all the friends I had among German refugees in New York I had known Karl Otto Paetel for the longest time. I had met him first in the late 1920s when we were students at the University of Berlin. But although we were both in Professor Petersen's class on the German romantics, that was not where we would or could have become acquainted. Professor Petersen was a zealous nationalist who used his lectures to praise war, and Karl Otto believed in the Gothic revival as part of Germany's rebellion against the humiliating Treaty of Versailles—as a means to liberate her from Western, rationalistic capitalism. I, by contrast, loved romantic poetry and would have liked to find the link between that artistic expression of human yearnings and Marxism. But such connections, even if found, never provided a basis for conversation between us. In fact, we never discussed anything seriously because we knew that, even where we seemed to agree, we did so for different reasons.

However, it had pleased the university administration to assign, to all student political clubs, bulletin boards in one and the same big niche of the lobby. Each society had a right to hang its emblem there so that beneath it one could meet for lunch, to exchange news, or just to show the flag. Sometimes we had heated discussions there, and it was an extremely unwise decision to force socialists, republicans, communists, nationalists, nazis, and zionists into such close

Reprinted with permission from *Salmagundi* (Summer/Fall 1977).

contact. By sheer luck, we never had a brawl in the lobby during my time.

Anyway, it was there that I first saw Karl Otto, a lanky figure of somewhat military bearing, fair-haired and blue-eyed as one would imagine a Nazi student should look, but with a slightly quixotic air—an impression which might simply have suggested itself because he was heavily gesticulating in front of a man in a storm trooper uniform. Not being far away, I could hear that they were debating Nazi doctrine, and someone whispered into my other ear: "Watch that one, he is a dissident Nazi." It was good news that the Nazis were splitting, but the information was slightly incorrect. Karl Otto never considered himself a Nazi. Of the six possible combinations of the words national, social, and revolution he had formed the label to which he stuck to the end of his life: He was a "social-revolutionary nationalist." He considered Hitler a petty-bourgeois demagogue who, moreover, had betrayed whatever anticapitalistic tenets had been in his program, and who had substituted anti-Semitism and anticommunism for socialism so that he could hobnob with the capitalists. The true German revolution, by contrast, Karl Otto held, could only be "socialist" and it could be victorious only in alliance with the Russian revolution.

This latter idea interested Boris Goldenberg, a brilliant Russian Jew who loved political adventure and who had just joined the Communist party. He also had a soft spot for national revolutionaries and later was to get himself involved in a Caribbean liberation movement. At that time he directed the propaganda work of the Communist Student Group, and Karl Otto had just the right idea for him: a German revolution with the Red Army's backing, an ideological fight between the mysterious East and the all-too-civilized West, a sort of cultural revolution that was coming to the aid of a Bismarckian scheme to overthrow the system of Versailles. These were ideas which then were circulating among students. They could have been voiced by Naphta in Thomas Mann's *Magic Mountain*, and they had actually been voiced by Moeller van den Bruck, the translator of Dostoevsky who had introduced the term "Third Reich" into political literature. They were not foreign to Count Brockdorff-Rantzau, the German ambassador to Moscow, or to a host of ideologists who called themselves "national bolshevists." Even Lenin had occasionally toyed with the idea of exploiting German nationalism, and Radek had written editorials for Nazi papers.

Some such national revolutionaries actually came over to the communists. The most famous case was one Lieutenant Scheringer who had started a small Nazi coup on his own, was sent to confinement in a fortress (a privilege for political prisoners who were not workers), there had met some of our student friends, and suddenly shook the world with a manifesto proclaiming his conversion to Leninism. There were quite a few defections from Hitler in the early 1930s and, each time, Boris and Karl Otto thought they were splitting the Nazi party down the middle. Alas, most of the commotion went the other way; in his former comrades' eyes Karl Otto was not just a lost soul but a traitor.

Above all, national bolshevist views had also occurred to the German youth movement, a romantic reaction to capitalism, urbanism, materialism, and rationalism. Karl Otto came from the youth movement and was able to mouth its confused ideologies. Boris saw to it that Karl Otto could address student meetings where he denounced the establishment Nazis and predicted the national and social revolution of the Germans under the Red Army's benevolent auspices. He showed that one could be patriotic and yet collaborate with the Communists, or at least look favorably to the Russians. He rejected anti-Semitism; he was an authentic German who despised Hitler. We went to Karl Otto's meetings, not because we liked what he said but because Boris felt he needed support and protection. After all, it took courage to attack Hitler in front of two hundred storm troopers. By dint of facing the same danger and marching together, some of our crowd became good friends with Karl Otto. Although we considered his ideas rather fuzzy, or hardly understood him, we respected him as an honest, decent, upright man. But he always kept his distance in this company, for he wished to continue being accepted as a person of the right. Even while praising the Red Army he made it clear that he would never be a man of the left; his views were elitist and he could not accept our proletarian theories. Later he told me that his deepest desire had been to be recognized by us as a "revolutionary," for very few people on the right could be so classified; but even to achieve that he would not part with his Prussian values, his ideals of a military order and of the barracks socialism that Spengler was then preaching.

This persistence was hard to understand in Karl Otto, for as a person he was most unmilitary and un-Prussian; he had an innate aversion to work, discipline, order. His room looked like an antique shop or, rather, like a secondhand bookstore. In fact he was bookish to a fault; even when he had to run for his life, he still carried a carton of books with him. He lived mostly on cigarettes and wine and shared what little he had with comrades from the old youth movement. They had a common language and quaint reminiscences. Some had never adjusted to civilian life nor grown up to fill their place in society; others were desperadoes. He was different from them in one respect, however, which matters in this particular setting. He did not love nature, not a bit, although this was incumbent upon a youth leader. He was a bohemian, or even, if that is possible for a Prussian socialist, a libertarian. He was always interested in liberation movements around the world (though of course not women's liberation); later on, in New York, he would support Castro, Ho Chi Minh, and Nasser, and even translate Beat literature into German.

But I am anticipating. When Hitler came to power, Karl Otto had to flee; soon a kangaroo court sentenced him to death—fortunately in absentia. (With a mixture of irony and glee, he often told his friends that a Nazi book on race included his photo: the prototype of the Nordic race.) He sought asylum in Sweden, but the socialist government of that country told him ever so politely that it could not afford to antagonize Hitler just for the sake of one "dissident Nazi." He made his way to Prague and later to Paris, where he was cut off from his own true comrades and brothers-in-arms, the national revolutionaries, the youth movement, the romantics, the mystics. Of necessity he was drawn to us more closely. His companions had to be Jews, communists, socialists, homosexuals. Boris was in Paris, and a girl of our crowd became Karl Otto's companion for a while; but it was rare that someone turned up in our meetings whom Karl Otto would spontaneously call "comrade."

The French government had even less understanding than the Swedish for the fact that there could be Germans, and patriotic ones at that, who were against Hitler. The first months of the war we were both in French internment camps; we got to America after the defeat of France.

But in America Karl Otto had to undergo his deepest change. For most refugees there was no problem when war came to America; in fact we had prayed for that moment to come. Every anti-Fascist, every democrat had to lend his hand to the war effort. But Karl Otto was no democrat and no liberal. He felt no obligation to defend either Western capitalism or Russian bolshevism. He was a German patriot who feared another Versailles after the war. Yet he worked in an intelligence office in New York. He felt that after the war there might still be a German revolution, and certain events seemed to point in his direction: Marshal Paulus with two hundred thousand men capitulated at Stalingrad and formed a committee to establish that friendship which Karl Otto had preached all his life. But on the day of Stalingrad he came to me and asked anxiously: Is it not time now to make peace? I replied: With whom? The answer came on July 20, 1944, when the flower of German nobility and officers rebelled against Hitler, lost ignominiously, and were executed en masse. Karl Otto felt that they had saved Germany's honor, though they could not save Germany. From that moment on, our relations grew tense again. We were looking forward to victory; he, to defeat.

One should have thought that the situation in Germany after the war would be hospitable to people of Karl Otto's persuasion. Why did this people in ruins not rebel? Why was there no fertile soil for the propaganda of national revolution? Karl

Otto was one of the first refugees to go back to Germany—
and return deeply disappointed. His Germany was dead; patriotism had become meaningless. He found friends but no
hope. He was of course indignant about the division of Germany, and for the sake of German unity he opposed NATO,
the founding of the Federal Republic, the cold war, American
policy. Although he had never been a pacifist, he now
preached neutralist philosophy. Mistakenly perhaps, he campaigned for Stevenson, Kennedy, McCarthy, and McGovern.
At his death, he had traveled far from his original commit-
ments, though he had not given up any of his basic philosophical attitudes. A book dedicated to him on his sixtieth
birthday was entitled *Upright Between the Stools*.

Karl Otto published books on the German youth movement
and on the ideology of national bolshevism. His life epito-
mizes the strange kinship between the romantic effusions of
the German youth movement and the tough policies of Third
World dictators. Military or intellectual elites presume to
make "revolutionary" history behind their peoples' backs, to
introduce "socialism" without democracy but in the name of
nationalism. They are liberationist without being liberal,
egalitarian without being humanitarian, and highly rational
in the execution of their plans without, however, believing
in Reason. The cultural revolution which they propose to
carry out does not bring culture to their nations; on the contrary, it is nourished by the anti-cultural, anti-intellectual
ideologies that were first developed in the murky grounds of
Richard Wagner's Niflheim, and have come down to us via
the proto-fascist movements of the first quarter of this century.

Karl Otto was too decent and too noble to draw from his
ideology the conclusions which the plebeians found so attractive. He was alienated from his own nation and never
managed to join any other. He had left the positions from
which he had started out, but he remained true to himself—
till his death in 1976.

11

Erich Mühsam (1878–1934):
A Centenary Note

IF there were justice, we would be commemorating the centenary of Erich Mühsam, the poet, the rebel, the irrepressible bohemian, the anarchist, the comrade. The Nazis killed him in a concentration camp after subjecting him to cruel and humiliating tortures; his clumsy appearance, recalling a Jewish teamster from the *shtetl*, was apt to excite the sadistic instincts of Storm Trooper types. They hardly needed to remember that, back in 1919, he had been "the enemy," one of the major participants of the abortive Räte Republic in Munich.

Some of us wondered, in 1933, why it was just Mühsam, of all the innocuous bohemians, whom they arrested, and we speculated whether by mistake the Nazis might have used an old blacklist. But reviewing Hitler and his crowd from hindsight now, I am sure that there was no mistake. They never forgot one they hated, and even as chancellor, Hitler remained the provincial he had always been. Back in Munich, Mühsam, a libertarian and mildly successful littérateur, had angered him. Mühsam played chess in the famous Café Megalomania and was the friend of all the artists who would not recognize Hitler's picture-postcard drawings. The irony of it was that the two had one thing in common: an estheticist idea of politics, an unprofessional, visionary expectation that the establishment would crumble at the sounding of the trumpets of Jericho. Mühsam conceived of his Räte (councils)

Republic as one great festival where everybody would love his fellow men; Hitler saw his revolution as a series of parades.

Mühsam's poetry was satirical and polemical, almost entirely in the service of the revolution as he understood it, or of humanity as he saw it—in the shape of the child, the vagabond, the outlaw. His most delightful verse is "The Merry Tale of an Elephant for Well-Behaved Children." As a pledge to his creed he was always poor, shared what little he had, and expected his friends to share what they had with him.

Of friends he had more than others have acquaintances— from Frank Wedekind to Else Lasker-Schüler, from the anarchist and avant-gardist Franz Pfemfert to the Social Democratic minister of justice, Gustav Radbruch, who visited him in jail. (For in contrast to Hitler, who served only one year for the Beer Hall Putsch, Mühsam spent five years at the fortress Niederschönenfeld).

He contributed to every avant-garde magazine, especially *Der Sturm* and *Die Aktion*, even to *Die Fackel* before Karl Kraus decided that he should be the only contributor. He performed in every cabaret. He published a monthly, which he wrote himself from A to Z; it was called *Kain* and dutifully supported every unpopular cause, from homosexuality to terrorism. He wrote the Max Hölz March in honor of the guerrilla leader who in 1920 haunted Thuringia for a few weeks.

Anarchism does not seem to be capable of a theory, and Erich Mühsam was certainly not interested in theory. He adhered to a sentimental socialism which combined all the worst features of Proudhon, Tolstoy, and Oscar Wilde, and he was closest to the saintly, noble and sensitive Gustav Landauer, the leader of the Munich Räte Republic and its first martyr.

Although he had written for Social Democratic papers before the first world war, and during the war kept in close contact with dissident Social Democrats, he never joined any party, not even the Spartacus group. He had no use for Marxism and organization and no understanding of economics. His socialism was neither one of planning nor one of nationalization. But after his release from jail he worked for front organizations of the Communist party, notably Red Aid, which raised money for political prisoners; he agitated for their liberation and denounced the political justice system.

With a childlike confidence he believed, to his last day, and even in the concentration camp, that eventually "humanity must prevail," and for all the scorn he heaped on the party bosses he never doubted that they would come around if only "the masses" would take the lead. Somehow, we need people like Erich Mühsam—or rather I should say: we would be lost the day we stopped feeling that we needed them.

MOTIFS

[12]

Irrationalism and the Paralysis of Reason: The Festering Sore

WHEN in 1885 Michael Georg Conrad started publishing a review, *Die Gesellschaft*, he said its purpose would be to "liberate literature from the dictatorship of high-school girls and old ladies of either gender." Bismarck's Reich having been consolidated, the citizens felt they should make up for the political revolution they had missed, by staging at least a cultural revolution. In the arts and sciences, there was ferment everywhere; sociology, psychology, and philosophy opened new frontiers. Architecture rid itself of baroque models and, in the big cities, created a functional, businesslike style. The intellectual avant-garde decided it had to represent urban culture and to deal with its very own problems, for better or worse but, at any rate, honestly. Its youthful zeal would overcome all the old traditions. That was how Gerhart Hauptmann's memoirs described a time of great hopes and new insights, where new fountains of energy and lust for life were flowing, where a new community was visualized, where a new culture, almost a counterculture, would come into being.

In the following decade the search for "the New" grew ever more intense. As Stefan Zweig saw it, "We found the new because we were looking for it, because we were starved for something that would be our own, . . . not our fathers'. In

Translated, and reprinted with permission from Horst Albert Glaser, ed., *Deutsche Literatur—eine Sozialgeschichte* (Hamburg: Rowohlt, in press).

this way our generation sensed, before our teachers became aware of it, that a revolution was brewing, or at the very least a transvaluation of values. The good, solid old masters—Gottfried Keller, Ibsen, Brahms, the painter Wilhelm Leibl—carried, we felt, all that circumspection of a secure world."[1]

This passage identifies the themes of a changeover of generations, even if to begin with there may have been just a literary-esthetic changeover. The new sensibility went with the new images of the world: a new image of man, of his relations to others, to himself, to God; a new attitude toward children, toward the other sex, in fact toward sex itself. The term coined for this new attitude was *Lebensreform*. Even people who were against all those newfangled notions could put forward their arguments only by newly discovering the old values or by finding in them new points of view. Some looked to the faraway shores of social and human liberation; others dug deep into the soul, the primeval world. They all basked in the joy of discovery; progress was exploding in all directions.

At that, there were two kinds of progress. One could see it as a straight line of achievements—as exploring a piece of geography which had been white on the map but hardly promised major surprises. Or else, one was willing to open new worlds—to create them if necessary; progress would happen in leaps and bounds with changes so bold as to call seemingly unshakable axioms into question.

Of course the transvaluation of values demanded by Nietzsche made its way by very slow degrees, though what Nietzsche really had in mind was less important than what it meant to the citizen. In the first place, a pagan-aristocratic moral was to be substituted for the Christian-bourgeois one. But soon this led to the problem of morality itself. After all, one could no longer exalt the new values as absolute, "higher" values; one could merely say that they better gratified real esthetic needs and fit more closely into a given life style, or— the main point—more effectively served racial or class interests. In England they called it pragmatism; Germans veiled the new truths in poesy and prophecy.

In the second place, one could no longer presume a perfect and lasting harmony between goodness, beauty, and truth. The value system was unmasked as a function of the particular life situation, as *relative*, as subject to existing life interests.

Where Marx conceived these interests as essentially rational, Nietzsche postulated the "will to power" which needed no vindication by reason. In a poetic vein, Nietzsche tied the realm of ideals to the Apollonian, the urge of the drives (which he also called the wisdom of the body) to the Dionysian. His treatise against David Friedrich Strauss, the humanist author of *Der alte und der neue Glaube* (1872), shows what he had in mind by rehabilitating the demonic. He resented the smug belief of Strauss, the "educated philistine" (in *Unzeitgemässe Betrachtungen I*, 1873), that Christian morality was going to stay valid even when "God was dead." Strauss claimed he had inherited the classics' cultural values; let them, said Nietzsche, decay in their bookcases, let sterile philologists write their innocent exercises about them—they will never help to build vigorous personalities.

So, following in Nietzsche's footsteps, his epigone Alfred Bäumler declared that "overcoming Weimar" with its refined humanism was the thing to do; and Kaiser Wilhelm II exhorted a conference for school reform: the task is not to train Greek boys but German men. In 1914 German army officers said proudly that they carried "the Zarathustra" in their knapsacks.

This attitude was thoroughly conservative; the remarkable thing, however, is that seen as a method it gave a thoroughly modern, even rejuvenating, impression. It was meant to fend off the new "mass age" with its commercial-militaristic "Reich," and at the same time it embodied that age's own ideology. What the age most particularly insisted upon was to follow any impulses for their own sake, to sever each purpose from the framework of a higher responsibility, to dwell "beyond good and evil" as Nietzsche claimed. Georg Lukács branded the movement that took off from Nietzsche as "the destruction of reason"; but this destruction liberated forces that helped the German spirit achieve unheard-of "break-throughs"—a very fashionable term at the time. All cultural values were completely secularized; science was made "value-free" as Max Weber put it and thus could be used for the most diverse purposes; as a matter of principle, all motivations were deemed to be of equal value. Pluralism of values, under imperialism, became a thing of value.

As early as 1891, the philosopher Wilhelm Windelband remarked that Nietzsche's anti-plebeian philosophy made him popular with the very people he despised. And even before Darwin, Herbert Spencer asserted that in the social struggle victory went to "the most competent" whom he naively identified as "the best." Development equaled progress, he felt, and progress justified a good deal of the misery created by early capitalism. Of course it also justified colonialism, which by now was winning the German liberals' adherence, too.

This economic doctrine of the prevailing liberalism, also called "social Darwinism," was considered the strictly scientific fruit of the new young science, sociology. On the continent, Ludwig Gumplowicz championed it vigorously. He proved, strictly "scientifically," that all of mankind's dreams ran counter to the realities of social life. Richard Wagner stated the same truth, profoundly, in his self-denial motive and Johann Strauss, frivolously, with "Lucky is he who can forget what cannot be changed." Gumplowicz did not believe in progress and underpinned his historian's pessimism with an anthropology which taught that racial struggle is the lever of action throughout the world.

Ludwig Woltmann, in his *Political Anthropology* (1903), said that society's division of labor rested on racial dissimilarities. The Nordic race, by divine mandate, was striving to dominate other races. While imperialists everywhere pleaded the cultural mission of the white nations, the Germans from the start conceived their global politics as the deployment of a specifically German "will to power." According to Heinrich von Treitschke and Hans Delbrück, this was the way for Germany to prove its manliness. Joseph Schumpeter discovered in imperialism an atavistic instinct that had forgotten its original purpose: the Germans sought power for its own sake and heartily despised the British who applied power for profit's sake.

To escape any suspicion of being utilitarians, the German ideologists bound themselves over to a faith in destiny which grossly contradicted their vaunted "idealism." This faith had nothing to do with old-time determinism; it derived from German historians' insistence on justifying whatever existed or, as they preferred to put it, whatever had grown into existence (*das Gewordene*). Wilhelm Dilthey's method of "empathy" and "understanding" categorically ruled out any judgment that criticized more than unimportant details; Friedrich Meinecke wrote (*Cosmopolitanism and the National State*, 1908), referring in so many words to the Prussian military state: "That which springs from the innermost essence of a natural being cannot be immoral." If destiny had chosen the Prussian state to solve the German question, and Bismarck to fulfill that decision, the new Reich now had to follow the fiat of the given situation and proceed from realpolitik to power politics. For in the final analysis, seen from the vantage point of German Historismus, a nation's destiny derives from the state personality and the structure of that nation itself. Similarly, Otto von Gierke argued in his many-volume *Deutsches Genossenschaftsrecht* (1881) that the state is not composed of individuals but has preceded them. What is more, the German historians believed that this unit and the thing it stood for pertained to Germans in particular; and the more deeply the Reich involved itself in global politics, the stronger grew the feeling that the individual existed for the sake of the state.

Add to this the race doctrine, itself oriented toward German "destiny," and political anti-Semitism (a term introduced by Wilhelm Marr in 1879). A professor of Semitic languages, Bötticher, had since 1873 been publishing his *Deutsche Schriften* under the pen name of Paul de Lagarde, preaching the Teutons' liberation from Rome and Judaism, the foundation of a German-pagan church, and the abolition of urban culture, of capitalism, newspapers, paper currency, and public schools: "Let us be not liberal but liberated; not conservative but German." For Eugen Dühring the decline (predicted by Marx) of small business meant "the victory of Jewry over Germanism." Konstantin Franz, a Catholic-romantic latecomer, demanded elimination of Jews from public life. The political economist Werner Sombart established a kinship between Jewish spirit and the spirit of capitalism. Adolf Bartels, a teacher of German philology, listed eight hundred Jewish writers who were displacing Germans from German culture. Adolf Stoecker, court chaplain, founded a Christian Social party; in Reichstag elections up to a dozen representatives won election as "anti-Semites." The Conservative party, too, adopted a "Christian" plank in its platform and supported the Pan-German program, which proposed that Germany rule the world on a racist basis.

In 1899 Richard Wagner's son-in-law, Houston Stewart Chamberlain, published a widely read, fuzzy-romantic inventory of all race myths, *The Foundations of the Nineteenth Century*. This earned him a compliment from the kaiser—a letter describing how the book had awakened in him "all that is primordial-Aryan-Teutonic [all das Ur-Arisch-Germanische] which has been dormant in Me, which has been layered in mighty strata, which has had to work its way up in hard struggle, which has come into open enmity to old tradition, and which has often expressed itself in bizarre ways as an obscure presentiment." It was a fitting comment on the book.

As a science, the race doctrine was rather rickety. As a political ideology, after the economic boom and bust of the early 1870s, it was able to attract those petty-bourgeois who had been frightened by the rush of urban-capitalist development. As a myth, it was the Germanolatry of stuffed shirts making commencement speeches, fed by Felix Dahn's and Gustav Freytag's historical novels, and closely bound up with other myths centered around two themes: the German race's unique spiritual essence and the destruction, by the Western-Jewish Enlightenment idea, of the German idea of community. Like some nations who were outstripped by other nations' modernization, the Germans flaunted their "soul" and their "depth"; especially educated people, the first to sense in themselves the effects of capitalist-urban alienation, were apt to find spiteful comfort in this self-conceit. Walther Rathenau experienced the mechanization process as "de-Teutonizing" and charged the Jews with narrow-minded purpose-worship: "Never before has mankind been dominated this thoroughly by the force of reason. As yet, this force is far from having reached its zenith; but it already carries the germ of death. At the bottom of its heart it dreads itself and longs for liberation from the chain of purposefulness."[2]

We find similar feelings in Thomas Mann's *Reflections of a Non-Political Man*, written during the war (published in 1919), but also as early as 1891 in Julius Langbehn's *Rembrandt als Erzieher* (published anonymously), which strongly influenced subsequent generations.

No doubt many of the stimuli sociology received from German ideology were quite valuable. Ferdinand Tönnies' *Community and Society* (1887) is a classic work of world literature; but no one can help hearing its nostalgic overtones. In contrasting *Gemeinschaft* with *Gesellschaft* the author dreads the loss of old community relations: "The big city and society are the nation's death." German sociology never got over this fear, and it also appears in Georg Simmel's *Philosophy of Money* (1900) as well as in Max Weber's studies on the spirit of capitalism, on modern accounting mentality and bureaucracy, and most distinctly in his sigh: "The world has been robbed of its magic."

Since German sociology had a regretful-critical attitude to capitalism, we should not interpret Weber's famous treatise, *The Protestant Ethic and the Spirit of Capitalism* (1904), as a rebuttal to historical materialism. His inquiry did not mean to determine whether the Reformation had created capitalism or vice versa, but whether there was an "elective affinity" between the two. Weber planned to explore scientifically the correlation between social and economic occurrences on the one hand, emotional development and ideas on the other. In the same way, Max Scheler laid the foundation of the sociology of knowledge. All these scholars sought to research irrational motives, but the research itself and its purposes were rational. And here is the difference: Charlatans raved about the irrational and thought they had intuitive knowledge of it; real thinkers sought to explore it and its roots.

Incidentally, most of these pioneers of a new science were liberals. Occasionally they would criticize the emperor's policies; later they would help build the Weimar Republic. Tönnies and Meinecke lived long enough to have the Nazis fire them from their university jobs. Yet, they were not democrats; rather they were elitists. Some worked with the "Society for Social Politics" and were gently derided as "socialists of the lectern" (Kathedersozialisten); but at most they wanted a "social emperor." Theodor Mommsen, who in 1902 received the Nobel Prize for literature, sided with Caesar in his Roman History (1854/56); Max Weber could conceive of no other way out of the mass-democracy dilemma than through a "charismatic leader," whom he thought he had found in Pastor Friedrich Naumann. Naumann, after leaving Stoecker, became leader of the Progressive party and changed it along social-liberal lines; he advocated a nonmilitaristic social imperialism.

Progressive though these men were in many ways, they shared the basically anti-revolutionary, anti-Enlightenment views of German Historismus—so easily used for patriotic apologies during the first world war. Even after the war, when Troeltsch in hindsight tried to take the edge off this antagonism, he was carried away into polemics against Western embourgeoisement with its cosmopolitan-egalitarian ethics, and against the mechanistic-utilitarian spirit of natural law. Beyond all that, he praised the German spirit of community, in which personality could thrive best: there the contract, here the tie; there progress, here development; there the unspecific-national, here the individual-heroic. Sombart concisely expressed this contrast in the title of his book, Merchants and Heroes (Händler und Helden), published during the war, while Klages extolled the German soul and called upon the tellurian forces rearing up against the shackles of reason.

They all were protagonists of this "conservative revolution" which was to reestablish the rule of the organic, primitive element over the artificial structures of civilization. In the publications of Diederichs Publishers and their magazine, *Die Tat* (started in 1909), these views found eloquent expression. Wilhelm Dilthey's "philosophy of life" as well as Hans Driesch's vitalistic biology supplied the scientific props.

Dilthey (older than Nietzsche, but for a long time eclipsed by the younger man's explosive power) taught that there were two kinds of sciences, the ones which "explain" and the ones which "understand." Thus, he became the father of modern hermeneutics and, indirectly, of Gestalt theory. He replaced the prevalent psychology, which dissected man into disparate traits, with a holistic appreciation of his character structure. In ideas, and *a fortiori* in *Weltanschauungen*, he saw precipitates of a fundamental life feeling; in a way he thereby anticipated Karl Jaspers' *Psychologie der Weltanschauungen* (1919). Dilthey tried to make the world of irrational experience accessible to rational analysis, but by being essentially an artist and uncertain in his conceptualizations, he prevented his inspirations from growing into a school of thought.

At the same time the Frenchman Henri Bergson, making the most of quite similar methods of intuition, was more influential. He elucidated the message of vital experiences with his catchwords, *élan vital* and *évolution créatrice*. Also at the same time Edmund Husserl, with his phenomenological vision of *eidos*, created the methodological space for this kind of abstract philosophizing which claimed to comprehend real experience.

No matter whether they called it "the wisdom of the body" (Nietzsche), "spirit" (Croce), "élan vital" (Bergson), the Id or Unconscious (Freud), the "archetype" (Jung), "intuition" (Dilthey), or "the demonic" (Thomas Mann), all these thinkers were aware that a force was there that could not be ruled by reason but that, on the contrary, made use of it.

Then there was Driesch's breakthrough in biology. From the observation that a sea-urchin's egg, part of which has been artificially excised, can nonetheless produce sound offspring, he concluded that organisms have been given an entelechy. Johann Jakob von Uexküll, starting out from similar experiments, arrived at the conception of organic "structures." Following these trains of thought, a scientific definition of the "soul" seemed possible. All this, again, was strictly scientific; but popular philosophy used it as evidence for irrational or religious tendencies.

Biology was on the rise. Where physics had served as the paradigm of science, now biology seemed to have taken its place; the concept of "the organic" was pitted against "mechanistic" materialism. Many failed to realize that by using vitalistic terms they were merely embellishing a crude biological materialism with pseudo-spiritualistic mysticism. Thus, Wilhelm Bölsche, in his three-volume *Liebesleben in der Natur* (1911), eroticized creation. Even the monism of Ernst Haeckel, the biologist, and of Wilhelm Ostwald, the chemistry scholar, introjected a living "soul" into matter and "overcame" the body-soul hiatus. Haeckel's *Riddle of the Universe* (*Die Welträtsel*, 1899) which within a short period sold 100,000 copies, ventured to understand all of nature, from a dead rock to feeling and thinking man, as a chain of ever-more-complex developments created by an ever-consistent life force—though that implied endowing every blob of albumen with consciousness. Ostwald, in his *Philosophy of Nature*, claimed "wisdom" for his "principle of energy."

In this way people's faith in the power of science well-nigh came to turn into a new mysticism or nature religion. They poeticized nature and estheticized science; perhaps it was not by accident that at this very moment they attributed to nature the one thing that man seemed to be most disastrously losing in the hubbub of the big city: his soul.

Eduard von Hartmann, in his *Philosophie des Unbewussten* (1869), had tried rather ineptly to restore the honor of the alogical. Although in higher circles this epigone of Schopenhauer's was well liked insofar as such people thought his writings could be used as an antidote against the spreading agnosticism, obviously such crass idealism could not combat the rising crass materialism. There seemed to be a better bet:

neo-Kantian philosophy. After the turn of the century, this mode of thought became popular among the educated, especially the liberal educated, and inspired a few outstanding works. Neo-Kantianism circumscribed the natural sciences and at the same time pointed out the limits of their relevance, thus saving the independence of the spirit from the frightening causality nexus and from sociological historiography as it had just then been developed in England and France.

Hippolyte Taine had drawn a superb picture of the "origins of contemporary France" as a great movement of masses wherein the individual's actions were submerged. Karl Lamprecht then offered a comprehensive, twelve-volume *German History* (1894 ff.). Building on Wilhelm Wundt's *System der Psychologie* (1889), he described a line of developments: from the "symbolic" age to the "typifying," to the "conventional," and finally to the "individualizing" age; for the present time he added the stages of "sensualism" and "sensitivity." Every nation and every culture, he felt, had to go through these stages. Lamprecht was so influential that after Treitschke's death, in 1896, he could apply for the position of chief editor of the prestigious *Historische Zeitschrift*; but the traditionalistic followers of Ranke prevented this invasion of "materialism" into German historiography. In the end Meinecke got the job, helped by his friendship with the south German neo-Kantians.

Heinrich Rickert, in his important work *Die Grenzen der naturwissenschaftlichen Begriffsbildung* (1896), drew a strict borderline between the "nomothetic" (law-giving) natural sciences and the "idiographic" or individuating cultural-social sciences or humanities (*Geisteswissenschaften*). The latter deal with the unique event or experience which will never be repeated and therefore can never be predicted nor probed by experiment; they deal with the realm of freedom, meaning spiritual, inner freedom—personal freedom rather than the citizen's freedom. The natural sciences, by contrast, can only explore and follow their own laws.

German liberalism has always cherished the individual and despised the masses. More and more intensely, the problem of agglomeration (*Vermassung*) or "automatization" came to be discussed by neo-Kantians and their friends: Simmel, Scheler, Emil Lask, Meinecke, Weber. They all belonged to that tired, resigned middle class which, while appalled by the enormities that the ruling system had spawned—beginning with the unpredictable kaiser—dreaded nothing as much as what might follow. A few of them, like Hermann Cohen and Paul Natorp, were ethical socialists. Although some of their studies, like those on alienation, point to our present problems, on the whole this philosophy retained its commitment to nineteenth-century issues and stayed loyal to the rational ideals of classical German philosophy. The same was true of the phenomenological research initiated by Husserl.

But there were revolutionizing impulses: on the one hand Nietzsche's catchwords, which grew effective around the turn of the century, on the other certain scientific discoveries, which were interpreted by some popular philosophers, though perhaps incorrectly, as vindications of irrationalistic and antirationalistic views. In biology, Hugo de Vries (*Die Mutationstheorie*, 1900) rediscovered Mendel's law of heredity, which seemed to contradict the old adage that there are no leaps in nature, or at least to offer chance an opening into the rules of nature's law. Then Driesch published his *Philosophie des Organischen* (1908), and J. S. Haldane's concept of holism was to corroborate his views. Quite unlike Haeckel's matter "animated by soul" (*beseelt*), a purposeful intelligence seemed to be at work here. In contradiction to the omnipotence of causality, which determined the natural sciences and threatened to seize the social sciences, from Dilthey's vitalism teleological principles were now deduced. We find them, applied to the life of nations, in Rudolf Kjellén's *The State as an Organism* (1915, 1917), in Meinecke's conception of Historismus, and later in Spengler's morphology of culture. While Uexküll's behaviorism never got a foothold in Germany, Driesch himself, by the obscure language of his organism theory, abetted its misuse for mystical-reactionary theories of state. The scientific world view had been put on the defensive; everywhere the revived romantic tradition, with weapons forged by the latest scientific insights, attacked science's claim to supremacy. At this late date, Enlightenment still was the enemy to be battled because it still smelled so suspiciously of democracy and egalitarianism.

In the past, the world view of mechanistic materialism had mainly been based on physics; but by now the hardest blows it suffered were felt by physicists. To be sure, certain axioms still were held to be irrefutable: that behind the appearances there was a *Ding an sich* (thing in itself) to be visualized as corporeal; that its relations to other bodies were subject to definite quantitative proportions; that the next solar eclipse could be predicted to the split second. These assumptions were so evident that Emil Du Bois-Reymond, in his famous *Ignoramus-Ignorabimus* lecture (1880), thought he could prove the existence of the unrecognizable simply by stating that the mechanical natural laws could not be applied just anywhere; he could not conceive of a different order of natural laws.

Then there was the idea of the cosmic ether, which once had inspired lyrical poets. It was imagined as a fine substance, solid enough to carry light waves, yet ethereal enough not to produce any ether wind against the earth's rotation. These absurdities were discarded by James C. Maxwell (1831–1879), who replaced the ether with an electric field and suggested: From now on, let us regard all metaphysical assumptions and corporeal models as just illustrative analogies; let no researcher pretend that prior to his research he knows the nature of what he is researching. Then, in 1889, Heinrich Hertz demonstrated the identity of electromagnetic, heat, and light waves; he no longer saw what happened in the electromagnetic field as a mechanical reaction of material units, but dissolved all matter into energy. The discovery of radioactivity, and the atomic physics derived from it, undermined the faith in the immutability of matter and the "thingishness" of the world.

In 1900 Max Planck, with his quantum concept, challenged the traditional ideas of the continuity of the physical world, which had been shared by Newton and the man in the street.

He proved that radiant energy is not emitted in a continuous flow but in discrete quanta. Later on, Einstein demonstrated that this quantum theory was universally valid and determined the structure of the universe. Based on this, Niels Bohr constructed his atom model, in which the minimal quantum played a part too.

For subatomic processes, therefore, the physicists had to recast the law of causality: there are indeed leaps in nature, but they can be predicted only as statistical probabilities. Determinism, up to then unquestioned, had been shaken, and many were eager to infer premature analogies for philosophy.

Even more exciting: Einstein's *The Special Theory of Relativity* (1905). So far everyone had supposed that whenever two experiments yielded conflicting results, better experiments would, finally, prove one of the results (or indeed both) erroneous and confirm the other one (or else, a third one). Einstein suggested modifying Euclid's and Galileo's mathematical-physical axioms in a way that would get rid of the contradiction. For instance, while we hear the siren of a passing ambulance becoming higher or lower depending on its relative movement, light waves have always the same speed, regardless of whether the observer approaches the light source or is receding from it. Einstein explained the phenomenon by no longer viewing space and time as givens, independent of each other, but putting in their place the observer's four-dimensional continuum. In the same way, he said, gravity is not a characteristic of things but inheres in their relationship to this continuum. And the result of these revolutionary ideas: Mass can be transformed into energy—the famous formula $E = mc^2$, which forty years later was to make history.

At that time, however, few laymen took note of this revolution; even scholars lacked the mathematical education to make use of it. (Ernst Cassirer, for one, in his *Substanzbegriff und Funktionsbegriff*, 1910, explained the new principles of natural science without mentioning Planck or Einstein.) Just the same, a certain uneasiness crept into the popular philosophy of the monthly reviews. The epistemological implications of the new natural sciences seemed threatening; sometimes it was even said, erroneously, that research itself had become untrustworthy and could perhaps produce postulates only. If even mathematics, the safest of all sciences, could be declared "subjective," who could blame obscurantists and miracle-believers for exploiting an opportunity to reconquer the territory lost in the nineteenth century? Spiritualism, occultism, various Oriental cults, theosophy, anthroposophy, faith healing, Jehovah's Witnesses found their followers in Germany.

Only the major churches failed to profit from the crisis of the sciences. They lost members when the secret was unveiled that the world was different from the way it looked to the naive eye. Agnosticism spread out and found its philosophical expression in empiriocriticism, founded by Ernst Mach and Richard Avenarius.

Both of them rejected all metaphysics. A thing, a body, a mind, they said, was just convention or makeshift—an artificial concept necessary to deal with the world, in itself it had no reality. By constructing the world out of pure sensory impressions, they meant to supply the new science with a methodology entirely free of premises. In 1912 Mach published his manifesto, *Für positive Erfahrungswissenschaft;* among others, Freud and Einstein endorsed it. Later on, Moritz Schlick and the "Vienna Circle" of neo-positivists expanded Mach's ideas.

This Weltanschauung plunged young Hugo von Hofmannsthal into a deep identity crisis. In its way, quite as Nietzsche had done in the realm of culture and philosophy, the new science helped disintegrate the middle-class individuum and call into question any "meaning" of life. Henri Poincaré, the French mathematician, felt entitled to say that theories were meant not to be true but to be esthetically pleasing. For Schlick, philosophy became merely "an enrichment of the philosopher's life." Bohr called the relativity theory "a great work of art and the deepest thought about nature, even if it should turn out to be beyond exact proof."

For the general public, to be sure, these ideas were too radical. Unfortunately, the one party who claimed the firmest determination in promoting progress had the least use for the new science. Marxist theoreticians might have seen dialectics substantiated by it; instead, they called it the decay of decadent bourgeois reason. Prewar Social Democrats had rejected naturalist literature, and in the same way they missed the connection with the time's most progressive ideas; they insisted they were the heirs of the classical ideas which the middle class had surrendered. For Marxist theoreticians like Karl Kautsky and Heinrich Cunow (and for Lenin too), "materialistic" equaled proletarian, "idealistic" equaled bourgeois, and that was that.

"At that time one anticipated a general, mighty collapse which, at the latest around 1900, would turn the world upside down . . ." or so said Gerhart Hauptmann in his novel, *Der Narr in Christo Emanuel Quint*. "Different people had different names for this apocalypse, but basically it was aroused by the same powerful longing for redemption, for purity, deliverance, and happiness. Some called it the social state, others freedom, again others the millennium."

This end-of-the-century utopian hopefulness had, as we have seen, yielded to skepticism. The unity of political, cultural, and social reform movements had been lost. New literature, new education, new social, youth and women's movements—each went its own way.

Sexual themes, implicitly tied to the women's movement, could no longer be kept taboo. As early as 1886, Richard von Krafft-Ebing published his *Psychopathia Sexualis;* twelve years later Havelock Ellis began his *Studies in the Psychology of Sex;* Magnus Hirschfeld fought for a more humane attitude to homosexuals and founded the "World League for Sexual Reform." In 1906 at long last, after fifteen years of waiting, Wedekind's *The Awakening of Spring* was staged; Strauss's *Salome* had preceded it by a year.

Taking off from the Frenchman Jean-Martin Charcot, Josef Breuer and Sigmund Freud in the 1880s began their studies in hysteria and hypnosis; in the 1890s Freud extended them into a theory of the unconscious; in 1900 his *Interpre-*

tation of Dreams appeared. Although in the ensuing decade barely a few hundred copies were sold, parallel views were soon to appear in literature, bearing witness to the timeliness of his theories. Even if people were not ready yet to abandon themselves to the irrational—which of course was not Freud's intention anyway—the time had arrived to recognize its existence and to come to grips with it. But then the Swiss Carl Jung (after seceding from Freudian-style analysis) and the Stefan George disciple Ludwig Klages initiated a fundamental change: research into the unconscious became worship of the unconscious.

Freud meant to help the intellect secure its control over instinctual drives; that was what he called civilization. But in 1910 the philosopher Wilhelm Windelband spoke of "the mysticism of our time" and its "urge to retire into one's innermost private self" (*Drang nach Verinnerlichung*). The writer Hermann Bahr, who as early as 1895 had "overcome" naturalism, wrote in an essay on education: "The challenge of our time is to make men of reason into men of the senses." The seed sown by Nietzsche had risen—the Dionysian was, at last, to take precedence over the Apollonian. Salvation from the perplexities of the spirit would be found by surrendering to the myth. The European spirit gave up; it reeled from the most sensitive subjectivism into a longing to experience community, even if that new community were only to be discovered in war.

When the war did break out, a collective intoxication gripped all. A great many important men (not excluding such cool, analytic heads as Stefan Zweig) have testified to the rapture of those days, when the ego was totally abandoned and an emotional communal experience carried all into transports of joy. In the trenches Ernst Jünger had that emotional "front experience" which formed a generation of young barbarians; gambling on their own death, they consecrated to destruction the middle-class world they despised. Their philosophy was "tragic realism": saying yes to pure will without hope. Thomas Mann in his war book still embellished it as "culture"; in futurism and expressionism, it appeared as a horrible exultation in destroying, or as a foreboding of being destroyed.

Finally, Oswald Spengler wrote *The Decline of the West* as a brutal-sober monument to his time: an immense historical panorama with cultures coming into bloom and dying, taking over from each other without learning from each other, leaving behind only graveyards, or else fossile empires glum in an everlasting twilight. But cynically, Spengler dedicated his book to the young Germans who were to abandon cultural pretensions and give themselves up to the pure will to power.

Were there other perspectives, more optimistic ones? Not within the system. Liberalism, imprisoned in relativism, had nothing much with which to thwart the armed demons; in fact, it hardly wanted to try. Insofar as it paid homage to social Darwinism, it could not dispute the right to life of whatever was triumphant. All it could do was try to salvage into cultural oases a few individual values from the bankruptcy of humanism. "Culture" now meant counterculture, criticism of "mass society," the lonely voice of the infinite in a world whose only purpose was the finite. Hence, the inner life became paramount to social concerns; irrationalism superseded intelligence, rebellion of the individual replaced the hope for universal happiness, and aggression transcended the impulse of civilization.

Aggression As Cultural Rebellion: The German Example

Of all the theories on fascism, racism, and imperialism, the most popular continues to be the thesis that goes back to J. A. Hobson and N. Lenin: that capitalistic enterprise, constrained by economic necessity, becomes aggressive and goes out to conquer markets abroad and to exploit less-developed races. Often enough, the appearances support that assumption. But the historian also finds, on the one hand, capitalists who would rather live peacefully than spend money on world-political adventures and, on the other hand, active imperialists whose motives are adventure and domination rather than profit.

There are even some ideologies of imperialism that have an anti-capitalist, anti-middle-class tinge. Arthur Rimbaud, whose poetic insurgency started the modernist revolution against bourgeois culture, may have made a fortune in Ethiopia. But he went to Africa as Gaugin went to Tahiti, for the same reasons that inspired Emil Nolde's terrible masks and Pablo Picasso's grimacing beauties—aversion to the society in which they lived but which they could not endure.

The biographies of famous colonialists such as Cecil Rhodes, Lord Cromer, and Dr. Carl Peters (the "Kurtz" in Joseph Conrad's *Heart of Darkness*) reveal a rogues' gallery of social misfits, outcasts, and failures. Hannah Arendt calls them "superfluous men" who would pay any price to inhabit

Reprinted with permission from *Centerpoint* (Summer 1978).

a world of irresponsibility. Like Mr. Heyst in Conrad's *Victory*, they were "drunk with contempt" for everything human. The folklore of imperialism was created by fantastic dreamers like T. E. Lawrence and romantic poets like Rudyard Kipling and D. H. Lawrence. No doubt, cold-blooded capitalists would take advantage of the imperialist mood to make a profit for themselves, but that mood had to be generated first, and those who planted the seed of empire were usually "outsiders" (in South Africa, a good many Jews) who could not make it at home or who had psychological, social, perhaps even criminal motives to seek an escape from home. Their admirers and supporters, the literary imperialists, were first of all romantics who were fascinated by the nonurban, anticultural, and antirational spirit, lured by the primitive, the mythical, the heroic, the sadistic, and the bestial.

The archetype of their fantasies, of course, was Thomas Carlyle's ostentatiously outrageous essay on "The Nigger Question," but Carlyle was also the fountainhead of populist and even socialist literature (Engels was influenced by him). As is well known, petty-bourgeois anticapitalism was often spiked with racism and anti-Semitism. Nativism not only worshiped the soil but also aimed to conquer more of it. Thus we find Pan-Slavism in league both with the czar's imperial designs and with his opposition's pleas for social reform. In France, the social protest of pre-capitalist strata against the *grande bourgeoisie* and the cultural protest of disaffected intellectuals merged in a movement that had many facets: it was estheticist, elitist, racist, chauvinistic, militaristic, anti-Semitic and syndicalist, anti-Masonic and anti-middle-class. The blood-and-soil nationalism of Maurice Barrès, the Catholic nationalism of Charles Péguy, the syndicalist nationalism of Georges Sorel, the elitist syndicalism of Charles Maurras—all reflected the bohemian's deep disgust with the *juste milieu* and all were led from there to the glorification of violence and imperialism. In Italy, the same combination: radical nationalism and militarism were married to a radical rejection of the bourgeois system by Marinetti; Mussolini, originally a radical socialist, embraced nationalism to form a fascist state. In Germany, Gregor Strasser, Hitler's second-in-command for a time, addressed himself to the "anti-capitalist nostalgia of the majority of our people," and at some time in the history of the Weimar Republic "national bolshevism" was considered a distinct possibility—not among the workers but in certain circles of intellectuals.

What all these movements had in common was a fanatical hatred of rationality and of the bourgeois system of values, life styles, and mental attitude (I use "bourgeois" in the sense American students attribute to "middle class"; it is so used in both French and German). They all derive from Nietzsche's devastating attack on the "educated philistine," his exaltation of power over economic reality, his praise of irrationality against the Enlightenment, his love of war as an alternative to peaceful mediocrity, his worship of aristocratic order as a bulwark against the anarchy of society. His contempt and disgust were shared by many members of the intelligentsia; they were both anticapitalistic *and* imperialistic or, more accurately, they tried to escape from the mediocrity of the "nouveau-riche" empire and of business materialism into the fantasies of a nobler existence of Wagnerian knights, noble conquerors, Superman instead of Everyman, a social order instead of wild competition, artistic values instead of mercantile hypocrisy and venality, respect for the great individual instead of democracy.

Although Nietzsche's influence spread rapidly to other countries, I shall concentrate, in the following pages, on the significance of the Nietzschean rebellion in Germany. I am not concerned with Nietzsche's philosophy or the philosophy of Heidegger, Scheler, and others; their merits as philosophers are not relevant to an examination of the effect which their exaggerated, distorted, and perhaps misunderstood formulations may have had on the development of the imperialistic ideology. I do not hold Marx responsible for Stalin, nor Nietzsche for Hitler, but this absence of responsibility extends only to the master's conscious intentions, not to the psychological and sociological mechanisms that made his attitudes and theories capable of turning into the ideology of a

movement. To describe Nietzsche's philosophy of Superman
as "an expression of the racist, imperialist bourgeoisie" or
his antirationalism as just a symptom of the "degeneracy of
bourgeois thought in the era of imperialism" (Lukács) is to
evade the question. How did the insight into the hollowness
of the bourgeoisie get into the head of a professor in Basel
who was the son of a theologian and who hated the bourgeoisie? It is my contention that, before these ideologies could be
adapted to the requirements of fascism, they had to be incu-
bated in a milieu that was alienated from the development of
German capitalism and nursed by a resentment directed
against that environment.

Nativist and imperialist ideologies, paradoxically, appear
first as protests against the coming of capitalism. Richard
Wagner's *Ring* attacks the accursed power of gold and shows
how a superior race, equipped with a good sword, fights the
dark forces of mammon. Wagner's epigones mobilized the
noble resources of German blood against the mercantile spirit
of Britain and the overrefined civilization of the French. They
defended Kultur and *Geist* against the sullen barbarism of the
Slavs and against the shallow, material civilization of the
West. In this demonology, the Jews incarnated all the evils of
capitalism, above all its impersonal anonymity and its cold
rationality. The petty-bourgeoisie and the peasants, who felt
outwitted and helpless vis-à-vis the rational-impersonal forces
of the market, were apt to hit back or to wish that someone
would hit back for them. Or they would seek compensation
for the decline of their economic fortune and their social status, whether in a romantic revival of their traditional virtues
and values, or in the aggrandizement of their race and nation.
It is an old recipe of imperialist statesmen: people who are
oppressed at home will be more willing to oppress others
abroad. Thus, out of *ressentiment* grows justification for racism and imperialism; the victory of business rationality is followed by the backlash of a revolt against reason. Anti-intel-
lectualism, anti-Semitism,and the cult of violence are then
welded into a monstrous "philosophy of life" which is presented as the precious fruit of German Kultur. In Ludwig

Oswald Spengler. "Oswald Spengler wrote *The Decline of the West* as a brutal-sober monument to his time."

Friedrich Nietzsche. "I do not hold Marx responsible for Stalin, nor Nietzsche for Hitler."

Elisabeth Paetel

Ernst Jünger. ". . . a Nietzschean superman, in the midst of horror he maintained his esthetic interests."

Deutsche Fotothek, Dresden

Gerhart Hauptmann. "Gerhart Hauptmann had forgotten that once he hoped to combine the politics of socialism with the anti-politics of art."

Klages' view the task of the German Siegfried is to liberate the forces of the soul from oppressive rationalism, from the conventions of bourgeois civilization. At the same time, Max Scheler could hail "the German war" as a "spiritual rejuvenation" and a "civilizing agent."

Werner Sombart, the famous historian of capitalism, expected the "true culture" to emerge from the breakdown of bourgeois civilization while Thomas Mann argued against his brother Heinrich—whom, in the *Reflections of a Non-Political Man,* he called derisively "the *littérateur* of civilization"—that in the first world war German Kultur was manifesting itself. Alban Berg, the composer of *Wozzek,* confessed in the first month of the war: "If the war were to end today, we would be back in the old rut." Rainer Maria Rilke, certainly the sweetest of poets in the German language, gave vent to this sentiment: "How can we rise if we give our strength to the wretched and oppressed? Let the lazy scoundrels perish. Let us be hard, terrible, and inexorable! A few great, powerful, divine men will build the kingdom with their strong, lordly arms on the dead bodies of the weak and crippled." Stefan George, whose nobly cadenced verse and cultist imagery had intoxicated idealistic youths, also sang of the good wars for the Reich and the Führer. Another poet, Gottfried Benn, a doctor who began his literary career with a series of provocative poems revealing gory, disgusting details of clinical surgery, found perverse pleasure in flinging the cruel realities of war and of the life of the race into the faces of the bourgeois; his purpose was no longer to amaze but to confound them. When the Nazis came to power, Benn claimed that now Expressionism would guide Germany and that Hitler would lead the Germans out of philistine mediocrity toward heroic deeds. Likewise, Oswald Spengler, known the world over for his philosophy of history which proclaimed the twilight of the West and which predicted the coming of the Caesars, exhorted the Germans to save themselves from the doom of Western civilization by cultivating the warrior virtues and following the path of "Prussian socialism."

These were the voices of some outstanding, even seminal,

thinkers, writers, and poets; not the raving phantasies of radical enthusiasts or rabid racialists, nativists and populists, but rather elitist voices. In fact, none of them got along with the Nazis. Thomas Mann and Max Scheler rallied to the Republic; Stefan George and Oswald Spengler, who had to flee the Third Reich which they had so ardently prepared, died in exile. Gottfried Benn was repudiated and withdrew into "internal exile." I have not cited them to demonstrate any particular characteristic of German intellectual life, for it would be easy to match their statements with similar glorifications of war from non-German sources. The point, rather, is the angle from which the peaceful life of the philistines was being attacked in this literature.

Professor Fritz Stern has assembled the ideas of some minor, though at one time very popular, writers (Paul de Lagarde, Julius Langbehn, Moeller van den Bruck) under the apt title: *The Politics of Cultural Despair*. These were not vulgar vigilantes of the Joseph McCarthy type but intellectuals of the highest caliber, steeped in the traditions of German literature and highly sensitive to the loss of meaning in twentieth-century civilization. They grieved that life was being demythologized. Choosing death is better than suffering, Thomas Mann's Naphta seems to say, or, with his creator's typical ambiguity: Life may be death, and facing death may be life. This suicidal mania is shown less equivocally, less philosophically, and more affirmatively, in the writings of a confessed terrorist and accomplice of murderers, Ernst von Salomon. He was one of the most admired writers of the respected avant-garde publishing house, Rowohlt, during the 1920s, and after the second world war he was able to speak once again for German Kultur by flinging back into the Allies' teeth their *Questionnaire* (1951) as a provocative protest against Western civilization.

Crucial here is the romantic idea of redemption through violence, the purging of a doomed or rotten society by the eruption of the primitive, the cleansing of civilization by soulful barbarians. The rebellious urge is not externalized and projected onto real outsiders; rather, the esthetic self is identified with the terrorist or with violent behavior. In Aristotelian or in Freudian terms, the naming and the presentation of these demonic forces did not lead to their exorcism nor to a catharsis but, on the contrary, it helped to legitimize and to activate them.

This can be shown in some detail for writers like E. E. Dwinger and Ernst Jünger. Both were storm-troop leaders in the first world war and came out of it with damaged personalities. Unable to find their way back into normal civilian life, they were successful in projecting their personal problems into a symbol of the German destiny. What is remarkable here is the directness of this sublimation and the acceptance of this literature—which soon was to become a school, with followers who wrote less from personal experience and more for patriotic propaganda. Dwinger and Jünger write about war as a deep personal experience, as a necessary form of life; they accept the destiny of failure and futility, for they need not sanctify war by any superior purpose, not even by the defense of the fatherland. The world is totally emptied of feeling. A mythology of destructive action is spelled out as though this were the natural human attitude. To overcome means to accept. "To say yea even though no: because destiny is cruel. . . . We need a cataclysm from time to time so that we can find our deepest self again" (Jünger).

The philosophy based on this perception is called tragic heroism—heroic because the person or nation must prove itself, tragic because no ulterior purpose is served. "Bearing," a Prussian expression from the military code of honor, and "style" are all. Those who have both are masters of their destiny and are aristocratic; the rest are an insignificant mass. It is only natural that this philosophy is deeply antidemocratic and even antisocial. Both Dwinger and Jünger belonged to the ultra-right during the twenties and propagated a new "ethos." Both were fascinated by the new technology and looked forward to an age when the worker would be reduced to a mere robot whose very sexuality might be allowed to wither. In war, too, the mechanized soldier fascinated them, as he did Marinetti. Interestingly, both became critical of the

Nazi regime as soon as they discovered that the Nazis were mean, plebeian, and cruel people. For cruelty had no place in the disinterested pleasure which mechanized heroism gave to the noble hearts of these Nietzschean supermen.

In 1939, Jünger wrote a courageous little novel, On the Marble Cliffs, which rather unobliquely expressed his horror of concentration camps and other Nazi crimes. During World War II, when he was a liaison officer in charge of relations with the French collaborationist intellectuals, he carefully entered in his diaries the hushed-up news of atrocities in the eastern war areas; but when he published these diaries after the war, he seemed to take special pride in his ability to maintain, in the midst of all the horror, his esthetic interests. The death of his son in the war evoked less comment than his acquisition of a book bound in rare morocco leather. When the Germans had to abandon Paris, he betrayed no sympathy with the fate of collaborators who had been entrusted to his care.

Jünger was not involved in the plot against Hitler, but after the war he circulated a pamphlet entitled Peace in which he emerged as a good European—with the same coolness of heart that had previously characterized his loyalty as a German army officer.

Since Nietzsche, the instincts have been ennobled and, more important, have been given independent status. Aggression has been isolated as an activity that fulfills an immediate human need; in its name war has been sanctified, not as an instrument for a purpose but as an activity in its own right. This, however, is only the consequence of a view of life which fundamentally rejects the values of "Western" bourgeois civilization and the Enlightenment. In the reaction to rationality, to universality, and the goals of the French Revolution, the irrational, the intuitive, and the arbitrary assume primacy. These reactionary values at once fuel and justify the ressentiment, not of the large-scale capitalists who may well profit from the ideologies of anticapitalist imperialism, but of the petty bourgeoisie which creates such ideologies and the climate of catastrophe as well.

[14]
Was Weimar Necessary?

The Räte Movement, 1918–1921, and the Theory of Revolution

IDEOLOGISTS tend to see the future in terms of the past. The image that the pioneers of the Great French Revolution sought to imitate was that of Brutus. The Bolsheviks in turn imitated the Jacobins, hoping to improve on their predecessors' performance while escaping their fate. Now the Bolsheviks serve as models by which other turning points in history are judged. Thus, critics of the Weimar Republic compare its origins in 1918 unfavorably with the enthusiastic faith of 1789 or with the social radicalism of 1917. There, they see the ever-deepening seriousness of the revolution, the emergence of ever-new strata from the depths of society, and the release of ever-fresh and unsuspected energies; here, the mere superseding of one leading elite by another,[1] and, after a brief interlude of revolutionary spasms, a step-by-step retreat into a new legality. No customary rituals of liberation and planting of freedom trees, no public rejoicing and dancing in the streets greeted the birth of the hapless Weimar Republic, born in despair and confusion. As soon as possible, with the adoption of a constitution on July 31, 1919, the new republicans tried to forget the revolution. Not the day of the revolution but the day of the Constitution was declared a national holiday.

Reprinted with permission from *Dissent* (Winter 1977).

Had this been the whole story, it would be incorrect to speak of a "November revolution" at all.[2] Yet, without that revolution it would be hard to explain two things: the hatred that the former ruling classes bore the Republic, and the loyalty of the working classes. Both were based on the abolition of the "servants' order" and of similar feudal laws, on the introduction of the eight-hour day and unemployment insurance, the recognition of collective bargaining, and other such matters that, however, were of little concern to the "Weimar intellectuals." Their contempt for the abortive revolution and its sorry product, the Weimar Republic, was based on the conviction that the collapse of the monarchy should have been followed by nothing less than a "total revolution." But neither was Kurt Weill a Rouget de Lisle nor Tucholsky a Danton nor Brecht a Büchner.[3]

Leninist theory asserts that only the treason of the Social Democrats prevented the creation of conditions that might have led to intensified revolution and civil war. But there is no evidence that the fear of bolshevism was warranted or that the masses were pressing for revolution. More sophisticated critics attribute the braking of the revolution to the old practice of collaboration between trade unions and management, culminating in the "agreement to cooperate,"[4] which might be called the real constitution of the Weimar Republic. The separation of political from socioeconomic actions, which also means separation of Marxist theory from the everyday practice of class war, was indeed one of the major charges that Rosa Luxemburg had leveled against Germany's prewar Social Democratic party.[5]

But in 1918 a new movement, the Räte (councils) promised, or seemed to promise, a way of overcoming the limitations of both the old-style parliamentary party, accustomed to a sterile opposition policy while accumulating votes—and old-style trade union reformism. The Räte seemed ideal instruments of a revolutionary policy: a means to unite the proletariat and exclude its enemies from political action, an executive and administrative organ to meet the emergency situation, and a two-way channel to electrify the revolutionary potential of all classes. Räte is usually, and correctly, translated as "councils" to distinguish them, on the one hand, from mere economic shop stewards and, on the other, from the Russian concept of *soviets* as instruments of a party dictatorship. The significance of this distinction will presently be clarified.

I shall try to show that a meaningful critique of the November revolution, and of the Weimar Republic that emerged out of it, is possible only from the viewpoint of the Räte movement, but not from that of the Jacobin ideology that still dominates the literature. The latter is ahistorical, since it presupposes a revolutionary ruling party, or at least a dynamic faction pushing the revolution toward radicalization. Neither existed, and with the two-stroke model of the Russian Revolution (or rather its legend: in February a bourgeois revolution, in October a socialist revolution) in mind, the easy conclusion follows: what happened in Germany in November 1918 can at best be compared to the Russian February 1917. Both had in common the heritage of a collapse, the contrast between vague hopes for a better future and awareness of the dire choices, of impending disasters, as well as the makeshift character of the provisional government.

But this indeterminate nature, which the two revolutions shared, conceals their great difference: successive Russian governments were unable to take root in Russian soil, while in Germany the republican majority—formed previously, during the last year of the first world war, by the opposition parties in the Reichstag—asserted itself rather quickly. In other words, unless one chooses to say that the German revolution began with its "Thermidor," one should study it as a phenomenon *sui generis* that followed a pattern of development totally independent of the French and Russian models.

The study of this pattern may be of more than historical or theoretical interest. Other countries now are facing situations that somehow resemble the condition of Germany in 1918. A regime dominated by traditional forces has broken down, leaving a mess of ill-placed investments and privileges; the new regime, searching for a balance between innovation and stability, must call on Socialist or even Communist parties to share responsibility. These parties must decide among three basic courses:

1. Lending conditional or critical support to a government that can be expected to push reform policies far enough to justify such support;
2. Joining such a government in order to gain positions of power and to introduce more decisive policies aiming at social transformation;
3. Fighting outside the government for more advanced programs, and against the government for total revolution.

Perhaps there is some relevance in the recent spate of studies and texts that deal with the Räte movement in the early days of the Weimar Republic and with its political sponsor, the short-lived Independent Social Democratic party.[6] After the violent overthrow of the Allende government in Chile and the narrow salvaging of the Portuguese republic, socialists in many countries are wondering whether a popular revolution is fated either to be stopped in its tracks before achieving its aims or to fall prey to a dictatorship—of the military or the party variety.

The Independent Social Democratic party of Germany (USPD),[7] which flourished briefly from 1917 to 1921, thought that radical policies were not only compatible with democracy but were essentially linked to it. This party had split off from the old SPD over the latter's support of the kaiser's war effort. When the empire crumbled, the two workers' parties formed a Council of People's Deputies (Rat der Volksbeauftragten), which derived its legitimacy from the nascent Räte movement but acted as a provisional government.[8] Here the Independents tried to keep things in suspense until the Räte could consolidate their power. The Social Democrats argued for an early convening of a constituent assembly, which would allow the whole nation to share responsibility for the painful decisions that had to be made. Moreover, the impending chaos and famine, pressure from the Entente powers, and the urgency of peace and reconstruction made it necessary to cooperate with the pillars of the ancien régime, such as the civil service, the army, and business.

Ever so reluctantly, the USPD leaders bowed to that reasoning. This is surprising. Should they not have insisted that the revolutionary government immediately depose the kaiser's judges, county presidents, and generals, indict the war criminals, abolish the *Länder* (the various separate German states), and expropriate the big landowners and industrialists? Should not the 1918 revolution, in one fell swoop, at least have finished the job which the aborted "bourgeois revolution" of 1848 had left undone seventy years earlier? Alas, the revolutionaries did not have enough trained jurists, economists, and managers to fill even the lowest cabinet positions—truly, a lame excuse for inaction! In Russia, the revolutionaries had charged ahead; they did not mind illiterate generals or commissars.

To be sure, even Rosa Luxemburg did not think that Germany was "ripe" for a socialist revolution, and the Independents were committed to a policy of peace at almost any price.[9] Indeed, 90 percent of the German people wanted first of all to see the boys come home, and if the high command wanted to keep the troops under the flag, it meant them to fight against the revolution. The homecoming soldiers, however, above all wanted jobs, and the Provisional Government agreed that its foremost task was the conversion of industry to peacetime work. A more radical policy might have provoked chaos and foreign intervention. The SPD majority was not prepared to run these risks of a socialist revolution.

But neither were the Independents. The character and constituency of the USPD was not uniformly Marxist and revolutionary. Founded in protest against the war, it was predominantly pacifist.[10] It had rejected Lenin's call to "transform the imperialist war into a civil war." Its leaders ranged from old Eduard Bernstein, the archrevisionist, and Kurt Eisner, the ethical socialist and pacifist, to the firebrand oppositionist Georg Ledebour and to Ernst Thälmann, who would soon become Stalin's handpicked leader of the KPD. The party's intermediate group included Karl Kautsky, the pillar of

Marxian orthodoxy and Lenin's pet villain, as well as Rudolf Hilferding, on whose *Finance Capital* Lenin based his theory of "imperialism." Political head and leading parliamentarian of the party was Hugo Haase, who never, until his assassination in 1919, abandoned hope that the two workers' parties, USPD and SPD, might reunite one day.[11]

This, obviously, was not the mood of the Independents' left wing: it hated both the policies and the style of the old SPD and trade union leadership; it hoped for a socialist revolution and believed that the Russians had made a good start. It included idealistic, quasi-anarchistic literati such as the playwright Ernst Toller, who was to found a Räte Republic in Munich, and also such Jacobins as Clara Zetkin, one of the first members of the Spartacusbund (nucleus of the KPD, which was founded as late as January 1919).

The bulk of the radical left, however, consisted of a new movement of shop stewards (*Obleute*), mostly active in the defense industries, who had first banded together to oppose wartime restrictions and deprivations but who then had turned to the pursuit of civil rights, political reform, and eventually revolution. Their leader was a metal worker, Richard Müller, who had syndicalist tendencies. Though a member of the USPD and later of the KPD, he tried to keep the political and the economic arms of the revolution apart. His theoretical companion was Ernst Däumig, a former theology student, soldier of fortune, and officer turned war-resister. Däumig was to become a leading spokesman for the Räte concept and later for affiliation of the USPD with the Comintern. What seems clear now to posterity, however, may not have been so to contemporaries: Däumig probably thought the Russian soviets were like the German Räte. Characteristically, he and Müller left the KPD a year after they had merged with it.

The USPD was the party of the Räte—an idea that was popular far beyond the circles of those who sympathized with the Russians. The Räte idea had emerged in the turbulent beginnings of the German revolution, in November 1918, as the only conception of popular power, the only organized source of legitimacy for the Provisional Government. Wherever people were gathered in political turmoil—in factories, the army, urban districts, even in villages—Räte were formed for every purpose. There were soldiers' Räte, housewives' Räte, and of course Räte of intellectual workers, Räte of the unemployed, and even the PTA began as "Parents' Räte." In Bavaria, Kurt Eisner's Volksrepublik was supported by hastily formed peasants' Räte. At first, Räte sprang up in haphazard, disorderly patterns—by usurpation, by simple show of hands, or by various election procedures. Often they were simply appointed by SPD or USPD committees. They usually decreed the reinstatement of suspended labor laws and civil rights and then got involved in the tasks of assuring supplies, issuing permits, and the like. However, the Räte failed to build up an independent structure of power on the national or even provincial level.[12] While they pretended to supervise the local or state administrative organs, most often they were used as the latter's public relations channel.

The Räte, though failing to substitute themselves for the executive power, were indispensable in providing an ideology for revolutionary rule. With the Social Democrats as junior partners, the Independents ruled in the name of the Räte over all of Saxony and Brunswick, using the larger towns as bases. Almost singlehanded, with merely a few sailors, the enthusiastic Kurt Eisner seized Munich and imposed on the rest of Bavaria a flimsy "Räte" scheme along with a new anthem which he himself had composed. The Council of People's Deputies in Berlin also was supported by an "executive council" (Vollzugsrat) of local Räte—though precariously and in constant rivalry over jurisdiction. Other councils, too, made erratic, despotic inroads into the routines of government; but nowhere did they supersede the established administrative departments or wrest executive power from the structures of the ancien régime. In fact, the first decree issued by the executive council ordered "all communal, provincial, national, and military authorities to continue their activities."

Politically, the Räte did not develop in the direction of the Russian soviets, and it is erroneous to describe the condition

of the German state at the turn of 1918–19 as a "dual government." Conditions in the young German republic did not resemble those in Russia between February and October 1917.
In Russia, the Provisional Government was legitimate, but the
power of the soviets was increasing, and the civil service system was falling into their hands. In Germany the Räte, rather,
were the *source* of power, but actual power was falling back
into the hands of the old civil service.

Lenin, as is well known, had called for democratic organs
of government that would combine the legislative's and the
executive's functions (*State and Revolution*). Later, in his anti-
Kautsky pamphlet, he identified the soviets as such organs
and described them as an ideal system of government. This,
however, was not the reality either in Russia or in Germany.
Even where the soviets were not a synonym for party rule,
they were simply an interim power intervening in emergency
situations with emergency measures. This difference was
stated clearly by Ernst Däumig at the USPD Congress in 1919:
"I should like to ask you to make this distinction. On the one
hand, Räte now are the means we have to use in order to
strive for socialism in the midst of chaos and destruction; the
soviet system as a goal is something very different."

Däumig saw the councils largely as political instruments
that would prepare the workers for the dictatorship of the
proletariat. The program the USPD adopted read more ambig-
uously: "The USPD supports the Räte in their struggle for
economic and political power. It aspires to the dictatorship
of the proletariat, *representative of the majority of the people,* as a necessary precondition for the realization of socialism" (my italics). This elastic formula could be interpreted as
an endorsement of parliamentary or of Räte government, of
majority rule or of dictatorship. Since the USPD was active
in both parliamentary campaigns and trade unions, in the
government, and in the Räte, its ultimate commitment remained vague. But many speakers at the USPD Congress argued that the Räte should be a means to unite workers across
party lines, to bridge the gap between unions of different persuasions ("red," "free," liberal-democratic, and "Christian"),

to close the gulf between partisans of the parliamentary republic and partisans of the dictatorship of the proletariat. Rudolf Hilferding finally saw the Räte as a means to democratize economic life, from the factory level up to the formation of a Supreme Workers' Council endowed with the right to initiate legislation and examine and veto bills before the Reichstag. Thus the Räte might be a strategic instrument of revolution, a tactical means of ongoing class war, or a republican institution.

These were not Leninist ideas but ideas based on Rosa Luxemburg's most exciting work, *Mass Strike, Party, and Trade Unions*, in which she demonstrated, in great detail, the cross-fertilization between political and economic struggle and minimized the need for party guidance of the masses. We must bear in mind that for all prewar socialists—left-wing and right-wing—the fight for democracy was axiomatic and that, in particular for revolutionaries, there could be no conflict yet between civil rights and proletarian dictatorship. They had conducted bloody strikes for the right to vote, and they would not readily throw that right away.

Karl Kautsky had described the relationship between revolution and democracy in his prewar book, *The Social Revolution*,[13] which every USPD militant must have known by heart. This pamphlet was remarkable for its many insights. Kautsky had recognized the significance of finance capitalism, trusts, department stores, and predicted the shopkeepers' flight into fascism. He foresaw the decline of parliamentarianism, and therefore assigned to the working class the historical function of rescuing and reviving parliamentarianism's "invaluable blessings." Democracy, Kautsky wrote, "is first of all a condition that makes the higher forms of revolutionary struggle possible"; and "democracy is an indispensable means to prepare the proletariat for the social revolution, but it is not a means to make such a revolution superfluous." He warned that *class war would be intensified* in the coming era, even in the countries where democracy had prevailed, and that it would continue for a long time *even after* the proletariat had seized political power.

This point, though of utmost importance, has not received any attention in the literature, which even today is totally enthralled with the Leninist conception of history: either the revolution is socialist or it isn't; either the proletarians have the power or they don't; either revolution leads to a parliamentary regime, and then it is bourgeois, or it leads to a soviet dictatorship, and then it is socialist. The February revolution of 1917 was bourgeois-democratic, the October revolution was socialist-proletarian. Kautsky, however, had called his pamphlet *The Social Revolution*, not "The Socialist Revolution." The radicals, even the most revolutionary among them, did not envisage the coming revolution as a takeover by the Socialist party in a single act but as a long process of socialization after winning democratic liberties and socialist-democratic majorities. This conception pervades even Rosa Luxemburg's great speech at the founding congress of the KPD: "It is an illusion to think that it suffices to install socialists in government and to issue socialist decrees." "Socialism cannot be introduced by decrees." The seizure of power "cannot be accomplished in one blow. It must be a progression of acts by which power is achieved on each level, one after the other."

The conception with which the USPD started the November 1918 revolution, therefore, anticipated two levels of action, a political and a social one. The Independents were preparing for a long period of protracted class struggle and therefore tried to prevent an early stabilization of the regime in the form of a constitution. Although their slogan was, "All power to the Räte," they had joined the Provisional Government. They failed to purge the civil service and to penetrate the executive with their own men, but they pressed to convene a national congress of workers' and soldiers' councils (a Räte Congress). They agreed that the constitution should be written by a national assembly—but not soon, and it should incorporate *faits accomplis*, which the Räte were to create in the meantime.

For the Independents, democracy and Räte were not contradictory—that was the way the bourgeoisie saw the matter:

either Räte or a constituent assembly. The bourgeoisie was trembling in fear of the word Räte. The Räte were proletarian and seemed uncontrollable. Here is the respectable *Vossische Zeitung* reporting, in December 1918, on the Räte Congress:

> Wild men, soldiers with war-frayed nerves, foaming at the mouth, babbling with excitement. Demagogues emerging from the deep dark, spouting evil thoughts and savage dreams . . . *and yet this is the only power in the whole Reich capable of exercising authority:* men in shirt-sleeves, sailors who were mute yesterday, incapable of mastering their own destiny, yet they are *now our masters.* (My italics)[14]

This rabble Congress, however, presented the Independents with a grave disappointment. The soldiers had elected mostly Social Democrats, and the majority refused to let Karl Liebknecht speak in favor of a Räte constitution. Instead, the Räte voted (400 to 50) to yield their power to a constituent assembly, which was to be elected at the earliest possible date. Under the one-citizen-one-vote rule, and with women voting for the first time, this assembly was almost certain to have a moderate majority. Däumig indignantly called the Congress a suicides' club. Müller, equally infuriated, acquired his nickname—the Corpse—when he exclaimed: "If they want to enter the National Assembly, they'll have to do it over my dead body!"

The Räte, though, had not completely abdicated their power. The Räte Congress (still the government's source of legitimacy) ordered the government to nationalize (*sozialisieren*) "without delay all industries that are suitable, especially mining." The Räte Congress also spelled out a thorough reform of the army (but since no socialist now wanted to serve in any army, the government had to rely on mercenaries who were indoctrinated by reactionary officers). The Congress finally called for a second Räte Congress that was to convene simultaneously with the constituent assembly; in the interim a "central council" was set up to keep an eye on the government itself.

Here the Independents made their decisive mistake. Exasperated by their defeat, they refused to participate in the central council, on the ground that it had been given insufficient powers. It is true that their experience in the first executive council of Berlin had not been encouraging; despite the more radical composition of that council, it had not been able to keep the government in check. And so, without the Independents participating, the central council withered away—that had been a self-fulfilling prophecy. Soon thereafter, the USPD withdrew its deputies from the national government too, on the even less plausible ground that Friedrich Ebert had used artillery against the mutinous sailors who had claimed allegiance to the USPD.[15] Instead of fighting to extend their own influence, the Independents left the revolution in the hands of Ebert, the Republic's future president, who already had made a deal with the kaiser's generals and who had appointed Gustav Noske to be "the bloodhound."

This all happened in December 1918. Very soon the troops came marching home, hailed by the middle class as saviors from disorder and ruthlessly used by Noske to suppress demonstrations.[16] In January 1919, Karl Liebknecht and Rosa Luxemburg were slain by murderous mercenaries, and the peaceful citizens went to the polls to elect a national (constituent) assembly. That new National Assembly then met in the little town of Weimar, far away from Berlin and Munich and the turmoil of revolution.

As predicted, the Independents had received only 8 percent of the vote, the Social Democrats 38 percent. At no time in the life of the Republic were the workers' parties—SPD, USPD, KPD—to command a combined vote of more than 46 percent. But the SPD also could take other partners. The parties that had pledged support for a republican government—the Social Democrats, the (Catholic) Center party, and the (liberal) Democrats—totaled 75 percent and formed the "Weimar Coalition"; these parties were to share power in Prussia until 1932. In Saxony and in the newly formed state of Thurigia, for a short time SPD-USPD majorities were able to govern constitutionally. But in Bavaria Eisner was disowned by the voters and fatally shot on the way to the Diet, where he planned to submit his resignation as minister president. There followed a Räte seizure of power that began as an operetta and ended in bloody suppression.

In Berlin, too, mass demonstrations scared the rump government into the use of violence. It is said that 1,200 demonstrators died in the streets—while Ebert declaimed on opening the Weimar Assembly: "The idealism of our great poets and thinkers must fill the life of our new republic." The Government was still so shaky and discredited that some adventurous national-bolsheviks were hatching a coup that, significantly enough, was to have delegated certain economic powers to the Räte; but, wisely, the USPD refused to participate in the harebrained scheme.[17]

Half a year later the republican constitution was promulgated with the compromise Article 165, which incorporated the Räte into the fabric of parliamentary democracy:

> Workers and salaried employees shall elect councils on the factory level, district councils by economic areas, and a National Workers' Council to represent their social and economic interests. . . . Social and economic legislation shall be examined by the National Economic Council (to be composed of worker, management, and consumer representatives). . . . Workers' and economic councils may be assigned to function as control and administrative organs in the areas assigned to them.

Although the article incorporated ideas by Hilferding, the left denounced it as an attempt to emasculate the political meaning of the Räte concept. Korsch charged that the more the Räte were assigned economic tasks, the less they would be able to act as organs of revolutionary ferment.[18] Soon indeed the Independents' political Räte lost all their power. In November 1919 Noske's troops were able to expel the Executive Council in Berlin (which by then consisted only of Communists and Independents) from its headquarters. Where municipal Räte survived, by now they performed merely narrow functions of supply, or acted as liaison for the administration; when the states stopped financing their offices, they ceased to exist.

Still not reassured, the Weimar Coalition proceeded to pull the few teeth Article 165 might have had. A new "shop steward law" restricted the Räte to little more than the role of grievance committees on the factory level. On January 23, 1920, forty workers marching in protest against this new law were killed and over a hundred wounded.

Over these developments, masses of workers left the SPD and joined the Independents. At the same time, the Räte idea began to change in the direction of its Russian meaning. From the concept of a specific organ of workers' power and workers' control on all levels of social and economic policy, it was transformed into the concept of an alternative form of government. Falling into disuse, the Räte ceased to be a living reality—the proletariat fighting for its place in society—and instead became a dream, an ideology. It was only consistent that workers now were looking to the political parties rather than to the direct organs of their class to represent them.

Only once more were the Räte called upon to perform an important political task. When in the spring of 1920 a military coup ousted the republican government, the workers arose to defend the Republic, called a general strike, formed Räte, and put "red militias" into the field against the militarists. This time the Räte hoped to seize the opportunity for a push toward socialism and beyond the bourgeois Republic.

Meanwhile, the Social Democratic workers also had had enough of Noske. Carl Legien, the president of the General Trade Unions' Confederation (ADGB), proposed that the workers' parties form a coalition, perhaps to be joined by the Christian trade unions. It would have been a new form of "workers' government."[19] But the Independents, by now dogmatically sold on the Räte idea, and unable to forget the Social Democrats' many betrayals, refused to participate. And so they gave Ebert another excuse to ally himself with the very forces that had just tried to overthrow him. The mutinous officers were pardoned or even promoted; workers who had defended the Republic were beaten down cruelly.

At the polls, in June 1920, Ebert received the answer: the SPD lost nearly half of its constituency. Its vote dropped to 22 percent; the Independents' rose to 18 percent. Since at the same time the Democrats also lost to the Nationalists, the

Weimar Coalition no longer had a majority. The bourgeois parties formed their own government, and Germany became "a republic without republicans."

Like the SPD before the war, the USPD now had to become a party of sterile opposition. Late in 1920, its majority decided to merge with the Communists. The minority was fated to drift back to the SPD the next year, there to play the inglorious role of "opposition" to the leadership's unpopular coalition policies. It has been estimated that about one-third of the membership went to the Communists, where they quickly became the ultra-left,[20] and that nearly one-third soon rejoined the SPD.[21] In the years 1921 to 1923—years of catastrophic inflation, civil strife, and foreign entanglements—workers again staged futile uprisings that only drove them deeper into alienation. Even in the brief prosperity period that followed, many German workers either did not take part in the political process of the Republic or lacked the habit of defending it with militant means. That habit could have been acquired only in the year of revolution, when the two causes of democracy and socialism were parallel or identical. The link between the two was cut during the last days of 1918 and in the gruesome experience of the class war of 1919–20.

Could this break have been prevented? In the early months of the revolution, both SPD and USPD had vivid memories of their recent split. To overcome the mutual suspicions might have required superhuman efforts on both sides.[22] Since each had to live down its past, an almost inexorable necessity drove them into different directions: the SPD into its obsession with procedural legalism, the USPD into declamatory revolutionism. Each in its way prevented the Räte from becoming a creative instrument of an ongoing revolution.

To tell the truth, the Räte themselves were sporadic, local, and unsure organs, often manipulated by the parties, and in themselves incapable of exercising executive functions. As for the socialist parties, they lacked the trained personnel needed to get rid of and replace the old civil service; where such persons were available, they often lacked the sense of power to institute a spoils system. Thus, the revolution became retrograde almost at its inception. Instead of radicalizing the masses, it stifled their revolutionary enthusiasm. Those who were interested in pushing on toward a social revolution could do so only by separating their cause from that of the Republic; those who were interested in securing a republic could do so only by denying it the chance to evolve into the social revolution—or so participants said they felt.

Thus, the SPD leaders eagerly seized upon the easiest excuses: the Entente threat of intervention, the impending famine, the fear of civil war, the need to bring the soldiers home. Well, the boys might have found their way home without the General Staff's help; the Versailles Treaty could not have been more onerous for a revolutionary regime than it was for republican Germany; food supplies were denied to prostrate Germany even after the Armistice; and civil war was launched against the Republic by those very civil servants whom it had neglected to fire.

All these scruples might have been overcome had the German people been prepared to act on its own behalf. But a significant part of the middle class, and notably the intellectuals, would have supported a revolutionary policy only if it had, at the same time, been a nationalistic uprising against the Versailles powers.[23] National bolshevism thus would have been the German version of French Jacobinism, the only alternative to the Weimar Republic. This price, the conversion of Germany into the battlefield of an international civil war, seemed too high to men like Hugo Haase and Rudolf Hilferding.[24]

Nor did the Räte develop a dynamism of their own. The revolution produced no great ideas, did not sweep great personalities to the fore, did not release creative energies. Everybody seemed too busy reconverting his own job and family life to peacetime, and the majority feared chaos more than it wanted change. The Räte never had more than local significance. They were strong in the factories but did not develop into the organ of mass democracy. Insofar as the German revolution of November 1918 aspired to fullest political, economic, and social self-determination of the people, to effective equality of the classes, to participation especially of the working class, the withering away of the Räte meant that democracy shriveled into the political power game of the parties, and only in this sense can it be said that the parliamentary regime fell short of the expectations of a significant part of the people.[25]

Weimar Culture—Nostalgia and Revision

WHEN the young German Republic called its Constituent Assembly to the little town of Weimar, my English teacher in a Berlin high school exclaimed: "The bastards! They are desecrating German culture." To him, a prototype of Thomas Mann's "Non-Political Man," the place where Goethe had founded the National Theater and where classical literature had emerged, belonged to the elite, the educated and leisurely classes, while politics was by its nature dirty and plebeian. When the Assembly in Weimar adopted as the national colors black, red, and gold, the flag used by the student volunteers in our "Wars of Liberation" (1813/14) and in the March Revolution of 1848, our art teacher pointed out that the imperial black, white, and red shone so much brighter.

Both teachers apparently had missed the point of the republican symbolism The Fathers of the Republic obviously wished to tell the middle classes that they had nothing to fear, that there would not be much of a revolution, that the Republic was to accomplish nothing more than what the classical writers, the patriots of a century ago, and the idealists of the aborted "bourgeois revolution" of 1848 had sought. Insofar as my teachers were typical representatives of the middle class, they did not get the message and did not wish to hear it. Thus the story of the Weimar culture began with a

Reprinted with permission from *Dissent* (Summer 1976)

triple misunderstanding. By invoking the ghost of old Weimar, the Republic denied the revolution from which it was born, but failed to mollify its enemies, and at the same time disappointed idealistic democrats who were looking for radically new symbols.

To us students "Weimar culture" meant only the mummified history of our great-grandfathers, their enshrined and perfumed values. It had nothing to do either with the ragamuffin smell of democracy or with the intellectual movements that were to blossom during the first German republic's brief life, nor with the bold, innovative, irreverent, bawdy, critical, or decadent antics that later came to be known as "Weimar culture." Nothing could better characterize the distance between this imaginary and the real Weimar than the fate of the Bauhaus: the citizens of the town of Weimar wanted no part of such an avant-garde institution and forced Walter Gropius to move to Dessau.[1]

In other words, whatever was alive in "Weimar culture" had to be in rebellion not only against the embalmed, prettified, hallowed, commented, and annotated spirit of classical Weimar, taught to and memorized by high-school students, but also against the living reality of political Weimar, the "republic of the burghers." Much of this avant-garde criticism was romantic and reactionary. The intellectual elite dated mostly from pre-Weimar days, and in rallying to the Republic the historian Friedrich Meinecke declared: "If we cannot have what we would love, let us love what we have." When Thomas Mann embraced the new state, he suggested that it was deficient in *Geist*. One does not need a finely trained ear to understand that these intellectuals had accepted the political state of Weimar without making any commitment to "Weimar culture."

Neither, of course, did those intellectuals of the left, like Bert Brecht or Herbert Marcuse, who later came to symbolize something of which they either had no notion or which they might have rejected at the time. For, to make a complex thing still more paradoxical, "Weimar culture" in exile came to mean something specific that had never existed and still does not exist in Germany. There are books in German about *Die Weimarer Republik*, meaning its political and social history, but none entitled "Kultur der Weimarer Zeit."[2]

Simultaneity of contrasting phenomena does not necessarily mean that they form a dialectical unity. If nevertheless we speak of a distinct "Weimar culture," embracing both the sublime and the mundane, from Heidegger to Brecht, from Marlene Dietrich to Goebbels, from Einstein to Josephine Baker, from the romantic youth movement to the Storm Troop goons, from the unruly students to the staid orchestras in provincial towns, ambiguity must remain its hallmark, as it was the hallmark of the political construction called the Weimar Republic.

Why Weimar, to begin with? If they needed a national monument, why not the venerable Saint Paul's Church in Frankfurt, where Germany's first revolutionary parliament had met in 1848? Quite obviously, that historical reminiscence would have hinted at sans-culottism and would have given the Republic a carrion smell of revolution—that *Ludergeruch der Revolution* (Heine)—which was to be avoided at all costs.

Thus the Republic tried to drape itself in the garb of German classical literature that could neither fit the real situation of 1919 nor appeal to the more dynamic elements of the educated classes, their young people, and their intellectual elites. Goethe was a subject for essay tests in high school but not a leader for Germany in the 1920s. Although Gerhart Hauptmann, by now an aging celebrity, was cultivating a spurious resemblance with the old Weimar Olympian's countenance, whatever was alive in contemporary German literature ran against classicism, just as whatever was forward-looking in German politics, had to be opposed to the previous century's idealism.

Unfortunately, an emphasis upon culture usually results in a lack of social-political background so that criticism of the Weimar intellectuals remains in the abstract. Too often one fundamental attempt at legislation is forgotten: a veritable social contract which had been agreed upon even before the Constituent Assembly was convened—the "agreement to cooperate" (*Arbeitsgemeinschaft*) between Hugo Stinnes, speaking for Germany's steel industry, and Carl Legien, leader of the German trade unions. Germany was to be a pluralistic state, and its first business was to assure peace and begin reconstruction; these moderates believed that Germany could afford neither a national war of liberation against the "Versailles system" and the former enemies nor a civil war between revolution and reaction.

The wisdom of this decision has been debated ever since; but it was confirmed by the voters, who gave none of the great ideological camps a majority. At no time during the Republic's short life did either the combined socialists or the combined reactionaries hold a majority in the Reichstag (which soon was reconvened in Berlin), and parliamentary government was possible only as long as moderates on both sides were willing to cooperate. This change of government would be the most polite and genteel in history; it would be inspired by that middle-class Kultur, the property of the ten percent who had gone to a Gymnasium.

But in its second meaning, "Weimar Culture" is the ferment among intellectuals, the ebullient fertility in the arts, in music, the theater, the novel, in philosophy, and the sciences. To be sure, most of the truly novel fruits of this new age dated back to the previous era: Expressionism, twelve-tone music, relativity, psychoanalysis, Rilke's poetry, Bauhaus architecture; but it is equally true that reception and diffusion of the new ideas and forms of expression did not begin until the 1920s and that many of the protagonists had to wait for recognition until the 1940s and remained "outsiders" during the life of the Republic.[3]

The "Tucholsky syndrome" consists in attributing this alienation of the intellectuals to a specific "German misery." Kurt Tucholsky himself lived in Paris while writing editorials for *Die Weltbühne* in which he complained that none of the republican politicians was a Robespierre. He was totally unaware that his revered French authors were as forlorn in their own country as he was in his.

The great problems of survival were to be solved by com-

promise and negotiation, often by dillydallying and logroll-
ing. There was to be no panoply of symbols, nothing to be
proud of, nothing to inspire young people. Politics was degraded to the status of a business; whatever intellectual, esthetic, or moral satisfaction a man sought had to be found
outside politics.

All of this went against the grain of intellectuals on the right
and on the left. Both sides objected to the lack of luster, of
dynamism, of inspiration. They would have liked to see either
the old glories of the monarchy or the new intellectual
triumphs of equality, justice, liberty, fraternity. Together, they
provided the splendors of a nostalgic counterculture: romantic, expressionist, nihilistic, erotic, libertarian—in retrospect
now called "Weimar culture." I have myself been guilty of
calling this ensemble a "Periclean age," and it is time to revise the judgment.

As far as Jews were concerned, it is true that they were
represented in the liberal professions more generously than
in the general population. Obviously, they were urban middle class, and as Professor Mommsen has shown, they were
especially well represented in those economic categories that
in the era of monopoly capitalism were on the decline. They
also tended toward "liberal" (in the European sense) philosophy and therefore to parties of the center of the political
spectrum. But they upheld liberal culture not as Jews but as
middle-class intellectuals. Romanticists, nihilists, and reactionaries found the Republic odious not because it was Jewish but because they realized that the Jews identified with it.
In many cases, the Jewish identity of a politician, actor, writer,
or department store owner was not known until some Nazi
researcher had found out. After Goethe had been appropriated by the republican establishment, some Nazi papers found
Jewish ancestors in his family and Jewish traits in his phy-
siognomy and short legs. They also found a secret Masonic
design on the Republic's coins, and they invariably attributed
the malaise of the middle classes, declining in that age of
modernization, to an international conspiracy—either of Wall

Street, of French imperialism, or of the Elders of Zion. They did not need Jewish authors to prove that the German language had been polluted by an alien mentality, nor Jewish doctors to prove that German science had been sold to materialists. The intelligentsia was "Jewish" because it was alienated, not the other way around.

Ironically, many Jewish leaders were patriotic and conservative (their association of "German Citizens of the Jewish Faith" was derisively dubbed "Jewish Citizens of the German Faith"). Alfred Ballin, the shipowner, was the only friend of the kaiser's who shot himself on the day of his flight; Ernst Lissauer wrote the only German war poem worth that name; Hugo von Hofmannsthal, half-Jewish, was a staunch monarchist and Richard Strauss's librettist; and Jews were swarming around the proto-fascist Stefan George. But none of these ideas or persons were ever denounced as "Jewish"; the image of Jewishness was attached to the Republic, just as a generation earlier the anti-Dreyfus mobs across the Rhine had attacked "la France juive." With only slight exaggeration, we can say that had the Jews not existed, the Nazis would have hated the Republic no less—or they might have invented another hate object (as in Italy, where the Freemasons were used for that purpose).

The French Republic survived the reactionary anti-Semitic onslaught; the German Republic did not. But the difference certainly was not that Weimar was less republican or Jacobin than France, as the intellectuals believed. If anything, Weimar was more liberal, more progressive than the "Third Republic." Weimar succumbed to the triple calamity of the Versailles Treaty, the inflation, and the Depression. Walter Laqueur thinks that the Republic did not have to fall but for "the loss of nerve, political and economic error." He also blames the intelligentsia's isolation and the lack of direction on the Left. He cites those who held that "Fascism is already here" and that therefore it would make no difference whether power was handed to Hitler. In his view it was not the Republic that failed but the republicans. But he fails to show why the republicans had no answer to those youths who had so conspicuously turned their backs on the Republic; why there was no dialogue between the antagonistic forces.

No history of culture can answer these questions because the Republic was not identical with its culture; it was its counterfoil. Weimar culture was one of polemics and of anguish. It was born out of protest against Weimar politics and Weimar's social structure. Weimar went down precisely because it tried to impose republican policies on a social-political structure that had not overcome its imperial antecedents. Judges, army officers, civil servants, most of the economic management were hostile to the Republic; newspapers and movies were in the hands of its enemies. Although the state was a republic in a purely legal sense rather than in a real sense, its culture was a true republic of letters.

CODA

[16]

On Being an Exile

An Old-Timer's Personal and Political Memoir

WHEN two comrades of our group were arrested I decided it was time to leave Berlin. My fiancée also had been detained, but thanks to her father's connections she had been released. She had been fortunate, too, in that it was not the Storm Troopers but the police who came to her home; at police headquarters the evidence was conveniently lost. In 1933 the police were still on our side quite often.

After Hitler's victory, Richard Lowenthal, my fiancée, and I had put out what was probably the first underground resistance paper, entitled *Proletarische Aktion*. But soon it was no longer advisable to print our little sheet in anyone's house. Most of us were too well known in the district. I learned one day that good people—comrades, socialists—were speaking highly of me; unfortunately, they publicly credited me with things I did not care to have advertised.

On a beautiful afternoon I noticed Vera in the street, an old friend who belonged to a most conspiratorial underground group. She hissed something like "Get lost!" and I had no choice but to act as though I had made a pass and she had given me the brush-off. I also ran into Wendt, a former president of the Communist Students' club; although I had been expelled from the Communist Youth many years earlier, I

Reprinted with permission from *Salmagundi* (Fall 1969/Winter 1970).

had occasionally written for his paper. He had always been very open-minded, so I talked to him frankly about the situation, indicating how one might perhaps coordinate underground work. He answered rather curtly; the next week someone told me that Wendt had gone over to the Nazis. That made my blood run cold; but to my knowledge Wendt made no use of what I had told him. Should he be alive, I wish to thank him publicly.

However, that revelation did it for me. I had to get out of Berlin; anyway my Jewish looks were a danger to any friend I visited, and all friends were comrades who in one way or another, more or less, for this or that group, were involved in underground work. By November 1933 I was tired of sleeping in a different bed every night.

But where should I go? It was not easy for a Jew to find a job anywhere in Germany. Besides, by December 1933 I had become convinced that Hitler was neither ephemeral nor temporary. I was not looking for a hiding place over a short period. The Nazis were going to last at least five years; they were not going to ruin themselves (abwirtschaften) to pave the way for a Communist comeback, as the Stalinists thought. I knew that the Communist apparatus was shattered. Desperately, some brave militants kept painting hammer-and-sickle signs on walls and chimneys; but they could not indefinitely prolong the optical illusion that the CP was alive outside the concentration camps. Their leaders, however, continued to send these young comrades into the arms of the police, ruthlessly exploiting their blind faith in early victory. It was criminal to continue such revolutionary gymnastics, but the Stalinist bosses could not admit that their party had been beaten.

The Social Democratic party's presidium had already gone to Prague. To the most militant among us it appeared that the old parties of the left were dead and that a new movement would have to be built—inside Germany by small circles which would meet very quietly, avoiding any foolish action-for-action's-sake; outside Germany by those who were able to formulate the new ideas and to publicize them. It was also clear to me that the place where new ideas would crystallize out of this ferment would have to be Paris, the birthplace of all European radicalism, every European's second capital, the probable center of any international action against Hitler. I knew that I would have to go to Paris to explain my four conclusions: that we had been beaten; that Hitler would last as long as five years; that Hitler would not be removed by the old parties; and that the birth of a new movement depended on a frank admission of these propositions. A further consequence was that Hitler could not be beaten by the German opposition alone but only in conjunction with foreign governments; but it took some more time to recognize what that meant for the movement and for me.

Before I left Berlin I explained to my comrades why I thought this was necessary, and they agreed. I also told them that it would be better for them to survive than to perish as unsung heroes. I suggested that they use every available device to camouflage themselves, and I encouraged the workers among them to join the Nazi shop organization (NSBO). Idiots among the American occupation authorities later screened people for their "affiliation with Nazi organizations"; little did they know, or imagine, what life was like in a totalitarian environment. Bertolt Brecht has written a beautiful poem about the brave men whose names and faces nobody ever knew; after it was all over, we unquestionable anti-Nazis must have given hundreds, or thousands, of affidavits of good faith to people of whom we had no firsthand knowledge but whom we felt we would have trusted under the trying conditions of the Third Reich. Still later we met people whom we would not have trusted at first: Prussian aristocrats and conservative churchmen who had become disgusted with Hitler only when he revealed himself more blatantly. One of them was my father-in-law, who had looked upon the Nazis as, at worst, misbehaved patriots but, at best, helpers against godless Communists. Under the dictatorship, no one knew how many of his kind were lingering inside Nazi Germany as "internal exiles."

The experience of the Third Reich made me more tolerant—or, better—more than tolerant. The great discovery of the 1930s was that the dividing line runs not between left and right but between decent people and political gangsters, between tolerant people and totalitarians; not between those who stayed in Germany (and perforce had to be involved in the daily life of the Third Reich) and those who emigrated for whatever reason, but between those who enjoyed the atmosphere of the Third Reich and profited thereby, and those who lived as aliens either in their own country or in another.

My own emigration was, of course, determined by the accident of my birth, which turned out to be a help in one respect: "Aryans" who had to flee from Hitler's jailers were suspect in the French authorities' eyes. These political refugees, simple members of the Republican Defense League, the Social Democratic, or the Communist parties, were not welcome in the country of liberty. We who had hoped that the French would consider us allies were sadly mistaken. To the French authorities the German left was at least as dangerous as Hitler. Like Professor A. J. P. Taylor they thought of Hitler as just a less polished version of Stresemann. It was quite a surprise to me that even French liberals showed a profound distrust of everything German and had little knowledge (and less appreciation) of the heroic efforts our republican government had made to pay Germany's war debt and to become reconciled to the West. It never dawned on the French that a more generous policy toward the Weimar Republic might have saved them and us from Hitler.

Later, during the war, they interned in camps all those who technically still were German citizens—Jews and anti-Nazi militants together with Nazis who happened to be in France when the war broke out, as well as discharged members of the Foreign Legion—real toughs who often were Nazis, too. When we tried to explain to our commanding officer that this created precarious, perhaps even dangerous, situations, he answered: "Some of you may not be *Boches* but you are still *Allemands*." A staunch French royalist, he had utter contempt for "Germans" who tried to make him believe that they were on the side of France in this war. After the defeat I told the story to a friendly farmer who had allowed me to hide in his barn; he looked at me without any sign of sympathy and said: "Sure, it's suspicious when a man denies his fatherland." This simple man expected me to side not with his country but with mine, and yet he sheltered me!

Try as I might, I never succeeded in being accepted. Yet I still consider France my second fatherland. I was poor there most of the time and I had to accept the oddest jobs, but I enjoyed every day of my seven years in France. I liked the people and I fell in love with the language; I began writing in French, too, and I even got involved in French politics. Nevertheless, it must be stated that in France I remained an alien in more than a technical sense.

In the beginning this was quite natural; one does not shed an underground existence so easily. I lived and worked for the day when we would all return openly. It is true that I had come to explain that this day was not going to dawn as early as the refugee colony in Paris thought; but in the beginning I made no arrangements to stay longer, and it did not matter that the French authorities did not even recognize my existence.

How strange it is to be a person without a passport! I soon had to fight very hard to obtain from the Paris police an expulsion order, for to be expelled meant to be recognized, and in the process of protesting the injustice one gradually acquired legal status until one eventually wrangled a permit to stay and, with luck, a permit to work. To achieve this, one had to learn the art of bribery. In a country that is largely governed by corruption, to know whom to pay for administrative services is really a sign that one has become acclimatized. The experience shattered both my Hegelian ideas of the dignity of the state and my liberal prejudices about France. As I said, our guerrilla warfare with the French authorities ended in our internment on the day the war broke out. The ghastly routine of evading the police and dealing with it prepared us for the Kafkaesque world which we finally came to recognize as our own.

Being an exile is not a matter of needing a passport; it is a state of mind. I discovered this only gradually. In the beginning I did not experience exile as a universal mode of existence. I still attributed my stance entirely to the specific and, so it seemed, transitory phenomenon of Hitler. We all felt that Hitler was something extraordinary, irregular, unforeseeable and, if rightly considered, impossible. According to the German philosophy which still was most commonly accepted and to which the Marxists also paid their tribute, this unthinkable phenomenon had no right to, and therefore did not, exist. Not really. Ernst Cassirer, the philosopher who was to be my neighbor in New York, once, at the time of Stalingrad, expressed it in a classic way: "You know, Mr. Pachter, this Hitler is an error (*Irrtum*) of History; he does not belong in German history at all. And therefore he will perish." This is what all decent people felt at the time. But History cared not for human decency—or German philosophy for that matter.

While I still felt that History owed us a rectification of her mistakes—a faith which forced our confidence to be placed in the eventual triumph of anti-Fascism—still I delivered my message that Hitler would last five years and that the condition of our rebirth was recognition of our defeat. They almost lynched me. All the has-beens expressed the fervent belief that nothing had happened to debunk their prophets: none of the political groups that met in the somber backrooms of some brasserie or bistro to deliberate the fate of the world could actually decipher it. Each was trying to prove to the others that its special brand of Marxism should have been followed and that other groups should not have betrayed the cause. There is nothing as inconsequential as émigré *querelles*, and in the midst of all that activity I soon felt more isolated than I had been in Nazi Berlin. I formed an alliance with Arkadij Gurland, who also had managed to be alienated from all groups and who was prepared to start thinking anew.

Recognition of the new conditions of our struggle had become imperative as early as 1933 when, in Berlin, we began to turn out our clandestine sheet. Richard Lowenthal played an important part in the discussions that took place. At the time he was working with Karl Frank's group, which later took the name "New Beginning," but which then was known, somewhat derisively, as "The Black Hand." The New Beginning people had, in my opinion, an exaggerated devotion to the Leninist theory of the vanguard and the virtues of that form of organization. But Richard Lowenthal had a keen, sharp mind and an elegant pen. He believed that the current situation was one where the philosophy of his group might be properly applied and leadership provided to other groups. We both felt that a sense of direction was needed, as well as a new assurance that socialism had a future so long as Hitler could be seen in historical perspective: that is to say as neither a horseman of the Apocalypse nor an Anti-Christ who preceded the millennium.

We took the position that fascism was a new form of capitalism, its third stage: after liberalism and monopoly, we believed, capitalism had passed into a stage which might be termed state capitalism or, as the French said more correctly, *économie dirigée*. We wished to show that at this stage dictatorial rule was necessary to prevent the capitalist system's social, economic, and political collapse; where such a dictatorship succeeded, it might even give the masses a share in prosperity and make them believe that they were enjoying greater security. In contrast to the Communist party, which counted on an early collapse of fascism, we sought to prepare our readers for the possible "success" of state capitalism under the Nazis. After all, we knew it would last as long as five years.

Many of us were forced to remain in Paris longer than that. Many of us, indeed, fell silent. The myth that exile produces Dantes, Marxes, Bartoks, and Avicennas certainly is not justified in general. More often exile destroys talent, or it means the loss of the environment that morally, socially, and physically nourishes talent. Even the musicians, whose idiom one might suppose is both personal and international, were surprised to find out how little their values were appreciated in a culture just next door. Only the few who already had world-famous names were able to carry on—living on reduced royalties, but not reduced to starting from scratch. Yet even in this category we have Thomas Mann's comically pathetic complaint that he had to live in a hotel room! Lucky also were those young enough to claim that their studies had been interrupted: benevolent committees provided the means for them to complete their education, and some endured hunger for the opportunity of a new start in intellectual life. But for most of us a new country meant more than a new language. Few found jobs in their fields, and most could not even find jobs that might be called tolerable. Hardly any one had a working permit, and the kind of work one could do illegally was poorly paid, never steady, and often demeaning. The more pleasant opportunities were *nègre* (ghosting)—i.e., a German dentist, lawyer, engineering consultant, research chemist, etc. did the job of a Frenchman who lent his name and took most of the pay. Many of the jobs I had were fraudulent, ridiculous, or repulsive. Having been taught by my puritanical father that work ennobles, I now learned that work can be more degrading than anything else. People who once had taken money for granted shared my feelings. One day Rudolf Hilferding, former finance minister and author of *Das Finanzkapital*, asked me with a sigh: "Did you ever have to work for a living?"

Each of us solved this problem in his own way, and not all did so honorably. Many had to rely on their wives, who could always find maids' jobs; but over this, many marriages collapsed. Others made an art of persuading backers and committees that we had a claim on their respect and money; even those of us who had not produced a line still represented that thin veneer of culture which stood between Western civilization and the new barbarians. Our physical and moral survival depended on this high-class form of extortion, and the piratical attitude we developed toward moneyed institutions prepared us for the games we later had to play with American foundations. We may even have helped to develop the art of thinking up research projects and writing outlines which now has become the mark of the academic operator in the Western world. (I suspect this because the percentage of German problems in American research, notably in the 1940s and 1950s, far exceeded our share in the academic population.) While one could not beat the Nazis one could still analyze them—hoping in one activity to keep the question of the century before the public eye and to justify one's existence.

It is no exaggeration to say that at that time we needed the Nazis as our *raison d'être*. They had become our obsession. Their omnipotence could not be illustrated more poignantly than by the way Nazism or Fascism affected our professional careers. Erich Fromm, a psychologist, wrote *Escape from Freedom*; Theodor Adorno, who had sparked the modern interest in Kierkegaard and was interested in the sociology of music, instead studied *The Authoritarian Personality*; Hannah Arendt, a gifted philosopher with little talent for politics, gave us the book on the origins of totalitarianism; Ernst Kris, Freud's co-editor of *Imago*, studied Nazi propaganda; Ernst Cassirer, who detested the entire area of politics and statecraft, nevertheless felt he had to write *The Myth of the State*. Remote fields like philology were raked over in efforts to discover strands of Nazi ideology in early German literature or in the structure of the German language.

How even the purest of sciences had been affected became apparent only much later when it was revealed that Einstein, Meitner, Bohr, Bethe, and other pacifists had contributed to the development of the atomic bomb.

Unfortunately, the Nazis were not alone in debasing the German language. We, the pure ones, the bearers and preservers of German culture, became guilty of something almost as bad: our language froze at the point of emigration, or it grew poorer for want of a dialogue with the people who create and develop speech every day. The sweet preciousness of the past which some of the famous cultivated was no substitute for living communion. By observing my Russian and Italian friends I had seen what happened to people who were reduced to inbreeding as émigrés. The Russian newspaper in Paris refused to use the simplified spelling the Bolsheviks had introduced. Were we similarly dated? We were writing about ghosts, writing for ghosts, and gradually turning into ghosts.

It was even worse when one decided to abandon German.

Working in a language which is not the language of one's dreams is to miss many over- and undertones, ambiguities and poetic notions, the spontaneousness and even the silences. Dimensions of thought and feeling must be replaced by a technique of significations, using spoken words in prefabricated, studied sequences which threaten to impoverish what they ought to enrich. Few succeeded in becoming creative writers in their second language, though they learned to express their ideas precisely in a technical Emigranto.

Observation: Uneducated people quickly learn to make small talk in canned phrases. Intellectuals learn slowly and tend to speak "translatese," painfully aware that it is one flight below the level they would like to inhabit intellectually. In New York I became able to guess from a person's German the decade of his emigration, and from his English which German city he hailed from.

The exile literature of those days is deeply steeped in the experience of defeat, of emigration, of the breakdown of hope. Alfred Döblin's *Babylonische Wanderung*, Thomas Mann's *Joseph* novels, Anna Seghers' *Seventh Cross*, Ernst Glaeser's *Last Civilian*, Erich Maria Remarque's *Three Comrades* (as well as his later *Arch of Triumph*), and Franz Werfel's *Jacobowsky and the Colonel* offer glimpses of the new outlook. Thomas Mann probably was unaffected in his Olympian serenity; he continued to write for an imaginary cosmopolitan audience. Anna Seghers for her part knew others for whom she wrote: the comrades of the Communist International. But Döblin told me that he did not know his audience any longer and was afraid his art might suffer from it; he then made a deliberate effort to *find* an audience: he wrote a Rosa Luxemburg trilogy.

It was, of course, not a question of having a publisher (which Brecht ironically called "the inner question") but of knowing that one was writing for a culture with a future; that no matter how gloomy its present content, one's play or novel would hold out hope for those to whom it was addressed.

Writers who had lost this faith, or who no longer believed that their audiences shared their faith, foundered and their style deteriorated. Some of the older writers who no longer knew which values they defended fell silent. Some younger ones who had shown promise were stopped in their tracks for want of an audience or a sympathetic environment. The only German writer to achieve world stature in exile was Hermann Broch; most of those who had gained it before failed to sustain their excellence.

But we shall never know how many good writers were broken by the shattering experience of loneliness. No unpublished masterworks emerged from secret drawers after the fall of the Third Reich. Joseph Roth died of drinking absinthe. Ernst Glaeser broke down and returned to Nazi Germany (where he became a hack, and after the war drank himself to death). In a moving letter to Walter Hasenclever, Kurt Tucholsky relates how someone asked Nitti, whose cabinet Mussolini overthrew: "What are you doing in Paris?" He answered: "I am waiting." Tucholsky comments: "I would not want to be like him." Both Tucholsky and Hasenclever took their lives. The same sense of futility caused the suicides of Stefan Zweig, Walter Benjamin, Ernst Weiss, and Ernst Toller.

Many who tried to avoid failure met regularly in the German Exile Writers' Club and assured each other that German culture was where they were and that Hitler could not suppress German literature. Other writers, we heard, had little circles in Prague, at the Côte d'Azur, in London, in New York, and even in Hollywood—though it also was reported that in this latter place they were unhappy and ineffective and received stipends rather than remuneration for services rendered. In Paris, at least, the indignities of our miserable life were compensated by the knowledge that our exile had significance. The closeness of refugee circles might give us a rather dim view of our leaders' human qualities; but as carriers of the great European heritage we saw ourselves, ten feet tall, bestriding the theater of history.

This sense of our mission received an enormous boost when the Communist International held its Seventh World Congress in 1934. After a long period of sterility, Stalin, for his own reasons, of course, returned to the humanistic and democratic wellsprings of Marxism. As he sought a rapprochement with the Western powers, he launched the Popular Front slogan and issued the "Trojan horse" directive. His propagandists engaged in a vast campaign of cultural mobilization, organized writers' congresses against fascism, created magazines, and promoted fellow-traveling enterprises. Reputable publishing houses which previously had been denounced as purveyors of mass deception now were infiltrated as vehicles of mass enlightenment; bourgeois culture, so far an object of derision, now became the heritage which the proletariat was to bring to new flowering. The refugee writers, more dependent and more malleable, eagerly seized the opportunities this well-heeled conspiracy opened to them and, knowingly or unknowingly, provided the core for the alliance whose outer fringes encompassed Aldous Huxley and Julien Benda. In these circles it was easy to meet André Gide, Aragon, Malraux, Nizan, Georges Friedman, and others. Although Gide was soon to voice his disappointment with the Soviet Union, it is fair to say that staying close to the Communist party did no harm to some lesser literary reputations at that time.

The German writers, indoctrinated and disciplined by our club, constituted a sort of cadre for this campaign. Our meetings were graced by the appearances of Heinrich Mann, Arthur Koestler, Erich Reger, and Alfred Döblin; but our discussions were dominated by the commissars and conducted in the style of the Moscow Writers' Club. Manès Sperber—then an editor of Gallimard publishers, today an important figure in Paris literary circles—bravely tried to stem the tide of party literature by emphasizing that art must speak to the deeper emotions too; but Alfred Kantorowicz remained plagued by the knowledge that his mediocrity condemned him to remain a partisan writer and a liar.[1] After the war he tried to act as East Germany's literary pope for a while, but eventually even he had to seek asylum in the West.

Another staunch defender of the party line was Arthur Koestler. Later he boasted that he had an anti-Soviet play

hidden in his desk; but at that time his job and his fame depended on the party, and the only time we met we clashed
rather vehemently. Despite his *Spanish Testament*, which at
the time was a deeply moving document, I still think that he
is no more than an intelligent reporter. After he broke with
the Communists, he found a comfortable niche in the liberal
establishment and retired to his private ivory tower. But his
later writings betray an acute awareness of the problem with
which I am concerned here: what it means to be a refugee
cannot be described in the simple terms of finding a job and
adjusting to foreign customs; it is a way of being, of constantly lingering between arrival and departure. No one has
told the story better than Koestler.

It would be tempting here to describe the intellectual excitement of the Popular Front in France and in Spain. Never
again was I to feel so close to the masses; never again did I
experience a similar unity of thought and action. Here was
the great cause that allied the future of European culture, the
achievement of social justice, the rise of the masses to a share
in power, and the fight against the evil dictators and usur-
pers. My own little monument to this episode is *España Cri-
sol Politico*—a book that tells of our hopes and how they were
shattered by our friends.

This is not the place to repeat the story of Léon Blum's
weakness, of Chamberlain's betrayal, of Stalin's gangsterism;
I am concerned here with the consequences for our mission.
The Spanish Civil War offered the peoples their last chance
to fight the dictators in a revolutionary way; thereafter, the
European intelligentsia could hope to fight Hitler only with
the great powers' help. Since many of us were pacifists, this
meant a split after the day of Munich; a split that rent parties,
families, and even individual consciences down the middle.

I sided with those who would have defended Czechoslovakia, and so did most Jewish refugees. But that placed us at
odds with many of our friends in the British Labour Party
and among the French Socialists as well as many intellec-

tuals. I did not know then, of course, that the "internal exiles" hoped the Western nations would resist and thereby give
them a chance to get rid of Hitler; but I felt that Munich made
World War II inevitable. Only the Communists understood
this too, but ten months later they drew the conclusion, quite
natural for them, that it was better to be allied with Hitler
than opposed to him, and resumed their attacks on the democracies.

These developments left a small number of us alone between two hostile groups of friends: those who stood on their
pacifist principles even if that meant victory for Hitler, and
those who wanted victory over Hitler even if that meant war.
War destroys principles and shakes men into alignments.
Soon the hour was to strike when men would have to choose
their comrades. Hatred of Hitler, bitterness over the defeat of
Spain, desire to avenge the rape of Czechoslovakia converted
most emigrants into unquestioning patriots of their host
countries or of any country that would join the alliance. (One
did not mention the Moscow trials as long as Stalin seemed
to hate Hitler as much as we did.) They became superpatriots
and worked for agencies from which the liberal intellectual
naturally shrinks, such as the Deuxième Bureau in France or
the FBI in the United States, even the GPU. Some forgave
Stalin after June 22, 1941; others looked for new allegiances;
Fritz Epstein, Stefan Possony, and others later forgot their native liberalism so far as to support Joseph McCarthy.

A few of us, however, did not see things that simply. Cos-
mopolitans and liberals, we could not turn into chauvinists
and militarists, and we doubted whether we had a right to
have French blood shed to redeem our defeat in Germany.
We wondered: Did we have a right to appeal, in France, to
the same nationalistic instincts we had condemned in Germany, from which we had fled, and which we pretended to
fight in the name of civilization?

Nor was Western civilization any longer as self-evident a
value as we would have liked to think. In France we had
become familiar with a new literature which ran counter to
our notions of humanism. Starting from Rimbaud, a series of

poètes maudits had rejected that civilization wholesale; the line ended with Montherlant and Céline in France, with T. S. Eliot in the United States, with D. H. Lawrence in England. The followers of Nietzsche in Germany had produced a similar revulsion from intellectualism, but we had dismissed its symptoms as a peculiar German disease.[2] The same disease now stared us in the face as a European phenomenon. Our cherished culture was sick, and whether Céline was right or was merely a symptom, his immediate success was proof that the enemy was not only on the other side of the Rhine. Moreover, some of these writers, like the revered Hamsun, the mad Ezra Pound (himself a voluntary exile), and Céline openly sympathized with fascism and were rabid anti-Semites. Worse still, the disease was not confined to the right. Sartre, a man of the left, published the deeply pessimistic *Nausea*, a sort of manifesto of despair. Western letters suffered from a failure of nerve. Though their mainstream was still represented by Jules Romains (*Men of Good Will*) and Galsworthy (*The Forsyte Saga*), the new and incisive literature tended towards totalitarian ideas and antidemocratic instincts. Were we fighting a rearguard action? Was fascism the wave of the future? Hemingway—whom the left claimed because of *A Farewell to Arms*—seemed to preach a vision of the hero that Mussolini would have liked. Would we be exiles from the age of liberalism in a coming age of beehive states that was dawning in all countries alike?

As Aldous Huxley and George Orwell in England and Harold Lasswell in the United States drew the caricature of the "garrison state," inside Germany the expressionist poet Gottfried Benn,[3] so we found later, had given this age the name of *Quartär*, quartary, following the tertiary order—the age where gigantic apparatuses would manipulate and dominate the minds of amorphous masses. Visions of 1984 were anticipated in a curious book, *La Bureaucratisation du monde* by B. Riccio, a Trotskyist; Rudolf Hilferding, a well-known Marxist, speculated in a Russian émigré paper about the possibilities of a totalitarian economy free of unemployment and crises.[4]

These discoveries posed a special problem for two kinds of intellectuals who otherwise have little in common: Marxists and bohemians. Neither can bear the thought of being out of step. The bohemians are constantly keeping up with the newest literary or artistic fashion, and the Marxists must be careful not to fall off the escalator of "Progress." The literati no longer were content with l'art pour l'art against society; they were graduating to l'art contre l'art and against all values. The Marxists always hailed the "next stage" and confused post hoc with supra hoc. Walter Benjamin already saw that the common interpretation of "historical materialism" needed serious revision, no matter what Marx had "really" meant. In the current version fascism was a "higher" form of capitalism, as the purges were a "higher" form of socialism and the literary mob was a "higher" form of criticism. Hannah Arendt soon was to describe totalitarianism as the action of lumpen-bourgeoisie, lumpen-proletariat, and lumpen-literati—all hell-bent on destroying the values of Western civilization. It required the stamina of an exile not to surrender to these dark forces of man's tribal past which had unleashed their fury in the name of progress, truth, and nature.

No; this war was not being waged between a more perfect and a less perfect totalitarianism but between a world that feared it might lose its humanism and one that was rushing to erase all vestiges of humanism. I had no doubt that among my allies in this war there were many traditionalists and reactionaries, and many who discovered too late that in the end the totalitarians must persecute them too. To have such allies is not easy, especially when one lives in a French internment camp and the only way to get out is by joining the Foreign Legion. Not even those whose citizenship Hitler had revoked were allowed to join the regular French army, or were promised French citizenship at the end of their service in the Foreign Legion.

In the camp I met Heinrich Blücher, a friend of Walter Benjamin and Hannah Arendt's second husband, who would become educational director of Bard College. He had been a movie writer, and he used his enforced leisure to read Kant.

He also gave a test to his fellow inmates: Those who liked
Brecht's "Legend of the Origin of the Book Tao-tê-Ching"
were invited to further confidences. Since I found the poem
particularly apposite to the exile situation, we quickly developed an understanding on the character of the near future
and on the values to be preserved for a far-off day.

The Blüchers helped many other refugees, and it might even
be said that they made a fetish of the exile condition. When
I met them again in New York, they were spending a fortune
to live in an uncomfortable hotel because they felt it was un-
becoming for people like us to have an apartment with furniture of our own. When I bought a secondhand car, they
remonstrated as though I had betrayed them. In Paris I had
only some garden furniture, which could be abandoned without loss, and even now some of my New York furnishings
have an air of the provisional. I suppose I shall never own
the heavy oak table and chairs my parents had in their dining
room. Contempt of the settled, bourgeois style of life is common to artists and to the exiled, as I have observed with my
Russian and Italian friends too, and along with it goes a generous desire to help others who are in similar conditions of
poverty and solitude.

Solidarity was the redeeming experience in the defeat of
France, the details of which I must skip here. It may sound
strange, but the months of insecurity in a little hiding place
in southern France belong to the happiest of my life. Everybody was hungry, everybody was fleeing somewhere, everybody shared what we had, everybody felt like everybody's
brother. We did not have much hope but we developed a
"nerve of failure," a dogged conviction that, even should the
Nazis win, life would go on and there would be new generations. Soon many thousand Frenchmen would be exiles in
their own country. Hitler was converting all Europe into a
refugee camp. Most of those who became martyrs had not
chosen to be heroes; history had thrown them into a role they
had not been prepared to play. It was natural that they could
not be sustained by the positive faith of those who deliberately had chosen to resist evil or who resisted in order to

help their cause. They found comfort and strength, however, in the new philosophy of Existentialism which—strangely, again—Sartre had introduced from Germany and developed into a philosophy of desperate affirmation. The myth of Sisyphus, as reinterpreted by Camus, taught them to return to the rock of history even as it had rolled down, and to begin again. In my only interview with Camus, after the war, he also said that the greatest problem for man was loneliness.

I was tempted to place as a motto over this section a verse by Max Herrmann-Neisse:

> Nun scheint mir alles, was ich schätzte, nichtig.
> Der Nebel draussen hüllt die Scham nicht ein.
> Ich weiss, ich lebte meine Zeit nicht richtig
> Und muss mein Leben lang erfolglos sein.[5]

(Now all I valued highly seems futile. The fog outside cannot cloak the shame. I know I failed truly to live with my age and I must be a failure as long as I live.)

An Excursus

I must confess that I was also a little annoyed by the new philosophy whose adepts proclaimed with sectarian zeal the new gospel of commitment—*engagement*, Sartre called it—as though no philosophy ever before had taught man to act in response to his fellow men's needs. Kant's categorical imperative in effect says nothing else; Hegel had developed the full dialectics of human interaction; and Marx's epistemology started out from the explicit assumption that social action is the only *human* way to know others. With his own categorical imperative Marx concluded: Man must join the action that leads to the liberation of all mankind. These activist, dialectical traits in Marx's thinking had been brought out by Lukács and Korsch even before J. P. Mayer published the "early manuscripts" which expound the concept of "praxis" in so many words. Erich Fromm now has given these ideas wide circulation.

In his own way, Sidney Hook, with whom I had been in Korsch's course, had found a convergence of these Marxian ideas with Dewey's logic of action. Dialectics, after all, is nothing but the recognition that in the humanities and social sciences the observer is always part of the scene he observes. Involvement, therefore, was nothing new to us, and we hailed "engagement" as a more poignant word—also for the possibilities of future development it seemed to open. Unfortunately, the word remained barren. Sartre just assumed that "engagement" always meant engagement on our side; he never showed why this was so and why one could not be engaged on the other side as well. In fact, most of the early existentialists were engaged on the other side. There is nothing especially "left" in Antoine de Saint-Exupéry, and it would not be difficult to make out Mussolini as an existentialist politician.

It has often been said that the same act done by a different person becomes a different act. It is just as true that the same act done by the same person at a different time is a different act. When the refugees introduced existentialism in America it already had become a fad, an empty attitude. Soon courses were held and systems were studied; every society lady could repeat the banality that existence came before essence, or find everything "absurd." Likewise, Hannah Arendt had the unfortunate intuition that America needed Kafka, and people who before the war had lived quite comfortably in the world he had scorned gleefully assured each other that they were living in a Kafkaesque world. Surrealism became the "in" thing and Dali made a fortune. To be accepted in the American literary establishment one had to mention Anxiety (Angst). A thread to which desperate people had clung in their great distress thus became the plaything of a literary cult. In the context of the American society we tried to enter by converting it, existentialism became, in Adorno's words, the last form of conformism. It was particularly suited for a society which no longer knew what it wished to conform to; perhaps it was meant to amaze the bourgeois, but it only tickled him.

I am, of course, not referring here to existentialism as a technique of philosophical inquiry or of psychotherapeutical intuition, but as *Lebensanschauung* or *Weltanschauung*. This aspect of it fulfilled a need in times of great ambiguity; but it could never be a revolutionary philosophy capable of guiding the perplexed out of their condition. After the war existentialism blossomed out into a full-fledged system, with various sub-schools—Marxist, atheist, Christian, humanist—fighting for precedence. Since this development must be considered a gigantic failure and existentialism was an exile philosophy more than anything else, we have to confess that philosophically the wartime emigration remained sterile. We produced no basically new idea and, in contrast to the Italians, no new political movement either.

At that time Paris was swarming with refugees from many countries and in 1938 they were joined by a wave of Spaniards. I had of course many friends among the two older emigrations that had preceded us in Paris—the Russians and the Italians. Their life was tragic. It seemed to me that the length of their exile had hardened rather than mellowed their sectarianism; especially the Russians had learned little and forgotten even less. Their attitude to the Soviet state did not change until Stalin called on their patriotic feelings, and then many thought of going back—precisely at the moment when the dictatorship exhibited its ugliest features.

A new attitude was struck by the brothers Rosselli and their group, Giustizia e Libertà. When they were murdered by Mussolini's agents, 200,000 of us marched behind their coffins to Père-Lachaise Cemetery, where so many of the earlier *fuorusciti* lie buried. Giustizia e Libertà was neither pre-fascist nor Marxist; it prepared a new humanist leadership for the post-fascist era. Ignazio Silone (and, as we found out much later, Carlo Levi) had a similar vision of Man in rebellion against the fascist state.

Since the fascist state was more porous than the Nazi state, it was possible for the *fuorusciti* to remain in contact with their homeland; but they could do little to organize an opposition inside the country. It was not until the war had

ALTERIVS NONSIT QVI SVVS ESSE POTEST

EFIGIES AVREOLI THEOPHRASTI AB HOHEN:
HEIM SVE ÆTATIS 47
OMNE DONVM PERFECTVM A DEO
INPERFECTVM A DIABOLO

1 5A† 40

Eugen Diederichs

Paracelsus, sixteenth-century scientist and innovator. Woodcut by August
Hirschvogel. "A veritable Dr. Faustus." "In a way, my *Paracelsus,* subti-
tled *Magic Into Science,* is my own autobiography."
His motto (at top): Let him be no one else's who can be his own.
Legend (at bottom): Effigy of Aureolus Theophrastus of Hohenheim at the
age of 47.

> "Every gift is perfect from God
> Imperfect from the Devil."

Oskar Maria Graf. "Oskar Maria Graf, a Bavarian poet and novelist, was as German—or to be precise, as Bavarian—as a beer mug both in appearance and in speech."

Heinrich and Thomas Mann. "The film *The Blue Angel* does not quite reflect the radicalism of [Heinrich Mann's] *Professor Unrath*, on which it is based."

"Although Thomas Mann later became the most prominent of antifascist intellectuals, his ultimate political stance still shows him as the artist who remains censoriously aloof from middle-class society."

brought disaster rather than glory to Italy that new groupings arose, that the partisans started looking for a new politics. Professor Parri's Action party and the men of Giustizia e Libertà then tried to lead this movement toward a democratic and socialist revolution; but they were small in number, and the revolution was betrayed by the big parties. A similar fate befell the Rassemblement, which emerged in France after the war. Inspired by Sartre, Rousset, and other intellectuals, it remained without influence on the masses. All practical politics quickly was taken over by the big parties and the traditional organizations. There was no European revolution after Hitler, and the Jacobin intellectuals remained exiles from the political process even in the democracies.

By the end of 1940, it had become clear that we would not be safe much longer in our little village. Even though ostensibly southern France was not occupied yet by the Germans, we had seen German soldiers and SS men in the streets of Marseille. Here I cannot deny myself the pleasure of giving thanks to the International Rescue Committee, called into being by Jay Lovestone, which was most effective in rescuing refugees. Its Marseille office, run by Varian Fry, helped us and many others obtain U.S. visas as well as Spanish and Portuguese transit visas. The trick was to have them all valid at the same time; if you had to wait too long for one of them, the others were bound to expire. Technically, the first thing you needed was the French exit visa; but even if you were the owner of an expulsion order, getting out of the country that was expelling you was quite a different story.

Most of us therefore decided to do without the exit visa, and the Marseille committee helped us get into Spain. It had young volunteers who had not achieved their American visas yet but who knew the Pyrenees. One of them guided us on a spectacularly beautiful path, with glimpses of the Mediterranean way below on our left, to the border. We found ourselves in Franco's Spain—slightly less perilous than Vichy

France—then in Salazar's Portugal; then there was the boat, and New York.

My thanks go also to the Emergency Rescue Committee, founded by Paul Hagen, which was most active in rescuing people and securing visas for them. The Jewish committees helped Jewish refugees once they were here, but they were more interested in promoting Zionism than in opening the United States to immigration. Secretary of the Interior Harold Ickes at one point suggested settlements in Alaska, but the Zionists exploited the refugees' plight for their own political purposes. They wagered the lives of many thousands whom Hitler had doomed to die, in order to force the opening of Palestine. Fortunately, in times of emergency the American government overcame the resistance of anti-immigration lobbies and obtained from Congress the power to grant visas outside the regular quota.

Going to Palestine (later, Israel), of course, meant to elude the fate of the exile—to end the *galuth*. Since an uncle of mine, the painter Hermann Struck, was a powerful man in Palestine, I could have obtained a certificate. But I told him that in my opinion the destiny of Jews was to be the salt of the earth.

Going to America also was an admission of defeat. But we were fortunate in preserving our lives, and we were glad that so many of us were able to escape from the destruction of Europe. Many had preceded us to these shores and prepared the mold for a different kind of émigré existence: here one tried to find a place in a society that was willing to accept the immigrant. One had the right to work and no need to feel excluded. Moreover, American society was engaged in a great revolution which seemed to continue where the Popular Front in France had failed; that revolution offered the progressive intellectual a special opportunity to experiment with utopias. An enlightened government was transforming the republic into a social democracy whose ideology was at the opposite pole from Hitler's and Stalin's.

At the same time, America was on the verge of a great reorientation in her foreign policy. She had been isolationist and secure in her own strength between two oceans. But Franklin D. Roosevelt's vision, combined with the shock of the fall of France, gradually produced the change that we refugees, perhaps erroneously, interpreted as a conversion of America to our political philosophy. We felt that antifascism and international security were really two facets of one policy and that we were able to explain her mission to America while helping F.D.R. educate his country for this new responsibility.

But to do this we also had to learn and to unlearn a lot. Americans did not react to the same appeals that moved us. Americans do not easily respond to abstract ideas. They don't admire a man for what he proposes but for the way he carries it out. They are forever trying out something new but are careful to keep it in the framework of old institutions which, however, are capable of infinite reinterpretation. They think that the term "pragmatic" implies something honorable and laudable and they conceive of their laws as guidelines that one circumvents, modifies, disregards, or adapts to. To a European mind all of this can be exasperating, most of all the ambiguity of that experimenting and temporizing: one never can tell whether "flexibility" will lead to utter corruption or to greater efficiency. Americans are gamblers, and to provide some European solidity for our program we had to gamble too.

The immigrants tried their best to understand this climate of general permissiveness and to blend into it, to prosper in it personally and to gain profit from it for their special cause. To enlist our new country in the service of humanity (and its good war), we were able to appeal to its own ideals, which we embraced ardently; but we also had to overlook some of its glaring blemishes and crying injustices. (Few of us then were aware of the full depth of the Negro problem or would even compare our own plight with that of the Afro-Americans.) To exploit the political naiveté of America, we had to flatter its consciousness of history which we knew it did not have. But we loved America for its promises, its youthfulness, its strength, and also because it was different from Europe in one important respect. America allows the individual to retreat from society and to have ties to various associations and bodies in many different ways; Europe always assumes that one is part of a social group whose every attitude and opinion one shares. In America a religious crisis does not entail a political collapse; an economic depression may leave the social structure intact; a revolution at the universities need not involve other strata. A man may be a racist and yet support the welfare state, or yet he may be a civil rights fighter and hate labor unions. This was almost incomprehensible to me in the beginning.

Later I found that herein lies the true secret of America's domestic security: each group is revolutionary in its own field at one time; no convergence toward a total revolution ever threatens the system as a whole. Since the refugees had no desire to be revolutionary in America, they thankfully embraced this system which permitted them to be dynamic reformers each in his own field. They accepted the so-called conformism which sits so lightly on most Americans' shoulders—precisely because it never seemed to affect vital interests of the individual; politics does not involve Americans with the totalitarian intensity of European party life. In the beginning of this century, European socialism immigrated into New York's sweat shops with immigrants. The refugees of the 1930s and 1940s, by contrast, had no quarrel with the American government, which had saved them from destruction. Eagerly they absorbed the gospel of opportunity. Many went into business or found positions that might not have been open to them in their old countries. In that respect they were luckier than earlier waves of immigrants; they rose faster to greater heights of prosperity.[6]

Beyond these purely personal and mundane reasons, however, the American creed held the promise of another mission for us in particular. We would return to postwar Europe as apostles of a global new deal. For once, it was possible to identify with a living state, and we gladly exchanged European ideologies for the absorbing and fascinating adventure of American pragmatism. I don't know what would have happened had we arrived here under Hoover. But Roosevelt and, after him, Truman persuaded us that our fight and America's fight were one, not only against Hitler but against all forms of totalitarianism, against hunger and backwardness, against colonialism and power politics.

During the war I worked for intelligence—no cloak-and-dagger operations but desk work, which is 95 percent of the job—and later found employment in market research. Unlike many intellectuals I knew a little about American business. But although I was a pretty good economist, I found economics less and less rewarding, the people I met positively boring, their manners appalling, their outlook distressing. I had considerable difficulty in getting "adjusted"—an American word that had not been in my vocabulary before—but this was hardly America's fault. My experience and outlook probably would have made it hard for me to adjust to any business community or to live by business-oriented values in any country. Yet America seems to have developed the purest strain of that culture, unadulterated by aristocratic or intellectual impurities. To make things worse, whiskey does not agree with me, and I loathe loud noise, television, and cocktail parties where one has to shout over the din of other people's chatter; I find baseball the most boring of sports to watch. I agree with Brecht and Sartre that the consumer culture of the American middle class represents a low point in taste and "engagement." Had my naturalization depended on my acceptance of the "American way," I would scarcely have passed the test. The same is true of some of my friends, though others have mastered the art of socializing in this country.

When I turned to teaching, my worries were not over. American students were not used to the freedom that was the pride of European universities. They were poorly informed, provincial, grade-conscious, and difficult to interest in problems of universal significance. When our daughter went to school, however, I began to understand why American education failed to stimulate and to slake the thirst for knowledge.

What is wrong with the college is the American high school and elementary school. My idea of education was based on the European model of an elite culture to which, one hoped, the masses could be lifted. American education seems to strive for an optimal compromise which however develops neither the highest cultural potential for the elite nor the maximum useful and relevant knowledge for the masses. The result is that the cultural avant-garde moves in a vacuum, unrelated to yesterday's cultures—which may or may not be taught in the schools and colleges—unrelated also to itself. I did not find in the United States, as in other countries, a cultural capital where a constant circle of conversation is spinning a web of intellectual relations. There were no coffeehouses—and college cafeterias are notoriously unconducive to talk. Writers in this country don't seem to congregate; they emerge from their respective farms or college-residences with a book every two or three years, and then disappear from public view, except on speaking tours for enormous fees. Academic departments, of course, congregate; but not with each other. They hardly mix for lunch.

I also found it hard to land a desirable position because I did not fit into any of the approved slots; I have written on fascism, on Renaissance medicine, on foreign policy, on propaganda—which makes people uneasy. I am not a cultural snob, but I find myself saying "we" when referring to Europeans of the period I happen to be teaching, and my students have learned to accept me as a witness or as an exhibit of what I am trying to demonstrate. Friends and other refugee scholars who have written memoirs report similar experiences, and unless those who are well adjusted are not talking, the Americanization of refugee intellectuals seems far less perfect than their outward success. Yet, this is not the whole story——

How much of an American one has become one notices only on one's first return "home," where everything then appears so small, so petty, so mean, so oversophisticated, that one is prepared to praise everything American, even the shortcomings. I took offense at the servility, the class spirit, the maid's constant "Ja, Herr Doktor," the chauffeur's heel-clicking, the overcorrectness of officials, and the air of importance in every business executive's anteroom. No matter how heavy the cultural heritage one carries on one's back, "you can't go home again." No matter how close the friends to whom you return, you come home as a stranger, or at least as a different person. Back in Europe, I loved America's freedom and generosity. The first time I returned, the Rosenberg case agitated the European intellectuals, and I found myself explaining the American system of justice.

As a result, I was constantly caught between two camps: explaining Europe to Americans and explaining America to Europeans. Carl Friedrich and Hans Rothfels are in a similar position, holding chairs in this country and in Germany. Others who have permanent positions at American universities like to spend a summer semester or a year at some European academy. Still more make it a habit to go to Europe at least for their vacation, or even own a house in the Alps—not to speak of the conferences and congresses they have to attend in Europe. This jetting about seems to indicate, not that European scholars have caught the American virus of restlessness but that they still live in two worlds. Despite success and adjustment, they seem to need a yearly replenishment of their previous cultural resources even while they elect to stay in this country.

In discussing this strange paradox of outstanding success in American academic life despite a nostalgic attachment to European culture, one easily comes upon two interconnected observations: perhaps we can be better Europeans in the United States than anywhere in Europe—unencumbered by special interests—and perhaps precisely this purity of our European idealism makes us marketable in the United States. Both sides of this equation are also related to my earlier remark on the permissiveness of American society and government: America does not either absorb or reject a person but allows many hundred flowers to bloom in its garden. Di-

vergency, dissent, even strangeness can be allowed to produce the sweet poison from which this enormously resource-
ful society may yet distil some useful drug.

The situation I have described was institutionalized at the
New School for Social Research in New York. Alvin Johnson
had invited a dozen great scholars from Germany to form a
graduate faculty. There were—besides some Social Democratic secretaries of state—Löwe, Köhler, Wertheimer, Led-
erer, Speier, Kahler, Kris, Schütz, Salomon. Then came the
French and Italians: Ascoli, Pekelis, Gourevitch, Mirkine-
Guetzévitch. Many others taught in the Adult Education Division, which after the war also developed a B.A. program.
The school was different from anything that existed in America—a true window on Europe. You had the impression that
an accent-free English would be conspicuous and improper;
the first time I entered my lecture room, unknown to the students, I heard a woman ask: "Does the teacher speak English?" Having mastered the language, many teachers went
from the New School to richer, more American and more normal institutions.

I stayed for fifteen years in various capacities, as research
fellow, lecturer, visiting professor at the Graduate Faculty,
and acting dean, until a new administration decided to com-
mercialize and Americanize the place—at the very time when
American education was experiencing a deep crisis and other
institutions had begun to imitate our methods. Already the
Middle States Association had given us its accreditation and
we were able to guarantee the grades our students earned in
unorthodox ways. (Up to then, the Ivy League universities
would accept our students, but some Southern state university might reject them. I admit that they were taking a chance,
for we might have spoiled the students for the American educational system, and that was worse than any "pink" opinion they might have picked up in class.)

The New School was a place of constant experimentation
and of complete freedom for teachers and students. I am

tempted to say that a place so European is possible "only in America"; it was endowed with the best of Europe without any of the drawbacks and reservations. The advantage of maintaining an exile situation is precisely that you can reject compromises—provided you are satisfied with low pay or even no pay. The New School, by the way, was not half as pink as its reputation. To be sure, we always had a house communist or even a martyr who had been in trouble with HUAC; but we also had a house reactionary—Ernest van den Haag, who likes to clown, played that role handsomely, a house mystic—Alan Watt, and several other oddballs. But on the whole the complexion of the faculty was social-democratic and New Dealish. During the McCarthy period the subversive Orozco murals in the old cafeteria were hidden by a curtain (which could be opened on request, however!), and the New School had a loyalty oath affirming allegiance to democratic institutions before anyone else.

What mattered, however, was the classroom situation, and there our audiences expected us to be left-of-center in domestic affairs and critical of the government in foreign affairs. Debate was essential, and the Communists paid me the special respect of always sending a heckler into my class. In the 1960s they also got a strong hold on the students' club until the Maoists took it away from them.

The New School used to have some links with the New York labor scene, and some of the older students in the Adult Education courses may still be coming because of a sentimental attachment to the 1930s' causes of which the school retains a flavor. But the majority now come simply for the opportunities it presents. It has a liberal admissions policy, and it is especially kind to older students who had to interrupt their curriculum for some reason or who cannot stand the spoon-feeding methods used elsewhere. In the 1940s and 1950s, however, students came to the Graduate Faculty because nowhere else could one get genuine Max Weber, genuine Gestalt, genuine phenomenology, or as close a reading of Plato as Leo Strauss taught his admiring followers.

The principal difference between New School teaching and

the methods of traditional American colleges was our higher degree of conceptualization. We taught that science is not a collection of more or less true facts but the crystallizing of ideas from facts. We were less interested in methods and more in ideas. More than any particular attitude to current questions, this insistence on concepts must have constituted one of the time bombs we placed on the American intellectual scene. The New School should have been extraterritorial in New York: it was pinkish and foreign in a deeper sense. Nevertheless, Leo Strauss's students now occupy important chairs across the country, Gerhard Colm became a member of the President's Council of Economic Advisers, Max Weber has become an oracle for American sociologists, and Alfred Schütz left behind a great number of graduates when he died.

Meanwhile, another group of refugee scholars had established itself uptown and solved its problem of exterritoriality in quite an ingenious way. The once-famous Institute for Social Research of Frankfurt, at the time the only Marxist academy west of Minsk, had transferred its headquarters first to Paris and Geneva, then to New York and, more specifically, to West 117th Street. Its letterhead ostentatiously announced that its telephone ran through the Columbia University switchboard, and thanks to Max Horkheimer's salesmanship or to the constellation of war, its members eventually succeeded in teaching courses at Columbia. They also served in war agencies of the U.S. government. Franz Neumann and Herbert Marcuse there bombarded Secretary of War Stimson with plans for a postwar Germany that would give democratic socialism a chance; they probably prevented the worst stupidities of which an occupation regime is capable. Neumann wrote what to this day is the best analysis of the Nazi regime, stressing its nihilistic attack on all the values inherent in the Western conception of state. Other members used European terminology to plant more time bombs: since Marx and Marxism could not be mentioned, they used Hegel or "German idealism" as code words. They said "alienation" when they meant capitalism, "reason" when they meant revolution, and "Eros" when they meant proletariat. In this way they hoped to assure Marxist philosophy an underground survival during the McCarthy episode. Fortunately their precautions proved to be unnecessary, and their "Aesopian" language became the fashion.

When the success story of the word "alienation" in America is written, the contribution of the Institute people will receive its due acknowledgement. In other respects too the Institute planted seeds. Adorno's *Studies on the Authoritarian Personality* is now a classic. Erich Fromm and Siegfried Kracauer, who originally were members but in this country struck out independently, became famous in their fields. After the war, Franz Neumann attracted many gifted students who now grace important chairs of history and government. He taught a Jacobin philosophy of politics, while his friend Marcuse went back to Rousseau or worse, preaching tomorrow's return to paradise. This won him the acclaim of students who do not understand the seriousness of his philosophy; his latest development confirms the suspicion that he never had contact with any real society.

With *Eros and Civilization* Marcuse was ten years ahead of the counterculture. But he was lagging ten years behind another German writer who combined Marx with Freud and preached the gospel of total gratification: Wilhelm Reich. A genius and a sort of racketeer, he died in solitude after having infected America with the "sexual revolution."

Horkheimer and Adorno went back to Germany after a stint in California. As a gesture of moral restitution, Chancellor Adenauer made Horkheimer the first "rector" of the rebuilt University of Frankfurt. Adorno continued to be productive and influential in esoteric European circles until his death. Fromm exiled himself to Mexico but continued to come to the United States as a highly respected psychologist, as an influential participant of the peace movement, and as a widely revered writer on sane man in a sane society.

Postwar, post-Hitler Germany offered many interesting jobs to returning exiles. Personally, I had no difficulty visiting

Germany. I talked to old friends as though I had left them yesterday. But should I stay? This would be a political decision. It was natural for Erich Ollenhauer, Willi Eichler, Ernst Reuter, and Willy Brandt—representing four distinct groups which now joined in the Social Democratic party—that they should return to redeem their exile image. They had to prove that one could continue where the Weimar Republic had left off. This was not so natural for me. One cannot step in the same river twice. Unless there was a really new beginning in Europe, a revolution in whatever form, I thought that the old powers would come back and that Europe's tragedy would be repeated.

In France one could discern the beginning of such a revolution, but the Communists quickly stifled it. In Germany no one gave a thought to a "new" beginning, except perhaps Richard Lowenthal, who earlier, under the pen name Paul Sering, wrote his impressive *Beyond Capitalism*. The Russians imported and imposed their system in the East, and the Western powers revived the old parties in their occupation zones. Karl Frank (Paul Hagen), whose group "New Beginning" had prepared itself for just such situation, did not go to Germany but became a psychoanalyst in New York. Some members of this group with excellent American and British contacts, however, infiltrated the Military Government and (I note this here as a footnote to history because the fact has nowhere else been recorded) helped prevent the merger of the Social Democratic party with the Communists in Berlin, saving the city from a Russian takeover. Two prominent members of the group, Richard Lowenthal and Paul Herz, became influential in Berlin. (This is not to diminish the importance of the Luxemburgist left and of the religious socialists, who also contributed to the revival of the Social Democratic party; but they were less strongly represented among the exiles.)

The head of the party came from the religious socialists. Kurt Schumacher represented the best of the internal emigration. He emerged from the concentration camp warped in body and soul, but his cadaverous appearance and the mystical glimmer in his eye made him a charismatic leader who could lead his flock through the wilderness of opposition policies. He was an exile by choice, capable of neither revolution nor construction, and he staked his party's political fortunes on a utopian nationalism.

Since I had concluded that neither Stalin and his successors nor the Western powers and their allies would allow Germany's reunification, I could see no place for me in a socialist party whose entire policy was based on this chimera. The Christian Democratic party was more realistic. But like its French and Italian sister parties, it had subdued its left wing so quickly that today hardly anyone remembers the possibilities of a political realignment in Europe during the late 1940s. Adenauer's restoration regime would not have deterred me, but neither did it inspire me, and as to its only redeeming aspiration—although I deeply care for a United Europe—there was little I could do for it.

Some five years ago Hermann Kesten published a curious book with two dozen answers to the question: "Why I don't live in the Federal Republic." German writers here explain their resentments against Germans and their disgust with the middle-class Bonn Republic, but none of them mention the reasons I just cited. At the time I reviewed that book. Looking at the review now, I find that I did not state these reasons either but frankly said: These writers, including myself, have grown so accustomed to the condition of exile that they are loath to abandon it. Writers do not communicate readily with real people, and while they are extraordinarily "engaged" at their desks with words and ideas, their actual involvement with the sordid details of political life is minimal. In exile one can project this alienation into the evasive dimension of linguistic and cultural differentials. But such differentials, I confessed at the time, also serve as a protective fence. They disengage me from other people and their worries in a way that might be impossible in a country whose most intimate fears and passions I had absorbed with its nursery rhymes. The nursery rhymes our daughter learned in America gave me clues to the minds of friends I had made in the new country, but there is a difference between learning them at the age of three or thirty-three. In his own autobiography, Les Mots, Sartre suggests that words separate people as much as they help them communicate. Action alone, concrete engagement unites people and constitutes reality. I think that for many the exile situation suspended the need to engage in action.

I wrote: "Once upon a time we were engaged too deeply; we dreamed that the intellectual's alienation can be overcome by political action. The error was costly. The punishment has left scars. Now we shun the fire that has burned us once." Perhaps that suggestion is being confirmed by the observation that some staunch German patriots such as Hermann Rauschning, after first returning to Germany, later came back to their American exile because the old fatherland refused to adopt their particular brand of patriotism. Karl Mannheim (who died in London in his second exile) developed the idea of the "free-floating" (socially unattached) intellectual when he still was living in his first exile, Germany. His one-time friend, Georg Lukács, who in the 1920s gave us the deepest interpretation of Marxism, thereafter sacrificed his intellectual powers because he could not bear to live without a spiritual home. Utopia is forever the locus where the intellectual must take his stand.

Paradoxically, therefore, my decision to stay in the United States was not a sign of my greater attachment to this country than to the country of my birth but, on the contrary, a sign that I could be less involved here and need not identify with the burning issues of national politics to the extent one does in Europe. There one can hardly avoid taking sides, and one is quickly isolated if one is consistently on the "wrong" side of every issue, as I was likely to be. In the United States the fringe area of possible dissent is so wide and the variety of eccentric circles so great that one can maintain one's autonomy even while participating.

I wrote for Dwight Macdonald's magazine, Politics, but later lost contact with him; he was too alienated for my taste.

This is perhaps a left-handed compliment to the United States and its pluralistic democracy: the convenience of the arrangement helped us over the shock of Hiroshima. I opposed the use of the A-bomb and wrote to several scientists asking them to declare a strike; but I am sure that my opposition would have taken more violent forms had a European government dropped the bomb. Then Joseph McCarthy's investigations put my admiration of America to a severe test, but meanwhile the cold war—the first rape of Czechoslovakia, the Berlin blockade, the Korean war—had forced us to identify American power with the cause of liberty. More important, we now identified ourselves closely with those American friends who were defending the cause of freedom abroad simultaneously with the American constitution. These same friends assured me that McCarthy was no Hitler, as we feared from analogy, but an ephemeral phenomenon. They were right. In America democracy provides a favorable fighting arena for democrats, in Europe it often does for its enemies.

Largely in this spirit, Erich Fromm, Horst Brand, Amos Vogel, Lewis Coser, and I took a hand in starting *Dissent* magazine. Its editors then included Norman Mailer, Meyer Schapiro, A. J. Muste, Stanley Plastrik, Norman Thomas, and George Woodcock. Michael Harrington and Michael Walzer joined the editorial board later—two very talented young writers, but with them I first encountered the generation gap.

They all were a dedicated group of radicals, mostly ex-Marxists, led by Irving Howe, who were striving for a democratic socialism and an undogmatic approach to politics. The words "radical" and "politics" may not go well together, but I suspect that Irving Howe would like to combine them. In practice, *Dissent* has been an ideological gadfly rather than a political animal, and to that extent I am engaged in American politics. Insofar as we are an opposition that "engages" the establishment, we "are engaged" with it in a dialectical relationship. The editors of *Dissent*, of course, are mostly college professors and thus beneficiaries of the establishment they criticize and attack. I do not deny that it would be possible to assemble a similar group of people with a similarly ambivalent attitude in Germany, but they are not active there and leave the field to the sterile "extra-parliamentary opposition"—or consume abroad the rich royalties that German publishers pay to extremists on the left. *Dissent* has been a frequent outlet for Günter Grass, but not for Hans Magnus Enzensberger.

We also published Norman Mailer's "White Negro," which is now, like many other pieces we first discovered, part of every anthology, but we did not like Eldridge Cleaver. We gave Frantz Fanon and Malcolm X respectful but not very sympathetic reviews; and although we have published plans to redistribute the world's wealth, we have condemned Che Guevara and other self-styled leaders of the Third World. We are hopelessly committed to "old left" internationalism and do not agree with those who equate socialism with the humiliation of the United States by small-time dictators. While some of us have been closely identified with the peace movement, we have not concluded that we must identify with the other side in the cold war. My own awareness of the long history of European imperialism and my studies of Soviet imperialism may have helped my friends to correct their own gut reaction to the power play of the postwar years. For American populists and radicals have a provincial preconception that Americans must be blamed for whatever is horrible that happens in the world, that Americans must atone for the sins of their past. I cannot conceive that they could obtain forgiveness by groveling before the destructive forces of black, yellow, and red nationalism. Having fought German, Jewish, American, Spanish, and French nationalism, I fail to appreciate how the cause of liberty, equality, justice, and abundance for all can be advanced by the victory of Third-World s-o-b's over our s-o-b's. For that attitude I have been attacked from two sides: the New Left thinks that one cannot be sincerely radical without being anti-American, and the FBI seems to agree with that reasoning. I must confess that the incomprehension on my left was less expected and more painful; that on my right was more annoying in practical ways—it cost me two jobs.

Writers who decided to stay and work in the United States are not, for that reason, necessarily apologists for its government. On the contrary, it is possible to make such a decision without even trying to relate to the American scene. Such is the case with many friends who should have gone back by every criterion in the book.

Oskar Maria Graf, a Bavarian poet and novelist, was as German—or, to be precise, as Bavarian—as a beer mug both in appearance and in speech. His politics were leftish, but since the Nazis fancied regional, peasant, and dialect writers, they did not bother him. On the day of the book-burning, therefore, Graf published a powerful "Open Letter" to the German government: he felt that it was an insult to have been excluded from the distinguished company of Thomas Mann, Brecht, etc. The letter ended with a passionate plea: Please burn me, too!

He did not learn a word of Czech in his Prague exile, and he lived in New York for over twenty years without learning any English. He despised German middle-class culture and stayed in New York in order to avoid any contact with the German establishment; as to its American counterpart, he was so happily oblivious of it that he could ignore it. He was committed to a Germany that exists only in literature, and he has written movingly about the influence which Walt Whitman, Ernest Hemingway, and other American writers have had on him, although he could read them only in translations. He loved the freedom of America and the circle of loyal emigrants who admired him. The city of Munich has provided a resting place for his ashes which is more dignified than any he had ever had in life.

By contrast, one cannot imagine a writer less Bavarian than Ludwig Marcuse, a cosmopolitan Jew, an urbane rationalist who first emigrated to southern France and later taught phi-

losophy at UCLA—unsuccessfully; his memoirs make it clear
that his students and he never learned anything from each
other. After the war he bought a farm at Miesbach, of all
places. To be sure, it is a beautiful spot at the foot of the
Bavarian Alps, but it also is the town where the Nazis published their first daily paper! Other writers, like Hans Habe,
also live in the Alps, but on the Swiss side. I suggest that
alienation is equally comfortable on both sides of the Alps.
As a German satirist said, "It's nice to grumble bravely from
afar."

A small group of activists who wished to be both aloof and
committed found shelter in the United Nations—a little society of international civil servants capable of maintaining
their own standards independent of any particular nation. I
regret very much that lately their jobs, through a quota system, have been given to people who simply represent their
respective governments and who are indifferent to internationalism.

The greatest opportunity for combining freedom with security is still provided in the American academy. It permits
a certain detachment or even dissociation from the establishment without destroying the dialectical relationship between
society and its critic. No doubt many who seem to be dissenters merely feel that, in a country where every disgruntled
general grabs the nearest microphone, they would be un-
grateful if they withheld their own dissent, which anyway is
offered for love of the country. They represent, with many of
their native-born colleagues, what Hegel called "the unhappy
consciousness"—awareness of unfulfilled ideals, the power-
less attempt to pit the American dream against the American
reality. More than any European institution, the American
academy allows the scholar to be an outsider with respect to
the mainstream yet at the same time an insider with respect
to itself. Success and failure can be combined almost seam-
lessly.

This does not entirely explain why unorthodox scholars and
teachers of foreign birth, expressing themselves in clumsy
English and using as their frame of reference examples which

were not within their audience's experience, could have had such outstanding success in America. Hajo Holborn—the distinguished Harvard historian, a disciple of Meinecke—has suggested that none of this might have happened twenty years earlier. In the 1930s and 1940s, the exiles achieved their stature not in spite of their alienation but because of it. America, deeply shaken by the Great Depression, was passing through a moral and cultural crisis. With intellectuals, now the "in" thing is to be "out"; conformism now expresses itself in conforming with nonconformism. In such a situation the ideal-type of exile can be very effective as a model; he represents alienation in his person and he describes it in his work.

But a deep misunderstanding occurs here. To him, dissent from society is radical and total; to his audience, dissent is only partial. The American society is porous and multidirectional; even radical dissent in one sector does not affect the whole; the meaning of alienation has become so fuzzy that the final effect of so much pseudo-alienation is no alienation at all. This misunderstanding caused considerable shock when people discovered what Herbert Marcuse really meant.

Let me turn now to another category of refugee scholars, a group situated at the other end of the spectrum of alienation—those who have experienced no problem of adjustment but, on the contrary, are swimming happily in the mainstream of American life and politics. They are government consultants or institutional experts; they fly from conference to congress to convention as veritable jet-profs, and they are part of the new power complex of industry, the military, and the intelligentsia. This is true whether they are Republicans like Professor Kissinger or Vietnam dissenters like Professor Morgenthau. Both have introduced a generation of American political scientists to the Metternichian and Bismarckian principles of cold power politics. But they have shown how conservatism can develop intelligently, provided it is not weighted down with nativist ideologies. In these cases, being foreign has an advantage which the American government can turn to good account. In the field of economics, Peter Drucker has made a similar contribution to the development of a progressive conservatism.

One wrongly assumes that refugees ought to be liberals. I might refer to Professors Hayek and Mises in economics, leaders of the Adam Smith–Robert Taft school of thought; to Professors Drachkovitch, Ulam, and Strausz-Hupé, outspoken advocates of the Cold War; I might refer to the role Dr. Teller played in the development of the H-bomb and in the Oppenheimer affair. Like most Irish who came to identify with America 100 percent, many German-born Jews have fervently embraced their new fatherland and are angry at those who doubt its righteousness or would like to soften its power. Indeed, Professor Karl August Wittfogel went so far as to inform on his American sponsor to the McCarthy Committee.

As the refugee generation grows older, it may develop a natural inclination to grow conservative, either by comparison with the new student generation, which has overtaken their old-fashioned liberalism, or in reaction to its rebellion. The black revolution also has passed us by on the left; those of us who do not feel totally guilt-ridden are apt to tell blacks that they must do like other minorities—smugly: Look at us!— and conquer a place in the American mainstream. Such arguments, of course, are ridiculous when coming from Jews who are Zionists or support segregated schools for their own group.

In this connection I remember my first meeting with America as it is, as opposed to the myth we had learned from our school textbooks. We had arrived in April 1941, and from habit I went to watch the May Day demonstration. I was shocked to see the ILGWU parading with posters demanding Palestine for the Jews, independence for the Puerto Ricans, colonies for the Italians; there were no labor demands and no Negro demands. The melting pot apparently had not done much melting in the ILGWU! Only gradually did I learn that America is not a unified society but a multidimensional jigsaw puzzle. Its national, racial, religious, regional, social-cultural divisions seem to be more important than the class divisions and the nation-to-nation divisions we accept in Europe. Many who came to this country with a European ideal of what makes a country and how a society is to be structured were bewildered when they saw the American model of a pluralistic society.

Europeans usually complain that children here have no respect for their parents and teachers, employees have no respect for their superiors, thieves have no respect for the police, the uneducated have no respect for the educated. This last disregard hurts most, and a certain Leon Lawrence Matthias has published a book saying that America is doomed because it is a society without ranks. Those who recommend European models to Americans, however, merely prove how little they know about the society they criticize. By European standards American society may be both compartmentalized and amorphous; but it is not unstructured. Peer groups and functional elites (a term I borrow from the Vienna-born sociologist Suzanne Keller) here are just as jealous of defending their privileges against outsiders and intruders as are classes in Europe. Most of us who have struggled to achieve status in American society know the power of "in" groups; but that which one is in or out of is not the same thing here and in Europe. I always tell European visitors that they should not be misled by the white skin and English (or near-English) language of the Americans they meet, that they will not understand America until they pretend that all people here have green hair and are playing a game the rules of which the observer is supposed to guess.

Part of this culture, two Britishers, Evelyn Waugh and Jessica Mitford have told us, is a ritualistic refusal to recognize death. Every educated European will tell you at the drop of a hat that Americans lack "depth" because they evade the question that puts every human being in his place. Personally, I think that this is nonsense and that Europeans too would be much better off if they could get rid of the notion that death is accompanying them wherever they go. Even so, the myth of death evokes, for us, two important categories of thought: tragedy and history. Americans tend to feel frustrated when a problem does not yield to scientific analysis, manipulation, and engineering. Europeans experience failure as proof of the final futility of all human endeavor; they positively resent a people that refuses to admit that some problems cannot be solved. We wallow in history while Americans are notoriously antihistorical. At best, they can be induced to admit that history can teach some lessons; but they see their own history as a success story, not as conflict and tragedy.

American literature has produced few great tragedies, and it does not deal with fate. Europeans believe that their tragic understanding of human life can add a missing dimension to the American dream—particularly by liberating it from the "shallow" notion of Progress and of the good-guy/bad-guy dichotomy. Hannah Arendt stirred America by stating the obvious: that evil is deeply embedded in every man's banal existence. Nor is it an accident that Lewis Coser introduced into American sociology the notion that "conflict" is a prime mover rather than an impediment to progress. Perhaps it would be fairer to state these contributions in a more modest way. It was a fortunate coincidence that precisely at the moment when America lost her innocent faith in everlasting harmony and progress, she became host to people whose nations had a longer memory of tragedy and whose personal experiences had made them singularly sensitive to the crisis of the Western mind. We often catch ourselves saying: Such an event reminds me of the German youth movement or of some other feature of recent European history. Our sense of *déjà-vu* sometimes tempts us to affect a slightly ironical stance vis-à-vis "one-dimensional" citizens. I don't suppose that such an impolite display of superiority must be attributed to any feeling of cultural differential. At best, it is the irony of wisdom such as we find in the multi-refractory style of Thomas Mann: a little tired, a little ashamed to reveal the truth without devaluating its relevance, somewhat decadent or at least aged, reflecting a knowledge that action may be necessary but not expecting that it will solve the problem for good or avoid creating new problems. Perhaps such a Brahmin attitude—that nerve of failure—was a necessary counterpoise for America at the moment when she was ready to make the century hers. Indeed, some refugees are proud to be citizens of this new Roman empire provided they can be its Athenian teachers.

An ancient Chinese manuscript, I am told, divides the animal kingdom into those animals drawn on paper, those belonging to the emperor, those crowing in the morning, and all others. My listing of refugee scholars must be similarly arbitrary, if for no other reason than because some are mentioned in existing bibliographies and others are not,[7] or because social scientists and psychologists research themselves better than others, or because atomic physicists, painters, and musicians blend better into an international pattern than stage actors, poets, and philosophers. To my knowledge, there are no statistics dividing the Jewish from the non-Jewish immigrants, or those who came directly from Germany from those who came after a stop in another country, or from that country directly, or for whom Germany in the first place had been a country of asylum. In the latter category belong the Russian Mensheviks and the Hungarian Communists. Later, America also received refugees from Austria, Hungary, Czechoslovakia, and other countries where different totalitarians were killing freedom, or refugees who did not want to go back to Soviet Russia. Add to this the Spanish Civil War refugees, and the political gamut runs from anarchists to persons far on the right; the motivations for seeking asylum vary from the purely personal to the intensely political, the immediate occasions for emigrating from dire fear for one's life to rank opportunism. It is obvious that besides Freiherr von Braun many others must be counted as immigrants but not as refugees.

There are still other distinctions which statistics might suggest: between those who came as established scholars, writers, or artists, and those who began their career in exile, like Peter Weiss in Sweden; between those who succeeded and those who, tragically, had to exchange the gown for some other trade. The most important distinction, however, must be made between those who returned to their country of origin after the war, and those who remained in their adopted country to become immigrants.

The National Refugee Service listed 7,622 professional and academic immigrants between 1933 and 1945. A bio-bibliography of exile literature published in 1963 by Professor Wilhelm Sternfeld comprises the names of 1,513 writers. Only a fifth of these returned to Germany or Austria. As early as 1936 a list of emigrated scientists carried 1,652 names. An exhibition of books, pamphlets, and magazines published by exiles between 1933 and 1945 contained 900 names of authors, 100 magazines and newspapers, 150 organizations, and 120 publishers. As we might expect, exile literature proper is more concerned with the condition of Germany and of Europe between 1933 and 1945, whereas later immigrant literature shows increasing concern with and adjustment to the conditions of the host country, as well as a widening spread among the various sciences and arts. This is quite natural, despite notable exceptions such as Peter Gay's sudden return to the Weimar Republic after a brilliant career in the field of French Enlightenment.

The cases of Peter Gay and Lewis Coser suggest an entire class of refugee scholars who arrived here young enough to attend an American university and to rise through the regular mill of an academic career. Refugee scholars proper had to break in from outside if they wished a status commensurate with their age and previous achievements. In some areas this proved more difficult than coming in on the ground floor. Some scholars and scientists (like Einstein, Köhler, Bethe, Erwin Panofsky, Schumpeter, Liebert, Röpke, or Ernst Cassirer) had been world-famous before the 1930s and merely took asylum in the United States, continuing the work they had been forced to interrupt. Others had been well-known in their own country but rose to world fame only through their work in exile. In this group belong Paul Tillich, Bruno Bettelheim, Erich Fromm, Karl Mannheim, Theodor W. Adorno, Franz

Borkenau, Eduard Heimann, etc. Some younger authors also continued the work they had begun before Hitler cut off their careers in Germany, and they went on to complete their careers in this country, publishing works that would have been written had their authors never heard of Hitler, or left Germany. The Renaissance historians Hans Baron and Paul Kristeller are distinguished examples of such a rigid separation between private experience and academic ambitions. Similar observations apply to historians like Felix Gilbert, Hans Kohn, Ernst Kantorowicz, A. Vagts, to art historians such as Panofsky, and literary critics like Auerbach, who introduced the methods of the Warburg Institute to America. Nor was the service some of us rendered to American scholarship lessened by the fact that it was first of all one of transferring and teaching a skill we had learned in the old country. American mathematics was never the same after Richard Courant settled at New York University, and American musicology was almost non-existent before we came—to name only two fields where the dispersion of ideas might have taken longer without personal contact.

I think there are four fields where the influx of European scholars accelerated a movement which might well have been under way but which took shape only after their arrival. One is the philosophy of logical positivism, which was greatly stimulated when Carnap founded the Encyclopedia of Unified Science. At the other end of the scale there is the enormous influence of the "theology without God" that Tillich introduced at Union Theological Seminary. Third, it is no accident that refugee scholars have been so much concerned with the philosophy of history (Meyerhoff here is a link to the Neo-Kantians, Hempel to the Viennese school, Löwith to existentialism, Stern to Ranke, Kahler and Heilbroner to neo-Marxian conceptions) and with the history of ideas as represented by the brilliant circle editing the *Journal for the History of Ideas*. (The method of the history of ideas also has its drawbacks; it can show by documents, for instance, that Max Weber and Karl Mannheim had been known to American sociologists long before C. Wright Mills struck his alliance with

Hans Gerth. But can anyone seriously deny that the European sociologists hit the American universities with an impact comparable to the invasion of classical studies by Greek scholars after 1453?)

The case of the psychologists and psychoanalysts is quite different. When the Viennese doctors arrived, America had been well advanced into the age of psychologizing. Freud, Jung, and Rorschach were well established not only in scholarly circles but in the public mind. It is not surprising, therefore, that the red carpet was out for European psychologists of all schools and that all flourished under the warm sun of increasing public interest. The father of child psychology, William Stern, and the founder of ego psychology, Alfred Adler; the teachers of the Gestalt school—Koffka, Köhler, and Wertheimer; the neurologist Kurt Goldstein; psychoanalysts like Otto Fenichel, Ernst Kris, Frieda Fromm-Reichmann, Theodor Reik, Otto Rank; independents such as the Brunswiks and the Bühlers were able to continue their work in new surroundings. There were others, however, who opened new frontiers. Though still European in their thinking, they conquered problems which were either posed by the new environment or suggested by the methods and facilities it placed at the disposal of research. Thus each in his or her own way— Karen Horney, Erich Fromm, Ernest Schachtel, Bruno Bettelheim, Rudolf Arnheim, and others—transcended the schools from which they had come. The most interesting case, perhaps, was that of Kurt Lewin. Originally a Gestalt psychologist, he quickly adopted the experimental methods of American psychology, made important contributions toward its conceptualization, proved with experiments on children that democracy is superior to dictatorship, and left, at his early death, an intellectual heritage which still bears interest.

With this observation we come to the fields where the influence probably worked in reverse. The refugee scholars who made themselves a name in political science and government had more to learn from their new environment than they could teach it. Whether profound or superficial, their studies in the mechanics of government or the laws of political behavior are more American than their authors probably would like to admit. That is true even of highly original works like Karl Deutsch's application of cybernetics to the art of government and Hannah Arendt's controversial book on Eichmann, which originally appeared in the "Reporter at Large" column of *The New Yorker* magazine. It is obviously true of studies whose subject matter is American or whose train of thought was inspired by American problems, like Hannah Arendt's *On Revolution* or Richard Neustadt's *Presidential Power*. Arnold Brecht's *Political Theory* certainly is more "American" in its relativistic attitude than David Easton's, and it points to at least one of the reasons why Europeans have become so well equipped to explain America not only to Europeans but to Americans, too.

They have indeed found much to admire and much to learn. They do not experience their American horizon as simply an addition to the European horizon but rather as a veritable new dimension which includes and comprises their old horizon. Moreover, the interesting observation has been made that many of the European scholars now teaching political science in the United States originally came from some other field. They had been open to new experiences, and when they had to organize that new experience into a framework of thought, they obviously could not use the bankrupt systems which they had learned in Europe.

All of this naturally applies even more to the scientists. The style of research in this country is so tempting that European universities now are complaining about the "brain drain." There are obvious dangers in this migration. Many scientists are being lured away—from subjects that might be of greater scientific value—to projects that are of interest to American corporations or to the American government. Science is no longer "free"; it is highly influenced and directed by state interests, and many physicists, obviously, might not be doing the work they are doing now in the United States had they remained in Europe under prewar conditions. But I have been led to understand that, personally, the European scientists here are happy not only with the conditions of life they can afford but, above all, with the research facilities and the professional prospects.

One more observation: science by now has become a highly international venture, and discoveries made in one country can be duplicated in others as well. Moreover, scientific research and technological invention has by now become so factorylike that we can speak of inventioneering. Discovery and invention are functions of input. Any government willing to pay the price can order, within definite time limits, any tailor-made material or device. Since America has the monetary resources, she can invite foreign scientists and inventors to use her laboratories and other facilities. American science thus has become the meeting ground of an international community with little consciousness of citizenship.

Furthermore, international corporations are spreading know-how across the globe while engineers and researchers merge with financial and commercial families to form one big international managerial class. As a group, scientists probably are the most widely traveled elite next to the jet set, with the most frequent changes of citizenship. Fulbright grants, international conventions, sabbaticals abroad, and service in United Nations organizations have made them into an international community where everyone is losing his ties to his native country and national government.

I have not spoken of artists, musicians, entertainers, and other fellow sufferers. Their statistics are less reassuring. Many have not been able to catch the American bus; as against a few outstanding successes—a Richard Lindner, a Martha Schlamme—we can cite sad instances of failure which cannot even be recorded by statistics because the contestant did not cross the threshold of the arena in the first place. With few exceptions, this memoir does not deal with young poets and novelists either; it would be dealing with buried hopes.

Ludwig Marcuse has said that Hollywood's cemeteries are the resting places of many Weimar personalities: the great director Leopold Jessner; several actors and actresses; Heinrich Mann, Franz Werfel, Bruno Frank, Lion Feuchtwanger. He could have added that Hollywood also became the grave-yard of many emigrant illusions: Alfred Döblin, Leonhard Frank, Alfred Polgar, Walter Mehring were unable to repay their host country's hospitality. Many of those who have not made an impact on their adopted country nevertheless de-serve to be remembered. They were sacrificed in the slaugh-terhouse of history. But there is the possibility of posthu-mous discovery, as in the strange case of Walter Benjamin.

In each of us there will be a little of Aharsuerus and also a little of the Trojan Aeneas, who became the ancestor of Ro-mulus. Our experience of exile has probably been summed up best by Bertolt Brecht in a quatrain which he set as an introduction before some unpublished poems. As if recalling an old legend about the wayfarer who carried a brick with him to show the world what his house had been like, Brecht wrote:

> Dies ist nun alles und ist nicht genug.
> Doch sagt es euch vielleicht, ich bin noch da.
> Dem gleich ich, der den Backstein mit sich trug,
> Der Welt zu zeigen, wie sein Haus aussah.[8]

Notes

1. Empire and Republic: Autobiographical Fragments

1. In fact, the view goes back to David Hume's skepticism. It was renewed, before the turn of the century, by the physicist Ernst Mach and the positivist philosophers, against whom Lenin wrote a book-length treatise, *Materialism and Empirio-Criticism,* without understanding them, though. In the 1920s, this school of thought was ably represented by the Viennese circle of Moritz Schlick and Otto Neurath, most of whom were Social Democrats. In the 1930s it was transplanted to London by Ludwig Wittgenstein and to Chicago by Rudolf Carnap, to Princeton by Philipp Frank, to California by Hans Reichenbach (who had been a founder of the Communist Workers' Party). I have had contacts with some of these men, and I find it hard to understand why the neo-Marxist school reserves its most vehement invective for these honest critics of metaphysical philosophy. Leszek Kolakowski, the Polish revisionist, has written a more discerning criticism of the school from a Marxist point of view. *The Alienation of Reason—A History of Positivist Thought* (Garden City; N.Y.: Doubleday, 1968).

2. Istvan Deak, *Weimar Germany's Left-Wing Intellectuals* (Berkeley: University of California Press, 1968), p. 14.

2. Expressionism and Café Culture

1. Soon this was to win distinction as Europe's first "family" beach where the two sexes were allowed to enter the water together.

2. The table where the "regulars" had their café get-together.

3. Whether or not that is the correct derivation, the term was rapidly extended to include every *schlemiel,* artist or not, and flourished in northern Germany, too.

4. Although the charge was not articulated, there may have been an anti-Semitic implication in the attack.

5. This was quite generous, considering that Becher's furnished room cost 30 marks and a meal 1.50 marks.

6. As Peter Gay has pointed out, this generation made hatred of the father a dominant theme. Moreover, in psychology, bohemia was the first to recognize Freud. Simmel's and Lask's studies of alienation were also discussed in the café, as is apparent from the writings of Kurt Hiller and Franz Jung. See Peter Gay, Weimar Culture (New York: Harper & Row, 1970).

7. This was the first generation to take its name, not from the content of what it had to say, but from the mere fact of its newness—just like fashion.

8. Only in translation does this point to the term "Expressionism."

9. Its upstairs floor was later transformed into the Kabarett Grössenwahn under Rosa Valetti's direction.

10. See the essay by Arthur Mitzman in Stephen Eric Bronner and Douglas Kellner, eds., Passion and Rebellion: The Expressionist Heritage South Hadley, Mass.: J. F. Bergin, 1982).

11. Even a radical like Rosa Luxemburg was conservative in her artistic tastes. See Stephen Eric Bronner's Introduction to The Letters of Rosa Luxemburg (Boulder: Westview Press, 1978).

12. Becher, Rilla, Piscator, Karl Liebknecht, and Rosa Luxemburg were Spartacists in the war and revolution period.

13. "Politics is for him [Péguy] not a business but the rustling of the blood."

3. The Intellectuals and the State of Weimar

1. The only exceptions I am aware of were the few brave men who denounced the clandestine rearmament of Germany: Felix Fechenbach, Emil Gumbel, Carl von Ossietzsky.

2. Cf. essay, "Friedrich Meinecke and the Tragedy of German Liberalism" in this volume. In the following notes, English titles are used where translations are available in print.

3. The universal estate, defined by Hegel as "having the general interests of society as its business; for that purpose it must either have private means or be compensated by the State" (Philosophy of Right, paragraph 205). Similarly, Theodor Geiger in Aufgabe und Stellung der Intelligenz in der Gesellschaft (Stuttgart: Enke, 1949), p. 109.

4. King Charles VII said that in The Maid of Orleans.

5. Heinrich von Gleichen-Russwurm, a descendant of Schiller, founded the June Club, which in the beginning attracted intellectuals of the right and the left—among others Rathenau, Hans Blüher, Brüning, Rudolf Pechel. It promoted the ideas of Stände and of People's Community; later it became the tool of the arch-conservative Papen circle and changed its name to Herrenklub. The highbrow magazine Die Tat propagated similar ideas and played host to parlor Nazis.

6. Hendrik de Man wrote *Psychologie des Sozialismus* (1926) and *Die sozialistische Idee* (1933). Having failed to rally his native Belgium to the idea of a plan, he hailed Hitler as the savior of civilization in 1939.

7. *Die Weltbühne* (1926), 22:412–415. These boys were giving daily battle to the storm troopers to protect Tucholsky's lecture hall, for instance; while appreciating that, he found them wanting in *Geist*. Heinz Pol even called the *Reichsbanner* "fascist."

8. *The Intellectual Migration*, Donald Fleming and Bernard Bailyn, eds. (Cambridge; Harvard University Press, 1969), p. 21.

9. These were cofounders of the Democratic party, which in the beginning attracted many intellectuals and students, among them a number who later became its most vitriolic critics—such as Tucholsky on the left and Hjalmar Schacht on the right. Its presidential candidate in 1925 was Professor Hellpach, and it produced Professor Theodor Heuss, the first president of the Bonn Republic.

10. See *Die Zeit ohne Eigenschaften, Eine Bilanz der zwanziger Jahre*, Leonhard Reinisch, ed. (Stuttgart: Kohlhammer, 1961), pp. 93–94.

11. Leopold Jessner, a Socialist, became director of the Prussian State Theater and provoked scandals with his revolutionary staging of old classics. In Frankfurt and Munich, daring new directors gave the stage over to Expressionist plays. Erwin Piscator, at the time a Communist, created his famous mass scenes.

12. Collected by Kurt Pinthus in *Menschheitsdämmerung*, 1919.

13. Bruno E. Werner, *Die Zwanziger Jahre* (Munich: Bruckmann, 1962), p. 41.

14. Other representatives of the new intelligentsia included Stefan Zweig, Franz Werfel, Max Brod, Rainer Maria Rilke, Joseph Roth, Robert Musil, Hermann Broch, Peter Altenberg, Arthur Schnitzler, Richard Beer-Hofmann, Karl Kraus and, of course, Franz Kafka.

15. See also Oskar Maria Graf's autobiographical *Wir sind Gefangene* (1927) and Ernst Toller's letters and poems from prison (in English: *Look Through the Bars*, 1936).

16. René König in Reinisch, *Die Zeit ohne Eigenschaften*.

17. Peter Gay, *Weimar Culture—The Outsider as Insider* (New York: Harper, 1968). The category of "outsider" also appears in Geiger, *Die Aufgabe*, p. 75.

18. Not all writers who stayed in Germany can be identified with the Nazi regime. Fallada tried to save a realistic style while evading reality by describing idyls; Ernst Wiechert and Günther Weisenborn, though at first considered nationalist writers, later found themselves in concentration camps; Ernst Jünger and Werner Bergengruen, shielded by the army, were able to publish thinly veiled attacks on the regime. Rudolf Alexander Schröder, Ricarda Huch, Stefan Andres, Manfred Hausmann, Hans Nossack, Hermann Kasack, and Elisabeth Langgässer felt they were emigrants too: "internal exiles."

19. The consequences of this classificatory raid can still be read in *The Destruction of Reason* by Georg Lukács (1953). On Communist infiltration in the Weimar press, see Arthur Koestler, *Arrow in the Blue*, and Margaret Boveri, *Wir lügen alle.*

20. Rudolf Hilferding, twice minister of finance, was sabotaged and did not have a Jacobin temperament to begin with; he led a double life, publicly supporting his party's lame policy and in private mocking his colleagues.

21. Paul Levi, Rosa Luxemburg's favorite student, was expelled from the Communist party, lived out an unhappy marriage of prudence with the Social Democratic party, and committed suicide after abandoning his followers. Other intellectuals as well—Maslow, Korsch, Werner Scholem, Rosenberg—were expelled from the Communist party.

22. In Reinisch, *Die Zeit ohne Eigenschaften*, pp. 50–81.

23. The film *The Blue Angel* does not quite reflect the radicalism of *Professor Unrath*, on which it is based.

24. This seems to be the view of Istvan Deak's *Weimar Germany's Left-Wing Intellectuals* (Berkeley: California University Press, 1968), and of Carl Schorske, "Weimar and the Intellectuals," in *The New York Review of Books*, May 21, 1970.

25. The ethical origins of Marx's thought had long been recognized by Lukács, Korsch, and Max Adler, who had emphasized the humanist side of the socialist class struggle.

26. The most fertile and most successful writer of love stories, Hedwig Courths-Mahler, was a pacifist and a feminist. But she separated her political from her literary activity by an impenetrable wall. Twenty-seven million copies of her books were sold.

27. See Fritz Stern, *The Politics of Cultural Despair* (New York: Anchor Books, 1965).

28. The Nazi charge that a conspiracy of Jewish publishers and Jewish critics favored Jewish authors, actors, and singers can easily be refuted, but it has been repeated by refugee authors who felt that culture left Germany with them.

29. Hermann Rauschning, *The Revolution of Nihilism* (1938).

30. Fritz Stern, *Cultural Despair*, quoting Moeller van den Bruck, p. 299. See also Karl O. Paetel, *Versuchung oder Chance? Zur Geschichte des deutschen Nationalbolschewismus* (Göttingen: Musterschmidt, 1965).

4. Friedrich Meinecke and the Tragedy of German Liberalism

1. *Weltbürgertum und Nationalstaat* (1908); English translation, *Cosmopolitanism and the National State*, with a preface by Felix Gilbert (Princeton, N.J.: Princeton University Press, 1970); references will be to *Cosmopolitanism*; translations are mine after *Werke* (Munich: Oldenbourg

Verlag, 1959–1965), vol. 5. *Die Idee der Staatsräson in der neueren Ge-schichte* (1924), vol. 1 of *Werke;* English translation under the misleading title *Machiavellism,* preface by W. Stark (New York: Praeger paperback, 1965); quotations are from *Machiavellism,* though the translations are mine. *Die Entstehung des Historismus* (1936), vol. 3 of *Werke;* not translated; references will be to *Historismus.*

2. *Die deutsche Katastrophe* (1946); English translation, *The German Catastrophe,* by Sidney B. Fay (Boston: Beacon Press, 1950).

3. Georg Iggers, 'The German Conception of History (Middlebury, Conn.: Wesleyan University Press, 1968); I quote from the German edition (Munich: DTV, 1971). Robert A. Pois, *Friedrich Meinecke and German Politics* (Berkeley: University of California Press, 1972); Kurt Sontheimer, *Antidemokratisches Denken in der Weimarer Republik* (Munich: Nymphenburger, 1962). Typical of the East German critique is Werner Berthold, *Grosshungern und Gehorchen* (Leipzig: Karl-Marx-Universität, 1960). Typical of the Jewish reaction are Shulamit Volkov, "Cultural Elitism and Democracy," in *Jahrbuch des Instituts für deutsche Geschichte* (Tel Aviv: Institut für deutsche Geschichte, 1976), and Pinhas Rosenblüth, "Friedrich Meinecke's Views on Jews and Judaism," in *Bulletin of the Leo Baeck Institute* (London: Secker & Warburg, 1976), no. 52.

More sympathetic evaluations in Richard W. Sterling, *Ethics in a World of Power* (Princeton, N.J.: Princeton University Press, 1958); Walther Hofer, *Geschichtschreibung und Weltanschauung* (Munich: Oldenbourg, 1950); Stuart Hughes, *Consciousness and Society* (New York: Vintage, 1958).

4. See Calvin Rand, "Two Meanings of Historicism," in *Journal for the History of Ideas* 25 (1964), and Iggers, *German Conception of History;* Stuart Hughes, *Consciousness and Society,* also retains Historismus.

5. *Werke* 7:72. All this happened many years before Horkheimer and Sartre shook the world with the discovery of "engaged science."

6. "Kausalitäten und Werte in der Geschichte," originally in *HZ* (1923), now *Werke,* 4:68 ff.; quoted from the collected essays, *Schaffender Spiegel* (Stuttgart: Koehler, 1948), p. 66. Meinecke's coining, Creative Mirror, is itself an expression of his understanding of the historian's work and function. Likewise, he says in the *Aphorisms* (1942), *Werke,* 4:239: "He who writes history must also create history."

7. "This contentment with the immediate past reflects an idea of freedom totally at variance with the classical liberalism of Western Europe." Iggers, *German Conception of History,* p. 264. I am much indebted to this valuable work.

8. *Machiavellism,* p. 1.

9. *Cosmopolitanism,* p. 83. For the categories "universal-individual" see text to note 4. My italics.

10. The German edition did not appear until 1917, but Meinecke may have seen the term in 1905 when it appeared in the preface of Kjellén's work, *The Great Powers.* He criticized geopolitics and Kjellén in a 1917

essay, but in his late work, The German Catastrophe, he placed him next to Jacob Burckhardt and Johan Huizinga (p. 111).

11. Urworte—Orphisch: Daimon (referred to in Machiavellism, p. 280).

12. Letter to Heinrich von Srbik, Werke, 6:194.

13. Cosmopolitanism, p. 190. Ranke, fully aware of the many wars they had fought with each other, nevertheless had been able to compose a History of the Germanic and Romanic Nations. After World War I, Meinecke quoted Benedetto Croce to the effect that "through this war both victors and vanquished have reached a higher spiritual life." Machiavellism, p. 432.

14. The German Catastrophe, pp. 56, 52. My translation.

15. Ibid., p. 110.

16. Werke, 4:192.

17. Werke (Historismus), 3:106. Meinecke hated Voltaire; mentioning him here was an expression of disapproval.

18. Werke, vol. 2. After World War I, his judgment on the Balkan Slavs grew much harsher. Machiavellism, p. 419. Although he had studied nationalism, he did not expect the virulence it was to assume in the 1920s.

19. Strassburg—Freiburg—Berlin, p. 137.

20. Werke, 2:365. Johann Gottlieb Fichte, the philosopher of identity, was known mostly for these patriotic lectures.

21. Werke, 4:154–160. For it to be asserted at the annual "Emperor's Birthday Lecture," 1916, this was almost a provocation.

22. Machiavellism, p. 44.

23. Geschichte der deutsch-englischen Bündnisverhandlungen (Munich-Berlin: Oldenbourg, 1927), p. 268. (Since the book clearly shows the limitations of cabinet politics, I don't understand Robert Pois's charge that its motivation was nostalgia for that practice.)

24. Werke, 2:411. It is regrettable that a former student of Meinecke should have written, without quoting the text verbatim: "In April 1926 he voiced opposition to the expanding cosmopolitan cynicism, and he specifically pointed to Jews." Rosenblüth, in Bulletin of the Leo Baeck Institute, 1976, p. 112. I cannot detect any sign of anti-Semitism in the above passage. It rather strives for sociopsychological explanation and, more important, pleads for understanding. Interestingly, Meinecke spoke much more harshly after the war, when most Germans tried to avoid the subject. The German Catastrophe, p. 32. Meinecke had many Jewish friends, like Walter Goetz, and maintained an intensive correspondence with those of his former students who had to emigrate. In 1933 he tried, vainly, to prevent the dismissal of Gustav Mayer. Mr. Rosenblüth does not quote any of the many passages in which Meinecke condemns Gobineau's and Nietzsche's race theories.

25. Schaffender Spiegel, p. 223; Werke, 4:367–378 and 61–89.

26. So still in Machiavellism, p. 11.

27. Ibid., p. 5. I shall use Reason of State when this meaning is clearly

intended, *raison d'état* when opportunistic Machiavellism is intended. Meinecke's usage does not always agree with his definition.

28. Quoted by Meinecke, *ibid.*, p. 301.

29. It is strange that Meinecke did not mention the novelistic and satirical treatments of *Ratio Status* in baroque literature. Grimmelshausen wrote a bitter pamphlet on *The Two-Headed Ratio Status*, and Daniel Casper von Lohenstein is a direct follower of Jean Bodin. Remarkable is a devastating counter-utopia by Anselm von Zigler, *The Asiatic Banise*, which tears reason of state to shreds; also Johann Michael Moscherosch's *Satyrical Wondrous and True Visions of Philander of Sittewald*, which deplores the displacement of justice by reason of state.

30. *The German Catastrophe*, p. 94, where this is applied to Hitler.

31. *Machiavellism*, p. 415.

32. Referring to Grotius, *ibid.*, p. 209.

33. *Ibid.*, pp. 214–215. Obviously, the critique of rationalism was not peculiar to Meinecke and Historismus but was fed from many sources during the 1920s.

34. Ranke, *Werke*, 33:153. The passage resembles Meinecke's statement in *Cosmopolitanism* (text to note 9).

35. *Machiavellism*, p. 426.

36. *Ibid.*, p. 426. Such formulations drew fire from indignant reviewers in the German press.

37. Introduction to *Machiavellism*; also *Schaffender Spiegel*, p. 220.

38. *Machiavellism*, p. 429.

39. *Historismus*, p. 265.

40. *Werke*, 4:81.

41. *Schaffender Spiegel*, p. 214.

42. "Causalities and Values" in *Werke*, 4:78 and 85. "Culture" (*Kultur*) is, of course, arts, philosophy, religion, and pure science.

43. *Ibid.*, p. 88.

44. *Machiavellism*, p. 407.

45. *Ibid.*, p. 369.

46. "Friedrich Meinecke is the Thomas Mann of German historical writing." Peter Gay, "Weimar Culture," in Donald Fleming and Bernard Bailyn, *The Intellectual Migration* (Cambridge: Harvard University Press, 1969), p. 66.

47. Interestingly, Oswald Spengler, whose *Decline of the West* Meinecke reviewed adversely, also attributed to Goethe a "historical world view based on a biological horizon" (1:75). It is strange that Spengler has not been claimed for Historismus. His view that each civilization has its own way of understanding numbers, its own *a priori* assumptions, its own *Schicksal*, is, at least in its method, a strong support of Historismus. But Spengler "was able to do justice to the singular only by transforming the great cultures into vegetative creatures like plants." *Werke*, 4:187. Meinecke further objected to the anti-intellectual, deterministic, vitalistic, Nietzschean strands

in Spengler's thought. He was repelled by Spengler's anti-democratic, anti-urban cult of barbarism; his summary of that cult: An expressionist copy of old counterrevolutionary ideologies, reminiscent of Adam Müller.

48. HZ (1941), 163:7.

49. Eckhart Kehr, "Modern German Historians," reprinted in Essays in German History, Gordon Craig, ed. (Berkeley: University of California Press, 1977), p. 181.

50. Machiavellism, pp. 368–369.

51. Werke, 3:588 and 590, from his speech commemorating the fiftieth anniversay of Ranke's death, 1936, with some interesting reservations on religion as a way out of historicism's dilemma.

52. Werke, 3:2.

53. Machiavellism, pp. 362–363.

54. Werke, 3:94.

55. Ibid., p. 53. A fairer appreciation of the Enlightenment is found in the "Aphorisms" of 1942, where he recognizes the turn of the philosophes away from a static conception of human nature and toward evolution, toward the variety of appearances. In 1932 Ernst Cassirer, the neo-Kantian, had written a monograph on the Enlightenment, showing that it was not as ahistorical as the German romantics had charged.

56. HZ (1934), 156:126.

57. "History and Personality," in Werke, 4:54.

58. "Causalities and Values," ibid., p. 87.

59. Meinecke suffered because he saw Hitler shooting his way into German, and into European, history.

60. The German Catastrophe, p. 86.

61. Werke, 4:206. See text to note 9.

62. Machiavellism, p. 408.

5. Walther Rathenau: Musil's Arnheim or Mann's Naphta?

1. Before accepting the post of foreign minister, Rathenau had warned that a Jew should not be given responsibility for the dire decisions that might have to be taken. But he was prevailed upon to serve because it was thought that his connections with "the Four Hundred" might help alleviate the burden of reparations for Germany.

2. Rathenau has been ill served by historiography. His first admiring biographer was the jolly gossip, Count Harry Kessler, who put later historians on the false track of seeking out the psychological complexities in Rathenau's character instead of analyzing the historical significance of his work and life. Even James Joll, in a superb essay which tries to be understanding and sympathetic, discards Rathenau's ideas as unoriginal and superficial, while focusing on the mystery man, on "his cultivation of the

incompatible—Prussian and Jew, capitalist and reformer, financier and philosopher." Professor Walter Struve, on the other hand, does take Rathenau's ideas seriously, but interprets them as proto-fascist and, with vulgar-Marxist blinders, attributes them to Rathenau's position as heir to the General Electric Corporation. See Count Harry Kessler, *Walter Rathenau: His Life and Work* (New York: Harcourt, Brace), 1930; also Kessler, *In the Twenties: The Diaries of Harry Kessler* (New York: Holt, Rinehart & Winston, 1971); James Joll, *Three Intellectuals in Politics* (New York: Harper & Row, 1960); Walter Struve, *German Elitists Against Democracy* (Princeton, N.J.: Princeton University Press, 1973).

3. Similarly Kessler, *Diaries.*

4. A typical entry in Rathenau's diary reads: "Had to preside over a Kaiser dinner in the Aero-Club. Metaphysical discussion with Prof. Nernst. Took along Jung to propose renting of power station. Sent reply to Diezelsky's essay on 'Jews and the State.' "

5. Mayer must have known that André Gide recorded in his diary: "He never let go of my arm," and that Rilke had also remarked on Rathenau's attempt to impress his physical closeness on his guests.

6. Kessler describes Rathenau in similar terms, and the unflattering portrait by Edvard Munch elicited from Rathenau the comment: "A great genius brings out the truth about his model."

7. Little did he know about a similar diatribe against Shylock by another Jew, fifty years earlier—Karl Marx—and there is an even closer resemblance between Rathenau and Benjamin Disraeli in their efforts to overcome their background. He was, of course, familiar with the figure of Fagin and, even closer to home, the cheap imitation of it in Gustav Freytag's novel, *Debit and Credit,* which was then very popular in Germany. If Heinrich Mann also is found in that company, one may wonder why Engels called anti-Semitism "the socialism of imbeciles."

8. "I am a German of the Jewish race. . . . Nature mixed both sources of my ancient blood in a foaming conflict: the urge to reality and the link with the spiritual." *Appeal to Germany's Youth* (1918), p. 9. Such inanities also have led biographers to muse about Rathenau's "two souls."

9. He saw that both liberalism and the national state had outlived their relevance, and joined Pastor Friedrich Naumann's call for the large-scale economy of "Mitteleuropa."

10. Kessler, *Diaries,* February 20, 1919, notes: "[Rathenau says that] at night he is a bolshevist—in the daytime not quite yet." The flirtation has often been a cause of amusement. Watching the debate between the fastidious Rathenau and Stinnes, the steel tycoon in the shabby suit, people would wonder which was the advocate of frugality and equality.

11. O. E. Schüddekopf, *Linke Leute von rechts* (Stuttgart: Kohlhammer, 1960); K. O. Paetel, *Versuchung oder Chance?* (Göttingen: Musterschmidt, 1965).

12. Still, he commanded sufficient respect on the right to act as a go-between in the "negotiations" to liquidate the Kapp Putsch of March 1920.

13. See note 1.

8. Heidegger and Hitler: The Incompatibility of Geist and Politics

1. *Die Selbstbehauptung der deutschen Universität* (May 27, 1933) (Breslau: Korn, 1934).

2. Heidegger, *Holzwege* (Frankfurt: Klostermann, 1950), p. 237.

3. "Der Ruf zum Arbeitsdienst," in *Freiburger Studentenzeitung*, Freiburg im Breisgau (January 23, 1934), p. 1.

4. Heidegger, *An Introduction to Metaphysics* (New York: Doubleday Anchor Books, 1959), p. 166.

5. *Ibid.*, p. 31 (italics added).

6. Stephen Eric Bronner, "Martin Heidegger: The Consequences of Political Mystification," in *Salmagundi* (Summer-Fall 1977). Also, note the obscurantist attack on this piece by Thomas Sheehan and Bronner's response in *Salmagundi* (Winter 1979).

9. Brecht's Personal Politics

1. "Einige Fragen an einen 'guten Mann,' " in Bertolt Brecht, *Gedichte* (Frankfurt: Suhrkamp, 1961), 3:164.

2. See Hugo von Hofmannsthal's ironic prologue to *Baal,* as quoted by Martin Esslin in *Brecht: The Man and His Work* (London: Eyre, 1959), p. 29.

3. *Arbeitsjournal (AJ)*, Werner Hecht, ed., vol. 1, 1938–1942; vol. 2, 1942–1955 (Frankfurt: Suhrkamp, 1973).

4. One person who understood, strangely, was Ernst von Salomon (the national-bolshevist, author of *The Outlaws*), who wrote: "Even the boldly articulated sentence, 'Eating comes first, then comes morality,' could not be interpreted as the breakthrough of an unheard-of insight, but had its effect through the naked brutality with which it named something that was commonplace, and also through the uncertainty as to whose leg was being pulled." *Die Stadt* (Hamburg: Rowohlt, 1932), p. 234.

5. See especially "Kleines Organon für das Theater" in *Versuche 12* (Schriften zum Theater 2) in *Gesammelte Werke*, vol. 16 (Frankfurt: Suhrkamp, 1967); *AJ* 8/40, passim.

6. Hofmannsthal in Esslin, *Brecht* (Prologue to Baal).

7. A similar device was used by Gerhart Hauptmann in *The Rats* (1910), one of the last naturalist plays.

8. Given the quality of teaching at the communist Marxist Workers' School, it is not astonishing that Brecht has not told us the names of any teachers he met there, though he claimed to have attended its courses.

9. As quoted by Esslin, *Brecht*, p. 19.

10. Fritz Sternberg's criticism of *The Measures Taken* cast the first shadow on the relations between the two.

11. Brecht, *Gedichte und Lieder* (Frankfurt: Suhrkamp, 1963), p. 160; translation from Bertolt Brecht, *Poems 1913–1956*, Willett and Manheim, eds. (New York: Methuen, 1976), pp. 319–320.

12. *Schriften zur Literatur und Kunst 2* (Frankfurt: Suhrkamp, 1967), p. 76.

13. HUAC, October 30, 1947. Appendix to Frederic Ewen, *Bertolt Brecht—His Life, His Art, and His Time* (Secaucus: Citadel Press, 1969).

14. In Comintern language, all this was "ultra-left"; had Brecht been a member of the Party, he might have been expelled.

15. Brecht, *Materialien zu Mutter Courage* (Frankfurt: Suhrkamp, 1964), pp. 86–90.

16. *Bertolt Brechts Gedichte und Lieder*, pp. 137–140; translated by John Willett, in Brecht, *Poems*, pp. 314–316.

17. Esslin, *Brecht*, pp. 158, 226; Ewen, *Brecht*, pp. 340f.

18. As quoted by Ewen, *Brecht*, p. 340.

19. *Merkur* (a West German magazine), 1973, no. 9.

20. The idea of the poem "The Ox" may have come from Emerson's essay on "Politics." There the state is compared to a cow, and Emerson says that he would feed it, not begrudging it the clover. But unlike Brecht, Emerson added: If the cow tries to gore me, I'll cut its throat.

21. *Me-ti, Buch der Wendungen* (The Book of Changes), *Prosa V* (Frankfurt: Suhrkamp, 1965), pp. 113–114. Although *Me-ti* was unfinished, it was meant for publication.

22. Ewen, *Brecht*, p. 327.

23. *Me-ti*, p. 9.

24. In *Me-ti*, Brecht gave an adequate account of Korsch's anti-Stalinist views (p. 140) but rejected his conclusions. Then he says (p. 142): "Under the leadership of [Stalin], an industry without exploiters was developed in the [Soviet Union]; farming was collectivized and industrialized. . . . [Trotsky] denied all progress in [the Soviet Union], even those aspects that were obvious. Outside [the Soviet Union] those who challenged the leadership of [Stalin] were soon isolated; those who challenged him at home soon were surrounded by criminals and themselves committed crimes against the people. In [the Soviet Union] all wisdom was devoted to construction and chased from politics. Outside [the Soviet Union] anyone who praised the merits of [Stalin], even those that were undeniable, was suspected of having been bribed." For further rejection of Korsch's libertarian socialism, see *Me-ti*, p. 147.

25. *Me-ti*, pp. 133–134.

26. Ewen, *Brecht*, p. 453.

27. Brecht, *Gesammelte Werke* (Frankfurt: Suhrkamp, 1967), 10:1009. Translated by Derek Bowman, in Brecht, *Poems*, p. 440.

28. *Ibid.*, p. 1008. Translated by Frank Jones, in Brecht, *Poems*, pp. 437–38. Brecht has expressed well what is the true relationship between the poet and posterity, or between poetry and its political effect. He expressed it in that little poem, written near the end of his life, where he speaks of coming upon a rose which had not been there the day before. He had not come to look for it, he says, but when he came, it was there, unplanned and undefined.

> Eh sie da war, ward sie nicht erwartet.
> Als sie da war, ward sie kaum geglaubt.
> Ach, zum Ziele kam, was nie gestartet.
> Aber war es so nicht überhaupt?
>
> (Unexpected till we came and saw it
> Unbelievable as soon as seen
> Hit the mark, despite not aiming for it:
> Isn't that how things have always been?)

(Brecht, *Gesammelle Werke*, p. 1020; translated by John Willett, in Brecht, *Poems*, p. 447.)

29. Wolfdieter Rasch and Iring Fetscher in *Merkur*, no. 10, 1963, and no. 11, 1973, seem to exaggerate Korsch's influence. Brecht used Korsch as a check on his own ideas and agreed with him on many negative points; but he drew opposite conclusions. Korsch was a Luxemburgist-syndicalist and in his later years highly critical of classical Marxism; Brecht was a Jacobin-Leninist and considered himself a Marxist. The one idea he took from Korsch (and perhaps from Heinz Langerhans, a student of Korsch) appears in Brecht's diaries (and perhaps in *The Caucasian Chalk Circle*) in a rather perverted, reified form: Brecht hoped that "productivity in the larger sense" might eventually supersede the rigidities of the proletarian dictatorship (*AJ*, 3/7/41). This goes back to the Sorelian myth of productivity which bursts the shackles of the system, and here artistic productivity and love also are seen as revolutionary. But Brecht uses "productivity" in the mechanical sense I have indicated: Stalin promotes productivity, the capitalists inhibit productivity, Lukács's literary criticism is not productive (*AJ*, 8/18/38, 10/16/43, and *Me-ti*, p. 89). The East German government would get more production out of its workers if it would talk to them.

Incidentally, Ewen has the wrong date for Brecht's introduction to Korsch. I am in a position to say that this occurred only in 1929—after the *Three-penny Opera*. Since Korsch was totally at odds with Western policy makers in the 1950s, the friendship was not disturbed by the cold war. By contrast, Brecht broke with Fritz Sternberg after the latter had become too anti-Soviet for his taste.

30. Ewen, *Brecht*, p. 486.

12. Irrationalism and the Paralysis of Reason: A Festering Sore

1. Stefan Zweig, Die Welt von gestern (Stockholm: Fischer, 1944), p. 62.
2. Walther Rathenau, Zur Mechanik des Geistes (Berlin: Fischer, 1913).

14. Was Weimar Necessary?

1. "The flight of one set of supervisors and the coming of another," said Walther Rathenau.
2. Geoffrey Barraclough even denies that the Republic deserves a special chapter in Germany's history. See "On the Periodization of German History," in The New York Review of Books, October 12, 1972, and my reply, March 17, 1973.
3. Rouget de Lisle, composer of the "Marseillaise." Georg Büchner's Dantons Tod and other revolution plays were restaged by Max Reinhardt in the early years of his Berlin Schauspielhaus.
4. Concluded between Carl Legien, president of the General Trade Unions' Confederation (ADGB), and, for the industrialists, Hugo Stinnes, owner of a steel, coal, and shipping empire, in November 1918, and enlarged in 1920.
5. See "The Marxism of Rosa Luxemburg" by Georg Lukács, in History and Class Consciousness (Cambridge: MIT Press, 1971), and Karl Korsch, Marxism and Philosophy (New York and London: Monthly Review Press, 1970).
6. David W. Morgan, The Socialist Left and the German Revolution: A History of the German Independent Social Democratic Party, 1917–1922 (Ithaca and London: Cornell University Press, 1975); and Hartfrid Krause, USPD—Zur Geschichte der Unabhängigen Sozialdemokratischen Partei Deutschlands (Frankfurt: Europäische Verlagsanstalt, 1975). Both books have ample bibliographies and biographical data and are useful for the wealth of information they provide but both offer little theory.

See also Karl Korsch, Politische Texte, Erich Gerlach and Jürg Seifert, eds. (Frankfurt: Europäische Verlagsanstalt, 1974). Korsch was the only theoretician of revolutionary syndicalism in Germany. His philosophy is now very influential on the Left within and outside the SPD. Korsch later repudiated some of the articles published in this collection. See Peter von Oertzen, Die Probleme der wirtschaftlichen Neuordnung und der Mitbestimmung in der Revolution von 1918 (Frankfurt: Europäische Verlagsanstalt, no date). See also his earlier Betriebsräte in der Revolution (Düsseldorf: IG Metall, 1963). The author is a leader of the left wing in the SPD, and coauthor of its controversial long-term action program. See Oskar Anweiler, The Soviets in Russia 1905–1922, translated from the German (New York: Pantheon, 1974).
7. The USPD was usually called either "USP" or "Independents." It was

briefly allied with the Austrian Socialist Party, the British Independent Labour Party, and like-minded "centrists" in the so-called 2½ International. The SPD or *Mehrheitssozialisten* was the (majority) Social-Democratic Party of Germany; KPD: the Communist Party of Germany (today the name is copyrighted by the German Maoists).

8. Friedrich Ebert had taken the precaution of having himself appointed Germany's Chancellor by the Kaiser's last holder of that office, Prince Max von Baden—constitutionally a doubtful procedure since Prince Max himself had declined the dignity of Regent of the Realm. Ebert was furious when Scheidemann proclaimed the Republic from a Reichstag window, undercutting his flimsy legitimacy. Indeed, until the January elections the government's legitimacy rested on the revolutionary power of the Räte alone. Karl Liebknecht, meanwhile, had proclaimed the "free Socialist Republic."

9. With the exception of some national-bolshevist authors, few writers recognized the cardinal point that in 1918 one could hardly have been for peace *and* pursue the revolution at the same time. Michael Freund, an ex-USPD member himself, admits this in *Deutsche Geschichte* (Gütersloh: Bertelsmann, 1960). See also note 21.

10. The USPD enjoyed the sympathies of non-Marxist intellectuals and artists. Neither Morgan nor Krause mentions Kurt Tucholsky, Carl von Ossietzky, Alfred Döblin (author of *Berlin Alexanderplatz*), and other *Weltbühne* authors who were USPD members.

11. Morgan wonders why the USPD held its founding convention at "remote Gotha"—why, that's where the Marxists and the Lassalleans had united in 1875! Morgan has little background in, and feeling for, the inner life of European mass parties.

12. Karl Korsch, in "Wandlungen des Problems der Arbeiterräte," *Politische Texte*, stresses that the National (*Reichs-*) Räte Congress was called by the government, not built up by the Räte themselves.

13. First published in 1902, amended in 1906 under the impression of the first Russian revolution (Berlin: Vorwärts, 112 pp.); it is Kautsky's best work—interestingly, not republished after the war. In his later writings, he lapsed into shallow legalism. See his *Der Historische Materialismus* (Berlin: Dietz, 1929), vol. 2.

14. Quoted by Walter Tormin, ed., *Die Weimarer Republik* (Hannover: Verlag für Literatur und Zeitgeschehen, 1962), p. 92. See also Arthur Rosenberg, *Geschichte der Weimarer Republik* (1935). Similarly divided sentiments are found in Harry Kessler's *Tagebücher* (Frankfurt: Insel-Verlag, 1961), which strikingly disclose how the most progressive faction of the bourgeois democrats, such as Kessler himself and Walther Rathenau, alternated between fear of the Räte and hope that they might be used to legitimize a *coup d'état*. And Thomas Mann at the time wrote: "Communism as I understand it has much that is good . . . it aims at . . . a de-poisoning of the world by de-politicizing it." *Briefe 1889–1936*, Erika Mann, ed. (Frankfurt: Fischer, 1961), p. 158.

15. Haase would have stayed but was forced to quit by his irate comrades. For particulars see Arthur Rosenberg, *Geschichte*, pp. 44–47. Rosenberg charges that the sailors wanted money, not revolution. But from the USPD point of view, their presence also meant power and the recognition of a proletarian force; the event had symbolic significance for both sides. Here was another turning point where the USPD had to choose between losing revolutionary credit and losing power.

16. Kessler quotes Rathenau as saying: "Noske is the only great man in the Republic." Kessler, *Tagebücher*. The same Rathenau just then published a pamphlet in which he argued for "co-determination"—using the very same word that fifty years later was to become the SPD's fighting slogan. Earlier, he had called for a confiscatory tax and designed a scheme of industrial self-determination, which influenced Hilferding's Räte idea.

17. In Kessler's fantasies, the Räte were to assure the resumption of "production," and the USPD was to "guarantee civil peace and work discipline." Kessler, *Tagebücher*, March 4, 1919. See also Thomas Mann, *Doktor Faustus* (Stockholm: Fischer, 1947), pp. 521 ff. and 558.

18. Korsch, *Texte*, pp. 31–32.

19. *Ibid.*, pp. 45 ff. The article quoted dates from 1923, when Korsch had joined the KPD, and refers to a different situation. He then defended "workers' government" against its ultra-left, "undialectical" opponents. These "workers' governments" of 1923 in Saxony and Thuringia were deposed by the army.

20. Arthur Rosenberg argues in *History of Bolshevism* that this was not accidental. The Räte idea by then had become utopian.

21. Some old-timers who had first joined the KPD returned to the SPD in 1921. The rump USPD continued under Georg Ledebour's and Theodor Liebknecht's leadership. It had the singular distinction of being the only party to oppose the nationalist "Ruhr Action" of 1922–23—the perverse "strike" of the miners, financed by the German government, against the French occupation power.

22. In his book, *Der historische Materialismus* (pp. 730 ff.), Kautsky blames "the split in the labor movement" for its failure. But he makes believe that the Spartacists (an insignificant sect in 1919) caused the split. This is a misrepresentation. The real split occurred down the middle, within the USPD, making that party incapable of deciding on a policy. Equally mistaken, or rather, unhistorical, is Morgan in blaming "class war" for the USPD's failure.

23. Cf. Michael Freund, *Geschichte*. Although an "alliance with Russia" also was the Communist Party's propaganda line, Lenin and Radek felt that a "Soviet Germany," too, would have to sign a harsh treaty.

24. Comintern President Grigorii Zinoviev, speaking for four and a half hours at the USPD's "merger" congress at Halle (1920), promised those willing to join that the spark of the world revolution, once permitted to set Germany aflame, would ignite the Western countries, "and ten years hence,

no one will remember what capitalism used to be like." Alas, even sooner he had to forget what people used to mean by socialism.

25. It may be of interest to trace a similar development in Italy, where syndicalism looked back on a great tradition. In 1920 the workers occupied the factories and formed "factory councils." Gramsci—now a saint of the PCI—was then fascinated by the idea of councils and based on it his theory of *stato operaio*. The Communist International refused to sanction this movement. At its Fifth World Congress (1924), it declared that soviets could be developed only *after* the Party had seized political power. After Gramsci's death, Togliatti denied that factory councils had ever been conceived as organs of revolutionary power.

15. Weimar Culture—Nostalgia and Revision

1. Herbert Bayer, ed., *Bauhaus 1919–1928* (Stuttgart: Hatje, 1955), p. 13.

2. Bruno E. Werner, *Die Zwanziger Jahre* (Munich: Bruckmann, 1962); Leonhard Reinisch, ed., *Die Zeit ohne Eigenschaften* (Stuttgart: W. Kohlhammer, 1961); Thilo Koch, *Die Goldenen Zwanziger Jahre* (Frankfurt: Athenaion, 1970) are typical titles. There are of course monographs on individual subjects, but nothing that matches Gay's and Laqueur's work.

By contrast, "Weimar culture," the title of Peter Gay's profound, analytical book (*Weimar Culture: The Outsider as Insider*), which appeared first as a chapter in *The Intellectual Migration*, Donald Fleming and Bernard Bailyn, eds. (Cambridge: Harvard University Press, 1969), is a fixed term in Anglo-American historiography. See also Walter Laqueur, *Weimar: A Cultural History 1918–1933* (New York: Putnam, 1974) and his contribution in the special "Weimar Culture" issue of *Social Research*, Summer 1972.

3. See Peter Gay, *Freud, Jews, and Other Germans: Masters and Victims in Modernist Culture* (New York: Oxford University Press, 1978).

16. On Being an Exile

1. When Kantorowicz came to New York, he was a frequent guest of Gerhart Eisler and took part in many private conferences of Communist writers, yet in his memoirs he pretends that he did not know who Eisler was. Even as an outsider I knew, and I know that many others of Kantorowicz's acquaintances knew, that Eisler was a grey eminence of the Communist party in the United States. Kantorowicz has also written that the Spanish Trotskyists had poisoned wells, and he never retracted this even after his eyes were opened about his source.

2. George L. Mosse still thinks the phenomenon of twentieth-century tribalism is purely German.

3. Although Benn was quite aware of the meaning of Hitler's dictatorship, he tried to idealize it as "expressionist politics"; after the war he ungraciously attacked the exiles for having spent the bad times abroad in luxury hotels. Another parlor Nazi, Ernst Jünger, also turned up on our side, surprisingly.

4. It is almost impossible for James Burnham not to have known about these two predecessors to *The Managerial Revolution* but he never mentions them.

5. Max Herrmann-Neisse, *Um uns die Fremde*. Printed with permission from Verlag Oprecht, Zurich.

6. Unlike the Irish and Puerto Ricans, we did not have to start from the bottom and work our way up. Thanks to benevolent committees, general prosperity, and the war, many of us were able to join the social class we had left in Europe. This was particularly true of intellectuals. In the beginning, many of us had to take positions that might be described as belonging to the "academic proletariat"; but eventually, many reached positions they might not have obtained in the old country. "Upward social mobility" is no myth, and despite a few cases of failure the percentage of successful careers is truly astounding. Even my friend W. J., whose great charm is not of the kind that goes with efficiency, and whose academic credentials are doubtful, achieved tenure.

Observation: one could be very poor and yet be sure that upward mobility existed for us; one might also be quite sensitive to discrimination and yet not be aware of the absolute limits to the social mobility of blacks.

7. One, published in vols. 10 and 11 of *Jahrbuch für Amerika-Studien* (Heidelberg, 1965, 1966), is extremely skimpy.

8. *Bertolt Brechts Gedichte und Leider* (Frankfurt: Suhrkamp, 1963), p. 87; translation by John Willett, in Bertolt Brecht, *Poems 1913–1956*, Willett and Manheim, eds. (New York: Methuen, 1976), p. 347:

> This, then, is all. It's not enough, I know.
> At least I'm still alive, as you may see.
> I'm like the man who took a brick to show
> How beautiful his house used once to be.

Index